SOCIAL JUSTICE IN THE LIBERAL STATE

SOCIAL JUSTICE

IN THE LIBERAL STATE

BRUCE A. ACKERMAN

NEW HAVEN AND LONDON, YALE UNIVERSITY PRESS

Designed by Sally Harris
and set in VIP Garamond type.
Printed in the United States of America.
Vail-Ballou Press, Binghamton, N.Y.

Library of Congress Cataloging in Publication Data

Ackerman, Bruce A
    Social justice in the liberal state.

    Includes index.
    1. Liberalism. 2. Justice. I. Title.
JC571.A135   320.5'1   80–12618
ISBN 0–300–02439–8
ISBN 0–300–02757–5 (pbk.)

10   9   8   7   6   5   4   3

FOR ANDREI SAKHAROV

CONTENTS

Part Two: JUSTICE OVER TIME

ACKNOWLEDGMENTS

This essay has taken up much of my time, and more of my energy, for the past ten years. It has been impossible to be my friend during this period without enduring countless conversations and scribblings devoted to one or another line of thought. As a result, my friends have contributed enormously to the final product. While I will refrain from a blow-by-blow account, this book would never have emerged without their ceaseless criticisms and encouragements.

It is easier to be more specific in detailing my other debts. Judith Shklar, by her personal example, introduced me to the reality of political philosophy while I was a student of hers at Harvard College. Proceeding to the Yale Law School in the mid-1960s, I encountered a group of teachers who gave Shklar's message a new force: Alexander Bickel, Robert Bork, Guido Calabresi, Ronald Dworkin, Charles Reich. While these people were very different from one another, they convinced me that political action was futile without systematic reflection.

Without this lesson, I would not have responded to the political turbulence of the late 1960s by taking a teaching job: first at the University of Pennsylvania; later, at Yale. Both these universities have been more than generous to me. Over the past five years, Dean Harry Wellington has provided invaluable moral as well as material support. Earlier on, my work was greatly assisted by the Dean of Pennsylvania's Law School, Bernard Wolfman, and by the Director of the Fels Institute, Julius Margolis. In the world beyond Philadelphia and New Haven, other institutions responded generously to my applications for support. During the early years, the National Science Foundation provided me with much-needed free time for a second draft of my essay; then, when NSF found my work insufficiently scientific, a Rockefeller Fellowship in the Humanities provided me with a chance to rewrite yet again. Finally, a Yale Senior Faculty Fellowship assisted me in attempting a last draft before publication. Throughout all these years of writing and rewriting, I have been very lucky in the people who have served as my secretaries: Damarest Robinson-Glasgow, Peggy MacKinnon, Diane MacDougal, Rosemary Boyce, and Marianne Basilicato. My thanks to you all for discharging a thankless task with great competence and good-will.

And finally, there is my greatest debt. I owe more than I can say to my wife, Susan. Her keen intelligence and gentle understanding have sustained me throughout.

PART ONE: A NEW WORLD

1

THE LIBERAL STATE

1. THE STRUGGLE FOR POWER

So long as we live, there can be no escape from the struggle for power. Each of us must control his body and the world around it. However modest these personal claims, they are forever at risk in a world of scarce resources. Someone, somewhere, will—if given the chance— take the food that sustains or the heart that beats within. Nor need such acts be attempted for frivolous reasons—perhaps my heart is the only thing that will save a great woman's life, my food sufficient to feed five starving men. No one can afford to remain passive while competitors stake their claims. Nothing will be left to reward such self-restraint. Only death can purchase immunity from hostile claims to the power I seek to exercise.

Not that all life is power lust. Social institutions may permit us to turn to better things—deterring the thief and killer while our attention is diverted. Even when our power is relatively secure, however, it is never beyond challenge in a world where total demand outstrips supply. And it is this challenge that concerns us here. Imagine someone stepping forward to claim control over resources you now take for granted. According to her, it is she, not you, who has the better right to claim them. Why, she insists on knowing, do you think otherwise? How can you justify the powers you have so comfortably exercised in the past?

A first response mixes annoyance with fear. Rather than justifying my claims to power, the urge is strong to suppress the questioner. There can be no question that her question is threatening: As soon as I begin to play the game of justification, I run the risk of defeat. I may not find it so easy to justify the powers I so thoughtlessly command. Perhaps the conversation will reveal that it is not she, but I, who is more properly called the thief in this affair. And if this is so, is it not better to suppress the conversation before it begins? This is no ordinary game; it may reveal that my deepest hopes for myself cannot be realized without denying the rights of others. If I succeed in suppressing the questioner, I may hope to live as if my power had never been challenged at all.

It is a tempting prospect, which becomes more seductive as my effective power increases. Power corrupts: the more power I have, the more I can lose by trying to answer the question of legitimacy; the more power I have, the greater the chance that my effort at suppression will succeed—at least for the time that remains before I die. Yet this is not the path I mean to follow; I hope to take the question of legitimacy seriously: What would our social world look like if no one ever suppressed another's question of legitimacy, where every questioner met with a conscientious attempt at an answer?

2. CULTURE AND RIGHT

And so we come to our first principle:

Rationality: Whenever anybody questions the legitimacy of another's power, the power holder must respond not by suppressing the questioner but by giving a reason that explains why he is more entitled to the resource than the questioner is.

The first thing to notice about this formula is its generality. No form of power is immune from the question of legitimacy. By framing the Rationality requirement in this way, I hope to avoid the familiar errors of partial critique: the blindness of the partisan of laissez faire who fails to recognize that the private-property owner must legitimate his power no less than the government bureaucrat; the blindness of the communist who avoids this first mistake only to insulate the power of Party leaders from the test of dialogue.

Nor are the institutions of property and government the only means by which some people get what others want. Each person comes into the world with a set of genetic abilities that helps determine his relative power position; each is born into a particular system of education, communication, and exchange that gives some great advantages over others. Finally, there is the tremendous fact of temporal priority: one generation can transform the cultural and material possibilities available to its successors—can deny them life itself. None of these power structures can be accorded the immense privilege of invisibility; *each* person must be prepared[1] to answer the question of legitimacy when *any* of his powers is challenged by *anyone* disadvantaged by their exercise.

This comprehensive insistence on dialogue forces a break with one of the great myths of philosophy—the idea of a "state of nature." While the myth takes many forms, it always tells a story in which actors acquire "rights" that are prior to, and independent of, their social interaction. How this trick takes place is a matter of some dispute— some say by a silent act of unchallenged appropriation, others merely stipulate the "rights" their actors possess when they "first" encounter one another in a social situation. The important point, though, is the myth's assertion that people have "rights" even before they confront the harsh fact of the struggle for power.

In contrast, the Rationality principle supposes that rights have a reality only *after* people confront the fact of scarcity and begin to argue its normative implications. If you were completely confident that no one would ever question your control over X, you would never think of claiming a "right" over it; you'd simply use it without a second thought. If you were transported to an alien planet peopled by entities whose symbolic code (if it existed) you could not crack, there would be no point in claiming "rights" in regulating your dealings with them. Instead, brute force would remain the only option open.[2] Rights are not the kinds of things that grow on trees—to be plucked, when ripe, by an invisible hand. The only context in which a claim of right has a point is one where you anticipate the possibility of conversation with some potential competitor. Not that this conversation always in fact arises—brute force also remains a potent way of resolving disputes. Rights talk presupposes only the *conceptual* possibility of an alternative way of regulating the struggle for power—one where claims to scarce resources are established through a patterned cultural activity in which the question of legitimacy is countered by an effort at justification.

1. Is it enough to be *prepared* to answer the question of legitimacy? Must we drop everything and *actually engage* in a conversation *whenever* anybody challenges any of our claims to power? It would be silly to spend our entire lives in a discussion of the single question of legitimacy—at the expense of all talk and action on behalf of our personal ideals. Nonetheless, I cannot be permitted to evade questioning to such an extent that others are uncertain whether they have the power to call me to account at mutually convenient times and places. See §§ 20.3, 56.2.

2. Of course, if the aliens were triumphant, you might try to warn earth that they did not recognize any "rights"—but that is plainly a derivative use of the term. See § 18.2.

Since the principle of Rationality conceives this dialogue as the foundation of all claims of right, it requires a subtler, but no less decisive, break with a second familiar myth—the idea of "social contract."[3] Although the parties to a social contract must speak to one another while negotiating its terms, this conversation is understood in instrumental terms only. It does not constitute the ground of the rights that emerge from the bargaining process but simply serves as a means to induce the parties to give their consent to the contract terms. Indeed, the most compelling versions of the contract myth try to cut through the chatter of precontractual negotiation by designing a bargaining situation in which no rational actor has any sensible choice but to sign on the dotted line. Protracted discussion about contract terms at the founding convention is often positively harmful—it can reveal strategic possibilities for bluffing and coalition formation that may make the terms of the contract indeterminate. And it is only each party's promise to abide by the contract that constitutes the basis of his social rights and duties—not the talk that precedes or follows the magic moment of promising.

In contrast, Rationality does not refer to some privileged moment of promising—existing apart from ordinary social life—as the foundation of everyday claims of right. It points instead to an ongoing social practice—the dialogue engendered by the question of legitimacy—as itself the constituting matrix for any particular claim of right. At a later point, I shall defend this view at greater length.[4] For now, though, it is enough to state the essence of my proposal: Rather than linking liberalism to ideas of natural right or imaginary contract, *we must learn to think of liberalism as a way of talking about power, a form of political culture.*

But there is another face to Rationality; one that deals with substance, not method. Consider, for example, the Nazi who answers the Jew's question of legitimacy by saying, "Jews are an intrinsically worthless people whose very existence is an insult to the morally superior races." While it is tempting to exclude such responses as ir-Rational

3. While "state of nature" and "social contract" are commonly joined in familiar classics, it is not obvious that this is a necessary connection. Thus, Rawls tries to free contract from the fallacies of the state of nature, while Nozick returns the compliment by rescuing the state of nature from contract. Since I shall be rejecting both myths on their merits, I need not consider the extent to which, as a conceptual matter, they are indissolubly tied together. But see § 66.1.
4. See Part Four.

under the first principle, I mean resolutely to resist.[5] Rather than isolating the distinctive features of liberalism all by itself, Rationality simply points the would-be liberal in the general direction in which such a discovery is to be found: *If* there is anything distinctive about liberalism, it must be in the *kinds of reasons* liberals rely on to legitimate their claims to scarce resources. Nazis are not liberals because there is *something* about the reasons they give in support of their claims that is inconsistent with the organizing principles of liberal power talk. And what might that something be?

Before I try to answer this question, permit me a single preliminary move that is, substantively speaking, even emptier than the last. As a second principle in my model of legitimacy, I insist that like cases be treated alike.

Consistency. The reason advanced by a power wielder on one occasion must not be inconsistent with the reasons he advances to justify his other claims to power.

Throughout the book, I shall remain content with an unanalyzed understanding of this second principle. The critical thing is that a power holder cannot justify his claim to X by saying, "Because Aryans are better than Jews" and then turn around and justify his claim to Y by announcing, "All men are created equal." Of course, Consistency simply requires the power wielder to resolve this tension in one way or another; it does not demand that he give up his nazism. Thus, when standing alone, Consistency hardly has an obvious claim to its preeminence—a state that killed all Jews is more illegitimate than one that muddled its way to saving some. But Consistency does not stand alone. Its function is to safeguard the intelligibility of the dialogue demanded by Rationality. When a Jew is told that he is being killed because "Jews are intrinsically vicious beasts," he will be appalled by the answer he has received, *but he will find no difficulty understanding it.* This is true, however, only because the Jew decodes the utterance with the aid of the interpretive assumption that the Nazi would not knowingly contradict himself. If the Nazi's assertion were set against the background of an equally emphatic declaration that "Jews are as good as the rest of us," it would be wrenched into a context that puts its

5. Certain minimal requirements for Rationality will, however, be advanced in chapter 2, § 11.

status as a reason into question. When a person is willing to assert R and $\bar{R}$ simultaneously, he has not given two reasons for his action. He has provided some noise that adds up to no argument at all.

3. CONSTRAINED POWER TALK

The first two principles do one important thing—establish the centrality of reason giving to the concept of right. Whenever nothing intelligible can be said in justification of a power, its exercise is illegitimate. A sustained silence or a stream of self-contradictory noises are decisive signs that something very wrong is going on.

All this, it may be said, is very true but very weak stuff. Yet appearances are deceiving; with the addition of one final ingredient, we may brew a political solution with enormous resolving power. The missing idea is that particular kinds of conversation are often constrained by special rules restricting what may be appropriately said within them. We could hardly run our everyday lives if every utterance opened us up to an all-consuming conversation about everything under the sun. Even the most egregious boor recognizes that a conversation with the telephone operator is not a suitable vehicle for a blow-by-blow account of his life. It is this familiar sense of conversational constraint[6] that I mean to put to a new use. Just as there are constraints imposed in other conversations, I also want to constrain the dialogues in which people talk to one another about their claims to power. Not that I wish to constrain power talk by appealing to social etiquette. Notions of conventional propriety presuppose the legitimacy of the power structure, rather than vice versa. The question, instead, is whether fundamental philosophical arguments can be advanced to justify one or another constraint on power talk.

Suppose, for a moment, that the answer is Yes. Suppose that I can convince you that no argument of type Z should be permitted to count as a good argument in conversations about power. Given this achievement, it is easy to see how my first two principles can be transformed into a mighty philosophical engine. While it is a safe bet that *some* reason can be found to justify *any* power relationship, P_i, all bets are off once the propriety of a conversational constraint, Z, is conceded. For

---

6. Elaborated illuminatingly by H. P. Grice, "Logic and Conversation," in Donald Davidson and Gilbert Harman, eds., *The Logic of Grammar* (Encino, Calif: Dickinson, 1975), pp. 64–153.

it might then turn out that the *only* reasons that can be advanced in support of P_i are among those eliminated by Z. Thus, once Z has done its work of exclusion, *all that may be left is silence*. And once a claimant to a scarce resource has been reduced to silence, Rationality requires him to recognize that his claim to power is illegitimate. In short, I propose to demonstrate the illegitimacy of a wide variety of power structures by reducing their proponents to silence. Call this way of delegitimating a power structure the method of *constrained silence*.

Now if this method can be deployed as a powerful engine of political appraisal, everything will depend on the choice of Z. To serve its purpose, Z must be designed with two ends in mind. First, the more reasons Z excludes, the more likely it is that at least some power structures will be unmasked as indefensible within the constraint it imposes. Ceteris paribus, the bigger the Z, the better. But this concern with quantity is worthless without an assessment of Zs quality. Thus, we will get nowhere with constraints of the form "*Only* reasons of Z type are good reasons in this conversation." For when the proponent of such a Z is asked to justify this constraint, he will be obliged to explain why Z is better than all competing substantive principles. Yet it is just this conversation which the constraint sought to avoid in the first place.

Things get more interesting if the constraint does not pretend to specify both necessary and sufficient conditions for a good reason but contents itself with stipulating only necessary conditions: "*No Z* is a good reason" rather than "*Only Z* is a good reason." When framed in this way, a conversational constraint may seem plausible to many different people who bitterly disagree about lots of other things. For example, both communists and liberals may agree that nazi arguments (defined in some clear way by Z) are bad reasons, though they reach this judgment by means of very different arguments—call them $[c]$ and $[l]$, respectively. Even more striking, the arguments contained in $[c]$ may be logically inconsistent with those contained in $[l]$. Nonetheless, *both groups will converge on Z by a process of argument that makes sense to them.*

Of course, the proposed "anti-Fascist" constraint is not, on its merits, a terribly incisive idea. Hitler may not have been smart enough to think of all the arguments for genocide. So if Z were carefully framed to exclude only the particular claims made by Hitler and his henchmen, our Z might not prevent someone from coming up with a new reason for genocide. If we are to hope for success from the method of constrained silence, we cannot frame our Z with a particular historical experience in mind but must proceed from more general philosophical considerations. Only in this way can we formulate a conversational constraint of such breadth that the proponents of particular power structures will find themselves speechless when called upon to defend their legitimacy.

But there are transparent dangers in broadening the constraints. The broader the Z, the harder it will be to frame a principle that will seem plausible to people with otherwise different views of the world. Nonetheless, the effort is not obviously hopeless; indeed, my object is to persuade you that the liberal tradition is best understood as precisely such an effort to define and justify broad constraints on power talk. Thus, I do not wish to claim any great novelty for the Z that will preoccupy us. To the contrary, constraints similar to mine can be found in any writer working within the historical liberal tradition.[7] The novelty is simply my claim that the notion of constrained conversation should serve as *the* organizing principle of liberal thought. When others have sought to give liberalism systematic form, they have turned to other ideas—most notably contract or utility—to serve as their organizing principle. In contrast, I hope to convince you that the idea of constrained conversation provides a far more satisfactory key to the liberal enterprise. And once the lock is turned, the liberal tradition will reveal unsuspected resources of methodological rigor and substantive depth.

4. NEUTRALITY AND CONVERGENCE

My particular Z taps the liberal's opposition to paternalism. The germ of the idea is that nobody has the right to vindicate political authority by asserting a privileged insight into the moral universe which is denied the rest of us. A power structure is illegitimate if it can be justified

---

7. Moreover, there are encouraging signs of a renewed appreciation of these constraints in recent liberal theorizing, see, e.g., Ronald Dworkin, "Liberalism" in Stuart Hampshire, ed., *Public and Private Morality* (Cambridge: Cambridge Univ. Press, 1978) pp. 113–43. No less encouraging is the emphasis upon conversational legitimation prevailing among the most creative workers in the Marxist tradition. See, e.g., Jurgen Habermas, *Legitimation Crisis* (Boston: Beacon Press, 1975).

only through a conversation in which some person (or group) must assert that he is (or they are) the privileged moral authority:

Neutrality. No reason is a good reason if it requires the power holder to assert:

(a) that his conception of the good is better than that asserted by any of his fellow citizens, *or*

(b) that, regardless of his conception of the good, he is intrinsically superior to one or more of his fellow citizens.

I will defer important questions of interpretation[8] to emphasize the main point—which is the way Neutrality promises to satisfy the two conditions we require for a potent Z. Since the breadth of the exclusion imposed by Neutrality is obvious, the critical question is whether the formulation suffers the defects of this virtue: Does its very breadth make it impossible to generate arguments that will justify its acceptance as a fundamental constraint on power talk?

Not at all. It is downright easy to think of several weighty arguments in support of Neutrality. The first is a skeptical argument: While everybody has an opinion about the good life, none can be known to be superior to any other. It follows that anyone who asserts that either he or his aims are intrinsically superior doesn't know what he's talking about. Yet this is precisely the move barred by Neutrality.

But there is no need to be a skeptic before you can reason your way to Neutrality. Even if you think you can *know* something about the good life, there are several good reasons for imposing liberal constraints on political conversation. Most obviously, you might think that you can only learn anything true about the good when you are free to experiment in life without some authoritative teacher intervening whenever he thinks you're going wrong. And if you think this, Neutrality seems made to order. But, once again, this view is only one of many that will provide a plausible path to Neutrality. Even if you don't think you need to experiment, you may adopt a conception of the good that gives a central place to autonomous deliberation and deny that it is possible to *force* a person to be good. On this view, the intrusion of non-Neutral argument into power talk will seem self-defeating at best—since it threatens to divert people from the true means of cultivating a truly good life. Assume, finally, that you think you know

---

8. For a definition of "conception of the good," see § 12; for a definition of citizenship, see Chapter 3.

what the good life is and that it is of a kind that can be forced on others; then the only question is whether the right people will be doing the forcing. A single glance at the world suggests that this is no trivial problem. People adept in gaining power are hardly known for their depth of moral insight; the very effort to engross power corrupts—at least if your theory of the good embraces any number of familiar moral ideals.

Not that it is absolutely impossible to reason yourself to a rejection of Neutrality. Plato began systematic political philosophy with such a dream; medieval churchmen thought there were good reasons to confide ultimate secular authority to the pope. Only they recognized—as modern totalitarians do not—the depth of the reconceptualization required before a breach of Neutrality can be given a coherent justification. It is not enough to reject one or another of the basic arguments that lead to a reasoned commitment to Neutrality; one must reject *all* of them. And to do this does not require a superficial change of political opinions but a transformation of one's entire view of the world— both as to the nature of human values and the extent to which the powerful can be trusted to lead their brethren to the promised land.

In proposing Neutrality, then, I do not imagine I am defending an embattled citadel on the fringe of modern civilization. Instead, I am pointing to a place well within the cultural interior that can be reached by countless pathways of argument coming from very different directions. As time passes, some paths are abandoned while others are worn smooth; yet the exciting work on the frontier cannot blind us to the hold that the center has upon us.

5. IS LIBERALISM CONSISTENT?

By the time we complete our journey, I will investigate the conceptual routes to Neutrality with greater care.[9] Before we engage in extensive road repair, however, simple prudence requires us to attend to sober guides who warn us that all these highways lead nowhere. According to them,[10] liberalism is incapable of formulating a self-consistent response to the struggle for power. It is doomed instead to lurch from one self-contradiction to another in a vain effort to save the myth of

9. Chapter 11.
10. See. e.g., Roberto Mangabeira Unger, *Knowledge and Politics* (New York, Free Press: 1976); Robert Paul Wolff, *In Defense of Anarchism* (New York: Harper & Row, 1970).

Neutrality. Rather than making the same mistakes again, we must have the courage to discard the myth of Neutrality and search for a Something whose nature can only be glimpsed darkly through the gray mist that liberalism has bequeathed us. And though this Something is certainly elusive, yet surely it is better than the self-contradictory Nothing that liberalism provides. On then, into the darkness—for only there will we find our hidden Humanity.

Now I take this argument seriously. Yet, like all arguments, this one can be no better than its premises. The choice is between an obscure Something and a self-contradictory Nothing only if it is conceded that liberalism is intellectually bankrupt, that it can propose no self-consistent way of resolving power conflict. And this is something that liberalism's critics are more apt to assert than prove. Not that I blame them: it is hard to prove a negative, and given their intimations of bankruptcy, they understandably prefer to spend their time on more constructive activities. For us, however, the case stands otherwise. There is a simple way to establish, once and for all, that the accusation of bankruptcy is wrong. And that is to provide a single example of a liberal theory equal to the conceptual task of providing a Neutral order to the struggle for power. In terms of our model of legitimacy, all we need propose is a single system for regulating power conflicts that can be justified by:

1. a self-consistent set of reasons (principles one and two) that
2. do *not* violate either branch of the Neutrality principle.

If there is even one such system of power relations, P_i, then the claim that liberalism is bankrupt is simply wrong. Of course, it may well turn out that any P_i that supports a thoroughgoing Neutral dialogue looks very different from the power structures within which we live our lives. But this means that liberalism, properly understood, requires a more sweeping critique of the existing power structure than is sometimes supposed. Rather than an empty bankrupt, liberalism emerges as a coherent set of ideals of enormous critical force.

Indeed, I may make an even stronger claim if the critics are only 99.99 percent right in their accusations of bankruptcy. Assume, for example, that a complete survey of the millions of possible reasons for claiming power reveals that *all but one* of them involved the claimant saying that he was intrinsically better than the next guy or that his ends in life were especially worthwhile. The discovery of such a unique reason, R, would have just the opposite consequences of bankruptcy.

As we have seen, people may be persuaded by any number of very different reasons to embrace the ideal of Neutral discourse. Since R happens to be the *only* reason that passes the test of Neutral dialogue, anybody who has been convinced (for whatever reason) to accept my three principles of legitimacy has *no choice* but to accept R.[11] Thus, we may glimpse the old liberal dream of a philosopher's stone by which a commitment to a particular procedure of dispute resolution—here, the process of constrained conversation—can be transformed into a commitment to particular substantive outcomes.

Not that such a demonstration would induce instant conversion among those who would lead us to authoritarianism in the name of Humanity. Yet there would no longer be any hope of a cheap victory over some pitiful blob of self-contradiction. Instead, the partisans of authority will confront at least one well-specified power structure, P_i, that can be rationally defended within the conversational constraints imposed by liberal principles. Before they can reject P_i, they must proceed to do battle on far more difficult terrain—where success requires them to free themselves from the complex web of argument that binds them to Neutrality and Rationality.

But, alas, there is no a priori reason to think that things will work out so neatly. While the constraints imposed by Neutrality are broad, they may nonetheless permit more than one R to break the conversational barrier. Rather than pointing to a single kind of substantive discourse, liberalism would then be the name of a family of different substantive arguments that may lead to very different substantive conclusions concerning the right way to resolve one or another power conflict.

---

11. The style of argument is similar to Kenneth Arrow's in his *Social Choice and Individual Values* (New Haven: Yale University Press, 2d ed., 1963). Like him, I propose to constrain collective choice by a set of principles each of which, taken individually, seems relatively uncontroversial. Given these constraints, I then inquire whether any principle for collective decision can be found that does not violate at least one of them. Unlike Arrow, however, I shall conclude that there is at least one R that does satisfy all constraints.

This conclusion, however, is not inconsistent with the famous negative result derived by Arrow's General Impossibility Theorem. Arrow works within the voluntarist tradition and is concerned with the problem of aggregating individual *preferences* into a consistent collective choice; I am working within the rationalist tradition and want to determine whether any of the *reasons* that can be given in defense of power survive plausible conversational constraints. If anything, Arrow's impossibility result can only invigorate inquiries of the kind attempted here. For if, as Arrow suggests, individual *preferences* cannot be aggregated in an uncontroversial way to legitimate social choice, it is even more important to isolate the kinds of *reasons* that may best legitimate the collective choices that must be made in the course of social life.

So much for Arrow's methods. The relevance of his more particular results will be noted in the liberal theory of democracy developed in chapter 9, § 61.7.

Nonetheless, while the P_is may differ substantively, they all will share one family resemblance: all can be fathered by a rational conversation within Neutral constraints. Of course, the fact of common paternity will not then suffice to satisfy all the requirements of political evaluation. We would then be required to reach a new stage of liberal theory and articulate criteria for choosing the most promising child within the liberal family.

Before liberalisms can multiply, however, we must first establish that the ground yields any fruit whatever. Thus, most of this book will try to show how one particular R can be articulated in a way that is conceptually equal to the task of regulating all important forms of power struggle. While I do not claim that mine is the only R that will turn the trick, I can report that my own searches among the universe of possible reasons has not turned up a competitor. Unless somebody develops a formal proof of my R's uniqueness, however, the search for alternative liberal rationales must continue apace.

6. LIBERALISM AND EQUAL RESPECT

Imagine that somebody finds that your claim to some resource interferes with his effort to pursue his good. Any resource will do—your questioner may challenge your right to use your body or some natural object or some cultural artefact or whatever. Anyway, he wants it and issues a conversational challenge:

Q: I want X.
A: So do I! And if I have my way, I'll use force to stop you from taking X.
Q: What gives you the right to do this? Do you think you're better than I am?
A: Not at all. But I think I'm just as good.
Q: And how is that a reason for your use of power?
A: Because you *already* have an X that's at least as good as mine is. If you take this X as well, you'd be better off than I am. And that's not right. Since I'm at least as good as you are, I should have power over an X that is at least as good as yours is.
Q: But haven't you just violated Neutrality?
A: Not at all. Neutrality forbids me from saying that I'm any better than you are; it doesn't prevent me from saying that I'm at least as good.

Q: But if I don't get this extra X, I won't achieve my ends in life.

A: That's not a good reason for your getting X, because the reason I'm claiming X is that I too want it to achieve my ends in life. And do you imagine that it is intrinsically more important for you to achieve your ends in life than it is for me?

Q: I can't say that within the constraints imposed by Neutrality.

A: So, then, what *can* you say in defense of your effort to get a better X than I have?

Q: And if I can't answer that?

A: Then you must recognize that I've given you a Neutral answer to your question of legitimacy, while you have backed up your power play with nothing that looks like a reason.

My purpose in producing this script must be kept clearly in mind. For the present, I do not care what you think of the *merits* of A's argument. Perhaps, upon finding out more facts about A, you will deny that he's as good as Q; perhaps, on thinking further, you will reject the idea that a person's assertion of *moral equality* implies a right to equality in *worldly possessions*. No such objection, however, defeats my purpose in presenting the script for your inspection. To pass the Neutrality test, I do not need to claim that A has presented a *convincing* argument for initial equality; instead, I need only establish that A has presented an *intelligible* argument on behalf of initial equality while keeping within Neutral ground rules. Even if you *disagree* with A when he says, "Since I'm at least as good as you are, I should have an X that is at least as good as yours is," there is something intelligible here with which to disagree. The only thing, then, that I want to say on behalf of my script is that *it can be said*.

And this, my reader, you already know to be true. For you've just read the dialogue and found no difficulty understanding it.

Yet this small concession is larger than it seems. It places the burden of articulation squarely upon those who seek an inegalitarian distribution of worldly advantage. While they may have all sorts of premonitions of superiority, they cannot engross a greater share of power within a liberal state unless they justify their claims in a way that passes the Neutrality constraint. And if they fail to articulate a Neutral justification, they can only succeed in the conversation over power by justifying a change in the conversational ground rules—explaining how they have reasoned their way free of all the arguments that lead to

Neutrality. And if they fail in that, they will have no choice but to attack Rationality, joining with Nietzsche in celebrating the power of the powerful to transcend all talk of good and evil.

And if they do declare themselves supermen, they surely will understand me when I say that I'm willing to fight for my rival understanding of the world.

7. FINISHING THE CONVERSATION

But I have gotten ahead of myself. There is lots of work to do before the stakes can get so high as this. To see why, consider two ways in which the first script is incomplete. First, the dialogue does not end with an unconditional conversational victory by A, but simply establishes that Q cannot expect to win his claim so long as he remains silent. There is, however, no certainty that Q will remain silent. Instead, he can respond in one of two ways. On the one hand, he may reject A's claim that Q's X is at least as good as A's is. On the other hand, Q may accept A's characterization of their power relation and try to frame a Neutral reason why his X *ought* to be better than A's. If Q succeeds in either conversational move, the burden of conversational initiative will shift back to A—obliging him to explain, consistently with Neutrality, why he finds Q's reason unpersuasive; and so on, back and forth, until somebody fails to meet his conversational burden. It is only when this occurs that the silenced party's claim has been unmasked as illegitimate in a liberal state. To use a helpful legalism, our initial script merely describes a way that A might establish a prima facie case in support of the legitimacy of his power over X. A complete theory, however, must move beyond this first, prima facie stage of the conversation and describe the kinds of power structures that would be legitimated in a dialogue in which the parties are free to talk until they have nothing more to say.[12]

---

12. An essay by H. L. A. Hart was important in suggesting to me the potential fruitfulness of this line of development. See his "The Ascription of Responsibility and Rights" in Anthony Flew, ed., *Logic and Language,* First Series (New York: Philosophical Library, 1951), pp. 145–66 in which the notion of a prima facie case is discussed in terms of "defeasible concepts." Unfortunately, Hart presented his analysis of defeasibility as part of a more ambitious—and much criticized—analysis of the nature of human action. See Peter Geach, "Ascriptivisim," *Philosophical Review* 69 (1960): 221; George Pitcher, "Hart on Action and Responsibility," ibid., p. 226. With characteristic thoughtfulness, Hart responded to these critics by abandoning his larger claims about human action. Nonetheless, even his critics recognize that Hart's point about defeasibility "seems to be true in one type of case, namely, that in which the action is bad and, in addition, is

As this dialogue unfolds, I hope to show that it resolves a central ambivalence that has greatly weakened the liberal analysis of power. The ambiguity concerns the place of equality in a just society. On the one hand, certain forms of equal treatment—say, formal equality in the administration of justice—have been central to the liberal tradition. On the other hand, there has been a recurrent fear of a nightmare world where all human diversity has been destroyed in the name of an equality that levels everyone to the lowest common denominator. Haunted by these fears, liberals have too often accustomed themselves to an awkward position on the slippery slope, unable to explain what in principle distinguishes the equalities they cherish from those they detest. My thesis is that an extended conversation is precisely the therapy required to dispel this nightmare equality from our vision. While, as we have seen, Neutral dialogue begins with the affirmation of a right to equal shares, subsequent conversational moves will define a liberal conception of equality that is compatible with a social order rich in diversity of talents, personal ideals, and forms of community. The articulation of this distinctive conception of equality—I shall call it *undominated* equality—will be one of my major purposes.

To accomplish it, however, will require a remedy for a second kind of incompleteness in the initial script. Here the concern is not with the prima facie character of the text but with the dim background against which Q and A recite their lines. The stage directions simply describe two citizens struggling over some scarce resource, X, which both of them desire. But in the world as we know it, the struggle occurs over more concrete resources and takes many different forms: assailant versus victim; trespasser versus property owner; dissident versus bureaucrat; child versus parent; handicapped versus talented; and so forth. To understand the practical implications of liberal conversation, we must grasp the way it can discipline the concrete power struggle of our everyday lives.

In bringing the script down to earth, moreover, we must be careful about the way we fill in the dialogic background. While it is impossible to analyze every concrete institution that regulates the struggle for

---

designated by a condemnatory verb" (p. 232). This is precisely the sort of case we are dealing with here. Q is condemning A's power play as illegitimate and A is trying to defend himself by asserting some reason in defense of his power.

For thoughtful efforts to save something of Hart's analysis, see Richard Epstein, "Pleadings and Presumptions," *University of Chicago Law Review* 40(1974): 556; Joel Feinberg *Doing and Deserving* (Princeton: Princeton Univ. Press, 1970), pp. 119–51.

power, we must resist the temptation of a grossly simplified account. This is, perhaps, the most common mistake made by partisans of the liberal tradition. Time and again, these people speak as if the only significant power in society comes out of the smoking typewriter of a government bureaucrat. While they are tireless in their efforts to constrain this power by exacting standards of Neutrality, they often react with shocked surprise at the very idea of subjecting the powers of "private" citizens to an identical scrutiny. Yet, first of all, we live in a world in which the powers of government are routinely called upon to enforce (as well as define) all of these "private" entitlements. Without this reinforcement, there is no reason to think that those presently advantaged by the distribution of "private" rights would remain so. Second, even if something like the status quo could be maintained without a central government, Q could still ask A to justify his possession of "private" powers that Q also wants to exercise. And unless A can frame a Neutral answer, the three principles require him to recognize that his "private" power is illegitimate. Of course, in the absence of a central government, A might find it very easy to suppress Q and maintain control over "private" powers he cannot justify. But this merely shows that a decentralized system of "private" power can be just as illegitimate as one in which a tyrannical central government holds sway. The task, then, is to deny *any* fundamental power structure the priceless advantage of invisibility—to define a world where *all* power is distributed so that each person might defend his share in a conversation that begins (but does not end) with the move: "because I'm at least as good as you are."

8. TECHNOLOGIES OF JUSTICE

It is one thing to count the ways our initial script is unfinished, quite another to "complete" the text. Indeed, since a single book can only supply a fragment of the required conversation, it is almost fatuous to ask what a *complete* script might look like. Yet it is only by asking this question that we can glimpse the relationship between the fragment presented here and other fragments provided elsewhere.

Consider, then, that a complete liberal analysis of power would contain two different parts. First, there would be an exhausting empirical exercise that would not only describe the power structure, P_s, into which people are presently born but every other power structure,

$[P_a \ldots P_n]$ into which P_s might be transformed through collective action. Then, having specified the "feasibility set," we could move to an equally exhausting normative exercise. Here we would consider each power structure separately to determine whether it would support a thoroughgoing Neutral dialogue. So far as the status quo, P_s, is concerned, this could be determined by considering the kind of power talk that actually takes place, noting especially whether questions of legitimacy are ever systematically suppressed or ignored or answered in a patently illiberal way. But so far as the other $[P_a \ldots P_n]$ in the feasibility set are concerned, we must instead imagine what people would say if they had a set of powers different from the ones they presently exercise. The only way to do this, of course, is to write imaginary dialogues between the incumbents of the various power positions specified by the particular P_i. If it *is* possible to write Neutral scripts for the various A's when they are confronted by the relevant Q's, then P_i would be legitimated as a liberal state operating under the three principles; if not, not.

There is, as I have already noted, no a priori reason to expect that one, and only one, P_i would pass this dialogic test. Instead, the discipline of Neutral script writing would sort the entire feasibility set into two distinct subsets. On the one hand, there would be a *legitimacy subset*, containing those P_is (if any exist) that support a comprehensive Neutral dialogue of justification. On the other hand, the *illegitimacy subset* would contain all the other feasible power structures. For those convinced of the merits of Neutrality and Rationality, *all* P_is in the first subset will seem superior to *any* P_i in the second. It is the class of power structures that fall within the legitimacy subset that I mean to call liberal states.

So much for the general program of liberal analysis. Given its amplitude, there is room for many different kinds of essay, each with different strengths and weaknesses. First, there will be empirical studies that attempt a realistic view of the shape of the feasibility set. Some will try to describe the consequences of transforming a particular power structure—say, the family or private property—in one or another way; others will attempt the more ambitious task of describing the feasible ways in which the entire constellation of power structures may be transformed. In addition to these empirical efforts, different kinds of normative work are also valuable. One kind takes advantage of the available empirical work to describe the feasible power structure that best supports the ideal of a Neutral conversation between all power wielders. While the virtues of this contextual approach are plain, so too are its limitations. Inevitably, the contextualist must heavily sacrifice breadth for depth. It is a rare contextual study that tries to describe a liberal policy for a subject as large, say, as the economy or the government or the family or the educational system. While such contextual assessments are important, we require a view of the forest as well as each tree: Can we not at least glimpse the overall shape of a power structure governed by liberal ideals?

This is the question that will preoccupy us here. As a consequence, our starting point will be different from the one adopted by the contextualist. Instead of beginning with a lengthy appraisal of the policy options that appear feasible in 1980 (or some other arbitrary year), I shall first imagine a polity possessed of a *perfect technology of justice*. That is, I want you to suppose that you live in a place where *there never is any practical difficulty in implementing the substantive conclusions of a Neutral dialogue*. So long as you and I can imagine a power structure, P_i, in which we might defend *all* our claims to scarce resources through Neutral conversation, the perfect technology of justice will costlessly permit us to shape our relations in the way specified by P_i. Not, mind you, that P_i is otherwise an especially attractive place. In particular, my ideal technology of justice has not abolished the underlying fact of scarcity that fuels the struggle for power. Just as in our everyday world, the people of "ideal" theory impose demands on resources that far outstrip the available suppy. My "ideal" assumption simply permits the polity to focus clearly on the question of ultimate objectives: Since we can implement any P_i that we want, the only challenge that remains is to define the kind of power structure worthy of collective support.

In short, a perfect technology of justice provides us with a clean-cut thought experiment to test the claim that liberalism is conceptually bankrupt. If we are unable to specify the way liberal theory can regulate the struggle over scarce resources under a perfect technology of justice, we can be quite certain that the ideal of a society ordered through Neutral power talk is an incoherent dream. If, in contrast, it *is* possible to specify liberal power structures that support a Neutral dialogue under a perfect technology of justice, we have at least located the source of liberal difficulty at a different place. The problem with liberalism would then lie, at worst, in the difficulties of *implementing* the ideal of Neutral dialogue under imperfect technological conditions. While these implementation problems are often extremely difficult, they are hardly what critics have in mind when they declare liberalism bankrupt. Indeed, it would be naïve to insist that a political ideal should be assured a trouble-free implementation; only a silent acceptance of the status quo can assure the absence of all tension between ideals and reality.

The first purpose of an ideal technology, then, is to serve as a kind of conceptual sorter, discriminating between the problems that liberal theory must answer in all possible worlds where people struggle for power from those that arise only under one or another kind of imperfect technology of justice. This conceptual clarification can serve the purpose of providing a framework for more contextual exercises in liberal evaluation. In any real-world problem, it is easy to lose one's way amid a babble of voices, each proposing a very different view of the status quo and its reform. These diverse policies, moreover, will be bottomed on disagreements of very different kinds. Some will depend on disagreements about the facts; others, about the range of feasible alternatives; yet others will involve fundamental questions of value. The success of a policy debate will depend, in part, on the participants' capacity to address the relevant issues in an orderly way. Nor is it enough to untangle empirical disputes; it is equally important to sort out the normative questions that divide the participants. One way of doing this is to ask the disputants to deal with their problem, for a moment, on the assumption that they were equipped with a perfect technology of justice. If their recommendations still diverge, normative differences are obviously of a fundamental kind; if not, the antagonists can proceed to identify the nature of the implementation problems that fuel their disagreement.

Beyond serving as a useful device for organizing debate over practical policy, there is a more general utility in an artful invocation of a perfect technology: it forces us to confront the feature of our political predicament that sets us apart—to the extent that anything does—from our predecessors. In earlier centuries, even the most audacious political thinkers and actors were constrained by the low level of prevailing technology. The most vicious tyrant was checked by the primitive control systems at his command; the most benign statesman could not escape the fact that many outrageous injustices were beyond all hope of remedy. This state of technological innocence is now beyond recall. Apart from the threat of nuclear holocaust, technology makes it possible for tiny elites to transform the world into a gigantic prison for the rest of us. Indeed, we already possess the power to induce people to forget that their world can be anything but an endless series of sedations. And it is only a matter of time before we learn to manipulate the genetic code in a way that will permit elites to design the kinds of underlings that suit their fancy.

Yet it is too late to respond to these dangers by a Luddite assault on our machines. Mass starvation—at least as horrible as nuclear catastrophe—would follow a great leap backward into an agrarian state of nature. Instead of an all-out war against an incredibly insidious foe, a perfect technology of justice points to a more hopeful possibility. It suggests that the vast scientific enterprise need not become an enormous engine of repression, but may instead serve to realize liberal ideals to an extent previously unknown. Of course, more than an act of imagination will be required before technology is transformed into the obedient handmaiden of Neutral dialogue. Indeed, even the most inspired acts of liberal statesmanship and mass vigilance may not suffice to avoid the worst. Nonetheless, without political imagination, liberalism will itself be devoured by the very technological forces that it fostered at an earlier historical moment. If we cannot even imagine a world where men and women master their technology through dialogue, the future is grim.

It is right, then, to begin systematic liberal theory with a perfect technology of justice; but it is wrong to end there. While our present technology is more powerful than our ancestors', it is hardly an ideal mechanism that can costlessly implement the conclusions of a comprehensive Neutral dialogue. Time and again, we will find that the resource costs of fulfilling liberal ideals are very high; indeed, our technology often permits only the crudest approximation of ideal liberal dialogue. These hard facts about the feasibility set generate a second series of normative issues which I shall group under the heading of "second-best" theory. One question stems from the heavy resource costs that efforts to liberalize existing power structures may exact: How is the liberal state to trade off the costs of implementation against the benefits of achieving a more liberal power structure? A second question confronts the fact that ideal liberal structures can never be achieved but only approximated: How are we to judge which imperfect solution is more liberal than the others?

My answers to such questions will have a similar form. On the one hand, I will locate a *family* of policy responses that *all* qualify as reasonable solutions to second-best problems. On the other hand, I shall deny that second-best theory is infinitely flexible—indeed, many familiar power relations *cannot* be fairly viewed as second-best approximations of the liberal ideal. It will be the function of the *theory of exploitation* to define these suspect power structures with care. Once this has been done, I shall argue that all liberals committed to the ideal of *undominated equality* must recognize that some familiar power structures impose a heavy burden of illegitimate *exploitation*. Liberal theory turns out to be neither an idle pipe dream nor a vindication of the status quo. Instead, it demands a discriminating approach to the world around us: some existing power structures already realize many of the possibilities of Neutral dialogue; others can do so with relatively modest reforms; others can exist only so long as Neutral conversation is suppressed. The political task, simply put, is to reform exploitative structures while preserving the liberal advances achieved by our predecessors.

9. OVERVIEW OF THE ARGUMENT

But before we lose ourselves in the complexities of practical statecraft, it is best to clarify some basic ideas. The First Part will strip the power problem down to its irreducible elements by imagining a world where there is only one resource, manna, which can be transformed into any of the familiar material objects of our own world. Predictably, this wonderful resource is desired by all the world's inhabitants. When all manna claims are added up, they exceed the available supply. Hence, the question of legitimacy arises, Q asking A why he is entitled to manna that Q also wants.

Enter now a final character, the Commander, armed with a perfect technology of justice. This means that the Commander will have no trouble implementing whatever decision she thinks just. Since she is a *liberal* Commander, she calls upon the two contestants to explain, consistently with the three principles, why each is justified in excluding the other from the manna that his competitor desires to appropriate.

The next two chapters consider the discussion that ensues. Chapter 2 attempts a general characterization of the conversational moves barred by Rationality and Neutrality, making a special effort to explain why some familiar kinds of political argument—say, utilitarianism—fail to qualify in Neutral discourse. Chapter 3 moves from the nature of the required conversation to the character of the political conversationalists: What does it take to qualify as a citizen of a liberal state entitled to claim rights in political discourse? Can any human being qualify? Any fetus? Any animal? Anything whatever?

By the end of Part One, I hope to provide a clearer view of both the conversation and the conversationalists protected by liberal theory. To make progress on these fronts, I shall content myself with a very simple model of the struggle for power. Not only will I assume that the conflict is limited to a single homogeneous good called manna, but I shall also stipulate that no prior conversation has previously established the legitimacy of any claims to the manna in dispute. To fix this idea, I shall ask you to imagine yourself on a spaceship that comes upon a new world where the available manna has not, up to now, been claimed by anybody. The task, on landing, is to conduct a political conversation that will allocate initial entitlements to the scarce good. This story, however, distorts the position in the actual political conversation in which we find ourselves. Rather than beginning political discourse with a clean slate, we come into a world in which previous generations have invested great energy in power talk.

It will be the task of Part Two to incorporate this basic fact into the dialogic theory of liberal legitimacy. Rather than limiting the conversation to a single generation, the liberal dialogue will be expanded to include the questions of legitimacy that a rising generation may ask of its predecessors. Analysis begins, in chapter 4, with the fact that the very existence of the next generation is within the power of the present one to determine. Do members of the next generation have a *right* to exist? If the present generation can use contraceptive techniques that deprive potential citizens of their very existence, can it also shape its successors in any way it likes? This question takes on added significance in the light of our increasing understanding of the genetic code. Even today, technology permits us to detect and destroy some fetuses who would otherwise possess unfair handicaps in life—if we think this is the right thing to do. Yet these primitive interventions are only a harbinger of things to come. Increasingly, it will become clear that genetic endowments are not immutable facts of nature beyond social control; like all other facts, we possess the power both to alter them and give them a wide variety of social significances. Nonetheless, liberals have had great difficulty confronting the possibility that the existing distribution of genetic resources may be unjust. It is here that the nightmare of equality becomes scariest: if we start to question the legitimacy of the existing genetic distribution, will we not be forced to conclude that the only just world is one where we are transformed (via a hideously "perfect" technology) into carbon copies of one another?

My answer is No. I hope to show how a commitment to Neutral dialogue will permit a political community to assert that a limited class of genetic handicaps are illegitimate while still retaining a general commitment to genetic diversity. It will be the task of the liberal theory of *genetic domination* to explain how to draw the line between liberal diversity and illegitimate advantage.

The next chapter, on liberal education, considers the next stage in the evolving power relationship between generations. Despite childish resistances, each youth is exposed to a wide range of sanctions if his forms of expression and behavior do not meet with parental approval. The way adults exercise these powers has an obvious impact upon the child's power to define and pursue a conception of the good in later life. The coercive aspects of education, moreover, have gained far more attention than the isomorphic problem of genetic domination. Not only has the liberal tradition recognized that educational authority can be exercised in authoritarian ways; liberal ideas have had a powerful impact upon modern child-rearing practices. Nonetheless, liberals have experienced difficulty in fully integrating their theory of education into their larger structure of political philosophy. Tension arises out of the liberal's systematic effort to prevent political authorities from viewing *adult* citizens as if they were errant children who could be restrained on the ground that Father Knows Best. Yet even the most committed liberal must suspect that a similarly absolute bar on paternalism is silly in dealing with children. To recognize this explicitly, however, threatens to erode the liberal's simple resistance to state paternalism when adults are involved. After all, if father *does* know best, why doesn't Father Know Best?

To avoid this embarrassing question, liberal theory shows a pronounced tendency to view education as a special case, treating the problem of justice in *adult–adult* relations as if it had nothing to do with the problem of justice in *adult–children* relations. Once again, my aim is to resolve this long-standing liberal anxiety. Education is not a special case ruled by special principles; it can be governed by the same Neutral dialogue that defines all other legitimate power relations. Only those special limitations over the young that can be defended consistently with the three principles are legitimate; the others are simply efforts by powerful adults to play God. This conclusion, as we shall see, does not require us to cease all self-conscious efforts at providing the young with a moral education; it permits us to refine and deepen already familiar understandings concerning the distinctive nature of liberal education.

I shall reserve the word *education* to denote interactions in which at least one side of the transaction is a child.[13] This leaves the task of defining a legitimate structure for adult–adult interaction to a separate chapter on free exchange. It is here where the liberal tradition is richest: notions of free speech, free contract, free competition, all press forward for recognition. The task will be to move beyond traditional labels and use the techniques of Neutral dialogue to establish the basic principles of transactional structure. Through dialogue, it will be possible to define a more abstract notion of *transactional flexibility* that will permit a clearer understanding of both the strengths and limits of more familiar and concrete slogans. This will permit us to distinguish the kernel of permanent value in traditional liberal formulations from the outworn husk of "free market" capitalism. Rather than eliding capitalism and freedom, liberal dialogue will reveal laissez faire as a very imperfect way of achieving the liberal ideal of free exchange within a flexible transactional structure.

The ideal of transactional flexibility will, in turn, bring us to a final dimension of the intergenerational power struggle. Even if each member of the elder generation begins life with an equal share of the world's material endowments, it is most unlikely that each will end up in the same egalitarian condition. By trading freely over time, some citizens may gain control of gobs of material wealth while others may trade away their birth rights. A new question arises, however, when the rich elders try to pass on their material advantages to their children. Can the disadvantaged members of the younger generation protest this use of their elders' power? May they insist that they have a

13. Of course, the conceptual line dividing "adults" from "children" must itself be clarified. See § 34.

right to begin life under the same conditions of material equality enjoyed by their predecessors?

A closely related question involves the right of the elder generation to deplete the stock of resources available to its successors. Can the elders simply consume as much as they like, leaving their children the crumbs? Or must they restrain the power given them by the sheer fact of temporal priority? It will be the task of the chapter on trusteeship to provide liberal answers to these questions, revealing a close link between our obligation to conserve the planet's finite resources for our successors and our obligation to respect each *individual* successor's prima facie right to an equal share of the wealth.

By the end of Part Two, then, our new world will begin to resemble a more familiar social reality. No longer will we be dealing with the effort by a single generation to resolve a single power struggle over a single resource through liberal conversation. Instead, liberal political dialogue will prove itself equal to the never-ending struggle over the genetic, material, and cultural resources that all of us require to define and pursue our ends in life. To state my conclusions in terms that only dialogue can make clear: A political community of diverse individuals can organize its power struggle consistently with Neutral discourse if it takes steps to assure that:

a. No citizen *genetically dominates* another.
b. Each citizen receives a *liberal education.*
c. Each citizen begins adult life under conditions of *material equality.*
d. Each citizen can *freely exchange* his initial entitlements within a *flexible transactional network.*
e. Each citizen, at the moment of his death, can assert that he has fulfilled his obligations of *liberal trusteeship*, passing on to the next generation a power structure no less liberal than the one he himself enjoyed.

If a social world fulfills all these conditions, I shall say that its inhabitants enjoy the condition of *undominated equality* that is required by an undeviating insistence on liberal dialogic legitimacy.

It is one thing, however, to define the nature of liberal ideals, quite another to implement the dialogic demand for undominated equality in an intractable social reality. To travel from the ideal to the real requires us to abandon our "perfect" technology of justice, to confront the costly and imperfect means we have at our disposal to reach a just solution to social conflict. As the discussion proceeds through the first two parts, I shall increasingly incorporate second-best factors into the analysis: after discussing ideal liberal education, I shall turn to second-best forms; and so forth. While these discussions can merely point to vast bodies of contextual work, I hope they suggest the power of general liberal theory to clarify the ongoing debate through which the polity seeks to legitimate its basic policy choices. Apart from these particular debates, however, there are two more general questions raised by the failure of a perfect technology of justice. It will be the point of the two chapters in Part Three to confront these questions head-on. The chapter on exploitation concentrates upon the hard choices required by the fact that justice is itself a scarce commodity. Given the resources eaten up by imperfect technologies of justice, it will no longer seem sensible for liberal statesmen to aim for a perfect condition of undominated equality. Moreover, different liberal statesmen will often disagree in good faith when it comes to deciding the best way of economizing on the pursuit of justice. Despite these ongoing policy disagreements, however, I shall argue that second-best theory places certain issues off limits as appropriate subjects of compromise. It will be the task of the theory of *exploitation* to define the cases in which victims of injustice have an *indisputable* claim that *all* statesmen must recognize upon pain of forfeiting their liberal legitimacy.

The next chapter begins by considering the problem of constitutional government that arises when liberal statesmen predictably disagree on a wide range of second-best issues of implementation. It is here that I shall explore, and vindicate, the liberal claim that majority rule is the best way of resolving—at least for a time—the wide range of issues upon which citizen-statesmen may legitimately disagree. As the theory of exploitation makes clear, however, there remain power structures that cannot be tolerated by *any* liberal statesman even when second-best conditions are taken into account. This leads to the second major question of constitutional theory: how to avoid a tyranny where government is used by elites to impose an exploitative power structure on the rest of us? It is here that I appraise the limits and strengths of traditional liberal solutions—bills of rights, checks and balances—as techniques for assuring the vitality of liberal dialogue in the face of authoritarian takeover.

By the end of Part Three, then, we shall have traveled a goodly distance from the early dialogues of our new world colony. By proceeding step by step, the hope is to gain an understanding of the way that Neutral dialogue can discipline the institutions that regulate the unending struggle within which we must somehow find our way. By the end of our imaginary journey, we shall glimpse a world that is committed both to individual rights and democratic decision; that uses the power of government to strike at the roots of exploitation while remaining conscious of the dangers of bureaucratic tyranny. In short, our commitment to Neutral dialogue has led us to a familiar form of polity—the liberal-democratic welfare state. Yet this familiar destination should not convince us of the futility of our journey. To the contrary, our act of political imagination has served to place the everyday world in a new perspective. The contemporary liberal state will no longer seem a random jumble of ideas tossed up by a century-long conflict between the partisans of Locke and Marx. Though this indeed is its historical parentage, modern liberalism has its own inner coherence when understood as a sustained effort to achieve a power structure in which all members of the political community can engage in a distinctive form of dialogue with one another.

Having seen this much, it remains, in Part Four, to consider the philosophical claims that liberal political culture has upon us. The aim will be to convince you—as much as philosophy can—to join the struggle for a polity in which liberal dialogue achieves a breadth and depth previously unknown.

2

WEALTH

10. A NEW WORLD

Imagine that you and I (and the rest of us) embark upon a voyage of discovery, forsaking our previous wealth and position to enter upon the quest. Coming unexpectedly upon a new world, we scan it from afar and learn that it contains only a single resource, manna, which has some remarkable properties. Most important, manna is infinitely divisible and malleable, capable of transformation into any physical object a person may desire. Further scanning reveals, however, that manna retains one basic similarity to familiar earthly elements—it is impossible to squeeze an infinite quantity of a desired good from a single grain of the miracle substance. Indeed, there won't be enough manna to satisfy the total demands of all the members of our party. A struggle for power is inevitable. Nonetheless, things could be worse, and so we decide to make this new world our home.

As we approach the planet, the spaceship is alive with talk. Since manna is in short supply and universally desired, the question of its initial distribution is on everybody's mind. We instruct the automatic pilot to circle the planet for the time it takes to resolve the question of initial distribution and proceed to the Assembly Hall to discuss the matter further.

There we encounter the Commander, the person in charge of the spaceship for the duration of our voyage. To set the stage for discussion, she has three preliminary announcements. The first reports the existence of a perfect technology of justice. The spaceship has been designed to be of value to the colony long past initial landing. The ship's computers can provide any information that we think relevant to our deliberations; its ray guns can be costlessly transformed into a perfect police force, giving constant protection to whatever distribution of manna we think right.

The second announcement concerns the Commander's role in the discussion. Although she is presently in control of the computers and ray guns, she has no intention of forcing us to do her bidding. Indeed, she has already instructed the spaceship's computers to protect her personal claims to manna only to the extent that the ensuing discussion reveals them to be legitimate. Instead of tyrannizing the rest of us, she will simply impose certain ground rules upon the conversation, notably the three principles demanded by the liberal conception of legitimate power talk. To protect the ground rules, she will rule out of order all distributive proposals that cannot be consistently rationalized within liberal conversational constraints. Each of us is free, then, to propose any manna distribution he likes before the Assembly; but unless the proposal can be rationalized in a way that is consistent with Neutrality, there is no chance that it will be adopted.

The Commander's final announcement tells us what we can do if we don't like the conversational constraints she has imposed on collective power talk. In a word: nothing. Before the meeting began, she has already designed a technology of justice that makes all attempts at revolution impossible. You and I are stuck with liberal ground rules; your only chance to get some manna is to frame a Neutral reason that explains why you are entitled to it even though your competitors wish to use it for their own, very different, purposes.

All in all, a very misleading story. As we shall see, one of the principal objects of a constitution is to assure that liberal government does not depend upon the will of a single, corruptible, Commander. Even if a single person could successfully impose liberalism on the rest of us, it would be wrong for her to do so without engaging in a metaconversation that tries to convince us that the three principles constitute the best form of political culture. Thus, the myth of the Commander serves to short-circuit two of the central tasks of liberal political philosophy. Nonetheless, it does serve to focus all our energies on a third task of no less importance. Given the Commander's tenacious defense of Neutrality, all the rest of us are obliged to think very hard about the internal resources of liberal political culture. Our very lives depend upon an ability to articulate a liberal argument that legitimates a claim for at least some manna. Can we, then, generate a political culture capable of regulating the struggle for power consistently with liberal principles?

If we answer this question affirmatively, it will be time enough to discard the Commander and design further thought experiments that will extend our understanding of liberal ideals. Moreover, for all its simplifications, the story remains faithful to our everyday situation in three vital particulars. First, the spaceship problem does not abolish the fact of *relative scarcity*; the discoverers of the new world cannot escape the struggle for power any more than the residents of an old one. Second, I have not asked you to imagine yourself an entirely different *kind of person* from the one with whom you are intimately familiar. At no point will you be called upon to look upon the power problem as if you were a benevolent ideal observer permanently removed from the struggle for power. Instead of pretending that you were some benign deity trying to maximize the happiness of your creation, I shall permit you to recognize that you are particularly concerned with your own self-realization. Moreover, I do not ask you to mask this sense of self with a veil of ignorance that deprives you of all knowledge of your personal life situation. Instead of hiding yourself from yourself, you are invited to confront the problem of social justice with as much self-understanding as you possess. The only special capacity I will require of you is the ability to determine whether your conversation conforms to the constraints imposed by the three principles. Third, the problem does not require you to think of your *social situation* as different from the one with which you are acquainted. In particular, life on the spaceship is not at all like any state of nature I have read about. The explorers may be conceived as representing each of the cultures generated by mankind during its stay on earth: rather than emerging from an innocent state of solitude, the future inhabitants of our new world can tap the collective experience generated by mankind in the course of social life on earth. Each is thoroughly acquainted with the reality of social constraint—though, of course, the particular substance of the constraints has varied enormously from one culture to another. The question is whether they can, through Neutral dialogue, forge a set of constraints upon the struggle for power that is their common fate.

There is a pattern, then, to the kinds of simplifications I have tolerated in my story. The goal, from the outset, is not to escape the familiar world but to point to a solution of a problem from which there can be no escape. Here we are, you and I, confronting one another over a scarce resource; while we happen to be on a spaceship, this hardly transforms the predicament generated by the fact of scarcity, much less the essential features of our self-understanding and social situation. Our story simply defines a social environment in which we are deprived of all the familiar cop-outs that permit us to evade the liberal question of legitimacy. Thus, neither you nor I are free to "solve" the power struggle by a show of brute force; nor can we fritter away our time by talking about important, yet ultimately secondary, issues of implementation; we are instead obliged to consider the central claim of liberalism—that it is possible for you and me to solve the problem of power by talking to one another under conversational ground rules that deny each of us the right to play God.

11. RATIONALITY

The meeting is called to order. The Commander reports that the spaceship's scanning device reveals that the new world contains a fixed quantity of manna (say, one million grains) and asks the Assembly whether this is enough to satisfy all their demands. Within minutes, it becomes obvious that demand outstrips supply. It follows that the group has a problem, one that can be solved only by framing a distribution rule that specifies the share of manna each colonist will receive as he begins a new life in a new world. In response, explorers come forward from all sides of the hall proffering a wide range of inconsistent solutions to the problem.

11.1. *Rational Distribution Rules*

Before recognizing the first speaker, the Commander must confront a procedural problem of her own: Should she permit speakers to string together any set of sentences they like to form their favored distribution rule? Or can she legitimately rule certain proposals out of order without further discussion?

I shall argue for the second, more restrictive, position. Not that the Commander may bar a proposal from the floor simply because she thinks it unwise. Nonetheless, distribution rules can be framed in such an inept way that they cannot conceivably solve the problem of scarcity that commands the Assembly's attention. It is these rules, and only these rules, that may be eliminated in the name of the Rationality principle.

To begin simply, assume there are not only one million grains of manna on our new world but one million citizens on our spaceship. Despite these facts, somebody proposes a rule that divides the colonists into two equal classes, A and B, and awards members of A two grains apiece and members of B one grain. This plainly will not do: as the total manna awarded under the rule is one and a half million grains, it cannot *conceivably* serve as a "solution" to the Assembly's million-manna problem. More generally, to satisfy the requirements of Rationality, all distribution rules must be *harmonious*: the material resources awarded under the rule cannot add up to more than the total available for distribution.

A second formal requirement seems no more controversial but is more important to the general argument that follows. Consider a decision rule that reads: "Whenever a person born on August 19 makes a claim for manna that conflicts with one made by persons born on other birthdays, the former shall win." The problem here is the rule's failure to specify a solution to all the conflicts that may be anticipated in our new world. Thus, if X and Y are both born on August 19, the rule does not tell them how much each is entitled to claim upon leaving the ship. Those born on unlucky birthdays will be in an identical predicament. While the rule insists that they recognize the superior rights of X and Y, it does not say what happens if the fortunate few let some grains fall unclaimed from their table. More generally, any admissible distribution rule must be *complete*: it must specify how *each* colonist will fare if the distributive proposal gains the Assembly's acceptance. Like the unharmonious rule, the incomplete rule cannot conceivably regulate the power struggle generated by the fact of relative scarcity.

Now, in any concrete case, the degree of elaboration required for completeness depends on contingent facts. If, for example, it turns out that I am the only person born on August 19, and I want to stake a claim on all the available manna, then the August 19 distribution rule will satisfy completeness. Since I am trying to write a book relevant to the real world, however, it would be silly to call a decision rule "complete" unless it is capable of resolving the manna claims generated by a large and diverse population of the kind familiar to an earthly traveler. Consequently, I shall require the proponent of any decision rule to explain how the rule would adjudicate the claims of *any* person whom we might plausibly encounter in real life.

This is not to say that a complete distribution rule need be an impossibly cumbersome and lengthy affair. If, for example, I advanced the rule "Bruce Ackerman should get all the manna while the rest of the colonists starve to death," this brief statement is perfectly complete (and harmonious as well). More generally, any distribution rule will pass the test if it explicitly defines a "residual class" that includes everybody who fails to fit within any of the other classes specified by the rule. Of course, even when this is done, a particular distribution rule may assert that members of the residual class are entitled to no manna whatsoever. But this is a problem with the substance of the rule, not its form; while it may be challenged under Neutrality, the rule escapes the strictures of the Rationality principle.

11.2. *Rational Justification*

After explaining that only harmonious and complete distribution rules are admissible, the Commander opens the floor to all comers. The results are overwhelming. Some rules distribute manna on the basis of merit, others on the basis of need; some classify people by their contribution to overall happiness, others consider their contribution to the worst-off class; some say manna should be distributed equally, others that it all should be the property of a named individual; and so forth. Worse yet, partisans of each approach soon discover differences within their respective camps: notions of "merit," "need," "happiness," admit of a wide range of different interpretations; even people who adopt precisely the same classificatory scheme may differ concerning the amount of manna that should be awarded to members of each group. For a time permutations and combinations are offered without end. Yet the collective imagination of the group ultimately exhausts itself. Speakers reach the platform only to find that their favored distribution rule has already been entered on the agenda. Finally, there is nobody who wants to expand the formidable list of solutions to the problem of scarcity.

The Assembly turns once again to the Commander, who confronts her second procedural problem. All the rules on the agenda are inconsistent with one another: each rule awards at least one person an amount of manna that is different from that which he would receive under any of the competing rules. The Commander's problem, quite simply, is to design a legitimate procedure for narrowing the agenda to a single solution.

The Rationality principle provides some first aid. It establishes that a distribution rule, before it can be legitimate, must specify a power structure in which each power wielder can support his claim to manna by giving a reason when challenged by any of his fellow citizens. This basic point immediately suggests an initial way of pruning the Assembly's agenda. All the Commander need do is call upon the proponents of each distribution rule to produce a "reason" in support of their preference. Any rule that fails to be supported in this way is to be struck from the agenda under Rationality.

Before adopting this procedure, however, the Commander must resolve an important interpretive question. Once again, she must decide whether the Rationality principle imposes some demands upon utterances before they can count as "reasons" for preferring a particular distributive proposal. Moreover, a misstep here can distort the entire enterprise. Suppose, for example, that the Commander dismissed as ir-Rational all conversations except the one, R, which seemed wisest to her. This easy use of "irrationality" as an epithet would not only undercut the idea of tolerance that is central to the liberal tradition; it also does grievous damage to this essay's central analytic point. For my aim is to develop a more complicated way of condemning power structures as illegitimate—the method of constrained silence. This method does not depend on an aggressive use of Rationality but on a demonstration that very few reasons survive the constraint imposed by Neutrality. Indeed, I *never* want to condemn any argument as irrational simply because I disapprove of its content. Instead, my exercise will parallel the one we have just completed in defining the class of admissible decision rules. There, the only utterances excluded were those that could not *conceivably* serve as a "solution" to the problem of scarce resources confronting the Assembly. Here, the definition of a reason will also be problem related. Now that all relevant distribution rules have entered the lists, the Assembly's problem is to pick the one that seems preferable to all others. Before an utterance can count as a reason, it must be interpretable in a way that is relevant to this objective. Once again, this point is not quite so innocuous as it may first appear. Some utterances fail to pass even this very low threshold of relevance.

Begin with an extreme case. Imagine that a group of citizens sneak out of the Assembly Hall, commandeer a space buggy to the new world, and stake claims to the manna while their fellows are circling the planet with talk. When the spaceship finally lands, the citizenry are confronted with squatters who say, "While you have been wasting your time talking, we have grabbed what we wanted. And, no matter what you say, we are determined to ignore your talk and keep what we have. So shut up and go away." While this response is perfectly intelligible, it does not purport to be a solution to the problem posed in the Assembly Hall. Rather than fulfilling Rationality, the squatters have attacked Rationality's legitimacy by glorifying the role of brute force unmediated by any dialogue whatever. More generally, a power wielder cannot legitimate his power by saying, "It is *inconceivable* that power can be exercised illegitimately." Such an assertion might serve as a reason for discontinuing the conversation, but it does not serve as an *answer* to the question of legitimacy. If a proposition denies the conceptual possibility that power may be illegitimate, it merely *glorifies,* and does not *justify,* power.[1] To count as a reason, a statement cannot contradict the very idea that power can conceivably be exercised illegitimately. Call this the *conceivability* test.

Once again, I want to emphasize the very weak restriction on discourse imposed by conceivability. Imagine, for example, that a citizen does not sneak out of the Assembly Hall but proposes an Oklahoma landrush solution to the manna problem:

RUSHER: I say that the first person who grabs a piece of manna should be recognized as its true owner.
COMMANDER: Well, this rule is both harmonious and complete. What reason can you give for thinking it's preferable to its competitors?
RUSHER: Because people who grab first are better than people who grab second.

Whatever else may be said of Rusher's remarks, they do not offend Rationality in the same way that squatter talk did. While the squatters reject the very idea that their legitimacy can be questioned, Rusher will have no difficulty satisfying the conceivability test. For he will have no trouble conceiving a situation that is illegitimate—notably, one where a second-grabber expropriates the power of a first-grabber.

Indeed, conceivability is such a weak test that it must be distin-

---

1. But don't the squatters have the right idea? Why shouldn't power be glorified rather than justified?

A good question. But notice that it arises on a different level from the one with which we are presently concerned. Rather than another move *within* a liberal political conversation, it denies the very *need for* such a conversation. While such attacks on liberal principles will be confronted in Part Four, especially in chapter 11, my present concern is to elucidate the political dialogue that proceeds within the ground rules imposed by liberal theory.

guished from more familiar criteria[2] that require speakers to universalize their value judgments. Thus, suppose Egotist rises in the Assembly on behalf of a proposal which would award him all the manna:

CHALLENGER: Why should you get it all?
EGOTIST: Because I'm the greatest thing there could possibly be.
CHALLENGER: Why do you think so? Isn't it even conceivable that somebody might be more worthy of praise?
EGOTIST: Absolutely not. While others might be smarter or nobler or kinder, they nonetheless would not be me!
CHALLENGER: So what?
EGOTIST: Its the meness of me that makes me great!
CHALLENGER: Awfully conceited of you.
EGOTIST: Say what you like, but it's the reason that I think I should get all the manna.

While Egotist may not be willing to universalize his value judgments, he finds it easy to conceive a world where power may be exercised illegitimately—notably, one in which anybody but himself exercises power. Given this fact, Egotist will have no trouble passing conceivability. While Egotist will confront conversational embarrassment when it comes to Neutrality, his answer *is* a possible solution to the Assembly's problem and, given its conversational relevance, passes the thin filter on collective discourse imposed by Rationality.

Given Egotist's success, it may be imagined that any and all responses (short of sneaking out of the hall) will satisfy Rationality. Yet this would be too strong. Imagine, for example, that I have entered the following rule on the agenda: "Bruce Ackerman should get all the manna, while the rest of you should get none." In response, you raise a dialogic challenge:

Q: O.K., Ackerman, why should you get all the manna? Why is this rule better than one which awarded *me* all the manna?
A: It's very simple really. My rule is better because the sky is blue.
Q: You call that a reason?
A: Absolutely. In fact, look out the porthole and tell me what you see.

---

2. See, e.g., R. M. Hare, *Freedom and Reason*, chap. 2 and 3 (Oxford: Clarendon Press, 1963); Marcus Singer, *Generalization in Ethics* (London: Eyre & Spottiswoode, 1963); Kurt Baier, *The Moral Point of View* (Ithaca: Cornell University Press, 1958), pp. 195–200.

Q: Well, the sky *is* blue.

A: Moreover, my statement passes the conceivability test. For if the sky weren't blue, I'd agree that my claim to power would be illegitimate. So why do you say that I'm being ir-Rational?

COMMANDER: Because, on the face of it, I don't see how sky color is relevant to the Assembly's present decision.

A: How so?

COMMANDER: Our present business is to determine whether your rule is preferable to Q's rule. Before a proposition can be relevant to this task, it must point to a feature of one of the decision rules that is *not* shared by the other. For if both rules possess the feature in the same degree, this could hardly be a reason for preferring one to the other.

A: I guess so.

COMMANDER: So tell me, can you link up sky color to some feature of your rule in a way that distinguishes its merits from the merits of your opponent's rule?

A: (*Silence*)

COMMANDER: Well, until you do so, I fail to see why the sky's blueness should count as a reason in favor of your rule rather than that proffered by your competitor.

We can reach the same conclusion in a different way by comparing the preceding conversation with the situation that would arise if nobody in the Assembly Hall had made any effort whatever to speak on behalf of A's rule. When confronted with this blank void, the Commander would have no choice but to find the A rule illegitimate under Rationality. Yet A's contribution has thus far advanced debate on the relevant question no more than silence does. Before the conversation can properly begin, somebody must say that one distribution rule has a distinctive merit that its competitor does not share. It is A's failure to pass this *differentiation* test that justifies a finding of a violation of my first principle.

Not that there is something about sky color that necessarily disqualifies it as part of a differentiating reason. Imagine, for example, that A responds to the Commander's final question by explaining that God has chosen to communicate with His people by color code, and that when the sky is blue, He is signaling his intention that A be given special preference. When faced with this explanation, there is doubtless much that Q would like to know about the divine color code. Nonetheless, he no longer will have difficulty understanding why A keeps emphatically pointing at the sky to differentiate their claims. To put the point more generally, Rationality does not deny conversationalists the right to differentiate their claims by invoking some feature of the situation whose existence cannot be verified by standard empirical techniques. It only insists that they *say* that this is what they are doing. Nor does the test require A to come up with some elaborate theology to qualify. To continue the conversation:

A: Well, I just have an overwhelming moral sense that the sky's blueness means that I win.
Q: But two can play your game as well as one. What if I say that my intuition tells me that blueness has nothing to do with your winning?
A: Well, your intuition must be wrong.
Q: Why are you so sure?
A: Because my intuitive capacities are intrinsically superior to yours.

A's final line plainly qualifies under the differentiation test: if it were accepted by the Assembly, it would count as a distinctive merit of A's rule that was not equally shared by Q's. Of course, as this dialogue suggests, A is hardly assured of final victory whenever he satisfies the differentiation test demanded by Rationality. Instead, the Assembly may find that it cannot publicly declare his reason persuasive without violating the Neutrality principle. But there is a big difference between something that is a *bad* reason and something that is *no* reason at all. And it is precisely the point of Rationality to mark this line.

Having made this much clear, we can generalize beyond the simple dialogue between A and Q with which we have begun. Rather than confronting a simple two-proposal agenda containing only the A rule and the Q rule, the Assembly's agenda contains a formidable list of competing decision rules. Moreover, its objective is not merely to reason its way to a rejection of a few proposals on the list. To solve the problem of scarcity, it must declare one—and only one—rule superior to *all* the rest. It follows that a proponent of rule X cannot simply propose a reason that differentiates his rule from one of its many competitors. Instead, he must give reasons to believe that his rule has merit when compared to *all* other proposals on the agenda. For it is only in this case that he may properly claim to have given the Assembly reason to declare his X preferable to all the competing ways of organizing power in the new world. This insistence on *comprehensiveness* represents the final requirement I shall impose in the name of Rationality.

I should emphasize, moreover, the purely formal character of this final test. It is true, of course, that only some reasons require little elaboration before establishing their comprehensive character. Thus, if A supports his decision rule by saying, "I should get everything because my moral character is infinitely superior to everybody else's," this is a reason that—if accepted—would vindicate the rule in a single blow against *all* comers, and so satisfy comprehensiveness without further elaboration. In contrast, other citizens will try to defend their more complex decision rules in a more "pluralistic" way, citing reason R_1 to differentiate their X from one subset of decision rules $[X_1 \ldots X_{10}]$, and quite a different reason R_2 to differentiate a second subset $[X_{11} \ldots X_{20}]$ and so forth. Despite this pluralistic commitment, a citizen will have no difficulty satisfying my formal notion of comprehensiveness—so long, at least, as he has some patience. All he need do is explain why his favored rule is preferable to each of the proposals on the Assembly's agenda, grouping these competitors in any way that will lead to an economical discussion. Indeed, since this may be a tedious exercise, it will suffice if the pluralist begins by explaining why he is rejecting a small subset of the agenda, permitting his competitors to pose additional test comparisons until the structure of his argument is sufficiently clarified.

In responding to these challenges, however, the pluralist must be wary of yet another formal constraint. For the second principle in my model—Consistency—denies him the right to decide test cases in self-contradictory ways. Nonetheless, it will always be possible to avoid a formal contradiction by reformulating the reasons that generate the conflict. Like Rationality, the principle of Consistency does not make it impossible for anyone to give any reason any weight he thinks proper. It merely requires the speaker to explain how important a particular argument is in his overall pattern of justification.

So much for formal constraints. If these were the only limits on the Assembly, our explorers would talk their lives away without ever beginning life in their new world. It is not enough for a citizen to propose a harmonious and complete distribution rule; nor is it enough for him to provide a self-consistent justification for his rule that differentiates its merits from that of all its competitors. The reasons he advances must at no point offend the substantive limits imposed in the name of Neutrality. And as these limits are better understood, it will become clear that the explorers cannot roam freely among the list of distributive rules that constitutes their political agenda.

12. NEUTRALITY

I shall call the first branch of Neutrality the bar against *selectivity*, for it denies speakers the right to say that some "conceptions of the good" affirmed by citizens are intrinsically superior to others. This formula, however, can only be as clear as its critical terms: How are we to recognize a citizen's "conception of the good" anyway?

Through dialogue. Each colonist in the Assembly Hall has, as we have seen, expressed a desire for at least some of the manna that is in short supply. It is by questioning the colonist about his purposes in demanding the manna that we will learn his conception of the good. Needless to say, the answers to this question will come in very different shapes and sizes. Some will say that they want the manna to become virtuoso pianists or to pursue God's will or simply to become good persons (of one or another description). Others will spurn all talk of virtue, excellence, or the divine plan. Instead, they will describe their purposes in more subjective terms: "I want manna because I like living better than dying." However complicated or simple the story, the important thing is this: each person is entitled to explain his purposes in the terms that *make most sense to him*; it is this statement that constitutes a citizen's conception of the good.

Now for some second-order cases. Suppose a person says that he thinks it a bad thing to work out his purposes in advance of concrete situations; he simply wants the manna to achieve whatever purposes he may happen to have when the spirit moves him. This proponent of absolute spontaneity has, if you will, only one "meta" purpose—and that is to have no particular purposes prior to the concrete situation. Yet this, for me, will be purpose enough. I shall draw the line only at utterances in which the speaker does not recognize himself as a being who could conceivably have a purpose in acting. While drawing the line here can be a tricky business, I do not think an elaborate exercise is necessary for the main point: the extraordinary diversity of conceptions of the good that our colonists will affirm in the course of living their lives. Given this diversity, each colonist will confront conversational embarrassment when he tries to justify his claim to scarce resources by affirming the value of the activity which his possession of manna will make possible:

A: I should get some of this manna.

Q: Why should you get it rather than I?

A: Because I'll use it to build a great cathedral (or . . .).

Q: But I too have a purpose in making a claim for the manna. I want it to keep my belly warm.

COMMANDER: What is it, then, about your purposes, A, that differentiates your claim from Q's?

A: Easy. It's better to build cathedrals than warm bellies.

Q: No it isn't.

COMMANDER: Well, I'm afraid that Neutrality prevents me from recognizing either of your assertions as admissible in political conversation.

A AND Q: Why?

COMMANDER: Because no citizen may rightfully expect others to recognize that he has the legitimate authority to define the goals that everyone must work to achieve. Neutrality denies the legitimacy of a power relationship when such a thing must be said in its rational defense.

Given the impasse generated by selectivity, the conversation in the hall will predictably turn in a new, but no less disturbing, direction. Here, the speakers will point to some feature they possess and claim that it justifies a preference in the struggle for power *regardless of the purposes for which they will use the scarce resource.* Yet it is just this move which is barred by the second branch of Neutrality, which I shall call the constraint on claims of *unconditional superiority.* Once again, notice the diversity of such claims. Some may advance a complicated story in which the deity or history or . . . has marked out the speaker or his group as superior; others will, less elaborately, assert that they simply intuit the overriding significance of this or that feature in marking their superiority over those competitors who lack it; and finally, there are the egotists: "I am intrinsically superior because I'm me, and you're not." In any particular case, some conversation may be required before it becomes clear whether a claim of superiority really is unconditional or whether a citizen's argument presupposes that he (or his group) is deserving of preference only so long as he keeps on affirming the intrinsic merit of some conception of the good. If this turns out to be the conversational outcome, a citizen will evade the second branch of Neutrality only to hang on the first—for it will then appear that his demand for manna depends on an illegitimately selective reason.

After a few citizens fail to sustain their claims of unconditional superiority, a silence falls upon the Assembly. Staking a legitimate claim to manna is harder than first appeared. It is time for more thought and less talk.

13. THE PURSUIT OF HAPPINESS

13.1. *Utilitarianism*

Pushpin is as good as poetry. Perhaps utilitarianism provides a way of avoiding the dilemmas of Neutrality. After all, Bentham was ostentatious in his contempt for people who thought they could legitimate power relations by appealing to the superior virtue of their goals in life. By measuring all goals in terms of subjective satisfaction, Bentham believed he had established an impartial calculus that could appropriately serve as the foundation for social judgment in a liberal society.

The past half-century, however, has not been kind to Bentham's project. Even the tribe most sympathetic to felicific calculation—professional economists—have come to the view that interpersonal comparisons of utility are "meaningless."[3] While this extreme position has been questioned in passing by philosophers who have noticed it,[4] there is no full-scale critique of the now conventional wisdom. The absence of a modern-day Bentham leads to an embarrassment in exposition. On the one hand, I myself believe that the conventional wisdom about interpersonal comparisons of utility is quite wrong: while there *are* very real (conceptual and practical) problems, I do not think they always make impartial comparisons of utility impossible.

---

3. The classic text is Lionel Robbins, *On the Nature and Significance of Economic Science,* chapter 6 (London: Macmillan & Co., 1932); for a fuller discussion, see I. M. D. Little, *A Critique of Welfare Economics,* chaps. 4–6 (Oxford: Clarendon Press, 2d. ed., 1957); for a rare willingness to move beyond the orthodox, see Amartya Sen, *Collective Choice and Individual Vales,* chaps. 7 and 8 (San Francisco: Holden-Day, 1970).

4. See, e.g., John Rawls, *A Theory of Justice* (Cambridge: Harvard University Press, 1971), p. 91; H. L. A. Hart, "Bentham," *Proceedings of the British Academy* 48 (1962): 340.

On the other hand, I can hardly take the time to do the utilitarian's work for him. The only way out of the impasse, then, is to deal with utilitarianism under two different presuppositions: first, that the conventional wisdom is right in declaring the very idea of interpersonal comparison meaningless; next, that a future Bentham will one day reestablish the idea that interpersonal comparisons may (sometimes at least) be impartially executed.

So long as we remain confined by the conventional wisdom, the dialogic treatment of utilitarianism can be brief. Imagine, for example, that two citizens, Manic and Depressive, each stake a claim on the same piece of manna. If Depressive gets the manna, he will use it to pursue a life of leisured conversation and philosophical reflection; if Manic gets it, he will use it to explore the mountainous reaches of the new world. Recalling past conversational debacles, Manic does not stake his conversational claim by glorying in the virtues of mountaineering; instead, he tries to invoke the principle of utility on his behalf. Unfortunately, however, he finds himself burdened by the conventional wisdom concerning interpersonal comparisons:

> MANIC: I should get the manna.
> DEPRESSIVE: Why?
> MANIC: Because it will yield more utility in my hands then it will in yours.
> DEPRESSIVE: But if you believe interpersonal comparisons of utility to be meaningless, you can't say that.
> MANIC: I guess that's right.
> COMMANDER: But that means you've failed to say anything that differentiates your claim from Depressive's. Unless you say something more, Rationality requires me to rule your manna claim off the political agenda.

Suppose, however, that Manic becomes more ambitious. Rather than settling for the conventional wisdom, he does the conceptual work needed to vindicate Bentham's claim, explaining the way utility experienced by different people may be measured by a common yardstick. Assume, further, that Manic can implement his conceptual analysis by writing a computer program that, given our spaceship's perfect technology of justice, will provide the Assembly with a utility index that indicates the utiles generated if manna is devoted to one use rather than another.

Assume, in short, that Bentham's dream of a perfect felicific calculus has at last been fulfilled on our spaceship. Once again, Manic turns to Depressive in an effort to explain why he should get the manna for mountaineering; only this time, he asks the ship's computers to compare the utiles he will gain with those that would be generated by Depressive's competing philosophical enterprise. After an appropriate number of bleeps and blinks, the computer reports that Depressive's use will generate ten utiles, while Manic's will gain one hundred:

MANIC: Well, I guess that does it. I should get the manna and you shouldn't.

DEPRESSIVE: Why?

MANIC: Look at the numbers, silly.

DEPRESSIVE: But do these numbers measure anything relevant? Are they any more significant than the fact that the sky is blue?

MANIC: They sure are. For they show that I'll get more satisfaction out of mountaineering than you will get out of philosophizing.

DEPRESSIVE: Not so fast. Perhaps they only show that you'll get more satisfaction out of *anything* you do regardless of your conception of the good.

MANIC: And what if this turns out to be true?

DEPRESSIVE: Well, surely you don't think I'm less deserving simply because, regardless of my conception of the good, I'm a less efficient utility generator than you are.

MANIC: Why not? It certainly seems a good enough reason to me for denying manna to you insipid types.

DEPRESSIVE: But you can't expect to have that count as a reason, given Neutrality's bar on assertions of unconditional superiority. So what other reason can you give for considering the numbers as relevant to our predicament?

MANIC: (*Silence.*)

DEPRESSIVE: Well, while you're thinking, let's ask the computer whether the numbers do measure a feature of our situation that obtains regardless of our conceptions of the good.

COMPUTER: Hypothesis falsified . . . numbers measure fact that philosophizing is a less utile-producing activity than mountaineering.

MANIC: So I don't have to stake my claim on an assertion of unconditional superiority.

DEPRESSIVE: But you have yet to break the other conversational barrier established by Neutrality—selectivity.

MANIC: But I don't see any trouble there. After all, I'm not saying that exploring is intrinsically superior to philosophizing.

DEPRESSIVE: How, then, is this utility number relevant to our discussion?

MANIC: It translates the value of philosophizing and mountaineering into a common yardstick: subjective satisfaction.

DEPRESSIVE: But surely there are other possible yardsticks. Why can't I, for example, construct a calculus that ranks all conceptions of the good in terms of the amount of philosophic wisdom they produce and instruct the computer to tell us how much of that good each of us will produce with the manna. (*He does so.*)

COMPUTER: Depressive scores one hundred units on the wisdom index; Manic scores 10 units.

DEPRESSIVE: Why, then, is your yardstick better than mine?

MANIC: Do I have to answer that?

COMMANDER: I'm afraid so. The Rationality principle requires you to say something that differentiates the merit of your rule from that of your competitor's. Apparently, your possession of a scale that measures the value of competing objectives is not enough to do the job. Since Depressive also has a measuring stick, you'll have to say why the Assembly should say that yours is preferable to his.

MANIC: Well, my scale measures the *real* value of both these goods. After everything is said and done, the value of all good lives boils down to subjective satisfaction.

DEPRESSIVE: But I refuse to evaluate my good life in these terms. Even though the process of self-examination may be painful, I think it is better to undertake it than to lead a happy shallow life.

MANIC: Say what you like, but it all boils down to subjective satisfaction in the end. Anything else is mere fluff.

DEPRESSIVE: But two can play this game. I say subjective satisfaction is fluff; the only yardstick that "really" counts is the one that measures the acquisition of wisdom.

MANIC: You can say it, but you're wrong.

DEPRESSIVE: It is you who are mistaken.

COMMANDER: We are reaching a dead-end, my friends. We search in vain for a neutral yardstick for measuring the "real" value of different conceptions of the good. To justify one yardstick over all the other possible ways of ranking values will require utterances that are inconsistent with at least some of the ideals affirmed by some of your fellow citizens.

Even if it were possible to compare utilities, then, there is a second aspect of utilitarianism that prevents its admission into liberal political discourse. And that is its self-confident hedonism—its conviction that the good consists entirely in subjective satisfaction. So long as anyone thinks it better to be a dissatisfied Socrates than a happy anything, the Commander cannot permit such a claim to stand as part of a reason for awarding manna in one way rather than another.

To put the point more broadly still, the problem with utilitarianism is its teleological character, its effort to evaluate distribution rules by how much "good" they produce. *Any* such effort requires a specification of the good that will be contested by *some* citizens who insist on measuring their good by a different yardstick, one that gives them more manna than their competitors. Once the issue is framed in this way, there seems to be no reasoned resolution of the conflict within the limits of discourse established by Neutrality.

13.2. *Equal Fulfillment*

But perhaps we have given up too soon; maybe there is a Neutral way to build a common yardstick. Call it the equal-fulfillment approach. Under this distribution system, each citizen is permitted to affirm *any* conception of the good he thinks best. Then the entire manna stock is distributed in a way that permits each citizen to get an *equal distance* to whatever goals he has set for himself. This leads, of course, to a distribution rule that gives different people very different quantities of manna, depending on how "expensive" their particular life plan happens to be. Yet this fact, standing alone, is hardly enough to condemn the proposal. Liberal theory does not begin with an ipse dixit on behalf of material equality; instead, it begins with a commitment to a process of constrained conversation. If an equal fulfillment standard can be justified within the limits of liberal conversation, its claim to dialogic legitimacy cannot be lightly discounted. It is important, then, to discover that more *can* be said on behalf of equal fulfillment than any of the distribution rules the Assembly has thus far considered. While, as we shall see, the rule's partisans will fail to satisfy their full conversational burden, it is only fair to begin on an upbeat:

MANIC: Well, then, let's find out what the computers have to say this time.

COMPUTER: Manic gets ten grains; after all, he needs all that hiking gear. Depressive gets only one; talk is cheap and Socrates was a vegetarian. Neither of you will get all the material stuff you need to achieve your goals perfectly. But each of you will get halfway to your goals—when judged by your own standards.

MANIC: There. I knew there was a reason I should get more than you.

DEPRESSIVE: What is it?

MANIC: I say that each conception of the good is entitled to equal respect, regardless of its substantive content. We follow this principle by doling out the manna so that each of us is free to achieve our particular good—be it mountaineering or philosophizing—equally well. And this means that I get ten and you get one. Any questions?

DEPRESSIVE: Yes, I don't like your principle. I think——

MANIC: Hold it. Before we start talking about the substantive merits of my argument, do you agree that it passes Neutrality?

DEPRESSIVE: Well, it certainly doesn't involve a claim of unconditional superiority. I'm less certain about selectivity.

MANIC: What's there to be uncertain about? Do you disagree that, with one grain of manna, you'll get halfway to your goal?

So far so good. But Manic's last question contains the seeds of his undoing. To see the problem, consider that equal fulfillment only makes sense in terms of life plans that have a very particular shape to them. Its partisans imagine that all of us conceive the good life as if we were mountaineers intent upon a slow and steady ascent to some high peak that signals final victory. It is only on this mountaineering metaphor that we can speak of two people getting "halfway" toward their ultimate ends. Yet many people affirm conceptions of the good that cannot be accommodated by the mountaintop metaphor. Most obvious are the strugglers among us who always affirm the value of yet another substantive goal if their previous ones have been satisfied. Given their infinitely receding horizons, how much manna do they receive under a rule that gives them enough to get a fraction of the way to their goals?

Then there are citizens—call them jumpers—who assert that an approach to their goals must necessarily be discontinuous. To take an extreme case, consider the mystic who says that you have achieved *nothing* of value until you have accomplished *everything*. On a more mundane level, consider the person who has staked a great deal on achieving one very concrete objective—playing a Stradivarius or building a masterwork. If he gets enough manna to achieve this goal, he will get, say, 80 percent of the way to his final objectives; if not, he can only get 20 percent of the way there. What is the fate of such people if there is only enough manna to permit each citizen to get half of the way to his final end in life? And there are many other troublesome cases.[5]

We confronted this problem before, albeit in a less controversial setting, when we considered the formal defects of a rule that stipulated, "People born on August 19 should always win conflicts with people born on other birthdays."[6] Like this rule, the equal-fulfillment standard is *incomplete*, leaving Manic open to the following embarrassment:

STRUGGLER: And how about me? How much manna do I get?

MANIC: The computer says that the answer is indeterminate.

STRUGGLER: Does that mean I can take at least a little bit of manna?

MANIC: No, it means that my distribution rule doesn't apply to your case. I can't tell you how much you're entitled to take.

STRUGGLER: Then you can't take any manna either.

MANIC: Why not?

STRUGGLER: Because if this is a liberal state, I have a right to a reason from you explaining why you should get the manna rather than me.

MANIC: And the rationale I gave Depressive on behalf of equal fulfillment won't suffice?

STRUGGLER: Not in the slightest, for you yourself have just told me it doesn't apply in my case. I'm waiting, then, for a reason why your claim to the manna is better than mine.

But incompleteness is only a formal defect; it simply means that Manic must supplement his equal-fulfillment rule with additional

5. To put the point in the technical language of economics, trouble will arise whenever there is a single citizen whose utility function exhibits a discontinuity at the manna distribution that would otherwise be selected under the "equal-fulfillment" approach.

6. See 11.1.

rules to cover the cases left out in the cold. Moreover, any number of rules will do the trick. The real difficulty comes when Manic tries to justify the selection of any one of them as an appropriate way of completing his solution to the power problem. In framing the "supplemental" rule, Manic will once again be confronted with the brute fact of scarcity: the more he awards people like Struggler, the less there will remain for people, like himself, who claim under equal fulfillment. However Manic resolves this trade-off, his particular solution will be open to challenge:

MANIC: I can now tell you how much you're entitled to.
STRUGGLER: I'm all ears.
MANIC: I think you should get five grains, while I should get eight.
STRUGGLER: Why so little?
MANIC: Well, appreciate my difficulty. Given your awkward conception of the good, I don't precisely know what to do with you. And five grains is nothing to sneeze at; indeed, it's a lot more than Depressive is getting.
STRUGGLER: I have only one question. Suppose I changed my life plan. Suppose I decided to adopt an expensive life plan on the mountaintop model. Could I then qualify for more manna?
MANIC: Absolutely. I make no claim of unconditional superiority.
STRUGGLER: So the only thing that prevents me from getting the manna is the character of my ideals.
MANIC: Yes. That's what my rule makes decisive.
STRUGGLER: But what reason can you give for making this decisive? Do you think that my life plan is intrinsically inferior to an expensive one designed on mountaintop principles?
MANIC: I can't say that, I guess.
STRUGGLER: Why else, then, should I qualify for more manna simply by striving for an expensive mountaintop?
MANIC: (*Silence.*)

As if this weren't bad enough, Manic is also faced with a final formal requirement of Rationality: comprehensiveness. To convince the Assembly to adopt his rule, he must defend its merits against all comers:

STRUGGLER: Even if I conceded the propriety of a special rule for strugglers, I still don't see why I should get only five grains. Why not a rule that awards me more—say, six?

MANIC: But if you got more, I'd get less.

STRUGGLER: On that reasoning, I should get zero. If you've gone so far as to give me five, why not six?

MANIC: Because you'd be really cutting deep into my success when you deprive me of that extra grain of manna.

STRUGGLER: But, on the other hand, my struggles would be more worthwhile if I started with six grains. So why shouldn't my gain compensate for your loss? Because struggling is a less worthy activity?

MANIC: I can't say that.

STRUGGLER: Well, then, what *can* you say?

Nor does the conversation get any easier if we try variations on the theme of equal fulfillment. Perhaps the most attractive permutation is a rule that distributes initial rights to manna in a way that assures each person an *equal chance* of fulfilling his conception of the good. This formula would have the advantage of eliminating the problem generated by jumping. It no longer requires the impossible task of giving the mystic enough manna to get X percent of the way to divine union; instead, it suffices to give the mystic a 10 percent chance of getting all the way there. While this formula does require formidable computational difficulties, this is not an objection in ideal theory—which posits the existence of a perfect technology of justice. When we turn to Struggler, however, it becomes plain that this new variation does not avoid the fundamental problem. While *equal chances* permits us to measure life's mountaintops in a different way, it does not help against a fellow citizen who denies that life is one long climb to a determinate peak. So long as such strugglers exist, no rule that tries to equalize fulfillment can survive the challenges of complete and comprehensive Neutral justification.

14. THE CASE FOR INITIAL EQUALITY

In the end, the partisan of equal fulfillment falls victim to the same difficulty that afflicted the utilitarian. When Manic talked like a utilitarian, he tried to vindicate his claim in terms of a common yardstick called "subjective satisfaction." When he shifts to equal fulfillment, he is *still* trying to impose his favorite yardstick upon you. Only now he is forcing you to express your life's meaning in terms of a particular formal structure. Unless you agree to express your purposes through the mountaintop metaphor, it becomes impossible to allocate manna in a way that permits each citizen to climb an equal distance toward his favorite peak.

It is this very search for an uncontroversial yardstick measuring use values that lies at the heart of the conversational difficulty. Different people want material resources for vastly different reasons. When these conceptions of the good are elicited through dialogue, the verbalizations come in countless variations. They do not have a common form, much less a common substance. Given this vast and tangled web of discourse, it is impossible to justify the selection of a common yardstick for comparing use values without labeling as deviant some conceptions of the good affirmed by my fellows. When I deny Depressive manna, I must be prepared to tell him he is wrong in thinking that philosophy is worth the pain it produces. When I deny Struggler manna, I must say that he is wrong when he asserts that life's meaning is not to be found on a mountaintop. Yet it is precisely this conversational assault on another's right of self-expression that is barred by Neutrality. In a liberal state, I cannot define the terms of political conversation in a way that disparages my fellow's right to express his ideals *in the words that make most sense to him.* I cannot force him to argue his claims for manna in terms that require him to deny the validity of his own answer to the question of life's meaning.

But if this is so, I must abandon the search for a yardstick that compares the value of my uses of material resources with those of my competitors. However important my particular goals may be to me, I cannot say that others ought to defer to me on their account. Instead, I must fashion a form of political discourse that vindicates my claim to material resources without requiring others to judge, in any way, the value of my particular aims and projects. In staking my claim to manna, I cannot talk of the value of cathedrals, of happiness or of mountaintops; I must content myself with the statement that I want the manna for reasons that seem sufficient to me. Equally confining, I cannot claim unconditional superiority on the basis of factors independent of my conception of the good.

Despite these stringent limitations, however, you and I are not fated to struggle silently over the manna that divides us. Indeed, it is only because the range of discourse has been so dramatically narrowed that certain dimensions of the power problem stand out in bold relief. While you and I may differ as to the meaning of life, neither of us is willing to starve to death while the other takes all the manna. Instead, each of us has affirmed *some* conception of the good that makes it seem sensible for him to live in the new world rather than starve in outer space. This provides enough common ground to permit the following conversation:

MANIC: I want the manna!

DEPRESSIVE: So do I!

COMMANDER: What reason can either of you give to support your claim?

MANIC: I want it to achieve purposes that seem valuable to me.

DEPRESSIVE: And I, no less than you, have purposes in life that require control over scarce resources if they are to be fulfilled.

COMMANDER: All this talk about purposes is very nice, but I fail to see how it helps us solve our distribution problem. After all, none of us can claim to possess a yardstick capable of measuring the relative social value of fulfilling your competing ends in life.

DEPRESSIVE: Well, at least I have identified myself as a being that *has* purposes.

MANIC: And I too am a person who has affirmed *some* conception of the good as my own.

COMMANDER: Congratulations! But I still don't see how this gets us very far.

MANIC: Will this help? I think it right to protect my claim to manna simply because I *am* a person with a conception of the good.

DEPRESSIVE: I agree. Regardless of his conception of the good, each citizen deserves manna simply because he has identified himself as a purposive being.

COMMANDER: So far, so good. Whatever the merits of this view, it passes Neutrality's bar against selectivity—for it does not distinguish the merits of competing conceptions of the good. But you have not said enough. Even if the Assembly accepts the idea that you are entitled to *some* manna simply for being a person who has affirmed *some* conception of the good, you must tell me how much manna each of you is entitled to.

DEPRESSIVE: Well, I can't say that I'm an especially deserving citizen for reasons that have nothing to do with my conception of the good. Nonetheless, the prohibition on unconditional claims of superiority does not bar me from saying that I'm at least as good as Manic.

COMMANDER: And what does that suggest so far as manna is concerned?

DEPRESSIVE: If I'm at least as good as Manic, I should get at least as much of this stuff that both of us desire.

COMMANDER: Well, then, Manic, you've heard Depressive argue for an equal distribution of manna. The time has come to decide whether his justification passes the tests of liberal legitimacy. What do you say?

MANIC: I haven't heard anything that violates Neutrality.

COMMANDER: And what of the constraints imposed by Rationality?

MANIC: Well, I certainly can't complain on grounds of completeness or harmony. A rule that gives each citizen at least as much as any other has no formal defects.

COMMANDER: And what of the argument presented on behalf of the rule—does it pass Rationality as well?

MANIC: I have to admit that it points to a feature that differentiates each citizen from every other—the fact that each has affirmed a conception of the good.

DEPRESSIVE: Moreover, I assure you that I'll be invoking this very same factor in every conversational challenge to my claim to an equal share of manna.

MANIC: So comprehensiveness is satisfied as well.

DEPRESSIVE: And it is easy to specify states of the world that would be illegitimate under my proposed rationale.

MANIC: So much for the conceivability test imposed in the name of Rationality.

COMMANDER: Well, then, what's troubling you?

MANIC: Frankly, I don't find Depressive's argument terribly compelling on its merits. I'm not persuaded that people are entitled to manna simply because they have affirmed a conception of the good life as their own.

COMMANDER: But you don't have a right to condemn as irrational every argument with which you disagree. The first principle eliminates only those utterances that could not conceivably count as justifications for a decision rule.

MANIC: Well, I must admit that Depressive isn't talking irrelevant nonsense—as in the case where sky color is invoked to justify a claim to manna. I *do* see how somebody *might* think that a citizen

was entitled to manna simply because he is a person who has affirmed some conception of the good.

COMMANDER: In that case, I must declare that Depressive has
discharged the initial conversational burden imposed upon him in a
liberal state.

DEPRESSIVE: Does that mean I get the manna?

COMMANDER: Not so fast. Perhaps Manic can turn your own
argument against you and show how, in the light of additional facts,
you shouldn't get an equal share.

MANIC: Or perhaps I can give an entirely different argument for
an entirely different decision rule that nonetheless passes Neutrality.

COMMANDER: And in that case we would have to design a procedure for choosing among competing proposals that all fall within the
legitimacy subset.

DEPRESSIVE: Ah, well, I see this may take some time. But, then
again, it may not. Everything depends on Manic and the others.
Perhaps they will not find it so easy to defeat my claim to equal
manna. For the principles of liberal conversation apply to them no
less than they apply to me.

So there *is* a way that you and I can talk about power without
claiming the right to judge the merit of each other's conception of the
good. While we may disagree about the meaning of a good life, each of
us is prepared to say that our own image of self-fulfillment has *some*
value. Otherwise, we should be willing to starve while the others took
all the manna for themselves. And once we are prepared to affirm the
value of fulfilling our own life plan, we may use this initial affirmation
as the foundation of a public dialogue of right. Without attempting to
evaluate the merits of our competing life plans, we may present ourselves to one another as persons who have undertaken to put a positive
value on their conception of the good. Our claims to manna can be
based on nothing more—and nothing less—than a dialogic exchange
in which each of us describes himself as a morally autonomous person
capable of putting a value on his life plan. Given this self-description,
it follows that *something* can be said on behalf of initial material
equality. While I cannot say that I'm an unconditionally better person
than you are, Neutrality does not forbid me from claiming rights based
on a description of myself as a person whose claim to moral autonomy

is at least as good as that of my competitors: Since I'm at least as good as you are, I should get at least as much of the stuff we both desire—at least until you give me some Neutral reason for getting more.

This is, at one and the same time, a very strong and very weak result. Strong, because it places a significant conversational burden upon the opponents of initial equality. Once these opening lines are spoken, Depressive's conversational opponents cannot content themselves with the bland assertion that they find the argument on behalf of initial equality unpersuasive on the merits. At a minimum, the advocates of equality have established that *something* rational can be said on its behalf, and Rationality commits the Assembly to the view that something is better than nothing. Depressive's dialogue, in short, suffices to establishes a prima facie case: so long as everybody remains tongue-tied, the Assembly has no choice but to recognize the legitimacy of equal initial material endowments.

Weak, because there is no reason to expect such a quick conversational victory. Even in our idealized setting, the colonists will find that they cannot conclude their discussion of manna without confronting other dimensions of the power struggle. Most obviously, there is the problem posed by genetic handicaps: if I am born crippled, should the cost of my wheelchair be charged against my equal manna allotment? Is it possible to argue, *consistent with Neutrality,* that I should get extra manna to compensate me for such handicaps? What, if anything, distinguishes crippled limbs from the countless genetic constraints that bind each of us? Suppose I am too stupid to understand the quantum mechanics that you find child's play; can I demand compensation for this disadvantage as well? If not, *why* not?

To make matters harder, my power position as an adult is determined by environment no less than heredity. Perhaps I too could transform my manna into beautiful music if I had only learned to play the violin as a youth. Should I be compensated for this disadvantage by getting more manna now? Can the idea of educational disadvantage *ever* be developed in a way that renders it admissible as a reason for special compensation?

These questions suggest that we have begun our spaceship story in the middle. An adequate theory of initial entitlements cannot imagine that all citizens emerge from the bowels of a spaceship as full-blown adults confidently asserting their particular ends in life. While liberalism is most at home treating people as adults, it cannot escape the facts of life without suffering an enormous loss of depth. More-over, I hope to show that we *can* talk Neutrally about genetic handicaps and cultural disadvantages in a way that sometimes justifies special efforts to compensate their victims.[7]

But before we press forward, it is best to consider our first step more carefully. While it is silly to anticipate all objections, I have found three clarifications helpful in locating Depressive's initial conversational move within the more general theory.

15. CONVERSATIONAL PRESUPPOSITIONS

15.1. *Egotism and Self-Sacrifice*
Up to the present point, we have been dealing with some pretty grabby people. However different Depressive may be from Manic, they are alike in one respect: both want more manna if they can get it. Moreover, the attention I have lavished on their competitive acts of appropriation may suggest that I embrace a baldly Hobbesian psychology where every citizen is an insatiable power monster whose only cry is "More for me!"

Not at all. While everybody must demand *some* manna in order to survive in the new world, many citizens may set an upper limit on the manna they desire. All my story requires is a general condition of *overall* scarcity where *total* supply is outstripped by *total* demand.Even if most people were ascetics, overall scarcity would exist if a small number of people affirmed relatively expensive life plans. Only a world where almost everybody imposed minimal demands on manna could escape the struggle for scarce material resources.

Not that I would be disturbed by the discovery of a planet where asceticism is universally practiced. People have a right to affirm any conception of the good that seems most sensible to them. If all citizens voluntarily choose ascetic forms of life, more power to them. If this means they never see the need for a bigger chunk of manna, I do not want to force the struggle for power on them. If, by chance, the citizens of an ascetic world happen to eavesdrop on our earthly conversations, they might well choose to ignore this Chapter as irrelevant to their worldly concerns. At best, they might view the chapter as a

7. See chapters 4 and 5, respectively.

lesson in the fragility of their social order and give thanks that no dissenting voices have yet arisen to disturb their peaceable kingdom.

For us, however, relative scarcity is no idle speculation but a fact of life that we must deal with every day of our lives. By positing the existence of grabby people, I do not pass judgment on the value of personal moderation. I only emphasize that in our world even the ascetic must deal with people like Manic and Depressive. Like the rest of us, the ascetic has but two choices when they demand things he requires to pursue his simple life: he can either answer their questions or refuse to answer their questions. And in a liberal state, neither personal asceticism nor any other character trait can permit a citizen to choose suppression over conversation.

It is wrong, then, to say that liberalism assumes that we are all people with insatiable appetites. Instead, the theory simply asserts that since the ascetic does demand *some* manna, he cannot exempt himself from the question of legitimacy engendered by overall scarcity. Given this principle, the existence of asceticism raises only minor analytic complexities. Assume, for example, that an equal distribution of the manna stock would entitle each citizen to five grains as he leaves the spaceship. Citizen Ascetic, however, only claims three grains and explicitly says that he has no use for more. What happens, then, to the other two?

Surely the Commander cannot force Ascetic to accept the extra grains on the ground that she knows his true good better than he does. If Ascetic thinks he's had enough of a good thing, no one is entitled to say he's wrong. It follows that the two grains should be treated as part of the unclaimed manna available to other citizens—and so should be divided into equal parts for distribution to those of his nonascetic brethren who still see a use in extra material resources.

Simple enough—until more complicated forms of asceticism come into view. Suppose, as before, that Ascetic needs only three grains of manna to provide him with his minimal requirements. He refuses, however, to renounce his claim to the extra two grains because he thinks his fellow citizens would use these extra grains in sinful ways. Better, he says, for the stuff to be destroyed than that it be abused. On this scenario, what is the fate of the two "extra" grains?

Ascetic gets to destroy the manna.[8] Indeed, it is a mistake to call him

8. Subject to a caveat concerning trusteeship for future generations, to be discussed in chapter 7.

an ascetic after all. No less than Manic or Depressive, he too has purposes in life that will be fulfilled by gaining control over more manna rather than less. By "destroying" the manna he is producing what he thinks is a good: saving another's soul from materialistic degradation. And surely the Commander has no right to declare such a use of manna "wasteful." Instead, she must protect a fellow citizen's right to manna without sitting in judgment as to the value of his ideals. Each citizen is entitled, prima facie, to an equal share simply because he is willing to affirm a conception of the good. Ascetic is entitled to his five grains of manna even though others would say that he is "wasting" his inheritance when he commits a chunk of it to the flames. Neutral conversation legitimates acts of self-sacrifice no less than efforts at self-affirmation. The key to liberalism is not one or another narrow view of human aims, but the perception that we live in a world where people have given *genuinely* different answers to the question of life's meaning.

15.2. *Satisfaction Guaranteed?*

Liberalism, then, has no difficulty vindicating the right of an ascetic to go his own way. Indeed, this very conclusion can be made the basis of a second common critique of the dialogic solution I have advanced. To see the problem, reconsider our simpler Ascetic who sees no need to claim more than three grains of manna. Assume, moreover, that once he has been guaranteed this modest portion, Ascetic will perfectly fulfill all his ideals in life.

Now contrast this state of self-fulfillment with Manic's discontent. So far as he is concerned, five grains of manna is a pitifully inadequate foundation for the good life. If he is obliged to begin in such poverty, Manic fears (correctly) that he will spend much of his time grubbing for his next meal. This means that he will never have the time for exhilarating mountain exploration. Behold, then, Ascetic's satisfaction and Manic's discontent. Given this comparison, isn't it bizarre to say that equality represents a *neutral* solution to the problem of initial entitlements?

This consequentialist objection—so powerful on its face— fundamentally misconceives the nature of the Neutrality principle. Neutrality is *not* a characteristic of the *outcome* of a decision rule; instead, it is a feature of the *conversation* through which a distribution rule is *justified.* It is not enough to point out the (undisputed) fact that some life plans are more manna-intensive than others. Instead, the consequentialist critic must introduce this fact into a rational political conversation that passes the test of Neutrality. Moreover, we have already shown that this conversational trick is not as easy as it looks. Thus, Manic cannot say that mountaineering is worth its extra cost because of its special contribution to the social good (measured in units of virtue, felicity, or whatever). Nor can he say that the manna should be divided in a way that permits all citizens to get an "equal distance" toward their respective goals. For the notion of equal fulfillment makes sense only in terms of life plans that are compatible with the mountaintop metaphor. Yet this metaphor, when questioned, is no less vulnerable in Neutral discourse than the bald claim that all life plans are "really" searches for happiness or virtue or whatever.

Even if this much is conceded, however, it does not preclude a narrower consequentialist critique. Here the goal is to convict egalitarians of the same crime of un-Neutral discourse they are so quick to find in their opponents' arguments. According to this critique, egalitarians are incapable of defending their rule Neutrally once the fact of unequal fulfillment is raised in political conversation. And if this is so, it would seem that the partisans of equality are on precisely the same footing as their consequentialist brethren: all are obliged to violate Neutrality if they hope to justify their positions rationally.

Fortunately, however, it is easy to design a thought experiment that can vindicate the conversational claims of equality against this narrow consequentialist critique. All that is required is a single script showing that the partisans of prima facie equality are not reduced to silence when the consequences of their rule are brought to their attention. This one should do the trick:

COMMANDER: My friends, you have just heard Depressive present an argument for the equal distribution of manna. Unless I hear any objections, we will land on the planet immediately and proceed to distribute the manna in the way he suggests.
MANIC: I object.
COMMANDER: What's the problem?
MANIC: While I'm condemned to a life of exquisite frustration, Ascetic will fulfill his life plan perfectly.
COMMANDER: And why are these facts relevant to our conversation?

MANIC: Isn't their relevance obvious?

COMMANDER: Not when you recall the fate of the equal-fulfillment decision rule. If it's invalid, I see no reason why we should think your frustration of special significance in deciding among decision rules.

MANIC: Your fancy phrases can't obscure the fact of my misery. You can't simply shut your eyes to the fate of a fellow being who yearns to fulfill himself.

COMMANDER: But I have not shut my eyes to your quest for the good. Indeed, it is only because you *have* affirmed a conception of the good life that you are entitled to an equal portion of manna in the first place.

MANIC: Nonetheless, I'm very unhappy with the situation in which I find myself.

COMMANDER: But this simple fact cannot be enough to justify a claim to more manna.

MANIC: Why not?

COMMANDER: Because we live in a world of scarce resources.

MANIC: So what?

COMMANDER: Such a world, by definition, is inhabited by some people who are dissatisfied with their initial share of manna.

MANIC: Well, I agree that *someone* must remain dissatisfied. I'm only complaining about the fact that the someone involved happens to be me.

COMMANDER: But if I respond by giving you more than an equal share, this will increase someone else's frustration.

MANIC: So what? It's more important for me to fulfill my life goals than for the others to gain their objectives.

COMMANDER: Easy for you to say. But Neutrality forbids me from making this the public ground for Assembly acceptance of a distribution rule. Instead, I declare that in a world of scarce resources, *no one* has the right to insist that the state give him a *special* guarantee that he will be successful in life.

MANIC: Where does that leave me, then?

COMMANDER: With an equal share of manna. While no one can be guaranteed success in life, everybody is guaranteed an equal right to the material endowments he thinks his success requires.

MANIC: But it would be a tragedy if mankind were mastered by the mountain range before us.

COMMANDER: The Assembly does not pretend to such ultimate

judgments. We cannot say whether you are the victim of cosmic tragedy or the pawn in some divine lesson plan.

MANIC: What *do* you say, then?

COMMANDER: That it is up to *you*, not me, to decide what the best use of this manna may be. Whatever your conception of the good, your claim to an equal share of manna is entitled to respect. But apparently you want a very different guarantee. You want a guarantee that you will become a success in life, and this guarantee we can't provide. You are no more immune from the harsh fact of scarcity than anybody else. We cannot guarantee you success while forcing others to content themselves with a smaller portion. Instead, it is up to you—like the rest of us—to make the best use you can of your initial share of initial endowments.

This dialogue is hardly the last word in political argument. As we shall see, Manic may well find something to complain about if his failures as a mountaineer can be attributed to genetic domination, cultural deprivation, or transactional imperfection.[9] The point the Commander is making here is a narrow, if fundamental, one. Her responses show the emptiness of the charge that egalitarians must make illiberal conversational moves when confronted with the consequences of their favored distribution rule. When confronted with Manic's complaint, the Commander does not deny the reality of his suffering or belittle the moral standing of sufferers. Instead, she forces Manic to see that, given scarce resources, the bare fact of frustration can *never* serve as a sufficient reason for gaining additional resources. To put her point in the more formal terms developed earlier,[10] a distribution rule that tries to fulfill *everyone's* wants must necessarily fail the harmony requirement imposed under the Rationality principle. Thus, it is simply wrong to say that the egalitarian will inevitably breach Neutrality when the simple fact of frustration is brought to his attention; instead, it is *only* the consequentialist who threatens to breach Neutrality whenever he tries to bring his desire to fulfill his goals into the political conversation.

15.3. *Manna and Private Property*

So much for the status of ascetic self-denial and insistent self-fulfillment. A third objection threatens our story from a very different

9. See chapters 4, 5, and 6, respectively.
10. See § 11.1.

angle. Rather than focusing upon the assertedly un-Neutral treatment of Ascetic or Manic, the "realist" aims his critique at the spacy way I have introduced the problem of distributive justice. According to him, there are so many important questions begged by a story that posits the existence of a liberal Commander, a perfect technology of justice, a founding moment, and so forth, that it is hard to know what the theory amounts to as a practical matter.

I am very sympathetic to this criticism. Indeed, by the time our exploration ends, I mean to take up the major oversimplifications in a systematic way, considering how Neutral dialogue must be complicated to do justice to earthly social realities. Only I propose to move slowly, especially at the beginning, for two different reasons. First, issues of principle are at stake even within the abstract and futuristic setting framed by our spaceship story. My central claim, after all, is that it is possible to conceive of a world where a band of citizens might solve their power problem *entirely* through Neutral dialogue. And if the citizens in my Assembly Hall are defeated by the manna problem, there is hardly any point in disguising the conceptual failure with realistic detail. Instead, I should simply abandon my theory and spend my time on more rewarding pursuits. Second, assuming I convince you that Neutral dialogue is a conceptually coherent option, only a step-by-step approach will permit us to confront a second intellectual challenge posed by life in the declining days of the twentieth century. While the past century has not been rich in normative liberal theory, there has been a superabundance of descriptive accounts and positive theories in economics, politics, psychology, child development, and many other areas of obvious normative significance. This overwhelming literature poses serious problems for liberal political philosophy. On the one hand, it is impossible for a single book or a single mind to pass judgment on all the relevant debates. On the other hand, it is wrong to ignore the important role that social science can play in the adaptation of liberal ideals to an intractable and complex reality. By complicating my model of earthly realities in a step-by-step way, I can frame empirical issues in ways that permit specialists to see the broader normative implications of their particular empirical studies. If this, in turn, induces them to force liberal philosophy to consider new empirical models, so much the better.

In this spirit, I shall defer realistic complications until the simple model is more fully developed. I raise the realism issue here only to warn against a common misinterpretation of the manna problem. Since manna is defined as infinitely divisible and fungible, it is easy to imagine that the political conversation will come to an end with the Commander dividing the stuff into little bits and distributing each bit according to one rule or another. Yet such a quick embrace of a purely individualistic form of property would be too hasty. After all, the Commander could *also* fulfil the equal-manna principle by breaking the manna into ten-bit chunks and assigning ten citizens to each chunk. The relative merits of such collectivist solutions can only be determined after further dialogues, to be considered in chapter 6. These dialogues will reveal the uncertain status of individualistic property in liberal theory: sometimes each citizen's right to an equal share of material wealth will be better expressed by giving him a share in collective, rather than individualistic, property.

16. UNIQUENESS

To sum up: I do not deny that an egalitarian decision rule will lead to a great deal of frustration, nor that some will feel more pain than others. Equality is justified not on the basis of what is *felt* but what is *said* by people trying to make sense of their predicament. While Neutral talk does not end the pain, it does provide a means by which each citizen can affirm his own sense of self-significance without impugning that of his fellows. And in the world as it is, this is an achievement not to be despised.

Nor do I imagine that the dialogues presented here represent the last word on the subject of material resources; they are only the first moves in a lengthy conversation, requiring further development as genetic, educational, and transactional power structures come into view. Despite these caveats, the fact remains that something *can* be said on behalf of initial equality, something that will survive the test of comprehensive and Neutral dialogue. When challenged to justify a claim to manna in a liberal Assembly, it is open to each of us to say:

1. I am a person with a conception of the good.
2. Simply by virtue of being such a person, I'm at least as good as you are.
3. This is reason enough for me to get as much manna as you do—so long as you have nothing more to say that will Neutrally justify a claim to additional manna.

Call this conversational move the liberal assertion of equality. Even if its Neutrality is conceded, however, we are still not home free. It remains possible that the liberal assertion of equality is only one of a number of Neutral conversational gambits that may be invoked to support very different solutions to the manna problem. Moreover, I have no formal proof establishing the uniqueness of the manna solution generated by the liberal assertion of equality. Nonetheless, this chapter has served to clear the conversational field of many familiar political alternatives. In particular, utilitarianism and many other teleological variants have been shown to require the use of political arguments that offend the principles of liberal conversation.

Yet even after all teleological theories are abandoned, familiar types of political argument remain untouched by the dialogues presented so far. Most important, one of the charms of social contract theory has been its conscientious effort to avoid ostentatious claims about the good. Like our spaceship story, the contract tradition begins with a group of individuals each asserting his own idea of self-interest. Writers like Hobbes and Locke tried to legitimate state authority in a way that respected each citizen's right to define his own good. Rather than appealing to the intrinsic merit of the public good, they tried to persuade each reader that the social contract was in his self-interest.

Moreover, if this move were successful, the contractarian would have an argument with real promise in our spaceship Assembly. In response to Q's question of legitimacy, A would then be in a position to say: "I don't see what you're complaining about. After all, Q, you yourself have agreed that this was my fair share of manna!" It is this assertion that must be attacked before contract theory can be eliminated from the field of liberal discourse. Nor is it enough to criticize the particular opinions of Locke or Rawls, but to show that the basic framework of the contractarian argument invariably requires its proponents to talk in ways that violate Neutrality.

Now this, in fact, is precisely my view. Nonetheless, I shall postpone my arguments until Part Four.[11] For, in the end, I do not aim to convict contract talk of certain analytic failures. Instead of winning some narrow technical victory, I hope to persuade contractarians to abandon their basic political metaphor and shift their allegiance to the concept of liberal dialogue. To accomplish this larger goal, it is neces-

11. See chapter 10, especially § 66.1.

sary to move beyond the simple question of manna distribution and show how the liberal assertion of equality generates conversational solutions to a vast range of social conflict—involving genetics, education, transaction, trusteeship—that eludes cogent contractarian analysis. Only then will a confrontation with the framework of contract argument take on more than technical interest.

Even if, however, I finally convince you that neither social contract nor social utility can serve as the centerpiece of liberal thought, it still does not follow that the assertion of liberal equality is the only surviving conversational element in the cultural field marked by Neutrality. In the absence of a formal proof of uniqueness, liberal theory retains its open-ended character. Perhaps somebody will come forward to elaborate a new kind of political dialogue that deviates greatly from the liberal assertion of equality yet satisfies the constraints imposed by Neutrality. And when such a spokesman arises, the liberal conversation will doubtless take many interesting turns—whose course cannot be predicted in advance. For now, though, we cannot afford the luxury of attending to hypothetical challenges from nonexistent liberal voices. It will be challenge enough to gain control over the egalitarian political dialogue we have only just begun.

3

CITIZENSHIP

17. THE QUESTION OF CITIZENSHIP

Up to now, I have been content to speak of Manic, Depressive, and the Commander as "citizens" of a liberal state without explaining what entitled them to this status. I took this shortcut to give you an example of the dialogic method in action. Now that we have glimpsed the resolving power of liberal conversation, this casual approach is no longer tolerable. By its very terms, the Neutrality principle extends its protection only to "citizens,"[1] leaving others at the mercy of a dialogue that is nasty, brutish, and short:

DEPRESSIVE: I want the manna. Why should you get it rather than I?
MANIC: Because I'm better than you are.
DEPRESSIVE: Haven't you violated Neutrality?
MANIC: Not at all, for I deny that you are a citizen of the liberal state. You're just another bit of manna to be exploited by me and my fellow citizens.
DEPRESSIVE: You're wrong about that. If this is a liberal state, you must recognize me as a citizen protected by the Neutrality principle.
MANIC: Why do you think so? But talk fast—I'm getting hungry.

Do not dismiss this script as too grotesque to deserve further analysis. *Something* must qualify as manna; otherwise, hordes of citizens will starve to death in our new world. If we are ever to conceive a well-specified liberal world, we must put words in Depressive's mouth that explain the conditions both necessary and sufficient to qualify him as a citizen of a liberal state. Only then shall we understand the class of beings whose claims of right must be guaranteed by any state that aspires to liberal ideals.

1. See § 4.

18. NECESSARY CONDITIONS FOR CITIZENSHIP: DIALOGIC PERFORMANCE

Begin, then, with the necessary conditions for citizenship. Are there any sorts of things that could not *conceivably* qualify for citizenship in a liberal state?

18.1. *An Easy Case*

Suppose "Depressive" were the name of a stone. Then I want to say that Depressive can't conceivably qualify as a citizen. Though Depressive may hit me on the head, I wait in vain for any communication that suggests the stone believes itself *justified* in engaging in this power play. And this symbolic void is decisive in determining whether a liberal power relationship can be established between the stone and me. Even if I started talking to the stone in an effort to convince it of the legitimacy of my power, it still would not follow that a liberal relationship had been established between us. While I might talk to the stone, it would leave my demand for a justification of its power unanswered; and a liberal power relationship is one where dialogue, not monologue, prevails between power holders. By virtue of its dialogic incompetence, Depressive cannot *conceivably* function in a way that will permit the formation of a liberal community with other entities.

Care should be taken with this conclusion. Simply because Depressive is not a citizen, it does not follow that it will be deprived of *all* protection in a liberal state. Even if all stones were treated like manna, citizens who believed in conservation will, in ideal theory, have no difficulty clubbing together to form nature preserves. Moreover, under second-best conditions, there will be additional liberal arguments for preserving things like the Grand Canyon.[2] While these policy arguments may lead the polity to grant the canyon certain "rights" to special protection, this legal fiction cannot blind us to the authoritarian relationship that still obtains between dialogically competent citizens and stones. A monologue cannot be transformed into a dialogue simply by shouting louder into the abyss. Even if we treated a stone as if it were a citizen, our power relationship remains one of brute force, unmediated by the kind of cultural interaction that consti-

2. See § 50; cf. § 22.2.

tutes the liberal state. While citizens need only invoke the concept of *Neutral dialogue* to vindicate their rights, noncitizens must depend upon the policy choices of *citizens* if they are to acquire rights on their own behalf.

This, in the end, will make a very big difference in the security with which citizens and noncitizens enjoy their rights in a liberal community. For I hope to convince you that the constitution of a liberal democracy should guarantee the basic rights of citizens even when they are threatened by a hostile majority. In contrast, the fate of noncitizens will be an appropriate subject for majoritarian politics.[3] It follows that the dialogic rights of citizens are grounded on a far firmer foundation than those that any noncitizen may possess.

18.2. *Harder Cases*

Now consider some harder cases, arranged in order of increasing difficulty. Imagine your claim to manna is challenged by an angry lion who roars his dissatisfaction as you leave the spaceship to take possession of our new world. Unlike the stone, the lion possesses a certain communicative competence. Nonetheless, it is insufficient to pass the dialogic test required for citizenship. While the lion, perhaps, is trying to say, "Stop grabbing that manna! I want it!" it is quite another thing to interpret his roar as raising the *question of legitimacy*: "Why should you get the manna rather than I?" Yet a liberal relationship is defined as a social condition in which power wielders ask and answer each others' questions of legitimacy. For a power relation to pass this test, it is not enough for the participants to roar their approval and disapproval. The ordinary lion cannot *conceivably* qualify as a citizen of a liberal state.

But how can we be so confident that we understand the true meaning of the lion's roar? Imagine that some expert in animal talk assures us that lions have been the victims of a tragic misunderstanding. Their roars, we are told, are interrogatory, not imperative. Indeed, the lion's question is precisely the one that inaugurates liberal conversation: he is trying to ask us why we should get the manna rather than he. The animal expert, in short, proposes a new way of translating lion roars into English that is inconsistent with our previous understandings. Is it possible, in response, to defend our linguistic intuitions against such a critique?

3. See chapter 9.

I shall not try to answer this question. Any effort to do so would require a serious confrontation with the writings of Chomsky, Quine, Wittgenstein, and others who have grappled with the problematics of translation. Not only is such a task beyond my powers, but it would divert us from the distinctive questions of *political* philosophy. As a consequence, I can only flag the question's importance by emphasizing that a complete theory of the liberal state requires a satisfactory theory of translation.[4]

Yet even waving a flag is sometimes useful. For the relationship between the theory of translation and the theory of politics has, I think, been ignored in recent liberal writings. Indeed, one often gets the impression that only the "sciences" of human choice—like economics and decision theory—are central to the concerns of liberal political philosophy. And since I will also call upon such techniques at later stages in the argument, it is important to emphasize that we are lost without the sciences of culture as well as the sciences of choice.

Nor should this be surprising in a liberal theory that places central importance on the ability of power holders to justify their power to one another. A liberal state *is* nothing more than a collection of individuals who can participate in a dialogue in which all aspects of their power position may be justified in a certain way; to participate in such a dialogue of justification, actors must be intelligible to one another; to be intelligible, one's utterances must be translatable into a language comprehensible to other would-be participants. It is this simple chain that links the theory of citizenship to the theory of translation. In the absence of such a theory, however, I shall simply assume that the imperative character of the lion's roar speaks for itself.

And, now, for a harder case. As the spaceship approaches our new world, scanners reveal a race of unfamiliar beings—call them Martians—who seem (to us) engaged in a complex form of communal life. Indeed, *if* we understand the Martian community rightly, the Martians have anticipated our quest for an ideal liberal state: whenever the Martians struggle over scarce resources, they also exchange symbols that seem (to us) translatable into Neutral dialogue; after talking their way to an ideal solution, they use their technology of justice to achieve the liberal outcomes suggested by their conversation.

4. And vice versa?

Despite all this, there is a single difficulty. Try as we might, we cannot establish direct communication with the Martians. They resolutely refuse to speak to our most skilled anthropologists and linguists. When our emissaries try to appropriate some manna, the Martians do not ask them why they think Earthlings merit the manna more than Martians do. Nor do they answer our emissaries' questions of legitimacy. Instead, when the Earthlings get in their way, they are simply pushed into a corner so that the Martians can continue without inconvenience. While the Martians may be citizens of *their own* liberal state, they cannot become citizens of *our* political community, nor we of theirs. How, then, are we to deal with them?

Perhaps by colonizing another planet and leaving the Martians in peace. But if we were running out of fuel, we would have no choice but to deal with the Martians in a way unmediated by dialogue. At best, we might treat each Martian *as if* he were a citizen of our polity, guaranteeing him a share of manna equal to our own. And we might constantly try to engage the Martians' attention so that we could explain to them why we thought this action justified. Yet even if we somehow convinced ourselves that the Martians were finally attending to our messages, this would not satisfy the requirements of common citizenship. It is not enough to conduct a successful monologue; a liberal state requires *both* sides to answer each other's question of legitimacy. Until a Martian answers an *Earthling's* question with a Neutral justification, all of us cannot function as citizens of the *same* liberal state. At most, there could be a condition of peaceful coexistence between liberal states.

To summarize: Before an entity can function as a citizen in a liberal community, he must talk about his power relations in a distinctive way. When he wants something claimed by another, he must be capable of asking the question of legitimacy: "Why should you get it rather than I?" (Call this the *inquiry* test.) He must also be prepared to answer the question of legitimacy in a Neutral way when it is asked by others, by saying something like "because I'm at least as good as you are." (Call this the *defensive* test.) Of these two tests, the "defensive" requirement appears more demanding. Thus, it is easy to imagine a person challenging another's claim but refusing to talk about his own power pretentions. In contrast, an entity who passes the defensive test but fails the inquiry test is a more unlikely being. As a consequence, I shall concentrate on the defensive test in the analysis that follows.

Having come this far, permit me one final animal story. While zoologists working with apes and dolphins have already engaged in primitive symbolic interaction, there is no conversation yet reported in which man and ape talk about the legitimacy of their relative power position. Nonetheless, we cannot exclude the possibility that some animal may pass the defensive test:

TRAINER: Hey! Where do you think you're going?
APE: Out of this cage.
TRAINER: Not if I have anything to say about it.
APE: Why *should* you have anything to say about it? I'm at least as good as you are, and I have my own purposes in life!

With these words, the ape has breached the cultural barrier that stands between him and citizenship in a liberal state. It is possible, of course, that the ape will be tripped up at some later point in the conversation. At the very least, though, the challenge of the talking ape is a formidable one: Are we to exclude the ape because he is too hairy or is it that we have a prejudice against the arboreal life?

18.3. *Human Beings*
I shall leave such questions floating in the air for a while and focus on a subject closer to home: the status of human beings under the defensive test. It should be clear that we cannot determine a human being's citizenship status by examining him apart from the other people with whom he interacts. While a scientist could determine an individual's brain weight or blood count in the silent isolation of a laboratory, such a setting tells us nothing about a person's capacity to engage in the relevant forms of defensive dialogue. Just as a Martian or an ape might—despite a different biology—demonstrate dialogic competence, so too an individual of the genus *Homo* might fail to deal with power in the way required for liberal community. In deciding whether an individual satisfies the defensive test, it is not his individual biology but his political culture that is of crucial importance.

Citizenship, in short, is a concept in political—not biological—theory. In claiming citizenship, an individual is—first and foremost—asserting the existence of a social relationship between himself and others. More specifically, a citizen is (by definition) someone who can properly claim the right to be treated as a fellow member of the political community. Since, in a liberal state, the polity is constituted by the process of dialogic interchange, an individual who lacks dialogic competence fails to satisfy the necessary conditions for membership. It follows that human beings are *not* liberal citizens from the moment of birth. Instead, each of my readers has passed through a predialogic period in childhood, where the complex skills required for the dialogue of legitimacy were painfully acquired. These facts will become important later when we turn to the problem of abortion and the theory of liberal education.[5] At this point, however, I shall focus upon the citizenship status of biologically mature *Homo sapiens* who have been socialized in any of the countless cultures developed in the history of human society. Does the defensive test exclude any of these individuals from citizenship status?

To begin with fundamentals, the defensive test does not require great mental acuity before it can be satisfied. While a citizen must defend his claims to power in conversation, all that need be said is: "I too am a person with ends in life. Since I'm at least as good as you are, I should get at least as much."[6] Nor is great loquacity required. Once having asserted his right to pursue his conception of the good, no citizen is under any obligation to defend the merits of his ideals in any forum not of his own choosing. Of course, some citizens will find philosophical conversation about moral ideals to be among the highest goods of life; many others will prefer to talk of other things; and still others will be bored by talk and prefer a life of vigorous action or solitary contemplation. Any of these life options may be pursued without denying a person's standing as a citizen. The minimal dialogue required for citizenship establishes a thin thread of mutual intelligibility among individuals who are free to disagree in all other respects. Having recognized each other's claim to self-respect, each may go his own way without endangering his standing as a full-fledged member of the political community.

18.4. *The Problem of Ideology*
The thin web of talk catches many in its net. Nonetheless, it may be doubted that its reach is as broad as I suggest. There are two problems—one raised by people who, as it were, talk too much;

---

5. See chapter 4, § 28, and chapter 5, respectively.
6. Indeed, even this is too strong. As we have seen, Ascetic may not *want* an equal share of manna but may content himself with far less (§ 15.1). In such cases, Ascetic need only say that his relative worth as a person is no less than that suggested by his relative share of manna.

another, by those who talk too little. Consider, first, the Nazi who goes everywhere proclaiming his infinite superiority to all Jews. Despite his authoritarian views, does he nonetheless fulfill the defensive test for citizenship?

My answer is a loud and clear Yes. I must emphasize, however, that we are not presently dealing with the problem that would arise if the Nazi tried to grab the manna that is rightfully the property of his Jewish fellow citizens. While we shall shortly be considering the problem raised by aggressive behavior, the question here is only whether the Nazi can *defend* the share of power that would rightfully be his if he qualified as a citizen of a liberal state. To test this issue, return to the spaceship's Assembly Hall and imagine the following conversation:

COMMANDER: Unless I hear anything more, I shall declare that everybody present in this Hall should start off with an equal share of manna. Are there any objections?

JEW: I object. I deny that this Nazi is a citizen of our liberal state. And since he isn't a citizen, he isn't protected by Neutrality. And since he isn't protected, I think we all should say he's a perfect swine and deprive him of all his rights to manna.

COMMANDER: But why do you deny that he's a citizen?

JEW: Because he fails the defensive test.

COMMANDER: Well, then, Nazi. What do you have to say to this?

NAZI: The Jew is wrong. While I do indeed think I'm better than he is, I need not make this strong statement to justify my claim to an equal share of manna. Instead, I need simply say that I am at least as good as a Jew and so am entitled to at least as much manna as he gets. This statement is certainly consistent with my true beliefs and fulfills the conversational requirement imposed upon citizens of the liberal state. I give you what is owing, though nothing more.

But what if the Nazi does not plead his case in so fastidious a manner? What if he says: "This despicable Jewish swine has no right to my manna. Destroy him at once!" Citizenship status is not to be determined by initial impulses or ill-considered turns of phrase. When confronted with such an outburst, the Commander must continue the dialogue further:

COMMANDER: To tell the truth, Nazi, I'm not interested in everything you have to say about Jews. All I want to know is whether you are willing to justify your claim to manna in a way that is consistent with the conversational obligations imposed upon all citizens.

NAZI: What is all this mumbo jumbo? Get the scum out of here!

COMMANDER: Let me help you out a little. For present purposes, all you need say is that you're at least as good as your Jewish competitor and are therefore entitled to as much manna as he is. Am I correct in believing that this statement is consistent with your beliefs?

*NAZI: I guess so. After all, if I think I'm *better* than a Jew, it follows by definition that I think *I'm at least as good* as a Jew. But let me tell you what else I think——

COMMANDER: Some other time perhaps, for you have told me enough to satisfy the defensive condition.

The critical conversational turn is marked by an asterisk. We should, therefore, scrutinize it with care: Was the Nazi really required to accept the Commander's helpful suggestion? Consider the alternative:

COMMANDER: It is your position, is it not, that Aryans are at least as good as Jews?

NAZI: Now stop putting words in my mouth. I say Aryans are *better* than Jews. And that's that.

COMMANDER: Don't get me wrong. I don't want you to say anything you don't believe. But as a speaker of ordinary English, surely you don't deny that a person who says "X is better than Y" is conversationally committed to the notion that "X is at least as good as Y"?

NAZI: I *do* deny it. Stick that in your pipe and smoke it!

COMMANDER: Well, then, what language *are* you speaking?

NAZI: What if I tell you I'm not speaking English at all, but some private language of my own design?

COMMANDER: Is this language translatable into English?

NAZI: Nope.

COMMANDER: Well, I must say I'm puzzled by your seeming ability to conduct a conversation that so closely resembles a language—English—that you say you don't speak.

NAZI: I don't care whether you're puzzled. Stop putting words in my mouth.

COMMANDER: I guess I have no choice. If you say you don't speak

English, then I must declare that this entire conversation should be treated as if it were unintelligible.

NAZI: What follows from that?

COMMANDER: That you are no more a citizen than a Martian is. But, mind you, the choice is yours. I'm perfectly happy to interpret your talk as if it were conversational English. Indeed, this would be the obvious interpretation but for your explicit denial.

NAZI: And what if I confessed that I was talking ordinary English?

COMMANDER: Then you are conversationally committed to the view that you're at least as good as the Jew. And if this is so, you readily satisfy the defensive test for citizenship. You may defeat the Jew's objection simply by affirming the obvious. Will you, then, permit us to assume that you are indeed talking English?

Now, in weighing his response, the Nazi would doubtless consider the consequences to him and his movement in accepting or rejecting citizenship status. By hypothesis, he has nothing but contempt for liberal conversation, cares nothing for its integrity, and only longs for its overthrow. Consequently, if he thought he could further his movement by making the conversation ridiculous, he might be tempted to remain steadfast in denying that he was an English speaker.

The conditions of ideal theory, however, permit us to put to one side all such strategic considerations. Given a perfect technology of justice, the Nazi has no reason to believe he can oust the liberal Commander from the ultimate means of coercion. From a material point of view, he has everything to gain and nothing to lose by conceding the obvious—that he is indeed a speaker of normal English. And the same is true of every other person who prefers any other authoritarian creed to liberalism. To qualify under the defensive condition, it is not necessary for a person to affirm the ideological superiority of liberalism to all other competing faiths. The defensive test does not require anyone to say anything inconsistent with his pretentions to superiority. Liberal conversation simply filters out these pretentions as irrelevant to the question of citizenship, leaving a thin, but fundamental, assertion occupying the entire conversational field: "because I am at least as good as you are."

18.5. *Solipsism*
But we have been making things too hard for ourselves. The ordinary Nazi would not deny that he is speaking ordinary English or

German or some other language readily translatable into these familiar tongues. Indeed, the last dialogue might be attractive only to a much rarer breed: the aggressive solopsist. This is a person who is not content with the occasional solipsistic daydream, but proclaims his radically idiosyncratic interpretation of reality in *every* interpersonal interchange. It is only such a person who might[7] take the Commander's puzzlement at the resemblance of his "private" language to ordinary English as an affront to his deepest convictions. He might, then, deny the intelligibility of his political conversation in order to save his belief in his own power to impose any meaning he likes on the reality he confronts. Such a person would indeed escape the web of liberal conversation. How, then, should he be treated?

I would vote to treat Solipsist *as if* he had satisfied the defensive test for citizenship. After all, even though he does not recognize us as self-interpreting beings, we surely can recognize him as one. And if a liberal community is a group of people who recognize each other's self-descriptions as morally autonomonous agents, surely it is in the spirit of such a community to extent an equal recognition to Solipsist?

Yet candor compels us to recognize that Solpsist's rights are—like the Martians we hypothesized earlier—on a more uncertain footing than those of full members of the liberal community. While, as a citizen, I would cast an emphatic Yes ballot for Solipsist's claims to citizenship, his rights cannot be grounded directly on the concept of Neutral dialogue in the same way that those of the typical Nazi can.

18.6. *Idiocy*

So much for people who speak too much. What of those who speak too little? Someone whose brain is so damaged that he is unable to master the most primitive moral vocabulary, who can never identify himself as a being with his own purposes in the world, who stares in blank incomprehension when asked, "Why should you get the manna rather than I?"

Once again, my present claim is a limited one. I do not deny that *true* citizens may well vote to extend the protective cloak of citizenship to such unhappy creatures. Instead, my point can best be made by comparing the present problem to the issues raised earlier by the talking ape. While the idiot human must base his claim on sympathy, the

---

7. Might, not must. I can imagine a solipsist who would take the entire question as just another one of his clever jokes and answer in the "obvious" way with an ironic spirit.

talking ape can assert that his rights do *not* depend upon whether his fellow citizens find him an attractive or horrifying character. Even if my flesh crawled at the prospect of recognizing the citizenship status of such a hairy creature, nonetheless a liberal must recognize that his personal likes and dislikes have nothing to do with the right of another individual to assert his moral personality. As soon as the ape can engage in a conversation that reveals that he too is a person with a sense of the meaning of his life, what reason can I give him to justify my own pretentions to moral superiority?

The rights of the talking ape are more secure than those of the human vegetable. Citizenship is a matter of political, not biological, theory.

19. NECESSARY CONDITIONS FOR CITIZENSHIP: BEHAVIORAL REQUIREMENTS

19.1. *The Behavioral Test*

Assume, now, that Manic and Depressive have no trouble carrying on a liberal conversation with one another under the special conditions established by the Commander in the Assembly Hall. Even so, there is still no guarantee that, upon landing, they will succeed in maintaining a liberal state. Once they have left the Assembly Hall, their worldly actions may prove unequal to their conversational obligations. Imagine, for example, that Manic charges out of the spaceship with but one goal in mind—to grab Depressive's manna before his rival comes on the scene. If he is permitted to succeed in this power play, the embryonic liberal relationship between Manic and Depressive has come to a premature end.

DEPRESSIVE: Manic! What in the world are you doing?

MANIC: Grabbing as much manna as I can.

DEPRESSIVE: But have you forgotten our conversation in the Assembly Hall so quickly?

MANIC: Not at all. But that was the Assembly Hall, and this is life. And never the twain shall meet.

DEPRESSIVE: If you say our Assembly Hall talk is irrelevant, so be it. But that means that you have yet to answer my question of legitimacy. So let me ask it again: Why should you have this manna rather than I?

MANIC: Do I have to answer that?

DEPRESSIVE: You do if you want to qualify as a citizen under the defensive test.

MANIC: And my talk in the Assembly Hall won't do?

DEPRESSIVE: You just said it was irrelevant. So if we are to get a liberal dialogue going, we'll have to start from scratch.

MANIC: I refuse. I now know where such talk will lead. It will require me to give up some of the manna I've just seized. To hell with your dialogue.

DEPRESSIVE: Say what you like. There is only one thing you can't say.

MANIC: And what's that?

DEPRESSIVE: That you and I are fellow members of a liberal state.

MANIC: And why not?

DEPRESSIVE: Because a liberal state is nothing else than a power structure in which each participant justifies his power when it is questioned by the other. And you have just declared yourself free of any such conversational obligation to me.

A liberal state exists, in short, only when *actual* power relations can be rationalized through Neutral dialogue. Whatever went on in the far-off Assembly Hall is relevant only as it informs the concrete power structure established in our new world. Before Manic and Depressive can function as members of a liberal political community, it is not enough for them to indulge in idle chitchat. Instead, their actions must conform to their talk. Call this the *behavioral* test for citizenship in a liberal state.

19.2. *Applications: Under a Perfect Technology of Justice*

What sort of beings, then, can satisfy the behavioral test for citizenship? The answer, once again, is not to be established through pseudobiological inquiry. To determine whether a person qualifies, we must see the way he behaves in the social setting in which he finds himself. If he remains content with the limited power that he can vindicate through liberal dialogue, then he qualifies under the behavioral test; if not, not. It's as simple as that.

Complexity arises only because the same person may behave differently in different social settings. It is possible, of course, to imagine a "liberal saint" who would conscientiously refuse to deprive *any* of his fellow citizens of their conversational rights under *any* circumstances. Only a self-righteous fool, however, can be absolutely confident that he is a perfect liberal saint. For most of us, it is pathetically easy to imagine situations in which we would succumb to temptation and pursue our self-interest by depriving others of their rights. Nonetheless, such daydreams need not jeopardize our standing as citizens. For the social setting in which we find ourselves may deprive us of any temptation to translate these fantasies into aggressive conduct.

Imagine, for example, that the Commander has a final surprise for us before we touch down on our new planet. As you approach her at the threshold, she hands you a remarkable ray gun for the purpose of aiding in the protection of your rights. The ray gun has been programmed to immobilize anybody who tries to grab the manna reserved for you. If, however, you try to use the ray gun to grab the manna reserved for another, it is entirely useless. Indeed, since she will be giving everybody a ray gun with an isomorphic program, your every effort to grab somebody else's manna will be doomed to failure. Assume, finally, that the programming has been done perfectly: there will never be a case where the wrong gun zaps at the wrong time. Given this perfect technology of justice, Manic will pass the behavioral test even though there is nothing he would like to do better than rip off Depressive. Every time he tries to translate his desires into action, he will be zapped by Depressive's ray gun. And whenever he asks why Depressive has the right to use this power against him, he will be greeted with the answer: "Because Depressive is at least as good as you are."[8] It follows that Manic's hatred does not prevent his interaction with Depressive from qualifying as a liberal power relationship. To function as a member of a liberal community, it is not necessary to be a liberal saint. So long as your aggressive impulses are controlled, your status as a citizen may not be impugned on behavioral grounds.

To forestall misunderstanding, I hasten to add that life in a liberal state hardly need be devoid of love and sympathy. As our story unfolds, we shall see our citizens establishing a rich variety of communities within which to explore the mysteries of personal association. Some will find love; others, that there are more important things. My point, rather, is that each citizen's right to material resources *does*

8. Nor can Manic say that he has the right to fulfill his conception of the good when this requires the theft of Depressive's resources. See § 15.2.

not depend on whether he tries to make himself lovable to his fellows. Given the diversity of moral ideals that will be pursued in a liberal polity, it is naïve to hope that all citizens will love one another; indeed, there will often be cases where my value commitments seem nothing less than hateful to some of my fellows.

It is, however, one thing for you and me to hate one another; quite another for you to deprive me of my rights to material subsistence if I do nothing to deprive you of yours. Indeed, there is only one word to describe a relationship in which my rights are secure only to the extent to which you find me a sympathetic character: slavery.

19.3. *Imperfect Justice: The Aims of the Criminal Law*

Take one small step toward earthly realities. This time deprive the Commander of her ray guns and give her a perfect criminal law. More specifically, assume (1) an ideal police force capable of discovering the perpetrators of all illegitimate power plays; (2) an ideal judiciary capable of adjudicating all cases with perfect accuracy; (3) an ideal punishment strategy which makes the citizen think himself worse off than he would have been if he had never committed his aggressive action in the first place.

Given this formidable set of structures, the principal ray gun result would carry over for the bulk of the new world's population. While the ideal criminal law has hardly induced everyone to love his neighbor as himself, this is not the goal of a liberal polity. Nor is the goal to transform Manic into the perfect liberal saint. Instead, Manic can function as a member of a liberal community if he merely possesses a minimal degree of prudence, the capacity to restrain his aggressive impulses in order to avoid more painful experiences in the future. So long as Manic is minimally prudent, his citizenship standing will be secure—regardless of his ideals, hatreds, and affections.

Yet, however minimal the requirement of minimal prudence, it does represent an important move beyond our ray gun world. There it was *completely* unnecessary to inquire into a candidate's motivational structure before he passed the behavioral test. Even the most imprudent person would be stopped cold by the ray guns in the midst of a hostile assault. So long as Manic passed the tests of *dialogic performance* he could not be barred from the full rights of citizenship by an appeal to the *behavioral* requirement. Now, however, it is possible to imagine a person who satisfies the dialogic tests but fails the behavioral one. He is somebody who is so blinded by momentary passions that he is incapable of reflecting upon the threat of future punishment. What, then, is such a person's status in liberal theory?

19.4. *Imperfect Justice: The Case for Special Restrictions*

Imagine, for example, that Estranged is minimally prudent in his dealings with all fellow citizens save one—Endangered, his former wife, whom he now hates beyond reason. So far as she is concerned, Estranged is simply uncontrollable—the next time he sees her, he will lash out and kill her. Fortunately, Endangered now lives on the West Coast while Estranged is happy with life in the East and only hopes to go West for occasional vacations. Would the Commander be justified in refusing Estranged permission to proceed with his holiday plans?

A realistic answer will turn on a host of contingent institutional realities. Thus, if judges were unable to predict future conduct accurately or if they selectively invoked the risk of future harm to suppress people they considered "deviant," then the dangers of illiberal abuse involved in preventive restrictions might well outweigh Endangered's right to physical security. While these second-best issues are of the greatest practical importance, I want to focus on the question of ideal theory involved: Is it even *possible* to conceive of circumstances in which preventive detention is legitimate?

To answer *this* question, assume that the liberal Commander can, with perfect accuracy, predict whether Estranged will be able to control himself when confronted by his former wife and has determined (correctly) that he lacks even minimal prudence in this regard:

COMMANDER: Stay East, my friend.
ESTRANGED: What gives you the right to restrict me in this way? After all, you let all my minimally prudent friends go wherever they like. What reason do you have for singling me out?
COMMANDER: I think it better for you to be restricted than for Endangered to be killed.
ESTRANGED: Doesn't your statement violate my rights as a citizen of the liberal state?
COMMANDER: Not at all. If you were permitted to roam around the country imposing illiberal relations on others, this would not make you a citizen of a liberal state; instead, it would transform the

polity into an illiberal state. It is only by virtue of this special restriction that you qualify as a member of an ongoing liberal community.

ESTRANGED: But I *want* to go West.

COMMANDER: Citizens of a liberal state are *not* guaranteed the right to get everything they want. In a world of scarce resources, such a right cannot be rationally justified.

ESTRANGED: What *am* I entitled to, then?

COMMANDER: A Neutral explanation.

ESTRANGED: And aren't you saying that Endangered is intrinsically better than I am?

COMMANDER: Not at all. I continue to affirm that when considered as a citizen, you are at least as good as Endangered. The only trouble is that before you can be considered a citizen, a special restriction must be imposed on you.

ESTRANGED: Who wants to be a citizen anyway? All I want is to go West!

COMMANDER: I'm afraid you'll have to lead a revolution against the liberal state before you can succeed in transforming all your wants into realities.

The point is a conceptual one. Just as it is (conceptually) impossible for me to establish a liberal power relationship with a stone, so too is it impossible for Estranged to establish a liberal relation with Endangered if he is allowed to confront her face to face. Consequently, if he hopes to maintain liberal relations with his former wife, he cannot be allowed to get close to her. This restriction is not a *violation* of Estranged's rights as a citizen; it is instead a *necessary condition* before Estranged can conceivably function as a citizen.

19.5. *The Least Restrictive Alternative*

Suppose that the Commander is emboldened by her last conversational success and seeks to restrict Estranged further. Imagine, for example, that she now proposes to impose special restrictions on the way he can use his manna while at home in the East:

COMMANDER: And, by the way, you'd better give half your manna away to charities.

ESTRANGED: Why?

COMMANDER: Because you're an especially vicious person, inca-

pable of controlling your murderous instincts without special restriction. It's right for you to do penance.

ESTRANGED: You can't say that!

COMMANDER: Why not? I could stop you from going West. Why
can't I tell you how to behave in the East?

ESTRANGED: Because the justifications for these actions are entirely different. You imposed the first restriction on the ground that
it was necessary to assure my citizenship status. But no such
rationale is available now. Once my travel is restricted, there can be
no doubt that I can behave like a citizen of a liberal state in my
dealings with all my fellows.

COMMANDER: I guess so. What follows from that?

ESTRANGED: Well, I thought you said that so long as I qualified as
a citizen, you recognize that I'm protected by the Neutrality principle.

COMMANDER: Right.

ESTRANGED: Then you can't justify this special restriction by saying I'm an especially vicious citizen.

COMMANDER: I guess not. That would violate Neutrality.

ESTRANGED: So then, I'm still waiting for a reason to justify this
particular power play.

To put the point another way, imposing a restriction on western
travel is the functional equivalent of providing Endangered with an
effective ray gun for warding off Estranged. Once an equivalence to
the ray-gun scenario has been established, however, we have shown
that Estranged's citizenship standing can no longer be impugned for
behavioral reasons. Only the *least restrictive alternative* that will satisfy
the behavioral test can be insulated from attack under the Neutrality
principle.

As a practical matter, this principle of the least restrictive alternative
will be one of the most important tools in the armory of liberal statecraft. In a vital liberal polity, all special restrictions will be periodically
questioned in an effort to determine whether they cannot be reduced
without undue risk of illegitimate aggression.[9] At this point, however,

_____

9. Not that all liberal statesmen will inevitably agree on the right way to answer the questions
raised by their ongoing inquiries. Apart from predictable empirical disputes about the relevant
facts, there will also be ongoing good-faith disagreement about the extent to which one pattern
of special restriction (say, a short prison term) is "less restrictive" than another (say, a long period
of probation). The general problems raised by the need to resolve such good-faith disagreements
will be discussed in Part Three.

I shall content myself with a single example that may suggest the principle's practical importance. Imagine, then, that Estranged treats all humanity as he does his former wife—lashing out homicidally against anyone who crosses his path. Acting on behalf of the liberal polity, the Commander has two—and only two—policy options available to her. On the one hand, she may execute the aggressor; on the other, she may use Estranged's share of manna to build an isolation cell where Estranged may live behind bars. The last conversation establishes the principled superiority of the second option. So long as he lives with the rest of us in peace, there is no need for Estranged to be lovable in order to claim the rights of citizenship.[10]

19.6. *Realer Worlds*

But, of course, things are never so simple in the world we presently inhabit. Instead of a near-perfect technology of justice, contemporary governments possess some very blunt instruments for deterrence and control. Rather than dealing with perfectly accurate and perfectly liberal Commanders, a realistic legal system must confront the difficulty of predicting the future and the ever-present risk that people in position of command may abuse their powers for illiberal purposes. It is here that the fundamental principles of liberal criminal law come into play: its suspicion of preventive detention, its insistence on the presumption of innocence, and its requirements of the highest standards of procedural regularity before a citizen is subjected to special restrictions because of his aggressive behavior. It should be emphasized, moreover, that these procedural rights are not grounded on anything so ephemeral and mutable as the general utility of the citizenry at large. Even if a mob were to shriek with delight at the prospect of Estranged's execution, this would not justify restricting his freedom of movement. It is only his breach of the behavioral criterion that limits his protection under the Neutrality Principle; given this, his violation of the condition must be made out in a convincing fashion.

This is not to say, however, that the liberal statesman will be single-mindedly concerned with the rights of those accused of aggres-

---

10. This is the dialogic core of the case against capital punishment in a liberal state. Nonetheless, a great deal must be said before the argument can be incisively applied in any particular second-best context. First, it is likely that Estranged's initial share of manna will be insufficient to purchase an isolation cell and a lifetime's supply of food. Second, the factors to be discussed in § 19.6 must be taken into account. Third, the entire problem must be viewed against the background of the theory of exploitation developed in chapter 8. Unfortunately, I cannot address the complexities these points require.

sion. As we have seen, the rights of innocent victims are at stake as well. A system of criminal justice cannot be so paralyzed by procedural safeguards that it is unable to deter criminal conduct by most prudent people most of the time. Indeed, given the difficulties of detection and proof in a liberal procedural system, it may be necessary to punish very severely the relatively few people whose crimes are brought to book. For it is only in this way that a level of deterrence may be achieved that will induce most prudent people to conform to the behavioral condition for citizenship.

It is not my aim, however, to design a model penal code for one or another concrete social situation. I only hope to suggest why the goals of a practical liberal system of criminal justice are *necessarily* complex and in tension with one another; and why, despite this tension, liberal criminal law takes on coherence when it is understood as a rough-and-ready effort to enforce the behavioral condition that may be justly required of all citizens of a liberal state.

20. FROM NECESSARY TO SUFFICIENT CONDITIONS

Imagine, now, that Manic has no trouble passing both dialogic and behavioral conditions for citizenship. It does not yet follow that he must be granted citizenship in any political community aspiring to liberal ideals. True, a person like Manic is fully capable of functioning as a member of a liberal community. But why can't a liberal state operate as if it were a private club, blackballing potential members who do not please its present constituents?

I shall argue that the analogy to a private club is misconceived. In ideal theory, *all* people who fulfill the dialogic and behavioral conditions have an unconditional right to demand recognition as full citizens of a liberal state.[11] After developing the conversational foundations for this ideal of universal citizenship, I shall consider the extent to which second-best considerations can legitimate a more restrictive attitude.

---

11. The arguments developed in this section not only apply to "law-abiding" citizens but also to people who find themselves specially restricted as a result of their specially aggressive behavior. Of course, the effort to protect the rights of specially restricted citizens may raise difficult problems of implementation. I cannot, however, treat these problems without attempting a much more contextual investigation than is possible here.

20.1. *Ideal Theory*

Imagine, then, that there are two spaceships—Explorer and Apollo—engaged in the task of discovery. Each contains an equal number of people who satisfy the necessary conditions for liberal citizenship. The Explorer, however, lands first, and the Commander of that ship gives each member of her landing party a single grain of manna with which to begin life. A split second later, the Apollonians arrive and demand equal standing in the burgeoning liberal polity:

APOLLONIAN: I want half your manna.

EXPLORER: Sorry, but I need all of it—and more—if I am to attain my ends in life.

APOLLONIAN: But I need it too! If personal need is a good reason for your getting manna, why shouldn't it count in my case as well?

EXPLORER: Do I have to answer that question?

APOLLONIAN: Absolutely. Rationality requires power wielders to answer the question of legitimacy whenever it is raised.

EXPLORER: But I want nothing from you!

APOLLONIAN: That doesn't mean you're not exercising power over me. I want half the manna and you're trying to stop me. That's enough to establish a power relationship requiring justification.

EXPLORER: Look, I didn't ask you to come. Why don't you just go away?

APOLLONIAN: I didn't ask you to come either. Why isn't that an equally good reason for you to go away and leave all the manna for me?

EXPLORER: Well, if you really must know, I'll come up with a serious answer.

APOLLONIAN: I'm waiting.

EXPLORER: I should get the manna because I'm a citizen of the liberal state we Explorers have established, and you're not.

APOLLONIAN: Progress at last. There's only one problem.

EXPLORER: What's that?

APOLLONIAN: Don't you remember the differentiation test imposed by Rationality? It requires you to point to a feature of our situation that differentiates your claim from mine. So, tell me, why do you think you qualify as a citizen and I do not?

EXPLORER: Easy. I landed on the Explorer, hence I must be a citizen of the liberal state we Explorers have established.

APOLLONIAN: That can't be right. After all, there are lots of things that landed on the Explorer that don't qualify as citizens. That hunk of metal, for example. (*Pointing to the spaceship.*)

EXPLORER: But I'm different from the hunk because I can justify my claims to power.

APOLLONIAN: So can I. Why then don't I qualify as a citizen along with you?

EXPLORER: And I can conform my behavior to the power structure required by a liberal dialogue.

APOLLONIAN: So can I. So why don't you say that both of us are different from the hunk in that we are both citizens of a liberal state?

EXPLORER: Because I landed in the hunk and you didn't!

APOLLONIAN: Awfully mysterious. This metal hunk doesn't even qualify as a citizen and yet it constitutes the decisive difference between you and me.

EXPLORER: But you don't deny the fact that, thanks to the Explorer, I got here ahead of you.

APOLLONIAN: I don't deny the fact. I just want to know why the fact should count as a reason justifying your superior power position.

EXPLORER: Because people who arrive first are better than people who arrive second.

APOLLONIAN: Reason at last! But this would plainly be an un-Neutral reason if given to a citizen of the liberal state.

EXPLORER: An irrelevant objection. I'm giving this as a reason for *denying* you citizenship. No Neutrality objections please; by its own terms, the third principle limits its protection to "citizens."

APOLLONIANS: And what about your children? Will they ever qualify as citizens?

EXPLORER: Of course.

APOLLONIAN: But they will arrive even later than I have.

EXPLORER: Do I have to respond to this point?

APOLLONIAN: Absolutely. The second principle requires power wielders to provide a consistent answer to the question of legitimacy, without any limitation restricting its scope to "citizens."

EXPLORER: Well, if you insist, I declare that the special superiority that I possess by virtue of my first arrival is passed down to my descendants forever and ever, while the special inferiority you possess taints your descendants as well.

APOLLONIANS: And suppose that I deny your claim, asserting instead that true moral superiority resides with those with a high IQ or those with a particularly beautiful body or those who are born black or those——

EXPLORER: Then what you'd say would simply be wrong. True moral superiority resides with the first inhabitants and their descendants. Only a fool would think otherwise!

APOLLONIAN: Aren't you troubled by the kinds of answers you're giving?

EXPLORER: An irrelevant question. All I've done is fulfill my conversational responsibilities under the first two principles of the liberal state. You've asked some hard questions, but I've answered them. Have I satisfied you?

APOLLONIAN: Not at all. In justifying your claim to citizenship, you have made precisely the same conversational moves that are generally excluded by the Neutrality principle.

EXPLORER: But I haven't violated its express terms, which are limited to "citizens."

APOLLONIAN: Yet you have entirely trivialized Neutrality's significance.

EXPLORER: How so?

APOLLONIAN: Well, don't you agree that citizenship is the most fundamental right a person could have in a liberal state?

EXPLORER: Why do you think so?

APOLLONIAN: After all, it is nothing less than the right to have conversational rights under Neutrality. And what could be more fundamental than that?

EXPLORER: A good point.

APOLLONIAN: Be careful. Even this small concession will get you in trouble.

EXPLORER: How so?

APOLLONIAN: If citizenship is the most fundamental right in liberal theory, how can you allow this right to be assigned for reasons you would never tolerate on less important questions?

EXPLORER: A good question. Do I have to answer it?

APOLLONIAN: Absolutely. Unless you want to deny that citizenship is the most important right in liberal theory. Otherwise it would follow a fortiori that conversational moves offensive in other contexts are illegitimate here as well. And this would mean that every time you insisted on a Neutral conversation in other contexts, you would argue inconsistently with the views you are expressing here.

EXPLORER: And this would require me to breach the Consistency principle?

APOLLONIAN: Precisely.

EXPLORER: You know, I really *do* wish you'd go away.

APOLLONIAN: I realize that. But I'm *not* going away. Like it or not, you are exercising power over me, and I shall continue to press my question of legitimacy. So tell me, isn't it obvious that citizenship *is* the most fundamental status question; after all, you're using it as the reason for denying me *all* my rights!

EXPLORER: Really, I have more important things to do with my time and manna than engage in such twaddle.

APOLLONIAN: *More* important things! Do you imagine that you are some divinity whose claim to dominion over me is self-evident? Why don't you answer my question?

EXPLORER: Well, frankly, I do find it difficult to deny that citizenship is central. After all, in order to establish my own rights to scarce resources, I am constantly relying on my citizenship status.

APOLLONIAN: Then you must concede the same to me.

EXPLORER: And if I do not?

APOLLONIAN: Then you must abandon the claim that you Explorers have established an ideal liberal state. For the first principle of such a polity requires each of its citizens to provide rational and consistent answers to the question of legitimacy whenever asked. And you have just failed this minimal test.

While I find this dialogue compelling, its structure is different from most conversations found in this book. In the typical dialogue, each participant tries to reduce the other to silence by showing that everything he wants to say in his behalf has been rendered unspeakable by Neutrality. But the third principle cannot, by its own terms, do its accustomed work here. To establish that the dialogic and behavioral requirements are not only *necessary* but also *sufficient* for citizenship, the Apollonian rests his case on the central place citizenship plays in the entire structure of liberal theory. Quite simply, citizenship is not just another question open for resolution by the political community. It is conceptually prior to all other particular power struggles, involving as it does the right to have one's rights determined through a Neutral conversation. To have *this* right determined by a political conversation that admits otherwise inadmissible dialogic moves would trivialize the liberal effort at conversational restraint from the very beginning.

To put the point more generally: We can make sense of citizenship only by rooting it in more fundamental ideas of political community. In liberal theory, the polity achieves its distinctiveness by a commitment to a process by which questions are, in principle, followed by rational answers. Nor can answers take any form the power wielders find convenient. Instead, when faced with the question of legitimacy, *the challenged party cannot respond by asserting the moral inferiority of the questioner.* It is this basic idea that is particularized by Neutrality's guarantee to all "citizens" of the liberal state. Yet this basic idea also applies to the conversation that determines the citizenship status of persons capable of participating in a liberal polity. The liberal state is not a private club; it is rather a public dialogue by which each person can gain social recognition of his standing as a free and rational being. I cannot justify my power to exclude you without destroying my own claim to membership in an ideal liberal state.

20.2. *Immigration in a Realer World*

But it is time to descend to earth. Quite unthinkingly, we have come to accept the idea that we have the right to exclude nonresidents from our midst. Yet, unless something further can be said, the dialogue between Explorer and Apollonian applies equally to the conversation between a rich American and an impoverished Mexican who swims over the border for a talk. The American can no more declare the intrinsic superiority of the first occupant than the Explorer can. Instead, it is only a very strong empirical claim that can permit the American to justify exclusion of the foreign-born from "his" liberal state.

To simplify the argument, divide the world into two nation-states, the poor East and the rich West. Assume further that Western domestic institutions are organized in a liberalish way while the East is an authoritarian dicatorship in which a small elite explicitly declares its superiority over the masses they exploit. Assume, finally, that as part of its second-best response to this dark reality, the West has adopted a forthcoming immigration policy, admitting a large number, Z, of Easterners on a first-come, first-served basis. Indeed, Z is so large that it strains the capacity of Western institutions to sustain a liberal political conversation. Any more than Z and the West's standing as a liberal society will be endangered; the presence of so many alien newcomers will generate such anxiety in the native population that it will prove impossible to stop a fascist group from seizing political power to assure native control over the immigrant underclass. Nonetheless, the Easterners keep coming at an awesome rate; the scene takes place at the armed Western border:

EASTERNER: I demand recognition as a citizen of this liberal state.

WESTERN STATESMAN: We refuse.

EASTERNER: What gives you the right to refuse me? Do you think I would fail to qualify as a citizen of an ideal liberal state?

WESTERNER: Not at all.

EASTERNER: Do you imagine you're better than me simply because you've been born west of this frontier?

WESTERNER: No. If that were all, I would not hesitate before admitting you.

EASTERNER: Well, then, what's the trouble?

WESTERNER: The fact is that we in the West are far from achieving a perfect technology of justice; if we admit more than Z newcomers, our existing institutions will be unable to function in anything but an explicitly authoritarian manner.

EASTERNER: But why am I being asked to bear the costs of imperfection?

WESTERNER: Sorry, we're doing everthing we can. But Z is the limit on immigrants.

EASTERNER: But you're not doing *everything*. Why not expel some of your native-born Westerners and make room for me? Do you think they're better than I am?

WESTERNER: Z is the limit on our assimilative capacity only on the assumption that there exists a cadre of natives familiar with the operation of liberal institutions. If some of the natives were removed from the population, even Z would be too many.

EASTERNER: So what am I to do? I'll be dead before I get to the front of the line of immigrants.

WESTERNER: Go back among your own people and build your own liberal state. We'll try to help you out as best we can.

A hard conversation. Nor should we be overly impressed by the faint optimism of the closing lines; there may be little realistic hope of liberal renaissance in this or that unhappy land. In the end, however, the dialogue is but another application of principles we have already developed. Compare the case of Estranged. There we saw that the Commander could stop him from moving west if this was necessary to prevent him from treating his ex-wife in a strikingly illiberal way. Rather than an un-Neutral restraint, the special restriction was a necessary condition for Estranged's recognition as a citizen of a liberal state. In the East-West dialogue, we confront the limiting case: if the Easterner is allowed to move to the West, this will not only threaten a single Endangered citizen but will destroy the *entire* liberal conversation that guarantees the rights of *all* existing citizens. Just as Estranged may be specially restricted without violating Neutrality, so too may Easterner.

The analogy between immigration and the criminal law, however, should not be overstrained. While Estranged may properly demand proof of his particular offense beyond a reasonable doubt, it would be silly to insist that immigration authorities make an individualized showing that the admission of a particular Easterner would lead to an illiberal upheaval. Since authoritarian revolutions cannot be predicted with accuracy, the most we can demand is that statesmen set an overall Z conscious of an immigrant's prima facie *right* to demand entry into a liberal state. Westerners are not entitled to deny this right simply because they have been born on the right side of a boundary line; nor can they escape the demands of dialogue simply because they would find sharing "their" wealth inconvenient. For the question is, precisely, why Easterners do not have a claim to an initial starting point that is equal to the position enjoyed by Westerners. After all, are they not at least as good as we are?

The *only* reason for restricting immigration is to protect the ongoing process of liberal conversation itself. Can our present immigration practices be rationalized on this ground?[12]

20.3. *"Internal" Citizenship Policy*
There is, finally, a more manageable set of second-best difficulties that arise in applying citizenship criteria to native-born residents of a

---

12. These themes are developed further in § 56.3.

liberal state. While a person's dialogic performance is critical in determining his citizenship standing, I do not mean to suggest that government bureaucrats should be permitted to deprive people of their citizenship rights on the basis of a casual chat. Given the obvious danger of authoritarian abuse, our citizenship rights should be guaranteed by the clearest possible rule: *Everybody* who has reached an age where a human being can typically satisfy the tests of dialogue and behavior should be *presumed* to be a full citizen of the liberal state. The precise age at which such a presumption should attach must await the next chapter's discussion of liberal education. For now, the important point is that once this age is reached, citizenship rights may be subjected to special restriction only on a compelling showing like the kind demanded by liberal principles of criminal procedure. Anything less than this fails to take seriously the risk of tyranny raised whenever an individual's standing in the public dialogue is threatened.

Even apart from the risks of tyranny, carrying on the public dialogue is a costly activity that must be kept within bounds lest it consume all the time a citizen would otherwise devote to the pursuit of his particular conception of the good. The times and places for dialogue must be restricted so that all life is not transformed into a weary "Because I'm at least as good as you are." This means that I should not risk my citizenship when I refuse to drop everything every time someone comes along and raises the question of legitimacy. Indeed, if I find it more convenient, I may ask someone else to speak on my behalf whenever my rights are challenged by my fellows. But these second-best points may never permit me to evade the question of legitimacy entirely. No second-best accommodation with liberal ideals can ever permit any group of citizens to doubt that they do in fact have the power to call me to account when my exercise of power trenches upon their important interests. For it is this thin chain of questions and answers that binds all citizens together to form a liberal state.

21. THE CITIZEN AS COMMANDER

So much for the necessary and sufficient conditions of citizenship. Only one conceptual issue remains before our sketch can pretend to adequacy. Up to the present point, our dialogues have in fact been trialogues, with the Commander participating along with Manic and Depressive in the struggle for manna. Yet it would be wrong to take the Commander too seriously. She stands, rather, as a placeholder for a complex process of government dedicated to the articulation and implementation of liberal dialogue. Rather than a distinct person, command is a distinct kind of power that one person can wield over another. The distinctive character of command can best be seen by contrasting it to the power manna brings. In ideal theory, manna stands as a compendious measure of all the material resources a citizen is given to achieve his objectives *within* the power structure established by a Neutral dialogue; in contrast, command represents an index of a person's power *over* the basic structure of the power system as a whole. To put the point in a more familiar vocabulary, we have thus far been speaking of a citizen's *civil* rights, but have failed to deal with his *political* right to share in the exercise of governmental authority. Moreover, as soon as the question of command is raised, it adds special conversational difficulties. Imagine, for example, a Nazi rising in the Assembly Hall to seize the chair from the Commander:

COMMANDER: Stop at once!

NAZI: Why should I? After all, I just won a share of manna equal to the Jew's. Why shouldn't I also have an equal share in the command of the Assembly?

COMMANDER: But if you take over, what will you do?

NAZI: Reprogram the ship's computers and ray guns so we don't have to carry on any more of these idiot conversations!

COMMANDER: Sorry, but my order stands. Keep away from the chair!

NAZI: You can't do this to me!

COMMANDER: Why not?

NAZI: Because I have rights to my fair share of power as a citizen of the liberal state!

COMMANDER: Indeed you do. But my action is not inconsistent with your rights. Just as in the case of Estranged or Easterner, I must impose a special restriction upon your behavior before you qualify as a citizen. Otherwise you will behave in a way that makes a liberal power structure impossible.

NAZI: But that's just what I want to do! What kind of liberal state is this anyway? Aren't I entitled to my own political opinions?

COMMANDER: Absolutely. You may think whatever you like; you may even try to form voluntary groups to put your beliefs into practice. The question here, though, is whether you can use the power of command to transform the polity into an authoritarian form.

NAZI: But that's what I *want* to do!

COMMANDER: A citizen of a liberal state is not entitled to do anything he wants. He must first justify his proposed power play in a Neutral dialogue. And nazism does not even try to justify its coup d'état in Neutral terms.

NAZI: I think this citizenship stuff is a lot of crap.

COMMANDER: That's for you to decide. Mine is a conceptual point: Your right to command cannot conceptually be recognized as part of the bundle of rights that you may claim as a citizen of a liberal state. For this very act of recognition would transform the state from a liberal to a fascist polity.

As in the case of the Easterner or Estranged, the dialogue is simply an application of the more general argument vindicating the behavioral test for citizenship in a liberal state. As such, it is subject to the same limitations on its abuse. Just as Estranged can only be restricted in his westward wanderings and could not be compelled to atone for his homicidal thoughts, so too the principle of the least restrictive alternative may be invoked on behalf of the Nazi's claim to positions of command. Indeed, it is possible to imagine a liberal world where even Nazis could properly demand a right to occupy the highest governmental positions. Given our governing metaphor, simply stipulate that a perfect technology of justice stopped the Nazi from sabotaging the ongoing liberal dialogue even if he occupied the Commander's chair. No matter how he might try, the spaceship's computers and ray guns prove impossible to reprogram; instead, the way he could best fulfil his thirst for grandeur would be to use the power of command as if he were a dedicated liberal and call upon the speakers to continue their Neutral debate. Given this stipulation, it should be plain that the last dialogue could not take place. Instead, the Nazi's equal claim to share in the powers of command would then be recognized by an ideal liberal polity.

I can make the same point by connecting it with an abiding hope of liberal political science. Rather than designing a foolproof computer, the traditional goal has been expressed through the rhetoric of "checks and balances." The aim is to divide command among a variety of offices, giving each office institutional incentives to check the actions of others when their incumbents attempt to abuse their powers in authoritarian ways. If such a design could be perfected, even a Nazi's claim to share in command could be given full recognition.

But the hopes of Madison and Mandeville will never be fully realized. Even in stable liberal regimes, the prospect of totalitarian takeover must be taken seriously. It seems best, though, to defer a serious discussion of this problem to chapter 9, where the problem of second-best government is taken up in a comprehensive way.

22. CITIZENSHIP IN LIBERAL THEORY

We have come far enough in our journey to wonder whether it is worthwhile, whether insight justifies exertion. So let us pause to inspect the landscape for signs suggesting that, though much remains unexplored, there may be a rewarding vista if ever we reach the mountaintop. A good way of orienting ourselves is to compare the emerging course of argument with more familiar lines of thought that proceed from ideas of contract or utility.

22.1. *Social Contract*

Consider the myth of social contract. Somehow or other, you are asked to imagine yourself an asocial monad encountering another monad for the "first" time. Your job is to come up with an agreement that will serve as the foundation of future social intercourse. Yet, however important this job may be, it remains derivative in an important way. Despite your asociality, the myth endows you with a developed consciousness of yourself as a person entitled to a set of "natural" rights. And happily for you, the other monads have an equal sense of themselves as autonomous individuals possessing "rights." Thus, all the monads need do is repackage their understanding of their "natural" rights into a social form better suited to the realities of social life. The contractual process itself is only a useful instrument by which this transformation takes place; it does not play a constitutive role in the process by which the monads achieve the consciousness of themselves as individuals whose rights are worthy of public recognition.[13]

---

13. Rousseau stands as a great exception to these (and other) remarks about contract theory. Throughout this book, I shall be unable to give him the attention he deserves.

In contrast, the citizens of a liberal state look upon dialogic processes in a less instrumental way. They do not come to their initial encounter as if they had been somehow provided (by God?) with a sense of themselves as creatures with rights. Instead, they achieve this form of self-consciousness by participating in a distinctively *social* process. Day after day, each citizen finds himself exercising power over scarce resources; at any time, he may be called upon by his fellows to justify his power; and when the question is raised, he must be prepared to answer: "Because I'm at least as good as you are." To achieve an understanding of myself as a person with rights, it is no longer necessary to imagine that I somehow "precede" the society in which I find myself. In a liberal state, the individual does not "precede" society; nor society, the individual. Instead, citizens create a *society of individuals* by talking to one another about their social predicament.

This dialogic method, moreover, not only permits self-affirmation but demands self-restraint as well. Since a liberal state is nothing other than a power structure regulated by Neutral dialogue, citizens cannot rightly protest against special restriction when they behave in aggressive ways that are inconsistent with their political talk. For in making their protest, they can say nothing on their own behalf that passes the tests of liberal conversation. Even if reduced to silence, however, people subjected to special restriction need never fear that their "breach" of the "social contract" suddenly transforms them into outlaws with no rights against the community. Instead, the principle of the least-restrictive alternative safeguards their continued standing as participants in the ongoing liberal conversation.

22.2. *Utility*
Surely the partisan of utility cannot be charged with the sins of social contract. A dose of Bentham is the best cure for anyone tempted by the vision of asocial monads giving contractual shape to their natural rights. Nonetheless, the utilitarian's solution to the problem of citizenship is very different from the one I am advancing. Rather than grounding individual rights in a communal process of Neutral dialogue, his aim is to make all talk of individual rights instrumental in character. The trick is to posit something so self-evidently good that anybody but a fool would see its desirability. And that is pleasure. Since pleasure is good, more pleasure is better than less. And so the world should be made as pleasurable as possible.

Now, as we have seen, this effort to propose an absolutely uncontroversial conception of the good is doomed to fail the test of Neutral dialogue.[14] Yet it is not this substantive weakness I want to emphasize here. Instead, I want to mark the point at which the path of Neutral dialogue diverges from that marked by utility. And for this purpose, the peculiar obtuseness with which the utilitarian approaches the problem of citizenship is most revealing. Speaking broadly, the present chapter has been concerned with a single problem disguised in many forms: How to define the boundary that separates members of a liberal political community from the rest of the universe. The utilitarian, however, simply fails to see the distinctive importance of these boundary questions. Not that the status of the immigrant, the revolutionary, or the criminal are thought to raise trivial issues. On the contrary, the sensitive utilitarian will offer an analysis of the felicific trade-offs whose complexity is equal to their importance; nonetheless, his method forbids him to recognize the depth of the boundary questions at stake. After all his exquisite trade-offs are elaborated and resolved, he is committed here, as elsewhere, to recommending the course that will maximize collective utility; yet, for the liberal, the peculiar poignancy of these disputes is the individual's rightful insistence that, as a citizen of a liberal state, he deserves the protection of the Neutrality principle without regard to the happiness others take in the assertion of his claims. It is just this point that the utilitarian cannot see.

Nor is this blindness easily cured. It follows directly from the utilitarian's failure to link individual rights to community processes. He would have us look beyond the ongoing dialogue in which I answer your questions and you answer mine. He does not see in this process of cultural give-and-take the constituting matrix of my confidence that I am indeed a person with rights that others have an obligation to respect. Instead, the only thing that concerns him is the subjective experience of pain I feel when my wants are frustrated. This—and this alone—commends my fate to his benevolent attention.

Since subjective pain, not communal dialogue, serves as the foundation of rights, the utilitarian can only look with sympathy upon all sentient creatures who fall on the wrong side of the liberal boundary line. So far as Bentham was concerned, the best world is one where the sum of all happiness is maximized, without regard to whether the

14. § 13.1.

sentient creature is a man, a lion, or a worm. And I think it is relatively clear that this standard requires very massive transfers of resources away from humans to the multitude of other creatures sharing the planet with us. Thus, to the clear-thinking utilitarian, talk about "citizenship" seems idle prattle concealing mankind's selfish insistence on obtaining more than its rightful share of the world's resources.[15]

For the partisan of the liberal state, however, this strong stand on animal liberation is but a striking example of the utilitarian's bland confidence that he has discovered a completely uncontroversial conception of the good. After all, it is not the animal itself who insists that we maximize overall utility. It is some person, like myself, who claims to speak on behalf of the animals. But why should I take his word for it when he says that the universe must be as happy a place as possible. Suppose I think that this is too syrupy a view, that we must recognize that the lion will never lie down with the lamb, that we may eat them both when we are hungry. Why isn't *my* conception of the universe entitled to community respect equal to that the community accords my fellow citizen?

Since we *cannot* enter into a liberal form of community with animals living beyond the conversational boundary, our relationship to them is *necessarily* authoritarian. And none among us can set himself up as a privileged spokesman for mute creation. This means that the first principle of the liberal philosophy of nature is not benevolence but agnosticism. No political faction may declare that it has finally unlocked the ultimate mysteries of the universe.

While the principle of agnosticism is clear, the best way of implementing the principle will be a subject of ongoing dispute. For some citizens, the right policy choice will seem simple. They will want to distribute all nature to the citizenry in the form of manna and leave nature's fate entirely to individual value choices. This does not imply that all noncitizens will be subjected to the kind of abusive treatment generally conjured up by talk of "exploitation." Groups of people will club together to preserve parts of nature—even if, like the peak of Mount Everest, it is not capable of sensation and so eludes the utilitarian's concern.[16]

15. See Peter Singer, *Animal Liberation* (New York: A New York Review Book, 1975). While Singer does not attempt a rigorous or straightforward utilitarian argument, his appeal for vegetarianism has many utilitarian strands and reinvigorates debate on an important question.

16. Moreover, a liberal government may well be justified in aiding these voluntary efforts if they would otherwise be undermined by a familiar range of market imperfections. See §§ 43–45, 50.

Such voluntary efforts will not, however, seem sufficient to some citizens. According to them, it is a fundamental mistake to give all nature out in the form of appropriable manna. This initial decision already offends agnostic principle since it requires the Commander to declare that all nature may be properly conceived as subordinate to the purposes of the liberal community. For these citizens, a truer agnosticism will require a collective decision declaring that at least certain natural objects must be preserved untouched by the citizenry—making it clear that liberal agnosticism extends to the question of whether nature exists merely to be exploited by the liberal community. For others, however, the notion that nature has "integrity" beyond the purpose of citizens is mere poppycock of the kind always indulged by political elites anxious to increase their power on the pretext that they have been appointed nature's guardian. Such people will oppose any effort to move beyond the preservationist steps that would ideally be taken by individuals acting on their own private initiative.

There can be no hope of ending this debate within the framework of the liberal state. Deprived of divine revelation, the liberal state must define its policy toward nature within a forum that explicitly recognizes the tentative character of any resolution reached. At a later point, I shall describe a democratic government best suited for this role.[17] For now, though, it is enough to contrast the confidence with which the utilitarian treats the subject of animal rights with the principled uncertainty that is the hallmark of liberal policy. While his rival confidently declares that the universe must become the happiest possible place, the liberal recognizes that all legislation protecting nature is essentially tentative and subject to revision over time. In contrast, the rights of people living on *our* side of the dialogic boundary have a depth and cogency that the utilitarian will never comprehend. Rather than depending upon another's sympathy, I stand before him with the question: Why should you, rather than I, possess this power we both desire?

What, then, is your reply?

17. See § 61.

PART TWO: JUSTICE OVER TIME

4

BIRTHRIGHTS

23. THE BIOGRAPHY OF EVERYMAN

Can we imagine a world in which *everyone* could provide a liberal answer to the question of legitimacy *whenever* it was asked by *anyone* who presented himself as a claimant for scarce resources?

If this is the central question of ideal theory, Part One only made a first step toward an affirmative answer. Most notable, perhaps, is the cavalier way with which Part One dealt with the problem of time. The simplification occurred on two levels. So far as each individual is concerned, the struggle for power hardly begins when we confront one another, as adults, over scarce material wealth. Instead, my position in the power structure begins to be defined at a much earlier stage—as my parents make decisions that affect the course of my future. A complete theory of the power struggle, then, must begin at the beginning, with the power of parents to control the upbringing of their children, with their power to deny their successors life itself.

But Part One oversimplified the problem of time in another, equally important way. Quite apart from the struggle that particular children have with particular parents, the rising generation, considered as a whole, can hardly pretend to be the discoverers of a new world full of unclaimed resources. Instead, they confront a preceding generation that tries to have some say in the way that initial wealth will be distributed to the newcomers. To complete the theory of legitimacy, then, we must trace the dialogues that will follow predictably from such efforts: Can the elders take advantage of their temporal priority to declare that only a few of their successors will inherit the earth and enjoy the labor of the dispossessed? How can the elders respond when their youthful fellow citizens deny their right to deprive them of an equal share of the wealth?

To provide a dialogic answer to these questions, the present part takes the form of a stylized biography of Everyman. Each citizen is first conceived (chapter 4), then socialized (chapter 5), then granted a share

of the material endowment that he may use to form mutually beneficial relations with his fellows (chapter 6) only to die and hand on the
world to his successors (chapter 7). At each of these points, Everyman's power to define and pursue his good is constrained in critical
ways by the power exercised by others. A comprehensive theory must
examine the distinctive way the question of legitimacy is discussed at
each of these critical stages in life's passage.

In discussing each citizen's progress through the web of power, I
aim to make as few empirical assumptions about Everyman as I can
without altogether losing sight of him. Frugality is required for two
different reasons. First, it is too easy to short-circuit normative discourse by simply positing that Everyman will do just what *you* think he
ought to do. Then anybody who deviates from Everyman's path can be
condemned as a pervert whose deviant conduct must be suppressed in
the name of an ideal we are "all" aspiring to fulfill. But this authoritarian gambit transparently begs the liberal question: What if the "pervert" disagrees with your version of the Everyman story and tells one
in which *his* ideals play the starring role? Why isn't his ideal Everyman just as valuable as yours? To keep this question in the foreground,
we must allow Everyman to do anything that it is physically possible
for human beings[1] to do—otherwise we will be merely disguising
normative judgments in pseudoempirical dress.

Which leads me to a second reason for frugality. Speaking for myself, I do not have a very clear sense of the ultimate biophysical constraints upon Everyman's behavior. I have not spent my life studying
genetics, child development, psychology, and the other disciplines
that speak to these issues. Given my ignorance, it seems wiser to take
an overly broad, rather than an unduly narrow, view of human
capacities. If I err on the side of overbreadth, my mistakes can be
cured by *empirical* research demonstrating that human beings cannot
engage in some of the power conflicts I imagine occurring. In contrast,
if I am unduly narrow, I have failed to consider the *normative* issues
that arise from some foreseeable power conflict. Since I aim to develop a normative theory that is, in principle, comprehensive, this
second charge is far more damaging to my mission. If, then, you do not
believe that Everyman would ever kill an infant or commit incest

---

1. I shall defer the problem posed by nonhuman citizens (§ 18.2) until such time as they
appear.

under liberal social conditions, simply ignore my treatment of such topics.

For all this, I have found it necessary to endow Everyman with certain minimal features before I can speak about his biography in a way I find illuminating. Most obviously, I assume Everyman does not come into the world as a full-blown citizen immediately capable of talking and behaving in the ways required for full membership in a liberal state. Instead, he is *first* conceived as an embryonic genetic program; *next*, he must endure a period of socialization before mastering the behavioral and dialogic performances required for citizenship; and *only then* can he establish his dialogic claim to manna and those transactional resources necessary for him to pursue his good. Other assumptions—both more and less controversial—will be invoked from time to time; the best I can do is flag them when they come into view.

24. FIRST AND LAST

To build a conceptual bridge from the last part to this, imagine that you and I are adult members of the spaceship generation setting out to build a society founded on liberal dialogue. As we circle the new world, somebody rises in the Assembly Hall to bring into question our obligations to future generations. May we simply ignore their potential interest in our conversation or must we somehow take their claims into account? To focus attention on the question of future generations, the Commander asks for a show of hands: How many among us plan to use some of our scarce time and manna to bring up children?

No hands are raised. The question is asked again. As always, all citizens are given the right to go to the ship's computers and obtain any empirical information or prediction they think relevant to their choice. Still, nobody thinks children worth the time and effort involved. You are Commander: What's your next move?

I say you should pass on to some other subject. Nobody in the hall is raising the question of legitimacy. Nobody will *ever* challenge the legitimacy of your decision to move on. Yet if no question will ever be asked, whom are we trying to answer? The conversation has exhausted itself; it has come to an end unless the Commander *orders* people to keep on talking.

But how can the Commander justify such a power? She cannot point to the first principle, which requires an answer to the question of legitimacy only when it is actually *asked* by somebody disadvantaged by an assertion of power. To the contrary, it is *her* effort to force her fellow citizens to keep talking that is subject to question:

> EVERYMAN: Look, I've already said that kids are not worth my time and effort. Why do you think I have to say more?
>
> COMMANDER: Well, this seems to me an awfully important decision.
>
> EVERYMAN: But apparently you don't think it's *so* important that you're willing to spend your own time and manna having a child.
>
> COMMANDER: That's right. I have better things to do with my personal life.
>
> EVERYMAN: And so do I. What justifies you, then, in forcing me to defend the merits of my conception of the good? Isn't it at least as good as yours is?
>
> COMMANDER: I guess you're right. I can't use my special powers as Commander to force you to talk when nobody else is asking the question.

But have I not been suffering from a lack of political imagination? Suppose that, in response to the Commander's request for a show of hands, a citizen steps forward, points to some empty space (or so it seems to me), and declares that he hears the voice of a disembodied junior demanding corporeal substance: "Let me in! I insist on a body! I'm at least as good as you are!" What then? How is this imaginary dialogue different from any of the others we have so eagerly considered?

While previous dialogues have made great demands on the political imagination, they have all involved the discourse of bodily creatures confronting a very worldly problem: how to deal with the condition of relative scarcity they all confront. Since the everyday world is hardly a place where this problem is always solved through Neutral dialogue, it became necessary to imagine what a more legitimate society would look like. Political imagination, in short, was not needed to *escape* the fact that we have bodies but rather to propose a legitimate *solution* to the problem of bodily conflict in a world of scarce resources.

When somebody posits the existence of a disembodied Everyman, however, we are confronted by a different sort of problem—one of theology, not politics. For one thing, it is not clear what is meant when such spirits are said to exist; for another, it is not clear how they communicate their wants to us; for another, it is not clear that they want bodies. This is not to say that a liberal Commander should take a hard materialist line on these issues. She need not deny the right of bodily citizens to define their life's meaning by positing the existence of spiritual beings and conducting dialogues with them. As we shall see[2], any group of like-minded citizens have the right to worship God in any way they see fit. All such spiritual communions, however, must be founded on a *voluntary* decision by each communicant affirming the value of his particular church's form of divine dialogue. Moreover, if a citizen—after divine communion—is convinced that God wants him to bring children into the world, there is nothing to prevent him from using his initial endowments to bring Junior into fleshly existence. But if nobody is willing to devote his fair share of resources to this purpose, the Commander cannot force the citizenry to engage in procreative activity. For this necessarily requires a public declaration that the elite's theology is intrinsically superior to other ways of defining the meaning of life. Childbearing, like every other activity, must vindicate its value through the free choices of a morally autonomous citizenry.

25. TRUSTEESHIP

Suppose, now, that the Commander's question gains a more positive response. Masses of citizens indicate their procreative intentions. Do they have the right to have as many children as they like?

As always, the way of proceeding is through dialogue. In contrast to the preceding case, the people in the Assembly Hall cannot suppose that the power they exercise will *never* be questioned by bodily creatures who claim the rights due fellow citizens of a liberal state. To the contrary, they specifically intend to bring *citizens* into existence, creatures who will come to question the decisions they make today. And if the Commander intends to preside over a liberal state that maintains its dialogic integrity over time, she must attend to the possibility that today's power play may generate a situation that requires illiberal talk tomorrow.

To see the problem, imagine that there are a million people on the

2. Chapter 6.

spaceship and a million grains of manna on our new world. In response to her question, 100,000 citizens indicate a desire to have one child each. At this point, however, the spaceship's computer printout conveys some disturbing news: if the present generation pursues its current plans, it will consume 950,000 grains of manna before its successors attain maturity. Given this prediction, the Assembly can anticipate the following challenge:

JUNIORS: We have come to claim our manna.

SENIORS: O.K. We'll give you folks half a grain apiece.

JUNIORS: Why so little?

SENIORS: Sorry, but that's all there is left.

JUNIORS: But you started out with one grain apiece!

SENIORS: True, but we've had a good time and now there are only 50,000 grains left.

JUNIORS: And why should we start off our lives with less than you received?

SENIORS: Sorry, but you weren't there when we began.

JUNIORS: Why should that matter? Do you think that citizens who are born early are intrinsically superior to those who are born late?

SENIORS: We can't say that—it would violate Neutrality.

JUNIORS: Well, then, how can you justify the fact that your starting point was better than ours promises to be?

SENIORS: (*Silence.*)

JUNIORS: While you are searching for a Neutral reason, let us give you one to support our claim. We think that all citizens are at least as good as one another regardless of their date of birth. And if we are at least as good as you are, we should start out in life with at least as much manna as you did.

Now there are two ways of avoiding this conversation. On the one hand, the present generation can cut the number of children to 50,000 so that each gets a grain apiece. On the other hand, it may arrange its affairs so that at least 100,000 grains are available when the next generation inherits the earth. Only one thing is clear: if we hope to maintain our liberal legitimacy over time, *we cannot tolerate 100,000 births while leaving only 50,000 grains of manna*.

I shall defer a detailed consideration of this population-manna trade-off to a separate chapter on intergenerational trusteeship. For now, it is enough to emphasize that a liberal political community cannot accept the idea that there is a "natural" right to have as many children as one wants under all conditions. While the present generation *does* have the right to refuse to have children, we cannot deprive our children of their fair share of manna *if* we choose to create them. This asymmetry between childbearing and contraception is not a result of some ad hoc prejudice fostered by Planned Parenthood. Instead, it is the *only* position consistent with a dialogic theory of liberal legitimacy. A spirit who will never gain an earthly body can never raise the question of legitimacy within our Assembly Hall; its nonquestions beget nonanswers. Yet once a child's earthly existence is assured, the intergenerational conversation we have rehearsed is a plain threat to dialogic legitimacy. A citizenry devoted to an ongoing liberal conversation must take steps now to assure that such delegitimating dialogues do not take place later.

26. GENETIC MANIPULATION

26.1. *The Master Geneticist*

Assume, then, that the Assembly has faced up to its trusteeship obligations, creating what we shall later call a "harmonious" population policy.[3] Under this approach, a citizen can bring a child into the world only if provision has been made to assure that the child will obtain a quantity of manna *no less than that guaranteed to members of the present generation*.

Even so, a final question remains before a citizen may exercise his power to bring a child into the world. The problem arises, distinctively, from a superabundance of resources. Each of us possesses more germ plasm than we can possibly use for our procreative purposes. In principle, this gives us great power over the genetic endowment of our children. Already doctors can detect an increasing number of genetic disabilities at an early stage in fetal development. If we abort the fetus on the basis of the information we receive, our superabundance of germ plasm permits us to try and try again until we conceive a fetus more to our liking. Since the future will transparently expand this awesome power, I shall begin by telling a science-fiction story that

3. See § 51.

emphasizes the full extent of the problem raised by genetic manipulation. After we talk our way to a solution in our spaceship Assembly, we shall be able to reason our way down to some earthly results.

Imagine, then, that the Commander introduces a Master Geneticist capable of making test-tube babies on command.[4] The Master has at his disposal a germ-plasm bank containing samples of all the genetic codes contained in the present generation's sperm and egg cells. He is capable, in short, of giving life to any permutation of genetic material that we can conceive through more familiar means. Moreover, before ordering an embryo into existence, the Master can tell us how the embryo will function under any possible environment in which it may find itself. Indeed, upon request, he can compare A's behavioral repertoire to those of any other embryo you might like to bring into existence, [B, C, . . .]. The question, then, is squarely posed: How should we make use of the powers technology may place at our command?

By talking about the problem under Neutral conversational constraints.

26.2. *A Master Race?*

Consider the dream of a "master race." Somebody, Noble, moves that the Assembly order the Geneticist to create a new generation composed of people capable of the greatest achievements he can conceive: let a thousand Beethovens, a thousand Einsteins, bloom. Note that Noble's proposal need not order the Master to mass produce a single genotype; he can mix genotypes so that they will add up to Noble's conception of excellence in all its splendor. Nonetheless, despite their variety, such proposals are subject to conversational veto:

COMMANDER: You have heard Noble's proposal. What do you have to say about it?
DEPRESSIVE: I object. I think some other genetic distribution will provide a firmer foundation for the pursuit of ideals that I consider good.
COMMANDER: Well, Depressive, I fear that your remark kills

---

4. For analytic simplicity, I shall first assume that all of us choose to have our babies by the test-tube method, deferring a systematic comparison of "artificial" and "natural" methods of procreation to § § 28–29 of this chapter.

your proposal as well as Noble's. For a liberal state cannot justify its use of power when this requires us to weigh the intrinsic merit of competing conceptions of the good affirmed by different citizens.

The task, then, is to devise a set of instructions to the Geneticist that somehow avoids the broad restriction on admissible argument imposed by the Commander's predictable ruling from the chair.

26.3. *Genetic Domination*

Begin simply by narrowing attention to only two of the possible genotypes, A and B, that the Master may produce. Can the spaceship generation *ever* say that B is *so* much worse than A that the Master should produce none of that genotype?

To avoid the preceding conversation, it will not be enough for any particular person in the Assembly Hall to condemn the behavioral capacities revealed by B's ability report as ignoble or perverse. But what if *every* member of the first generation agreed that B was less capable of achieving his favored conception of the good than A? Then the following conversational move appears to view:

NOBLE: I say that we should tell the Master Geneticist not to produce any Bs.
COMMANDER: What reason can you give for using our power in this way?
NOBLE: I think that B will be at a relative disadvantage in pursuing those lives that I think are good.
COMMANDER: Are there any objections?
(*Silence in the Assembly Hall.*)
COMMANDER: You mean that despite all the different conceptions of the good maintained by people in this Assembly, *nobody* is prepared to say that B is better prepared than A to define and fulfill a good life?
EVERYMAN: That is correct. However much we differ in other respects, we believe that B is at a relative disadvantage.
COMMANDER: Then accepting Noble's argument does not, in this conversational context, breach the Neutrality Principle—for it does not require me to declare that some conceptions of the good affirmed by my fellow citizens are intrinsically superior to those affirmed by others.

MASTER GENETICIST: So you are prepared to begin instructing me?

COMMANDER: Yes. Do not create any Bs.

But, once again, haven't I forgotten *B's* interest in this affair? Can't somebody step forward on behalf of the unconceived B and insist that B would prefer to live rather than remain a mere conceptual possibility?

I have already answered this question. In affirming the present generation's right to become last, we considered the claim of a citizen who asserted that he could communicate with the spirit world. While such dialogues have a place in church, nobody in the Assembly can assert that his form of spiritual communication is superior to another's. If a citizen agrees that B is at a relative disadvantage in pursuing the good, he cannot pretend to be a privileged communicant with the disembodied B and assert that B would nonetheless prefer to be born.

26.4. *Drawing the Line*

To exclude improper objections, then, the Commander should frame her question carefully. The issue is not whether Citizen X (through some form of spiritual communion) thinks that a conceivable B would "prefer" to come into existence even though he has defective genetic equipment. Instead, X is to compare the genetic endowments of A and B under the conception of the good that X is willing to affirm as *his own* ideal in life. If *every* X in the Assembly Hall says that B's genetic equipment places him at a disadvantage to A in the pursuit of the good, as X understands the good, then the Commander may declare that A *genetically dominates* B. In contrast, a relation of *undominated diversity* obtains if some citizens say that A's genetic code equips him better than B, while others place an opposite evaluation on their respective genetic equipment.[5]

While this basic distinction seems clear enough, there are a number of obscurities lurking in the background. The most important problems involve the relationship of genetic domination to other concepts

---

5. What if somebody says that A and B have *equivalent* advantages in the pursuit of the good, but nobody is willing to go further and say that B is at a relative *advantage* when compared to A. This judgment of equivalent endowment seems to me enough to require a social judgment of *undominated diversity*. But there may be complexities lurking here that deserve further exploration.

in liberal theory that have not yet been developed. To fix ideas, suppose the Master's report reveals that A would be a typical human specimen possessed of the powers of sight, hearing, locomotion, and so forth. B's report, in contrast, reveals a distressing prospect—a person who is blind, deaf and crippled. Having read the report, the Commander asks for your judgment: Given your conception of the good, would A or B be placed at a relative disadvantage by its genetic endowments?

Speaking personally, I have no trouble with this question. While it may be possible for B to fulfill many moral ideals, I have no trouble concluding that B's genetic bundle places a person at a relative disadvantage in pursuing those forms of life that I consider good. Yet it will take more than my say-so before B can be declared dominated. Suppose, for example, that Imposer rises in the Assembly Hall to speak on behalf of B. His eye has been attracted by one feature of the Master's report that I have failed to mention. It appears that if A turns out to be Imposer's child, he will pose all sorts of trouble to him as he tries to socialize the bawling brat into a condition of liberal citizenship. In particular, the report indicates that A will come to hate Imposer and everything he represents. In contrast, B will prove a more pliant student. However deficient in other respects, he will find it easy to worship Imposer and the good he represents. After thinking the matter over as soberly as he can, Imposer announces that he thinks it is better for B to exist than A. How should the Commander respond to Imposer's announcement?

By ruling it irrelevant to the question of genetic domination. As we shall see in the next chapter, no parent has a right to view "his" child as a mere instrument for the gratification of his personal conception of the good. Instead, the pursuit of Neutral dialogue will establish that parents have an obligation to provide their children a *liberal* education— with cultural equipment that permits the child to criticize, as well as affirm, parental ideals. Yet if this is true, Imposer's genetic strategy bears an insidious aspect. Essentially, Imposer is trying to gain his illiberal *educational* objectives by *genetic* means. Since he cannot prevent his child from criticizing his ideals once he has been born, Imposer wishes to cripple the child's genetic capacity to question his ideals. But if illiberal education is illegitimate, so too is programming the child to make liberal education ineffective.

This principle—call it the principle of liberal restraint—has a

broader application than the particular effort by Imposer to undermine the impact of liberal education. Thus, after a child is educated, he
will enter a transactional structure regulated by principles developed
in chapter 6. These principles will suggest that people like B will
typically confront illegitimate disadvantages in their effort to deal with
their sighted and more mobile contemporaries. Yet one can imagine
an Imposer trying to take advantage of this foreseeable problem by
insisting that the Master Geneticist provide him with an abundance of
"suckers" so that he may continue his pursuit of self-advantage as the
next generation comes on the scene. Since this objective would be
illegitimate when pursued directly, it may not be used as the dialogic
foundation for liberal genetic policy.

Assume next that the members of the Assembly have universally
followed the principle of liberal restraint. It still remains possible that
somebody may say that B is better off than A is. Suppose some explorers happen to believe that people like B have the divine mark of
approval emblazoned upon them. Blind, deaf, crippled though he be,
B is understood as possessing a uniquely valuable insight into the
meaning of the universe. Thus, if B finds himself in this subcommunity, there will be a general celebration; and when no B is present, the
members long for a sign of divine approbation. On this scenario, a
member of the community of B worshippers would be entirely within
his conversational rights if he protested Noble's assertion that the B
genetic bundle placed its holder at a relative disadvantage in the pursuit of the good. When faced with the B worshipper's protest, the
Commander cannot order the Geneticist to avoid B creations without
impugning the value of a conception of the good affirmed by some of
the very citizens she confronts in the Assembly Hall. *So long as B worshippers exist*, she has no choice but to declare that a condition of
undominated diversity exists and that both A and B may become part
of the next generation.

Having presented situations that fall on either side of the line, I shall
conclude with a hard case. Imagine that the *only* person protesting
against Noble's characterization of B is somebody called Idiosyncratic. Unlike the B worshippers, Idiosyncratic does not engage in any
concrete practice which suggests his commitment to a B-ish value
system. Nonetheless, he loudly asserts that B would have the mark of
divine approbation upon him, and so denies that A dominates B.
Should the Commander take Idiosyncratic's say-so as a sufficient rea-

son for declaring that the genetic differences between A and B amount
to nothing more than an instance of undominated diversity?

My uneasiness, I think, has its root in second-best problems of
proof. If she just takes Idiosyncratic's word for it, the Commander will
leave the door wide open for Imposers to disguise the illegitimate
reasons for their opposition. Hence, as a second-best matter, it may
well be wise to insist that at least a few *existing* communities actually
accord people with B endowments greater esteem than those with A
endowments. But these (important) second-best considerations
should not befog the conceptual clarity of the line separating dominated from undominated genetic relationships. In principle, so long as
anyone conscientiously believes that B is better able to achieve a good
life than A is, no assertion of genetic domination can survive challenge
in a liberal state.

26.5. *Genetic Domination in a Large Society*
Thus far we have narrowed our view to two of the many genotypes
that the Geneticist may produce on command. Instead of a single
pairwise comparison, however, the Master's germ bank calls into
question an almost infinite set of genetic relationships. How does this
complicate the notion of genetic domination?

On one level, not at all. For example, in evaluating three
genotypes—A, B, and C—the Assembly must attempt three pairwise
comparisons—AB, AC, BC—before it can tell the Geneticist which
genetic distributions will give rise to a finding of genetic domination.
And as the number of genotypes increase, the number of pairwise
comparisons required increases in a way determined by the law of
permutations.

While increasing the number of genetic permutations does not
change the basic process of evaluation, it does complicate the analysis
in other ways. Most important, as any embryo, A, is compared in a
pairwise fashion with all other genetic possibilities, it will often turn
out that A is genetically *dominant to* one subset of potential citizens,
genetically *dominated by* a second subset, and has an *undominated*
relationship with a third.[6] Assume, for example, that the spaceship
generation contains no group of B worshippers who place a positive

6. While it is possible for a potential citizen to be genetically dominated by *all* his fellows,
only an omnipotent God could be confident that he genetically dominated all other beings.

valuation on children born blind, deaf, or crippled. Even so, this will hardly imply that *all* blind embryos will be genetically dominated by *all* sighted embryos. For many blind people will have other valuable attributes that permit them to maintain an *undominated* relationship with many sighted people despite their serious handicap. Indeed, the *only* person who is certain to dominate a blind B is an otherwise identical twin who has the power of sight. Moreover, while a blind B may be *dominated by* some sighted A's, B may also *dominate* some C's—say, those who are both crippled and blind.

This means that the Assembly must frame its instruction to the Geneticist in a more abstract way than was previously suggested. Rather than giving the Master a list of particular genotypes to be avoided under all circumstances, the Assembly will frame its instruction in terms of the genetic characteristics of the next generation taken as a whole: the only embryo distributions $[A_1, B \ldots Q]$ that can be forbidden are those in which at least one member of the set genetically dominates at least one other member of the set. Thus, it is perfectly possible that a blind embryo will be brought into existence in a perfectly liberal world—so long as it has other attributes that permit it to establish a relation of undominated diversity with each and every one of the fellow citizens with whom it will share the planet.

27. UNDOMINATED DIVERSITY

The number of permissible distributions that pass this threshhold test will depend, in part, upon the diversity of ideals held by the members of the present generation. If there are B worshippers on our spaceship, a whole range of possibilities that would otherwise go unrealized must be recognized as admissible outcomes of a liberal genetic policy. Even if (as I shall assume) nobody says that being blind or crippled or deaf from birth is, taken by itself, a positive advantage, an enormous number of genetic permutations will generate conditions of undominated diversity. Within a particular generation, there will be people with the capacity of becoming athletes, botanists, clairvoyants, drummers, educators, farmers, or generous and honorable human beings. So long as *somebody* says that A is better endowed than B while others say B is better than A, and so forth, the distribution cannot be impugned because it fails to conform to someone's private dream of a master race.

This result gains added importance when viewed against the back-

ground of the Assembly's earlier efforts to distribute manna. When
the conversations about genes and manna are read together, they give
the lie to the familiar claim that liberals who preach the equal distribution of material wealth are somehow committed to a nightmare world
where all of us are genetic look-alikes. To the contrary, the same
liberal conversation that legitimates each citizen's prima facie right to
equal manna also legitimates an enormous range of genetically diverse
outcomes. Rather than some nightmare identity, liberalism affirms an
ideal of undominated equality, where very different human beings
have an equal right to use material resources to pursue the ideals that
seem best to them. Moreover, the reason why the same conversation
leads to such seemingly different results need not be shrouded in
mystery. Quite simply, the problem with manna is that it is in *short*
supply; the problem with germ plasm is that it is in *over*supply. While
the distribution of each of these resources has an enormous impact
upon the power structure, the differing character of the distributive
decision leads the liberal in different directions—for germ plasm, to
voice a concern lest possibilities be excluded when some citizens find
them good; for manna, to insist that each citizen, regardless of his
conception of the good, obtain a share that is not inferior to that
claimed by any other citizen. The differing conversational outcomes,
in short, respond to the fact that, in one case, the Assembly is *dividing*
a *finite* resource while, in the other, it is *selecting* one genetic possibility out of *countless* others to be actualized. The differing character of
the problems compel different substantive solutions—whose common character is revealed only by the conversational process that
provides each with a liberal legitimacy.

Despite this conversational synthesis, however, the Assembly cannot conclude its discussion of genetic endowments with a simple affirmation of the value of undominated diversity. Even after he has
taken pains to avoid genetic domination, the Master Geneticist must
still, in some way or another, bring into being one, *and only one*, of the
genetic permutations that remain within the set of admissible social
choices. How is this power to be exercised?[7]

27.1. *Parental Design*

Consider the "parental design" solution. On this approach, each
parent would tell the Master Geneticist what bundle of genetic attrib-

---

7. In more formal terms, if the Assembly failed to answer this question, it would violate the
completeness requirement imposed by the Rationality principle. See § 11.1

utes seemed best; after checking to assure against genetic domination,[8] the Geneticist would provide the parent with a child whose genetic endowment satisfied parental specifications. If you want a brown-eyed girl who is relatively good at chemistry but relatively weak on aesthetic sensibility, that's what you'll get. All very simple; but does parental design represent a legitimate way of determining the next generation's genetic endowments?

Once again, the way to answer this question is to imagine the kinds of conversation that the parental design option makes possible. Consider, for example, the following script. The scene is set twenty years after the parent exercises his design option; the brown-eyed daughter has, after a liberal education, become a fellow citizen of the liberal state:

DAUGHTER: I hate chemistry!

PARENT: But you're so good at it!

DAUGHTER: Couldn't care less. What I'd love to be is a great artist!

PARENT: But you'll never be better than mediocre.

DAUGHTER: So what. It's better to be a mediocre painter than a first-class chemist.

PARENT: Well, you're a citizen now. I guess I can't force you to use your talents in a way that seems best to me but not to you.

DAUGHTER: But you *have* in the past used your power to force me down the path of your choosing.

PARENT: What do you have in mind?

DAUGHTER: When you approached the Geneticist, you ordered him to make me good at chemistry and bad at art. What gave you the right to use your power over me in this way?

PARENT: I guess I can't say that science is intrinsically better than art.

DAUGHTER: Nor did you have the right to impose your preferences on me during my period of liberal education. Hence, you must have recognized that I could well detest the attributes you have forced upon me.

PARENT: But aren't you grateful to me for bringing you into existence?

---

8. There are technical problems concealed by this clause. Since I shall be rejecting parental design on more basic grounds, I leave them unexplored.

DAUGHTER: That is not an answer to my question of legitimacy. It is rather an assertion of your power to do whatever you like without answering my question of legitimacy.[9] What more, then, can you say in justification of your decision to shape me in the way you think good but I think bad?

The conversation reveals parental design as a variation on the forbidden theme of the master race. Earlier on, Noble tried to design his particular conception of the good into the genes of an *entire* generation; here Parent is "merely" trying to impose a genetic design upon a *single* member of the next generation. Yet liberal theory does not discount the question of legitimacy simply because it is asked by a single person. The Rationality principle requires *all* power wielders to answer all questions if the state is to hope for perfect legitimacy.

It follows that the Commander must rule parental design off the agenda of a liberal Assembly's deliberation. While citizens have a right (subject to trusteeship) to use their share of manna in the way that seems best to them, they do not have an analogous right to design their children in the way they find most pleasing. The reason for placing greater restrictions on parental power over genes is simple enough: human embryos will one day come to insist on an answer to their question of legitimacy, while no piece of manna will ever (by definition) ask: By what right did you assume the power to shape me in the way you thought good?

27.2. *The Genetic Lottery*

I can see only one way out: hold a lottery in which every undominated genetic distribution is given an equal chance of success. Tell the Geneticist to take a random draw out of the grab-bag of undominated possibilities. Whichever distribution he draws will constitute his recipe for the next generation. Such a procedure permits the following conversational defense when your frustrated chemist raises a challenge:

DAUGHTER: Why wasn't I given a richer endowment of aesthetic sensibility?
PARENT: A good question. I myself have asked it often.
DAUGHTER: You can't get off the hook so easily. After all, you

9. More technically, an unlimited appeal to gratitude violates the conceivability test imposed in the name of Rationality. See § 11.2.

were there when they were passing out the genes. Why didn't you see to it that I got a better deal?

PARENT: Because I could not expect the Assembly to accept the idea that art was to be favored over science or vice versa. The rational way to proceed, then, was to refuse to exclude *any* admissible option from the range of choice.

DAUGHTER: But you still had the power to choose!

PARENT: But by means of a procedure that gave each admissible option an *equal* chance of realization. After all, if none of the admissible distributions is any worse than any of the others, none should be given a better chance than any other.

DAUGHTER: But the outcome of this decision rule has made me miserable.

PARENT: It is up to you, not me, to say which activities will best make use of your talents. But while you are entitled to affirm the value of artistic creation, you are not entitled to insist that your ideals be fulfilled to *your* satisfaction. Given relative scarcity, no polity can rationally make such a promise to *all* its citizens. And given this fact, the liberal state refuses to make such a guarantee to *any* of its citizens at the cost of deepening the frustration of others.

Instead of guaranteeing you happiness, your fellow citizens discharge their obligations to you by providing you with a Neutral justification for the decision that brought you into the world with your present abilities. I have just fulfilled this burden.

28. ADOPTION, ABORTION, INFANTICIDE

Before the Master Geneticist proceeds with his random draw, a final objection echoes through the Assembly Hall. A motion is made to reject the Geneticist's offer of his services; indeed, to pass a law denying anybody the right to create test-tube babies for any purpose whatsoever. The reason for the motion is simple enough: the fear of tyranny. Even though we have shown that the Geneticist's power *can* be tamed by liberal conversation, it is only with our ideal Commander and her perfect technology of justice that we can be confident that the Master *will* be tamed. And if some authoritarian faction ever did seize control, their mastery over the Geneticist might permit them to achieve a final victory over the liberal spirit. It is far better to destroy the technology and leave procreation to more familiar, decentralized processes.

This is, transparently, a powerful objection—though, like all second-best points, its particular weight can be determined only after an empirical study of the particular society and institutional framework in which it is raised. Instead of attempting such a study here, I hope to show that our thought experiment is not in vain even if you are persuaded by second-best arguments to destroy the Geneticist's germ banks. For the story provides a framework for assessing claims of injustice arising out of the traditional system of "natural" procreation.

28.1. *Sterile Parents*

Suppose a couple cannot conceive a child through the familiar means. Shouldn't *they* have the right (subject to trusteeship) to ask the Master Geneticist to assist them in their pursuit of the good?

Surely a law forbidding the Geneticist to help cannot be justified by an Assembly declaration that "natural" procreation is intrinsically superior to "artificial" insemination. Instead, the *only* justification is the second-best fear of tyranny—the threat that once the genie is out of the bottle, it will be much too easy for liberalism to lose in the end. In a second-best world, we must often make do with the lesser evil. While it is wrong to deny would-be parents the power to fulfill their good by having children, it would be wronger to risk the complete destruction of liberal dialogue through totalitarian manipulation of the gene pool.

I will defer a fuller consideration of such second-best arguments to Part Three. Nonetheless, it should be apparent that a liberal statesman will not deny prima facie rights unless he is convinced that he has no other reasonable choice under the circumstances.[10] Even conceding the serious risk of tyranny, can't some safe way be worked out to permit people with no other options to draw at random from the Geneticist's germ banks?

Suppose, alas, the answer is No. The risks are just too great. Then, it would seem incumbent upon liberal statesmen to provide some

---

10. This is merely an application of the more general principle of the least-restrictive alternative developed in § 19.5.

mechanism by which infertile parents can pay others to bear their babies for them. As chapter 6 will argue, the liberal state has a general obligation to provide citizens with a flexible network within which they may transact to their mutual benefit. This general obligation is all the more pressing if the state cuts off citizen access to "artificial" means of procreation. Infertile citizens cannot be fobbed off by talk of an inscrutable divine will; they are no less entitled to fulfill their good than others who are differently endowed by the genetic lottery.

28.2. *Contraception*

In an ideal world, fertile couples would *also* have the right to choose artificial over natural procreation. Given the availability of the natural alternative, however, the second-best statesman may think this a good place to draw the line on access to the Geneticist's germ banks.

Even if this line is drawn, our thought experiments illuminate a range of perplexities. First, just as the sterile parent has a prima facie right to have a child, so too the fertile parent has a prima facie right to *refuse* to have a child. Indeed, of the two rights, the latter is the more absolute. For we have shown that would-be parents must first satisfy a "trusteeship" obligation before they may people our new world with a second generation; in contrast, the present generation has a perfect right to call it quits forever. This right was entrenched in the Master Geneticist story, for the Master did not force children on unwilling parents but only responded to citizen demands. Moreover, thanks to our perfect technology of justice, citizens made their requests only after obtaining any empirical information about their futures they considered relevant.

But natural sex is not like that. Unless they take precautions, fertile citizens will have children even when they affirm child-free sex as part of their conception of the good. Moreover, the state cannot ban efforts at contraception when the only thing said on behalf of a ban is some official proclamation defining the Truth about Sex. Even if we resolve to keep the full-blown Master Geneticist myth locked away on some science-fiction shelf, the liberal statesman cannot embrace the myth of "natural" sex. Instead, contraception must be recognized as a fundamental right of all citizens.[11]

---

11. Like all rights, the right to contraception obtains only so long as nothing Neutral can be said to justify its restriction. Imagine, for example, that there was only one small liberalish state

28.3. *Abortion*

Abortion is more complicated. I can think of four reasons a person may wish to abort a fetus; two are plainly legitimate; one, illegitimate; one, troubling.

The first rationale proceeds from the fact that we do not possess a perfect technology of justice that guarantees the right of contraception. As a result, unwanted embryos are conceived; more subtly, but no less wrongly, embryos are conceived before the parents have had time to decide whether they really want to be parents. If, after thinking the matter over, the parents decide that it is bad to have a child, the state cannot tell them they are making the wrong decision.

Nor can it intervene on behalf of the fetus's rights as a citizen of a liberal state. The simple truth is that a fetus is *not* a citizen of a liberal state. While it may possess a humanoid body, we have seen that citizenship is not a biological category. A liberal community does not ask what a creature looks like before admitting it to citizenship. Instead, it asks whether the creature can play a part in the dialogic and behavioral transactions that constitute a liberal polity. The fetus fails the dialogic test—more plainly than do grown-up dolphins.

But the fetus is a *potential* citizen—shouldn't that matter? We have already answered this question in the First and Last scenario that began this Chapter. We dealt there with somebody who claimed to have access to the world of disembodied spirits, who insisted that these spirits wanted bodies regardless of the wishes expressed by the present generation. Such unmediated conversations with the spirit world, however, have no place in a liberal Assembly. They cannot justify a law forbidding parents to abort when their reason has to do with failures of contraception. Not, mind you, that believing Catholics cannot find the *existence* of the fetus a sufficient reason for changing their mind about the desirability of parenthood. The question is not whether a citizen can be forced into an abortion when she thinks child rearing is a good thing. Instead, the only question is whether the Assembly, on the basis of some conversation with the spirit world,

---

whose very existence was threatened by populous authoritarian neighbors. Given this dire threat, liberal statesmen might well conclude that an increase in population was necessary for the survival of *any* liberal dialogue whatsoever. A prohibition on contraception might then be justified as the way to increase the population with the least overall destruction of liberal values. I shall not, however, attempt a systematic canvass of such third-best arguments in this book. For a more elaborate definition of third-best argument, see § 53.1.

may deny citizens their right to decide that child rearing is not worth the effort.

Suppose, however, that this is *not* the reason the parents want to abort the fetus. While they are happy to affirm the value of child rearing, they want to abort the *particular* child on the basis of genetic information provided by their doctors. Are "therapeutic" abortions always legitimate?

It is only when the fetus can be said to be a victim of *genetic domination* that the liberal state can unambiguously say that it is acceptable to replace this embryo with a "better" one. If, however, the parents want to use the "therapeutic" label to conceive their favorite embryo—aborting a blue-eyed boy to get a brown-eyed girl—then this exercise of power fails for the same dialogic reasons that felled the parental design option in the Master Geneticist story.

This leaves a final, terrible case. Suppose a couple simply *enjoy* abortions so much that they conceive embryos simply to kill them a few months later. Cannot the state intervene to stop such brutality?

If a majority so choose. While the threatened fetuses are no more citizens than those who are aborted for other reasons, chapter 3 established an alternative ground for protecting some noncitizens some of the time.[12] In brief, treating everything as if it were manna for citizen exploitation may be taken as an unsatisfactory expression of the liberal community's principled agnosticism about the "proper" relationship between the state and the larger universe. Thus, the citizenry might choose to preserve the Grand Canyon or some other natural monument in its pristine condition as a mark of its collective uncertainty about the extent to which it may exploit the world for its own purposes; in the same spirit, it may restrain acts of wanton cruelty where the *only* reason a citizen has for abusing an animal is to see it suffer. And if this is deemed an appropriate response, what better place to start than by restraining the wanton abortion we are presently contemplating?

28.4. *Infanticide*

By the time a fetus is viable outside the womb, the problem has changed in two respects. First, the biological parents have had time to consider whether they *want* to be parents. While the right to abortion

12. See § 22.2; cf. §§ 18 and 50.2.

typically protects against the failures of contraception, this rationale seems weaker when the parents allow so many months to pass. Second, once the infant is viable, some other adult may want to take on the task of child rearing. The question, then, is whether a "natural" parent has the right to kill the child rather than transfer it to a parent who wants to "adopt" it.

This is *not* a rhetorical question. We have already seen, in chapter 2, that Ascetic *does* have the right to burn his fair share of manna despite the fact that others think he is "wasting" it.[13] Moreover, a day-old infant is no more a citizen than a nine-month fetus. What is required, then, is a liberal argument for denying citizens the right to kill their newborn children while saving their right to consume other forms of material reality in the way they think best.

I can think of at least two. The first emphasizes the rights of the adoptive parents. To make the case easy, assume that the adoptive parents are infertile and that, for second-best reasons, they are denied access to a test-tube baby. It follows that these people have been consigned to a power structure that denies them a prima facie right they may value dearly. A *very* minimal second-best response might be to guarantee them access to children who would otherwise be killed by their "natural" parents.

A second argument extends the principle against wanton cruelty developed in our discussion of abortion. In the present case, the "natural" parents have it within their power simply to pass the child on to another, yet they prefer to kill it instead. What other reason can they give for their action but their desire to impose pain upon mute creation?

29. BIRTH DEFECTS

Now imagine a child born with some terrible birth defect, a deficiency that places him in a genetically subordinate position to many, if not all,[14] his fellow citizens. Such tragedies are another injustice of "natural" procreation. They would not occur if our Master Geneticist had avoided all genetic distributions scarred by domination. Yet the

13. § 15.1.
14. Recall: a blind and crippled child may dominate a child who is blind, crippled, and dumb; yet this does not prevent him from being dominated by countless sighted and mobile fellows. See §§ 26.5 and 29.2.

fact that the child has come into existence radically transforms the dialogic problem. While, as we have seen, therapeutic abortion would be justified, a liberal state cannot force a woman to cut into her own body if she thinks it would be sinful to give her consent. And this is just the position we can expect in the real world: though many religious people might agree that it would have been better if a genetically dominated child had never been conceived, their moral ideals demand that they preserve the child once its body takes on a human form. And once the child is born, either natural or adopted parents might freely choose to lavish their care on it rather than turn their backs upon the afflicted creature. Yet a time will come when the infant will become a citizen and hold his caretakers to account:

> DISADVANTAGED: I have been placed, by your decisions, at a plain disadvantage from my very birth. While my peers could run and see and play, I am confined to a small and dark place. How can this be justified?
>
> CARETAKER: I agree that this is a tragedy. If it had been within my power, I would not have wished you into existence. Nor would any of my fellow citizens.
>
> DISADVANTAGED: So why did you save me?
>
> CARETAKER: Because, disadvantaged though you are, I thought it was still possible for you to live a meaningful life.
>
> COMMANDER: And given this affirmation by my fellow citizen, I have taken care to assure you a power position in which you, no less than any other citizen, have a right to fulfill your own conception of a meaningful existence.
>
> DISADVANTAGED: Indeed, you owe me no less; for I *am* at least as good as you are. There is only one problem.
>
> COMMANDER: What's on your mind?
>
> DISADVANTAGED: Since I'm at least as good as you are, I'm entitled to start out in life with a set of endowments that is at least as good as yours is.
>
> COMMANDER: Speak on, for I can detect no breach of Neutrality in your talk.
>
> DISADVANTAGED: Yet you yourself must recognize that my genetic endowment is inferior to the one with which many of my fellows have been endowed.
>
> COMMANDER: Yes. While you doubtless can do much that is

good, there is no question that your genetic endowment makes it more difficult for you.

DISADVANTAGED: But if this is a liberal state, an unjustified power disadvantage cannot be permitted to stand.

COMMANDER: I guess you're right. There's only one problem.

DISADVANTAGED: What's that?

COMMANDER: I don't know what I can do that will effectively correct the power disadvantage under which you are laboring. I'm not a miracle maker, you know. I can't change your genes for you. And even if I could, perhaps it would be too dangerous to give me this power.

DISADVANTAGED: Yet you can help out in other, less drastic and dangerous, ways. Like giving me special equipment to permit me to move about, special books and typewriters to permit me to communicate freely, special education to permit me to make the most of what I have.

COMMANDER: But all this will cost a lot of manna.

DISADVANTAGED: True, but if I'm relatively disadvantaged *genetically*, you'll have to give me relatively more *manna* if my overall share of initial endowments is to be at least as good as that enjoyed by my fellow citizens.

COMMANDER: But *how much* more manna must I give you to compensate for your genetic handicap?

DISADVANTAGED: A good question. But before we address it, let's get the basic principle clear: My limited power over the physical environment is of a kind that entitles me to special assistance beyond the equal share of manna that would otherwise be my due as a citizen of a liberal state.

I shall continue this conversation in chapter 8, where the question of the *amount* of aid due will be treated within a more general framework. For now, only two issues need be clarified.

29.1. *The Limited Range of Genetic Injustice*

It is important to distinguish the problem of genetic domination from the more frequent case in which one *undominated* citizen covets the talents of another. To trivialize: Say you can be a fairly good athlete but would much prefer to be a decent pianist. If you are able to beat the pianist at tennis, you cannot complain when he beats you on the keyboard. And so on, for other, more fundamental genetic capacities. So long as there is *some* conception of the good at which you are comparatively advantaged, you cannot verbalize your sense of grievance in a way that survives the conversational constraint imposed by Neutrality. This is not to deny the *psychological* reality of the frustration a person feels as he comes to recognize that his talents do not measure up to his ideals. However frustrated he may be, the piano player cannot rationally hope to convince the Assembly that he is at a comparative disadvantage, unless he can say that tennis playing is an inherently inferior activity to the one upon which he places a higher value. Yet it is precisely this move which is denied to all participants in a liberal political conversation.

29.2. *Second-Best Classification*

Pick any two people out of the population. Compare their genetic endowments. In principle, two—and only two—conclusions are possible. Either A genetically dominates B and B may properly demand compensatory assistance; or A and B stand in a relation of undominated equality, and B gains no relief—no matter how envious of A's talents he may be. If we continued this process of pairwise comparison long enough, we would finally obtain a map of the domination relationships generated by the "natural" genetic lottery.

The genetic topography would have a distinctive structure. Most of us would find that we would stand in an undominated relationship with most other citizens: I have the ability to do some good things better than you, and vice versa. Similarly, almost all of us would find that we dominate at least a few other people. Yet the people I dominate will not necessarily be the people you dominate. Suppose you could be a good athlete and I could be a great mathematician. Suppose we compare ourselves to a blind person who could be a good—but not great—mathematician. Then it is quite conceivable that *I* dominate the blind man and you do not: someone who believed that mathematics was the highest form of spiritual activity might well choose to be a blind mathematician rather than a good athlete; while *none* would choose to be a mediocre blind mathematician rather than a brilliant sighted mathematician. And it may be possible, of course, to find somebody you dominate and I do not.

For practical purposes, however, it would be impossible to operate a policy under which some of my taxes went to a fund to compensate all the people *I* personally dominated while some of your taxes went to a *different* fund dispensed only to those people *you* dominated, and so forth. Instead, we must content ourselves with a policy that marks out substantial groups in the population who are dominated by large numbers of their fellows. This will inevitably lead to second-best problems of over- and under-inclusion. For example, assume that all blind people were treated as a genetically dominated group for purposes of second-best compensation. Then blind geniuses will get some compensation they do not deserve from a tax fund to which sighted dummies may contribute; meanwhile, some people who fail to qualify as "handicapped" under any of the rough rubrics of second-best policy will in fact be genetically dominated by significant portions of the "normal" population.

This is too bad and should prompt recurring efforts to rethink prevailing compensation practices. Nonetheless, the inevitable crudity of practical categories cannot be used as an excuse for jettisoning the day-to-day effort to aid the handicapped. Rough justice is better than callous injustice.

30. GENETIC MANIPULATION IN LIBERAL THEORY

Having talked our way to a particular response to childbirth, we can now compare our results to those that may be generated by more familiar approaches: What are the likely utilitarian and contractarian responses to the problems we have canvassed?

30.1. *Utility*
Begin with the utilitarian, since the general outlines of his position may be readily discerned. After all, no problem is too big for the greatest happiness principle. When provided a perfect technology of justice, the clear-thinking utilitarian would be utterly opposed to the liberal use of a lottery to select a genetic distribution out of an almost infinite set of undominated options. Instead, he will take advantage of the Geneticist's information to arrange genes in a way, X, that maximizes overall utility. Now, of course, in choosing his favored X, the utilitarian will confront familiar problems in defining happiness more precisely and explaining how it may be summed to an overall societal total. The important point, however, is not these familiar difficulties but the consequences that follow upon their "successful"

solution: an ideal utilitarian policy contemplates far more sweeping genetic manipulation than that tolerated by liberal theory. To make matters worse, there is no guarantee that the utilitarian's X will avoid the limited class of cases—involving genetic domination—that the liberal will place beyond limits. If, for example, Imposers will gain a lot of "happiness" by the birth of a few blind and crippled children, this may offset the "unhappiness" suffered by the offspring and so justify their inclusion within the "optimal" X. This difference in genetic doctrine reflects more basic conceptual differences we have already noticed. Thus, the utilitarian's willingness to manipulate genes for the sake of happiness presupposes the legitimacy of a political effort to define the good. In contrast, the liberal's insistence on a lottery among undominated options follows from his effort to organize power relations in a way that permits each citizen to participate in a Neutral dialogue. My aim here, as elsewhere, is to suggest that this difference in basic theoretical structure is of more than theoretical interest; it generates strikingly different results in every fundamental area of the power struggle.

This is not to say, however, that the utilitarian cannot try to soften the illiberal tendency of his genetic doctrine. Most obviously, he will remark upon the danger that a Master Geneticist will abuse his power and select a Y that will bring happiness to an elite while immiserating the mass of the population. Consequently, the utilitarian—no less than a liberal—will take steps to assure that the Geneticist's power will be carefully controlled—perhaps abolished entirely. Nonetheless, this second-best calculus will differ from the liberal approach in countless particulars. As we have seen, the liberal statesman will be obliged to take steps to ameliorate a variety of genetic injustices that flow from "natural" procreation: facilitating adoption, guaranteeing contraception and abortion, aiding the handicapped in their effort to lead a good life. While the utilitarian will surely be sensitive to the unhappiness generated by these problems, there is no assurance that he will protect the rights of both parents and children as they are elucidated through Neutral dialogue. As a matter of principle, the utilitarian will treat the complaints of the handicapped person or frustrated parent as if they were no different from the cries of pain generated by countless other complaints. For the liberal, however, a sense of frustration, *however real*, can never establish an injustice unless it can be translated into a conversation that conforms to Neutral principles. It is only when the processes of "natural" birth fail to measure up to this dialogic test that those disadvantaged by it may assert their rights. And when a vindication of birthrights is dialogically required, it cannot be defeated merely because others find it inconvenient. This point, however, is systematically ignored by the utilitarian's single-minded search for collective happiness.

30.2. *Contract*

While nothing is too difficult for the greatest happiness principle, the entire question of genetic justice threatens to outstrip the contractarian's methodological resources. Under this approach, one tries to solve the problem of social justice by consulting the will of hypothetical contractors trying to further their self-interest by bargaining their way to a social contract. When the subject is genes, however, our view of these contractors is more obscure than usual. Can we really talk sensibly of the preferences of a *disembodied* "contractor" as he picks and chooses among alternative genetic distributions? Such a creature is so removed from our common experience that the nature of his preferences remains altogether mysterious. If, however, the theorist tries to make the preferences of his hypothetical contractor more intelligible by endowing him with a *physical body*, then it becomes difficult to speak of the contractor as *choosing* one genetic distribution over another. Instead of choosing a distribution, the contractor has instead *been given* a body by the theorist so as to make his *choices on other subjects* intelligible to us. How, then, is the contractarian to respond to the Master Geneticist without making his talk of the contractor's "choice" of a genetic distribution either mysterious or question-begging?

It is a great virtue of John Rawls's theory that it promises a way out of this impasse. By placing his contractors behind a veil of ignorance, Rawls does not suggest that they are entirely disembodied. Rather, they simply *do not know* the genetic program which will control their bodies' particular functioning. Hence, it is at least possible to ask how Rawlsian contractors would respond to the Master Geneticist. Not that I find it easy to put myself in the position of a person who has lost touch with his body in the striking way that Rawls supposes. Nonetheless, for purposes of the present exercise,[15] I will concede that Rawls

---

15. For a challenge to this assumption, see chapter 10.

has cut the Gordian knot and provided an intelligible way for contractarians to talk about genetic manipulation. How, then, would a Rawlsian instruct the Master Geneticist?

An explicit answer cannot be found in *A Theory of Justice*. While Rawls condemns the existing genetic distribution as arbitrary, he refuses to talk about the possibility that the "natural" lottery may be "improved" by eugenic policy. Instead, his contractors attempt to ameliorate the impact of the initial genetic distribution by designing compensatory educational and tax schemes. While I can see no reason why Rawlsians would reject the Master Geneticist's invitation out of hand,[16] I am quite reluctant to engage in an elaborate guessing game: extension and refinement of a theory is best left to those who believe in it. It seems best to content myself with a few obvious points.

A good place to begin is with Rawls's most general statement of the principle that his contractors will adopt behind the veil of ignorance:

> All social values—liberty and opportunity, income and wealth, and the bases of self-respect—are to be distributed equally unless an unequal distribution of any, or all, of these values is to everyone's advantage.[17]

Now genes obviously have to do with several of Rawls's social values: opportunity, income, wealth, and self-respect. And if Rawls's principle is given a simplistic interpretation, it can authorize genetic manipulation that would destroy much or all of the genetic diversity legitimated in a liberal state. "Opportunity" is particularly troublesome. While it is not impossible to arrange things so that different genotypes receive equal income or wealth, there is an obvious sense in which people with different genes do not have equal opportunities. Though neither Manic or Depressive may genetically *dominate* one another, Manic may have a better chance of becoming a great musician, while Depressive has a greater chance of succeeding on the stage. The only way to eliminate all such inequalities would be to make all people into carbon copies of one another.

Yet, in other contexts, Rawls seems to settle for a more metaphoric conception of equal opportunity which, if applied here, would leave some room for genetic diversity. Central to the metaphor is the idea of an index of primary social goods which may be used to "measure" each

---

16. Rawls presents none when he glimpses the problem on page 107 of *A Theory of Justice*.
17. Ibid., p. 62.

group's access to income, wealth, opportunity, and the other basic values. Applying the metaphor to our present problem, one might imagine a Rawlsian Indexer putting a number indicating the value of Manic's chances on the stage and comparing them with Depressive's greater opportunities in the world of music. If, for example, the Indexer judged these countervailing advantages equally valuable, he would give them an equal score on the opportunity index. Obviously, a great deal of diversity may be saved by a sufficiently liberal use of index numbers. Indeed, it is possible to manipulate the opportunity index to justify *all* forms of genetic diversity that a liberal statesman would consider legitimate. Unfortunately, I cannot say how much diversity Rawls would find tolerable: the text is virtually silent on the entire indexing problem.[18]

If, however, we assume that the Rawlsian index is not calibrated along liberal lines, a second move is open to those Rawlsians who wish to prevent their ignorant contractors from destroying undominated genetic diversity. For the contractors, as we have seen, do not insist on strict equality if inequality will make all of them better off. Thus, if Depressive's life is enriched by Manic's greater musical talent, and vice versa, then perhaps diversity will be justified after all. Indeed, it might even be possible to justify a condition of *genetic domination* under this approach. It will all depend upon the way the Indexer uses his awesome authority.

In short, while it is possible to manipulate the Rawlsian system to legitimate the liberal's ideal of undominated diversity, it is also possible to generate Rawlsian arguments for positions ranging from genetic uniformity to genetic domination. While I think that Rawls himself would give the Geneticist a set of instructions that would not greatly depart from liberal principles, this should not obscure the ease with which his system could generate very different substantive results.

We have come, then, to a doctrinal pattern that will recur repeatedly in these excursions into comparative analysis. While the utilitarian's

18. The single paragraph explicitly devoted to the problem concedes that "we admittedly rely upon our intuitive capacities" in constructing the index (*A Theory of Justice,* p. 94). What, then, to do when the intuitions of different indexers differ?

Perhaps an answer may be found much later in the book, where Rawls expands on his idea that self-respect is the most important of the primary social goods (pp. 440–46). This suggests that the proper way to index the relative importance of different opportunities is to determine their strategic role in developing self-respect. Unfortunately, Rawls's comments about self-respect are sufficiently abstract and ambiguous to permit any number of (very different) interpretations in hard cases of the kind we are imagining.

method of analysis promises to support a disciplined inquiry, his conclusions will often be antagonistic to basic liberal doctrine; while it is
easier for the contractarian to reconcile himself to liberal doctrine, he
deprives his assent of much value by failing to ground it in a systematic
and disciplined mode of analysis.

5

LIBERAL EDUCATION

31. BEYOND HORTICULTURE

Children are born radically incomplete. Barring genetic handicap, each can function in a bewildering variety of human cultures. The particular use a child makes of his cultural freedom, however, depends on us. If we talk English, the infant will learn English; if Greek, Greek. Our models of behavior provide the starting points for the child's evolving patterns of conduct.

These facts are a source of perplexity for liberal and authoritarian alike. Only they respond to the childish mixture of freedom and dependence in different ways. The authoritarian exploits the child's cultural dependence to limit his cultural freedom. Infancy is a time to plant the seed in good moral ground; childhood is a time for the weeding and pruning needed to transform good young saplings into extra-fine timber. By maturity, a well-educated person can only look with contempt upon the stunted and deviant growths that, unaccountably, inhabit so much of the forest.

Such horticultural imagery has no place in a liberal theory of education. We have no right to look upon future citizens as if we were master gardeners who can tell the difference between a pernicious weed and a beautiful flower. A system of liberal education provides children with a sense of the very different lives that could be theirs—so that, as they approach maturity, they have the cultural materials available to build lives equal to their evolving conceptions of the good.

Yet as soon as this is said, doubts begin to form. Isn't there a difference between being a liberal educator and being wishy-washy? When your child hits some other kid over the head, surely you shouldn't ignore his misdeeds. More generally, does liberalism require educators to pretend they are somehow indifferent to all the ideals that compete for attention? If so, liberalism seems to require adults to deny their very souls when dealing with their children. If not, how is the liberal to distinguish the legitimate use of educational authority from an illegitimate attempt to constrict the child's moral universe?

I will view these questions from the vantage point provided by the liberal theory of dialogic legitimacy. My thesis is simple enough: If we talk about the evolving power relationship between young and old within the constraints imposed by Neutral dialogue, we will find ourselves elaborating a theory that rejects horticulture without denying our right to try to impress our children with the things that are most important to us.

As always, liberal theory begins with the realities of power. A child wants something, encounters parental resistance, cries in frustration. The parent sometimes relents, sometimes does not. But always there are questions: What gives the parent the right to decide whether the child's wishes will be fulfilled? Why not some other adult? Why not the child himself?

Yet while these questions can always be asked, they cannot always be asked by *the child himself*. This provides the foundation for a critical distinction. During *primary* education, the child has not yet mastered the cultural skills necessary for his own participation in liberal dialogue. Thus, the question of legitimacy can only be asked by other adults. During *secondary* education, the child *can* raise the question of legitimacy. This fact, I shall argue, transforms the kinds of coercion that are justifiable in the name of liberal education.

32. PRIMARY EDUCATION: THE PLACE OF THE FAMILY

Before he can begin to participate in liberal dialogue, the child must develop an awesome series of cognitive, linguistic, and behavioral skills. The simple question "Why should *you* get it rather than *I*?" requires the child to recognize that "you" are not merely a part of "I." Yet Piaget's path-breaking experiments suggest that the construction of a dichotomy between subject and object is a triumph of the second half of the first year of life. After this first conceptual breakthrough, it is still a long time before an infant can talk and act in ways that qualify him for liberal citizenship. For present purposes, however, only two assumptions about child development are critical. First is the idea that no single method of child rearing can pretend to provide the unique path to liberal citizenship. While different parents will present vastly different dialogic and behavioral models to their children, the outcome, so far as liberal theory is concerned, will typically be very much the same. By the age of four or five, children will come to the reluctant recognition that their claims to scarce resources will not go unchallenged unless they can be defended through forms of symbolic interchange established as appropriate by their particular upbringing. At this point, they will not only cry when their desires are frustrated; they will sometimes challenge the legitimacy of their constraints by manipulating the symbolic forms placed at their disposal by their primary culture. Such symbolic behavior begins to qualify the child for liberal citizenship under the dialogic tests developed in chapter 3.

Similarly, there are innumerable ways in which the child may be brought to recognize—with even greater reluctance—that it is wrong for him to persist in his actions if he cannot defend his claims to power through culturally approved techniques. This uneasy psychological recognition will provide an essential foundation for the behavioral requirements imposed on citizens: the demand that each of us curb our self-aggrandizing instincts when these lead us to destroy the rights that others establish through Neutral dialogue.[1]

So much for the first assumption—call it the *multiplicity* of paths to citizenship. My argument also requires me to assume that these multiple paths have one thing in common. Each recognizes the infant's *need for cultural coherence*. While an infant may learn English or Urdu or both, there are limits to the cultural diversity he can confront without losing a sense of the meanings that the noises and motions might ultimately signify. Exposing the child to an endless and changing Babel of talk and behavior will only prevent the development of the abilities he requires if he is ever to take his place among the citizenry. While the degree of cultural coherence required is a matter of great dispute, it will be enough to assume that the infant needs *some* coherence if he is ever to find himself in the ranks of a liberal citizenry. Once this assumption is allowed, a liberal theory of the family appears to view.

Given the infant's need for cultural coherence, a random concatenation of grown-ups cannot necessarily discharge the tasks of primary liberal education. They may instead provide such a chaotic cultural environment that the child will be unable to develop the dialogic and behavioral competences required of citizens. Once these minimal conditions for cultural coherence are satisfied, however, a liberal pol-

---

1. See §§ 18–19.

ity will suffer conversational embarrassment if it seeks to restrict the right of an individual or group to socialize a newborn infant. Imagine, for example, that a group of men and women think it good to socialize their babies through a kibbutz-like communal arrangement:

NOBLE: What gives you the right to impose your bizarre values on these innocent children?

COMMUNARDS: You might think them bizarre, but we say they're at least as good as yours are.

NOBLE: But these kids will be so perverted during their infancy that it will be difficult, perhaps impossible, for them to recognize the error of their ways later on!

COMMUNARDS: We deny we're perverting them. After all, they are receiving an upbringing that will equip them to discharge the dialogic and behavioral requirements of citizenship.

NOBLE: But there are any number of ways of achieving this minimal objective. What gives you the right to impose the *particular* form of primary education you have selected?

COMMUNARDS: Because we think it's the best one.

NOBLE: Just as I thought. A breach of Neutrality!

COMMUNARDS: Not at all. We can justify this power consistently with liberal principles.

NOBLE: I'm waiting.

COMMUNARDS: After all, we're not claiming the right to monopolize the primary education over *all* kids. All we need to say is that each citizen, *regardless* of his conception of the good, has the right to discharge his power of primary education over his own children in the way that seems best.

NOBLE: But why not permit *everybody* to talk to *every* infant? Isn't this just as valid a form of liberal education as the one you propose?

COMMUNARD: Not at all. Such a Babel of talk would prevent any child from attaining liberal citizenship.

NOBLE: I guess I can't deny that the child does need some form of cultural coherence.

COMMUNARDS: Why, then, can't we give the child the cultural form we think best—so long as we concede an equal power to you?

NOBLE: But if I can't prevent you from poisoning your kids, what can I do?

COMMUNARDS: Have some of your own. Our decision rule gives you the right to wield your power as primary educator with the same freedom we claim for ourselves. After all, we don't say we're doing any better at the job than you could.

NOBLE: But I really don't want to take the trouble to raise a kid.

COMMUNARDS: You're perfectly entitled to use your freedom in this way if you think it best. Only don't try to deny us the right to use our power differently.

NOBLE: You mean that I can only participate in primary education if I join some particular child-rearing group? Can't I give educational instruction to parents in general?

COMMUNARDS: You sure can. Only don't complain if some of us don't take your advice. You can't say it's any better than that given by your countless rivals.

Two cross-references are required to locate this script in the evolving pattern of liberal talk. Both involve the possibility that Noble may not, as the Communards suppose, be able to have children of his own to educate. On the one hand, Noble may be biologically incapable of having children. When this is so, the present dialogue presupposes efforts, like those discussed in chapter 4, to guarantee Noble adequate rights to obtain children through adoption.[2] On the other hand, Noble may be biologically fertile but confront a trusteeship restriction limiting the number of children each parent may have. A full discussion of population policy, however, must be deferred to chapter 7.

33. PRIMARY EDUCATION: ABUSE AND NEGLECT

But what if Noble's critique goes deeper? Suppose he asserts that the Communard "family" is failing to provide the cultural coherence necessary for a child to develop the competences required for citizenship? How are such claims to be treated?

With caution. The potential authoritarian abuse is obvious: bureaucrats seizing children from "deviants" on the pretext that they are failing to fulfill their responsibilities as primary educators. Great gobs of speculative social psychology are presently required before a particular family—let alone an entire mode of family organization—could be condemned as depriving the child of the cultural coherence he needs for citizenship. Given these facts, any second-best liberal

2. See § 28.1.

state will—if it does not ban all governmental intervention—restrict it to the most egregious cases.

For present purposes, however, these second-best concerns are less important than the issue of principle: *Can* a liberal dialogue be written which legitimates the removal of an infant on grounds of the family's incompetence as a primary educator?

To fix ideas, imagine that a citizen—call him Naturalist—informs the Assembly that he intends to place his child in solitary confinement for the first ten years of his life. The purpose, he assures us, is the advancement of science: once and for all, he aims to establish that children deprived of all human culture will be incapable of making up the deficit in later life. To establish his humane intentions, moreover, he plans to treat his child as decently as the conditions of his experiment permit. Thus, the child will be given a broad enclosure and plentiful food and shelter—though he will never be aware of the human identity of his benefactors.

NOBLE: This is unspeakable perversity!

NATURALIST: There you go again. How many times do I have to tell you that I'm at least as good as you are?

NOBLE: I do not deny it. Only it hardly follows that you can use your power over the child in any way you wish.

NATURALIST: Why not? If you don't like the way I'm bringing up the kid, have one yourself and educate him the way *you* think best.

NOBLE: But you're not educating him at all. You're treating him as if he were just another piece of manna—to be used in a way that gratifies your curiosity.

NATURALIST: What's wrong with that? And please, save the un-Neutral sentiments for the church of your choice. I happen to believe that the pursuit of science is the greatest thing there could possibly be.

NOBLE: But this child might one day raise the question of legitimacy concerning your treatment of him. And, *then*, how will you respond?

NATURALIST: No need to worry. I have overwhelming reason to believe that this child will *never* engage in normative discourse. Indeed the whole point of this experiment is to prove the empirical truth of my theories. And isn't the pursuit of truth a good thing? At least as good as the ideals you profess?

NOBLE: Certainly. But you can't demand the right to pursue your good when your power to do so can't be justified under liberal principles.

NATURALIST: Sure. But if the child will *never* talk, I fail to see why I can't treat him as if he were just another piece of manna—to be used in the way I think good. It's up to you to give me a reason—a *liberal* reason—for rejecting this analogy.

NOBLE: If you insist, permit me to compare two states of the world. Under A, the child is talking and interacting with the rest of us in a liberal way. Under B, the child is mute and we are obliged to interact with it without the aid of liberal dialogue. I say that the A way is better than the B way.

NATURALIST: But you've only managed to restate your preferences one more time. You've merely said that it's better to mediate a power relation through liberal dialogue than organize it through brute force. And it is precisely *this* I deny. At least when the pursuit of science is at stake, force *is* justified, even when unmediated by dialogue.

COMMANDER: I'm afraid that I must rule this remark out of order within this Assembly. For a liberal state is, by definition, a place where all power relations that *can* possibly be mediated through dialogue *are in fact* legitimated by liberal conversation.

NATURALIST: But *why* should this Assembly be committed to liberal dialogue? Why is a liberal state better than any other form of power relationship?

COMMANDER: A good question—and one to which we shall return in the concluding part of our conversation. For now, though, the question on the floor is not whether the liberal state is a good thing, but whether you can give a reason that passes liberal conversational constraints. And, so far, you have failed to answer Noble's question in a way that does not challenge the very principle of liberal dialogue itself. Unless you modify your educational program, I will have no choice but to take the infant away from you—if this is the only way to assure that dialogue will ultimately mediate our power relations with it.

To put the dialogic point in a broader context, compare the Naturalist's case with the (relatively) permissive position on abortion developed in the last chapter.[3] After all, the abortionist also proposes to treat the fetus at Time One in a way that makes it impossible for him

3. § 28.3.

to function as a citizen at Time Two. Why then will the Assembly often *permit* the parent to kill the fetus, while it intervenes to save the infant from the Naturalist's experiment?

Not because the infant is a citizen and the fetus is not. At Time One, *both* beings fail to qualify for protection under the Neutrality principle. The difference resides entirely in the way that the Naturalist's program threatens the integrity of *future* patterns of communal life. Quite simply, if the aborted fetus exists at all at Time Two, it exists as a purely spiritual being—with whom we could not conceivably talk in a way that is cognizable within a liberal Assembly. The Naturalist's victim, however, stands before us in the everyday way; indeed, he has many of our wants and anxieties. Yet whenever he grabs something, he is oblivious to our questioning. He turns blankly away from us as we invite him to reason together in an effort to resolve the perplexity to which we have all been condemned by relative scarcity. While such a relationship cannot be avoided in dealing with the animal, vegetable, and mineral kingdoms, it cannot be the affirmative aim of education in a community whose very being is constituted by the common effort to discipline power through the rule of Neutral dialogue.[4]

34. THE DECLINE OF PARENTAL AUTHORITY

Consider the younger generation as it emerges from infancy. Not only can each child communicate, but each has begun to master the special talk required by the dialogue of citizenship; similarly, with the help of the complex controls established within his "familial" group, each child has begun to master his aggressive impulses in the name of cultural norms. These common themes, however, do not do justice to the unimaginable diversity and intensity of the educational variations: children talking every language, acting out the billions of cultural scripts that constitute the living inheritance of past generations. Children testing, changing, restoring, transforming; parents teaching, adapting, cajoling, commanding.

Commanding—that is the problem. I assume that no form of primary education perfectly socializes any five-year-old to the point where he *never* resists the demands made by his "parents" in the name

4. Imagine that Naturalist somehow evades detection and proceeds with his experiment. Would we then be justified in forcing Naturalist's victim to talk—say, by giving him drug therapy? For a discussion of this point, see § 74.

of his primary culture. Resistance, in one area or another, is to be expected. And when it comes, the liberal dialogue takes a new turn. By definition, the successful product of a primary education can himself raise—albeit in a hesitant and primitive form—the question of legitimacy: "Parent, why are you entitled to boss me around?"

And once the question is asked, Rationality requires an answer. Moreover, the very act of questioning his parents' legitimacy begins to qualify the child under the dialogic tests for citizenship. Hence, his question cannot, in principle, be suppressed or dismissed with an answer that does not respect the child's rights under Neutrality. A liberal political community cannot support the exercise of coercion when the only thing that can be said is that elders are intrinsically superior to younger citizens; nor can it flatly assert that parents necessarily know what's good for the child better than the child does himself. These moves are flagrant violations of the Neutrality principle. But if this is so, what *can* be said in defense of parental authority beyond the age of five?

34.1. *Control*

We have already, in the chapter on citizenship, developed the ideas needed for a liberal answer to this question. Recall the effort of a homicidal Estranged to search the West Coast in quest of Endangered.[5] While Estranged was otherwise capable of behaving like a liberal citizen, he could not complain when the Commander imposed special restrictions upon him to protect Endangered's dialogic rights to bodily survival and material subsistence. The special restrictions on Estranged's behavior were not violations of Neutrality; instead, they were necessary conditions for his qualifying as a citizen with Neutrality rights in his other relationships.

An identical rationale for restricting the child's behavioral freedom is available here. Not that the typical five-year-old has the power to act out his homicidal fantasies. Nonetheless, the training the child receives between five and puberty is an important factor in the way he will deal with his increasing power to injure others in later life. The subtle and continuous reinforcement of cultural norms within the family may reduce the chance of an aggressive breach of the criminal law upon maturity. And so long as this is true, a liberal statesman must

5. § 19.4.

confront a perplexing trade-off: on the one hand, when a youth is forced by his educators to do something he does not want to do, these special sanctions *do* restrict the youth's prima facie right to act in the way that seems to him best; on the other hand, authorizing special controls during childhood may increase the youth's capacity to remain free of the special restrictions imposed on aggressive adults by the criminal law. The task, in short, is to design a set of behavioral limitations *over a citizen's entire lifetime* which promise to minimize the overall weight of special restrictions imposed upon him. Just as Estranged could not protest the special restriction imposed on his West Coast travel, so too Junior cannot protest special restrictions in childhood that free him from greater restrictions imposed in later life. Rather than violating Junior's citizenship rights under Neutrality, such limitations are necessary conditions for the maximum recognition of his dialogic rights over his lifetime.

This means that there is an important relationship between liberal criminal law and liberal family law. Assume, for reasons we have already discussed,[6] that the criminal law governing aggressive adults is structured along conventional liberal lines, demanding the highest levels of proof of an actual hostile act before special restrictions on liberty are imposed. It follows that an enormous weight must be put upon the subtler forms of "control" administered during infancy and childhood if the overall level of aggression is to be kept down to tolerable second-best limits. In saying this, I do not suggest that we should change the basic terms of trade-off between criminal law and family law, making it easier for the police to restrain adults and harder for parents to restrain youths. The important point is one of principle: authority over children is not justified by adult pretentions to moral superiority. Instead, parental control appears as a less restrictive means of permitting a child-turned-adult to escape the yet more intrusive restrictions imposed by the criminal law.

It is, however, one thing to state a principle, quite another to work out the particular shape of parental control that is justified within a particular institutional setting. Indeed, it seems plain that different liberal statesmen will reach different conclusions as to the extent of parental control that is justified. Not only will many relevant facts be contested, but different liberals will disagree about the best way of

6. § 19.6.

comparing the overall level of restriction imposed by parents and jailers of various types. The best way to resolve such good-faith differences of opinion will be the subject of the theory of liberal democracy developed in chapter 9. For the present, it will be enough to assume that the political discussion concludes with a vindication of *some* forms of parental control during the period lasting, say, from ages five to sixteen. Given this decision, the next question is the way parental control should evolve over this extended period of restriction.

It is here that a basic liberal principle emerges: The *more* successful the parents are in discharging their controlling functions, the *less* justification they have in continuing to impose their own conception of the good on their children. Despite the air of paradox, this conclusion follows directly from the rationale for parental control. Parents are given the right of control because the child must internalize habits of self-discipline if he is to deal with his aggressions in a way that steers clear of criminal sanction. It follows that as the child successfully internalizes the basic controls imposed by his primary culture, the parents may not view their initial success as warranting the imposition of more elaborate forms of their favored routine. A liberal education is not an advanced form of horticulture, with parents clipping their young sapling to achieve the pattern they most desire. In a successful liberal education, childish resistance at the age of eight must be taken more seriously than at four; at twelve, more seriously than eight.

An isomorphic argument generates a second paradox: the *less* successful the parents are in discharging their controlling functions, the *more* justifiable the continuing exercise of adult authority. At this point, however, the argument takes a different turn. It hardly follows that the people who have botched the job of primary education should exercise the task of remedial secondary education. Once again, however, the power to remove children from their primary families must be exercised with caution, both out of a justifiable fear of tyranny and a recognition that removing the child from its primary environment may itself undermine the child's capacity to deal with his aggressions.

34.2. *Guidance*
As the control rationale fades over time, a second rationale—which I shall call "guidance"—takes on independent weight. While control and guidance are inextricably intertwined in real life, I shall ignore this fact in giving a conceptual account of legitimate guidance.

Assume, then, that a proper restriction of parental control leaves it up to the child to decide whether he wants to be a good baseball player. Assume, further, that Junior *does* want to excel in the Little League; he finds it difficult, however, to deal with the fact that a lot of boring batting practice must be accepted as a necessary cost of baseball mastery. It is here, once more, that adults familiar with the child can be of assistance. Aware of his inexperience in the prudential judgments required in comparing means to ends, they may find ways of suggesting to the child that, *even when taken in his own terms*, he has misestimated the costs or benefits involved in the activity in which he has become interested. Most obviously, the child may be the victim of simple empirical mistakes: perhaps he thinks that once he has learned to bat a ball, he will be able to command all other objects to fly through the air. Once disabused of this error, Junior may change his mind and say that piano practice is better than batting practice.

Less obvious, but no less important, will be childish mistakes about the *social* reality that awaits him beyond his family. In particular, a child is apt to assume that people in the world beyond his "family" will act toward him on the basis of cultural patterns with which he is already familiar. Such an assumption is hazardous in a liberal society. While citizens will be free to look upon their fellows with love and admiration, they are also free to look with indifference or even contempt upon the way others live their lives. Once again, parents are often in the best position to realize that their child's actions, *even within their own terms*, make sense only on an unrealistic assumption as to the motives and intentions of people in the larger world.

Yet, the legitimacy of these special powers of guidance will also erode over time—though often at a different rate than the power of control. As the child gains more experience in matching means to ends, more experience in the world beyond the family, it becomes increasingly implausible to think that his disagreements with his parents are based upon mere imprudence; an ongoing pattern of dispute will increasingly suggest that the young adult dissents from family ideals and that the parents are using their powers of guidance to mask their illegitimate desires for control.

35. SECONDARY EDUCATION: THE LIBERAL PRINCIPLE

Thus far, we have been trying to define the extent to which parents are justified in overpowering childish resistance. But there is a second perspective from which to view the confrontation: the child's. And since we have shown that the parents have a diminishing claim to overpower childish dissent, a complete theory of liberal education must take a more sympathetic view of the child's "disobedience" than that of the disappointed parent.

From the child's point of view, there is, apparently, something troubling about the parental command. Yet he will experience predictable difficulties in expressing precisely *what* is troubling him. After all, his entire "primary" education comes from his parents and their delegates. Yet they, by hypothesis, are telling him that he is being a "bad child." Is the child entitled to learn, however, that his parents' view of the matter is not unchallenged within the liberal community? Do his parents have a right to stop other adults who seek to persuade the child that his resistance is not a sign of evil but contains the promise of a better life than the one his parents offer?

Imagine that some adult citizen—Noble—has viewed a particular parent–child relationship as it developed from the child's birth. During the child's "primary" education, however, Noble was barred from all interchange with the infant, the parents thinking that his influence would impede their efforts to provide the baby with a culturally coherent environment. The time has come, however, when the parents' success has begun to undermine their claims to control the child's ends and actions. Assume, in particular, that an interchange between Noble and the child will *not* have the effect of undermining the parents ongoing training in aggression control. Nor will Noble prove an unreliable guide; he will be sensitive to the problem of inexperience and help the child make prudent choices within the context of the child's developing conception of the good. The conversation proceeds:

PARENT: Daughter, how many times do I have to tell you that you shouldn't be playing with your brother's trucks. Play with the dolls instead.
DAUGHTER: But why can't I play with the trucks?
PARENT: I've had enough of this! Stop this truck stuff, I say!
DAUGHTER: (*Cries.*)
PARENT: This is ridiculous. Go upstairs to your room and stay there until you're more sensible. (*The child obeys. The doorbell rings and Noble appears.*)
PARENT: And what do *you* want?
NOBLE: I'd like to talk to the girl.

PARENT: What do you want to tell her?

NOBLE: I want to say that maybe she's right to play with trucks despite your efforts to suppress her. Now, can I proceed?

PARENT: Not if I have anything to say about it!

NOBLE: O.K. What *do* you have to say in defense of your effort to bar my access to her?

PARENT: First of all, she's *my* child, not yours. So get out of here!

NOBLE: You're wrong. She's not "your" child in the same way that this chair is part of "your" manna. Instead, she is a citizen of the liberal state.

PARENT: How can you be so sure?

NOBLE: Wasn't she questioning the legitimacy of your authority when I rang the doorbell?

PARENT: True. But she still must be subjected to special restrictions.

NOBLE: I don't deny it, but as a citizen of a liberal state, your daughter is entitled to the least restrictive environment consistent with her dialogic and behavioral development. A fair application of this standard does not entitle you to deny me access to her. (*Explains how this claim is consistent with Parent's residual rights of control and guidance.*)

PARENT: Suppose I accept your explanations for the purposes of this argument. What follows?

NOBLE: That you have yet to present a reason for barring me that will pass muster in liberal discourse. You don't assert, for example, that your daughter would be uninterested in my conversation.

PARENT: To the contrary. Your talk will only encourage this truck business of hers.

NOBLE: And what's wrong with that?

PARENT: Playing with trucks is a bad thing for a girl to do.

NOBLE: I'm afraid you'll have to do better than that. For I say that it's good for her to play with trucks.

COMMANDER: And given this conflict of opinion, *I* say that neither assertion can count as a legitimate reason for power wielding in a liberal state.

PARENT: Well, we seem to be at an impasse. While I have yet to come up with a Neutral reason for excluding you from my daughter, you have yet to come up with a Neutral reason for imposing yourself on her environment. Before you speak to her, you must answer *my* question of legitimacy: What gives you the right to the power that you seek?

NOBLE: A good question, but I have an answer. I say that each citizen has a prima facie right to decide for himself which communications he thinks it most profitable to hear. After all, every citizen is at least as good as every other. Unless something Neutral can be said in a particular case, it follows that no third party can claim the right to censor the flow of symbol in which each citizen is engulfed.

COMMANDER: I don't find anything in these remarks that offends Neutrality. What follows for the present dispute?

NOBLE: Unless Parent comes up with a Neutral reason for censoring my communication, I have the right to talk to the girl. She and I have the right to talk together if we think it a mutually profitable way of spending our time.

COMMANDER: Well, Noble, I find that you have satisfied your conversational burden. You shall gain the power you seek—unless Parent can come up with a Neutral justification of his continuing effort to monopolize his daughter's moral vocabulary and perception.

PARENT: Perhaps I'd better reconsider some of the concessions I made earlier for the purposes of the argument. Perhaps I can persuade my fellow citizens that Noble's intrusion will undermine my continuing efforts to develop my daughter's self-control. Moreover, I doubt that Noble is a trustworthy guide, given the girl's inexperience.

COMMANDER: Such empirical arguments are always welcome; but, of course, Noble must be given an equal opportunity to develop his own version of the relevant facts.

This conversation has implications that transcend the parent–child conflict generating it. The dialogue serves as the foundation for the next chapter's more general discussion of liberalism's hatred of censorship in all its forms. For the present, however, the point to stress is the dialogue's critique of all horticultural theories of education. Parents are not permitted to view childish resistance as a kind of weed that destroys the beauty of their private garden; they must increasingly recognize the right of others to provide the child with cultural materials with which she may forge the beginnings of an identity that deviates from parental norms. Indeed, our last script was appropriate only in the earliest stages of secondary education, where Daughter simply cries when confronted with a show of parental authority. Increasing contact with the outside world will provide her with the cultural capacity to take a more active role in the conversation, to insist upon her right to talk to Noble or anyone else who will be useful in clarifying her evolving self-conception. As time goes on, Daughter will speak more for herself and may assert her independence from both Parent *and* Noble—until the day comes when she has gained sufficient control over her aggressions and sufficient experience with the larger world to claim the right to define and pursue her own conception of the good, like every other full citizen of a liberal state.

In emphasizing the centrality of interpersonal tension and dialogue in liberal theory, however, I do not wish to exaggerate the liberal hostility to parental authority. Most important, a liberal education is *not* intended to persuade the child that his parents' values are rotten and that he had better convert to some official ideology prescribing the behavior of the Ideal Man of the Future. Rather than *personal conversion*, its goal is to provide the child with the materials he will find useful for his own *self-definition*. Despite Noble's access, Daughter may conclude that her parents were right after all—and come to see that playing with trucks is, indeed, unbecoming a growing girl. The liberality of a child's education is not measured by the outcome of her decision; its only index is the extent to which she has been given access to cultural materials that provide her with the tools she may find useful in making sense of her earlier resistance. If, after confronting the possibility of alternative cultural interpretations, Daughter embraces her parents' models, this is a perfectly legitimate outcome of the educational interchange. Surely a liberal Commander must recognize that parental values are no less entitled to respect than Noble's.

36. THE ROLE OF THE SCHOOL IN LIBERAL THEORY

To lay bare the dialogic foundations of liberal education, I have introduced the subject through a single conversation between Parent and Noble at a single moment in a child's socialization. But, of course, a child's questioning cannot be answered once and for all. Not only is the child's socialization extended over time; parental commands will typically be challenged by a large number of secondary educators from a number of very different—often contradictory—perspectives. Thus,

when the child resists parental authority, the "correct" thought experiment is one that imagines a *group* of Nobles ringing the door simultaneously, each demanding the right to provide different moral vo-
cabularies and environments within which the child may understand
his resistance to his primary culture.

This cacophony at the threshold generates its own distinctive problem of legitimacy. Even if a single Noble may be admitted into a child's
environment without undermining the parental project in aggression
control, it hardly follows that a five-year-old can suddenly confront
the full force of liberal society without undermining his developing
capacities to deal with aggression. The complex controls imposed
within the family do not depend merely upon the superior force of the
parents but upon their capacity to maintain their child's respect and
affection. These subtle ties could not survive an environment in which
parental models were subjected to constant ridicule and condemnation. While the child's questions of legitimacy must be treated with
respect, parental control cannot be eroded at a rate that outstrips the
child's capacities for self-control. The need for restricting, without
entirely eliminating, access by outsiders generates the problem of
liberal curriculum: Given the continuing need to control access, how
does one select among the different citizens who offer themselves as
secondary educators?

A plethora of would-be secondary educators also raises the problem
of guidance to a systemwide level. Mechanisms must be designed to
deny access to adults who seek the educator's role simply to further
their own self-interest by taking advantage of the child's inexperience.
I shall call this the problem of *trustworthiness* and will not say very
much about it, for its solution depends upon subtle facts about particular societies. In contrast, I do think something general can be said
about the problem of curriculum.

36.1. *Liberal Curriculum*

I shall define a school as any place where secondary liberal education occurs. As such, a school is not to be identified with a particular
building or bureaucratic structure. Indeed, many school buildings are
nothing more than an extension of the child's primary culture, with
"educators" interested only in weeding and pruning youngsters so that
they will better accord to the parental design. In contrast, a liberal
school has a different mission: to provide the child with access to the

wide range of cultural materials that he may find useful in developing his own moral ideals and patterns of life.

There can be no thought, then, that a single substantive curriculum can be imposed on all children attending a liberal school. Each child arrives in school with his own distinctive attitude to his particular primary culture—his own special resistances, his own distinctive affirmations. It is the liberal educator's task to take each child as he finds him and provide those cultural materials that will help the child interpret his own resistances and affirmations in a way that makes the most sense to him.

This challenging task is complicated further by the liberal educator's limited authority over the child. As we have seen, the child's family will typically exercise continuing powers of legitimate control and guidance. And many parents will inevitably be threatened by a school curriculum that equips the child to question, as well as affirm, family values. This means that the relationship between the liberal school and family heads will never be tension free. On the one hand, school curriculum must be respectful of the parents legitimate—if declining—authority over their children. On the other hand, parents have an obligation to refrain from using their residual authority in ways that sabotage the child's right to a liberal education.

The concrete form of these mutual responsibilities will depend on particular institutional facts; nonetheless, the sharing of control between parent and school precludes extreme solutions. On the one hand, parents may not use physical force to prevent their children from attending secondary school: nor may they impose an incestuous sexual relationship upon the child in an effort to pre-empt the challenge of liberal education. Instead, the liberal educator may rightly insist that sexual energies should be channeled outward into an exploration of extrafamily meaning. On the other hand, a liberal school cannot run roughshod over parental sensibilities, but must give family heads the right to press a panic button if a particular form of schooling threatens to overwhelm the family's efforts at control and guidance. In what follows, however, I shall not try to address the complex questions that will arise in managing the ongoing tension between school and family. Instead, I will focus on the problem of liberal curriculum that remains even after the problem of coordination with the family has been satisfactorily resolved.

From this point of view, the liberal educator confronts an embarrassment of riches. Each child's resistances can be given a large number of different cultural interpretations. Perhaps a girl's desire to play with trucks is a protest against her parents' overly bookish habits or rigorous sex typing; perhaps it is a sign of mechanical aptitude or some combination of these and other things. Even subtly different diagnoses may point the educator in very different directions as he searches for a curriculum that the child will find most useful for her problem of self-definition. Moreover, the liberal educator obviously cannot solve his problem of diagnosis by declaring that some ideals are intrinsically superior to others. But if he cannot do that, how *is* he to resolve his curricular problem?

There are at least four pedagogic strategies for ameliorating, if not entirely eliminating, this difficulty. First, during the early years of secondary education, the curriculum must be especially respectful of the strong parental interest in continuing control over the child. Hence, the early stages of a liberal curriculum will content themselves with the elaboration of life options relatively close to those with which the child is already familiar. By beginning with the relatively familiar, moreover, the child will find it easier to grasp the idea that his resistance to parental commands may not (as his primary culture suggests) be the sign of perversity but may instead represent a more satisfying way of expressing his developing self-understanding. As the child ages and parental interest in control declines, a firm foundation will have been laid for confrontations with cultural forms that provide more challenging interpretations of the youth's evolving pattern of resistances and affirmations.

Second, the liberal educator must beware of an overconfident diagnosis of the child's cultural needs. Rather than labeling a seven-year-old as a future mystic or entrepreneur, the early effort must provide the child with skills that he may find useful in a variety of self-definitions. Even more important than any particular skill will be the cultivation of the child's independent moral judgment, his sense that he need not remain content with the values his parents taught him in early childhood, that it remains open for him to adapt and reshape his values so as to recognize the validity of the moral insights of other groups in a liberal society.

Third, the problematics of diagnosis must be kept in mind as the child's curriculum evolves over time. The child's responses during one year should guide the curriculum he receives in the next. The aim is not a curriculum in which the child "succeeds" in learning the year's lessons and then is "promoted" to the next set of tasks in lockstep with his fellows. Indeed, if the child experiences no "failures," this is a sure sign that his educators are not using their power over the child's environment in the proper way. For it is through "failure" as well as "success" that both the child and the educator may learn which dimensions of liberal culture may be left unexplored and which are deserving of more intensive scrutiny. Moreover, people have the right to choose ideals even though they may fail in their pursuit. An easy success may seem less worthwhile than a noble failure.

Which brings us to the fourth principle. As the child gains increasing familiarity with the range of cultural models open to him in a liberal society, the choice of his curriculum should increasingly become his responsibility, rather than that of his educators. More and more, the educator, like the parent, becomes simply a guide whose authority depends solely on his greater experience with the flood of meaningful symbol and action generated by a liberal society.

These four principles, however, will predictably fail to point the educator to a *unique* solution to the problem of liberal education posed by any individual child. Inevitably, the educator's initial diagnoses of the child's cultural resistances and affirmations will be questioned by some elements of the liberal community. They will predictably protest when the educator's diagnosis of a girl's truck playing suggests that other cultural models have more to offer her than the one they advance. And while a liberal curriculum may give the dissidents some access to the girl at a later stage of her development, this may not provide a complete answer to their question of legitimacy— for the partisans of a particular culture may properly argue that they have lost the chance to carry their messages to the child at a time she is most impressionable.

Yet, given the very limited time available for any child's liberal education, this injustice is inevitable in any particular case. There is a sense, however, in which the entire secondary educational system, when considered as a whole, can be more liberal than the sum of its parts. An effort can be made to expose children with similar primary cultures to *different* secondary environments: while the educational diagnosis of a girl's delight with trucks is interpreted in one way in one case, it can be interpreted quite differently in the next. Such systematic diversity will permit the liberal educator to tell his fellow citizens with even more credibility:

> In exercising my power over the young, I have not used it to indoctrinate them into one or another of the competing ideals affirmed by members of our political community. In my capacity as liberal educator, I do not say that any of these ideals is worthy of greater respect than any other. Instead, my aim has been to provide each child with those cultural materials that—given his imperfect self-control and inexperience—he would find most useful in his efforts at self-definition. After all, these children are citizens of our liberal state. Although they may be subjected to special limitations when necessary to assure their future standing as citizens, they may not otherwise be denied their right to pursue their good in the way they think best. For are not they at least as good as we are?

It does not follow from this justification, however, that the liberal school will be a bland and colorless place. While each child's *entire curriculum* will be organized on liberal lines, he will typically confront *particular educators* with the most diverse set of skills, passions, and beliefs. Indeed, many secondary educators will be confident that the lessons they teach, both in words and actions, represent *the* truth for humankind. Such intolerance may often be pedagogically useful—so long as it is not permitted to envelop the child for too long a time, it will often be best for the child to assess a culture's strength when it is presented by its wholehearted enthusiasts. The entire educational system will, if you like, resemble a great sphere. Children land upon the sphere at different points, depending upon their primary culture; the task is to help them explore the globe in a way that permits them to glimpse the deeper meanings of the life dramas passing on around them. At the end of the journey, however, the now mature citizen has every right to locate himself at the very point from which he began— just as he may also strike out to discover an unoccupied portion of the sphere. For the liberal state is not committed to a system of liberal education because it wishes to indoctrinate children in one vision of the good rather than another. An Amish child, turned adult, has every right to follow his Amish parent; the New Yorker, the New Yorker. The liberality of an education is to be measured not by outcomes but by the extent that the growing child's question of legitimacy is taken seriously. The ideal liberal education is one that permits the child to move from his initial resistances to an ability to define his own objectives in the light of the universal culture defined by all humankind.

36.2. *Deschooling Society?*

Having glimpsed the liberal ideal, I will bring the discussion down to earth by criticizing some fashionable proposals to restructure American public education. Not that I mean to serve as an apologist for the narrow, authoritarian stuff that goes on in the country's classrooms; but some remedies may be worse than the diseases with which we are familiar. Consider, for example, the reform prescribed by Professor Milton Friedman, which has become popular in many circles.[7] Friedman, characteristically, attributes the repressive character of public education to the fact that school teachers are not held accountable through the marketplace. As a consequence, he would have schools compete for children, giving parents the right to cash a voucher at the place they think gives their child the best available education. The result, according to Friedman, will be a system far more responsive than the one that presently exists.

But responsive to whom? Surely most parents will refuse to spend "their" vouchers on anything but "education" that strives to reinforce whatever values they have—with so much effort—imposed on "their" children during infancy. Thus, Friedman's plan legitimates a series of petty tyrannies in which like-minded parents club together to force-feed their children without restraint. Such an education is a mockery of the liberal ideal.

This is not to say that parents have no role in defining the aims of a child's secondary education. Not only do they have more knowledge about the child than anyone else, but their legitimate role in the overall "control" system still bulks large. But this is a long way from saying that parents should be given the exclusive voice. If I may overstate the case in a Friedmanesque manner, the problem with the public schools is *not* that they are insufficiently responsive to parental views but that they are *already* overly concerned with reinforcing, rather than questioning, the child's primary culture. Somehow Friedman assumes that children can be legitimately made the subjects of moral indoctrination so long as the people doing the indoctrinating are called "parents." Liberal dialogue, however, seeks to control the exercise of superior

7. *Capitalism and Freedom*, chapter 6 (Chicago: University of Chicago Press, 1962).

power in *all* its forms, insisting that—so far as possible—uses of power be justified in a way consistent with the dialogic rights of those who happen to be powerless.

While Friedman's reform is a striking symbol of liberal myopia, it is the more fundamental criticisms of writers like Ivan Illich which suggest the dangers of a misguided reformist impulse.[8] Illich sees clearly that Friedmanesque alterations will do little to change the coercive structure that modern schooling imposes upon the young. The fundamental fact, for Illich, is that the contemporary school-teacher has been granted the power to determine the ultimate social status each of his students will attain in the bureaucratized, technocratic order characteristic of modern societies. As keeper of the keys to society at large, the school, whether "public" or "private," induces the child to conform to dominant technocratic mores. Whatever the particular subjects taught, the conventional school teaches the child that his success in life depends on his ability to move from one rung to the next in the educational (later, social) hierarchy; that all relevant knowledge is packaged in technocratic modules insulated from one another; that his unhappiness today is capable of a successful solution tomorrow if only he rises far enough in the bureaucracy. So long as the school is the handmaiden of bureaucratic and technocratic values, the progressive educator's dream of presenting himself to his class in a nonauthoritarian way is impossible. Whatever an individual teacher may say about the importance of self-definition, the larger structure will carry a very different—and far more powerful—message.

While Illich's indictment may be overdrawn, it contains powerful insights—that must be taken seriously in any liberal effort at curriculum design. Yet Illich wants more than this. He wants to destroy *all* education that occurs in "schools" that exist apart from other institutions in society. Freed from the incubus of schooling, people will rediscover the untapped educational opportunities of their primary social institutions, integrating the task of learning with that of living in society. Since abstract intellectual mastery will no longer be a key to bureaucratic advance, human beings will rediscover the pleasures of learning for its own sake. Deschooling society will generate a rebirth of living culture.

8. *Deschooling Society* (New York: Harper and Row, 1972).

If taken as an empirical prediction, I find Illich's prophecy so wildly implausible that it makes Milton Friedman's free-market economics seem sensible by comparison. If they were forced to do without separate places called "schools," I would guess that modern business could readily maintain itself by providing "on-the-job training" that would seem narrow and repressive even when judged by today's modest attainments in liberal education. Nonetheless, I do not wish to rest my case against Friedman or Illich on the factual accuracy of their predictions. My point against both is that even if their reform worked according to plan, the results would be antagonistic to liberal ideals. So assume, with Illich, that adults will rise to the educational challenge and educate children in the deeper meanings of the activities in which they are engaged. Even this, however, fails to satisfy the demanding requirements of liberal education. It is not enough to indoctrinate the child into the patterns of life he happens to find at hand; what is required is a cultural environment in which the child may define his own ideals with a recognition of the full range of his moral freedom. There is no reason to think that ordinary adults, in the heat of action, will take much time to deal with the expression of doubts as to the underlying merit of their enterprise. Yet a liberal education requires toleration—indeed, encouragement—of such doubts. It is only by questioning the seeming certainties of his early moral environment that the child can begin to glimpse the larger world of value that may be his for the asking. More generally, the liberal educator's methods of doubt, imagination, and independence must necessarily come in conflict with whatever moral ideals happen to dominate society at large. It is this unending conflict that makes the institutionalization of liberal education—in "schools" relatively insulated from the rest of society—a matter of the first practical importance. Without special institutions devoted to the ideal of liberal education, the social pressures on children to conform to the received wisdom of their particular concrete environments will seem overwhelming.

Illich does not see this as a threat because, like Friedman, he concentrates so intensely on one form of coercion that he is blind to all others. Just as Friedman associates coercion with government, Illich links it with technocratic training for the bureaucracy. But the truth is that *any* system in which the elder generation uses its superior power to "educate" the young is coercive. A preindustrial family that forces its children into unquestioning obedience to its norms is no less coer-

cive than a school that induces unquestioning acceptance of technoc-
racy. The task is not to undertake a vain search for the coercion-free
educational system, but to consider ways in which the inevitably coercive aspects of socialization can be justified. No educational "reform"
can hope for success unless it recognizes the problematic character of
any effort by *any* power holder to inculcate an uncritical acceptance of
any conception of the good life. However radical Illich's reforms may
seem, they represent yet another effort to suppress the question of
legitimacy in the name of education.[9]

37. THE PLACE OF EDUCATION IN LIBERAL THEORY

My task, however, is not to provide a roadmap for the next hard steps
in educational reform, but to demonstrate that there *is* a coherent
theory of liberal education that can animate a reform enterprise.
Moreover, I hope I have convinced you that education cannot be
treated as if it stood apart from the more general problems of liberal
political philosophy. Instead, the distinctive character of liberal education has been established by the same dialogic methods used to discipline seemingly unrelated power struggles. The illumination gained
through liberal dialogue, however, cannot be appreciated until it is
compared with more traditional ways of linking liberal political theory
with the idea of education.

37.1. *Education in Contractarian Thought*
Modern contract theory was born in protest against a metaphor that
would liken the problem of legitimate *political* organization to the
problem of legitimate *familial* organization. Instead of viewing society as an extended family owing obligations of loyalty to a king-father,
Hobbes and Locke sought to reconstruct the concept of political obligation so that it might be worthy of a liberal society of free individuals.
Yet this effort to extricate the state from the family inevitably called
the continuing legitimacy of the family into question; if our idea of the
state should be reorganized on individualistic lines, should not the
family also be conceived in the same spirit?

The question is dangerous, for it may turn out that no conceivable
notion of parental authority can withstand the liberal's corrosive in-

9. Related discussions of educational finance (§ 56.1) and civic education (§ 64.3) may be
found in other chapters.

quiry into the legitimacy of power. Whatever may be said of adults existing in a prepolitical state of nature, it is obviously silly to say that infants have consented to subordination by their parents. Yet if there is no familial compact analogous to the social compact, on what ground could the child's obligations of obedience be based?

Several answers are possible, but all have difficulties. One may, for example, say that the family is a "natural" institution that needs no further justification in larger political terms. The idea of "natural" obligations of obedience, however, is not easily cabined within bounds the liberal might find endurable. If the child owes a natural duty to his parent, why does not the parent owe a natural duty to his king? To answer this question, the liberal seems required to develop an entire theory of natural obligations, which it was the very point of contractarianism to avoid.

To avoid this prospect, the contractarian may say that it is only because the child is unable to give his *intelligent* consent to the social compact that nonconsensual subordination is tolerable. On this line of reasoning, the family is seen as a limited exception to the general principle of consensual obligation, justified only by the fact that the child comes into the world an unreasoning brute not yet capable of comprehending and acting in accordance with the social contract's provisions. While this liberates the child from the family once he has reached the age of consent, it only serves to legitimate his total subjugation until this moment is reached. Since the youth cannot rely upon the social compact, and there is no familial compact, his status during his minority seems to be regulated by no compact at all. Thus, the family turns out to be a petty tyranny, limited in the temporal extent of its dominion but not in its essential nature.

In contrast, liberal theory has no difficulty recognizing that a child's questioning must be taken seriously despite the fact that he is not yet capable of controlling his aggressions in a way required of full citizens. Long before the child reaches political maturity, he can establish rights for himself by participating in the dialogue that constitutes the liberal state. Citizenship is not a sudden acquisition, grasped through the (metaphorical) signing of a social compact, but the product of a long and painful process by which we master conflict in the name of a common political culture. It is this process which both justifies, and limits, the claims of the family over the young.

37.2. *Education in Utilitarian Theory*

While the idea of contract is too weak to cast much light on child-hood, the idea of utility shines so bright that it blinds us to the distinctive aspects of the problem. As always, education presents no special difficulties for the utilitarian. And that is just the point—something vital is missed in the bland assertion that educational institutions should be arranged to maximize overall felicity.

To see this, consider the suspicion with which a clear-thinking utilitarian will greet my idea of a liberal education. An education that provides the child with cultural assistance in his resistance to parental values exacts a heavy price in human anxiety, agony, pain. And it is far from obvious that a utilitarian will find these pains offset by the pleasures gained from the experience.

Before toting up the pains generated by a liberal education, however, I do not wish to belittle its distinctive pleasures. Some children who would have bitterly followed in their parent's footsteps will find happiness in the cultural opportunities provided them by a liberal education. And there is a peculiar joy that comes when, after moments of doubt and despair, a person discovers that there *is* a conception of himself which is worthy of affirmation. Moreover, free competition between partisans of different ideals may spur creative innovation that redounds to the general felicity in the long run.

Nevertheless, after giving these pleasures a full accounting, the utilitarian must turn to the heavy task of enumerating the extra pains generated by the liberal system. Life may be happier for most children if, instead of facilitating a challenge to parental values, secondary educators seek merely to reinforce them. If children suppress, rather than explore, their early resistances, perhaps they will be spared much agony and self-doubt, enjoying a tranquil happiness. Even if authoritarian methods do condemn a large number to angry rebellion or sullen acquiescence, the interests of the elder generation must be taken into account. Who can ignore a parent's deep joy when his child follows upon the path marked out for him? Yet this great satisfaction is put at risk by a liberal secondary education. Even if a large fraction of the young complete their liberal education convinced of the value of parental traditions, the mere existence of a potentially subversive educational system may strike profound fears (i.e. pain) in the hearts of the elder generation. And the clear-thinking utilitarian cannot refuse to give these pains their proper weight in the overall felicific calculus.[10]

In the end, then, the utilitarian can only condemn the liberal ideal sketched here as simplistic and one-sided. Instead of facilitating the childish expression of doubt and youthful experiment with cultural alternatives, he would seek to devise a mix of authoritarian and liberal policies that maximizes social satisfaction of young and old in both the long and short run. Moreover, the utilitarian's policy mix will depend upon the educational tools available for use. If a new technology makes it possible to diminish (at low cost) the anxieties of the elder generation, this innovation serves as an argument for increasing the liberality of the optimal education. If a scientific discovery increases the accuracy with which a secondary educator can predict the sort of goals that will in fact maximize a particular child's happiness, this will justify an adjustment in the optimal mix in a repressive direction, for the probable felicific benefit of encouraging the child to search out his own ideals has been reduced. While the "optimal" mix of repression and liberalism will change over time, there is no reason to think it will tend in the liberal direction.

The source of the difference is easy to locate. While the utilitarian sees the schools as simply another place to jolly up society at large, the liberal sees education as a coercive relation subject to special abuse if not handled with sensitivity. Educators may never justify their controls by saying that they know where a child's ultimate happiness resides; instead, their authority resides in their ability to establish an environment in which the youth may perfect his capacities for aggression control while increasing his familiarity with the alternative forms of self-definition affirmed in a liberal society. If this process leads the child to generate anxiety in his parents, this pain cannot be taken into

10. One may, of course, soften the utilitarian critique of liberal education by adopting Mill's expedient of distinguishing "higher" from "lower" pleasures, weighting the former more heavily than the latter. So long as the higher pleasures are defined as those related to the development of the moral imagination required by the liberal ideal, the utilitarian can then discount the pains involved in introducing the child to moral confusion. Nonetheless, this procedure does not permit the utilitarian to ignore the fears that liberal education will generate in the hearts of parents. Moreover, it is easy to manipulate the higher-lower distinction so as to legitimate a very authoritarian education by defining "higher" to include only those cultural activities that happen to be in momentary favor in society. More fundamentally, the utilitarian embrace of a distinction between higher and lower pleasures comes at an enormous cost to the general enterprise of liberal political philosophy, since it cuts the heart out of the liberal's search for a theory that will enable decision makers to legitimize their uses of power without claiming the right to declare that one conception of the good is better than another.

account if all the parents can say is that their children have adopted mistaken ideals in life. Similarly, the polity cannot call liberal education to a halt simply because the child experiences some anxiety when he confronts the fact that his secondary curriculum does not provide an authoritative answer to his moral problem, but simply provides him with the tools to answer it on his own. A high level of anxiety and frustration *can*, of course, serve as a signal that the child may require a firmer "control" system if he is to master his aggressive impulses in the way required of citizens. Nevertheless, while the sources and level of the child's anxiety should play a role in determining proper educational tactics, they do not call into question the liberal's ultimate educational objective: to bring the child to citizenship in a way that, as nearly as possible, respects the questions of legitimacy he raises as he develops his own distinctive pattern of resistances to, and affirmations of, his earliest culture.

6

FREE EXCHANGE

38. PARTIAL SYNTHESIS

We have been exploring our new world in a cautious, even pedestrian, way. Rather than straining for a comprehensive view, we have glimpsed one aspect, then another, of the ideal power structure—dealing first with control over material resources, then citizenship status, then genetic endowments, then cultural inheritance. While this piecemeal approach permitted analytic depth, we may now build a more synthetic vision.

Imagine, then, that we have put our interplanetary journey to good use, each explorer taking advantage of the time to gain an ideal liberal education for himself. Stipulate further that conditions of undominated genetic diversity obtain; while the spaceship contains citizens with very different capacities, none can claim a genetic disadvantage within the constraints imposed by liberal conversation. Speaker after speaker is reduced to silence as he tries to justify an inegalitarian solution to the manna problem. Finally, the Commander herself takes the floor to announce that every adult citizen will, on landing, be awarded an equal share of manna:

> CHALLENGER: I want more than an equal share. What gives you the right to deny it to me?
> COMMANDER: Because your fellow citizens are at least as good as you are. And if they're at least as good, they should have at least as much manna to pursue their good, whatever it may be. Now that I have given you a reason for an equal distribution, can you give me a reason for your getting more?
> CHALLENGER: I will use the manna for better purposes than will the others.
> COMMANDER: Reasons of this sort are blocked by Neutrality's bar against selectivity.
> CHALLENGER: I am made of intrinsically better stuff than the

others and deserve more manna regardless of my conception of the good.

COMMANDER: And that move is blocked by Neutrality's bar against claims of unconditional superiority.

CHALLENGER: I am unhappy with my education and insist on compensation for the way my teachers have used their power over me.

COMMANDER: But throughout your childhood, we have taken your questions of legitimacy seriously and have restricted your environment only to the extent necessary to assure your successful growth to full citizenship.

CHALLENGER: I am unhappy with my native abilities and insist that those who are more fortunate share their advantages with me.

COMMANDER: But I cannot, consistent with Neutrality, recognize your genetic bundle as inferior to that of any other citizen. What, then, do you have to complain about?

CHALLENGER: (*Silence.*)

COMMANDER: Well, until you find something to say, I shall support an equal distribution of manna.

Our more particular efforts to talk about power in a Neutral way support a unified doctrine of initial endowments. It is only when the separate liberal ideals are taken together—*equal* material resources, *liberal* education, *undominated* genetic diversity—that they describe a power structure that supports a thoroughly liberal form of political discourse. Moreover, the simple dialogue we have rehearsed can serve as a foundation for the more complex conversations required in second-best theory. Thus, if some people are victims of genetic domination or illiberal education, they may well assert a claim upon the rest of us for more manna than would otherwise be rightfully theirs.[1] While determining the precise *amount* of compensation due will often be a tricky business, it will be the job of Part Three to analyze these complexities. For now, the important point is that so long as the compensation problem is resolved in a liberal way, the last dialogue will apply to victims of genetic or educational disadvantage with the same force that it applies to their more fortunate fellow citizens.

1. See, e.g., the dialogue, in § 29.1, written on behalf of the handicapped. An isomorphic dialogue could also be written on behalf of the educationally deprived, see § 55.1 of chapter eight as well as chapter five.

Yet, for all this, we must beware the pleasures of partial synthesis. By cultivating the art of liberal conversation, we have defined some of the basic terms upon which the first generation will begin social life together on their new world. More talk will be required, however, before we can build a solid bridge to earthly realities. We must follow the first generation after it lands upon its brave new world. What forms of power struggle will emerge as adult citizens deal with one another over time? We must pursue the first generation to the very end when it confronts the inevitability of death and tries to set the terms upon which its successors will live after generation one has passed away. Only then will we transcend the new world metaphor and establish that liberal dialogue can govern a world like our own, where material wealth does not merely depend upon ownership of natural resources but on the effort by individuals and groups to transform material reality through processes of labor, exchange, and inheritance.

39. TRANSACTIONAL FLEXIBILITY

After hearing the last dialogue, a hush falls on the Assembly. Nobody comes forward with a competing distributive principle that can be defended through Neutral dialogue. The conversation has exhausted itself, and the Commander declares the Assembly committed to the only principle that has survived liberal discussion: undominated equality. In triumph, she is about to adjourn the Assembly sine die when a new question comes to the fore.

To see the problem, consider the variety of property arrangements that are consistent with egalitarianism. At the individualistic extreme, the Assembly might divide the manna into as many bits as there are citizens, giving each citizen one bit; or it might adopt a collectivist solution in which the manna is divided into, say, ten-bit chunks and assign ten people to each chunk; or it might adopt some complex mix of individualist and collectivist forms of property ownership. The question, simply put, is the form of property ownership that will provide the best way of packaging the Assembly's commitment to undominated equality.

39.1. *The Uncertain Foundations of Individualistic Property*
This is a question that liberals have found all too easy to answer in the past. Once the right to an equal share of manna is recognized, it has

seemed but a short step to adopt the *individualistic* concept of property, dividing the manna into as many bits as there are citizens and giving each citizen one bit. Despite its roots in the liberal tradition, however, the individualistic solution leads to embarrassment when put to the dialogic test.

Imagine, for example, that upon leaving the spaceship, you hope to establish a commune devoted to work and philosophy with a group of like-minded individuals. Unfortunately, your future comrades are scattered far and wide among the sea of humanity in the Assembly Hall. When faced with the individualistic solution to the property problem, you and your like-minded friends take the floor:

LIKE-MINDED: We protest. If you give out the manna in an individualistic form, it will be very expensive for us to locate one another and join together in mutually advantageous enterprise.

COMMANDER: What would you have us do then?

LIKE-MINDED: Adopt a form of communal ownership over largish chunks of manna and assign us all to one chunk. This would make it much easier for us to start our commune.

SOLITARY: But it will make life harder for me. I want nothing better than to live in solitude and work my manna in peace. If you give out the manna in bigger chunks, I will—at best—have to spend a lot of time and energy before I sever my little bit of manna from the communal chunk to which I have been initially assigned.

COMMANDER: How, then, are we to proceed? And please don't present a plan that requires me to say that a commune of like-minded associates is any better or worse than the solitude of the hermit.

The dialogue reveals the need to distinguish between three closely related concepts in liberal theory. First, and most fundamental, is each individual's right to *dialogic recognition* as a citizen with equal standing in the ongoing political conversation. Second is each citizen's prima facie right to an *equal* share of material reality. Third is the idea that an *individualistic property system* is the best way of permitting an individual to acquire control of material reality so that he may pursue his conception of the good. While the first two principles have deep roots in liberal theory, an individualistic property regime has a far more uncertain place. Indeed, it is only the perfect solitary who believes that such a regime provides the best way of establishing his control over material reality. Even slightly more communal types would prefer to save the transaction costs required of them to repackage their property rights into more collective forms that facilitate the interpersonal relationships they think good. Rather than declaring individualistic property an "inherently" superior starting point, the Commander must try to deal with the objections of the Like-minded in a Neutral way.[2]

39.2. *The Master Designer*

Begin by considering the problem with the aid of a perfect technology of justice. The Commander introduces a Master Designer who can engineer any transactional system the citizenry thinks will solve the problem revealed by the last conversation. Is there a design, then, that will permit the Like-minded or Solitary to respond Neutrally to their Commander's question?

Begin by viewing the problem from Solitary's point of view. He would prefer to avoid the transaction costs that may fall upon him if he began life as a part owner of a communal chunk and had to bargain with his fellow owners before he could sever his bit of manna from collective control. Since he cannot say that these transaction costs ought to be born by communards instead of solitaries, there is only one condition under which he will be able to justify the choice of private property over communal property: if the Designer can construct a scheme that will permit the Like-minded to repackage their individualistic property rights costlessly into a form of collective ownership that better suits their purposes. Under a design that involved no *negotiation costs*, Solitary can respond: "Don't take the Assembly's individualistic specification of property rights too seriously; thanks to the Designer, a system is available which will permit you to locate the Like-minded costlessly and mutually agree upon the form of communal ownership you think best."

---

2. Moreover, the Commander cannot adjourn the Assembly before it has reasoned its way to a solution to the property question. Until each citizen knows the legal form in which he will acquire manna, he would not know, upon leaving the spaceship, how to go about identifying the chunk of material reality that has been assigned to him as his rightful share of the new world. He would be condemned to wander about the new world asking: Is this the piece that is my rightful share?

Less metaphorically, the Rationality principle requires every distribution rule to be "complete"—it must tell each and every citizen where he stands in the struggle over scarce resources. See § 11.1. Yet this formal requirement cannot be satisfied until each citizen is told how to identify the manna in which his claims will be vindicated in preference to those made by his competitors.

Now consider the same conversational problem from the point of view of the Like-minded. If chunks of manna were initially distributed to groups of people who seem like-minded, they must contend not only with the perfect solitaries but with people (call them deviants) who think that they would be better off under some different form of collective ownership than the one preferred by their chunkmates. Just as Solitary could not defend individualistic property by saying that the Like-minded ought to bear the negotiation costs, so too the Like-minded cannot say that Deviant is a "bad" collectivist who ought to bear the exit costs out of his own pocket. To legitimate a collectivist proposal, the Like-minded must instruct the Designer to develop a mechanism that would permit every citizen to *exit* costlessly from his initial collective together with an equal share of manna. Then, so long as the deviants can take advantage of a costless negotiation system to locate potentially like-minded fellows, the collectivists would have a conversational response isomorphic to the one with which Solitary defended the individualistic property solution.

Putting the ideas of costless negotiation and costless exit together yields the liberal ideal of perfect *transactional flexibility*. A design that fulfilled this requirement would permit a Neutral defense of *any* form of property ownership that was selected as the legal package in which manna is initially distributed. *So long as transaction is perfectly flexible, the initial property package is irrelevant.* Not that transactional flexibility is a panacea for all the ills of a liberal citizenry. Perhaps I would love to live in a commune in which a group of a hundred like-minded friends owned their manna in common, spending it on fine music, exquisite wines, and philosophic conversation. Suppose, however, that each of us receives only one grain of manna and that the communal plan I have in mind requires two hundred grains to get off the ground. Thus, even if I (costlessly) found ninety-nine like-minded associates, we would only have half the wherewithal required for our communal ideal. While this would make me unhappy, my complaint would not be with the perfectly flexible transactional system but with the *underlying fact of scarcity*. An ideal transactional design does not guarantee anybody success in life—any more than does the guarantee of undominated genes, liberal education, or equal manna. It simply permits a Neutral defense to the foreseeable questions that arise when the Assembly tries to justify its decision to give out the manna in one legal package rather than another. So long as perfect flexibility obtains, the Assembly may respond: "If you don't like the form of property holding we have provided, you may costlessly repackage your bundle of property rights in a way you think better. Do not imagine, however, that you are the only person who will be provided with this power of transactional flexibility. Everybody else will also be guaranteed an identical power over his initial bundle of property rights. After all, they are no worse than you are. Shouldn't they have the same transactional freedom you demand?"

40. TRANSMITTER-SHIELDS FOR ALL

After listening to the conversation, the Designer sets to work. As our spaceship lands, he hands a piece of equipment to each of us. What would it look like?

40.1. *Costless Negotiation*

I shall call the object a transmitter-shield. Turning first to the transmitter, it will be a two-way device that permits each person to send and receive signals to any or all of his fellow citizens.

The message-sender is easier to describe. Suppose I am interested in establishing some relationship, R, with one or more of my fellow citizens. Then the sender permits me to beam a description of R to anybody I want to interest in my project. It is up to me to determine the size and identity of my R audience. I am free to broadcast R costlessly to all mankind or a select few. Moreover, each citizen can use the communication medium he thinks will best transmit his meanings. A universal telephone and/or mail system is not enough—the medium must be perfectly plastic. Otherwise, the Designer could not justify denying some people the power to transmit offers in *their* favorite medium while forcing others to communicate through media they think distort their message.

The receiver must be designed to meet even more demanding requirements. Obviously, it must permit me to receive any R offer beamed in my direction; otherwise, the excluded citizens can raise a powerful question of legitimacy. The real problem is the design of a mechanism that will permit me to cope with the billions of R offers that will probably be beamed in my direction. Since I can only consider a very few Rs seriously, I must be equipped with a selection device that permits me to receive only those that I will think most promising. While this ideal of perfect discernment is formidable, it must be recalled that each of our citizens—thanks to his liberal education—already has a sense of the life options most attractive to him. The task, then, is not to design a system for a completely unformed person but to permit each citizen to make use of his present values to search efficiently for those message domains that seem most promising to him, giving him ample opportunities to backtrack and search different message domains as values evolve.

40.2. Costless Exit

Aided by his ideal transmitter, Depressive has located the associational options that seem most attractive among all those beamed in his direction. Assume, for example, that Depressive is willing to dedicate half his manna endowment to a life of music if he can find a suitable person to share it with him, and that Manic and Noble appear the best available music-mates. The ideal transmitter, however, carries bad news along with the good. It appears that Manic and Depressive have initially been assigned neighboring manna chunks; as a consequence, Depressive must contend with the noise pouring out of Manic's window whether or not he plays along. While this would be a delight if the Manic-Depressive duet got off the ground, it would be a maddening distraction if Depressive chose Noble instead. Thanks to the initial specification of property rights, then, it will cost Depressive a half-grain of manna to say No to Manic, for he must then sound condition his property. In contrast, it will cost him nothing extra to say No to Noble, whose initial manna holding is safely out of earshot. Thus, if Depressive is initially endowed with a single grain of manna, he will spend it *all* if he establishes a relationship with Noble but will keep a *half-grain* if he sticks with Manic. On these facts, Noble would have the right to question the legitimacy of the original specification of property rights. Why wasn't he, rather than Manic, placed next to Depressive by the initial property specification?

It is here where the Designer's shield comes into play. Each citizen may costlessly use the device to shield his manna from any undesirable effects that would otherwise be imposed upon it by other citizens. At the flick of a switch, Manic's noise may be cut off at Depressive's manna frontier. No longer can some citizens impose exit costs of a kind unavailable to others because they were initially assigned to a neighboring manna chunk. If Manic, rather than Noble, is successful in convincing Depressive to play a duet, this cannot be the product of an advantage generated by the initial form of property holding; instead, Noble's failure must be attributable to Depressive's considered judgment on the merits of the competing offers: "I'm sorry, Noble, but I think I can play more meaningful music with Manic. And you have no right to say I'm wrong. For my judgment on these matters is at least as good as yours is." Manic and Noble must compete for Depressive's favor on transactional terms that do not require either of them to make a conversational move that breaches Neutrality.

In introducing the ideal shield, I began with the most obvious dilemma it is designed to solve—where, thanks to the initial system of property holdings, some citizens can impose exit costs on Depressive while others are denied an identical power. Yet such obvious forms of un-Neutrality only constitute half the problem solved by the shield. Just as a property system may give Manic the right to impose special *exit costs* on Depressive if he fails to cooperate, so too it may give him special rights *to take a free ride* on Depressive's activities which are not granted to other property owners. Imagine, for example, that Manic likes nothing better than to listen to a Depressive-Noble duet. Moreover, thanks to the initial system of handing out manna, Manic finds that he is Depressive's neighbor and so can overhear the duet for free. This disconcerts Noble and Depressive no end, for they would vastly prefer to play a trio in which Manic also participates. Yet, so long as the property system gives him the special right to a free ride, Manic stands aloof. On these facts, Noble and Depressive have a just complaint: Why is Manic given the right to hear their concert for free while property owners at other locations can only hear it with the duo's permission?

Once again, there is a design that undercuts the dialogic force of this question. Simply stipulate that the Designer's shield not only permits each citizen to *screen out* all undesirable impacts at his manna frontier but also permits each citizen to *screen in* any activity originating in his space which he wants to keep private. This will permit the Assembly to defend itself even if it chooses to specify a collectivist mode of property holding to govern the initial property distribution. In response to an individualist's protest, the Commander may simply respond: "If you prefer a more individualistic package, simply use your shield to restrict the special powers given your neighboring chunkmates. These shielding powers are available to every citizen, regardless of his conception of the good, to do with as he thinks best. It is not up to me, but up to you, to decide which property form is best for you in a world of scarce resources."

To forestall misunderstanding, do not imagine that each citizen will *in fact* use his shield to cut all free riders off from all benefits. To the contrary, Noble and Depressive may choose to make a gift to the rest of the world by allowing their duet to pass through their shields. And the rest of the citizenry will allow these gifts to pass through *their* shields to the extent that they think them good. Thus, each citizen may be as altruistic with his shield as he thinks proper. The only thing the shield system prevents is the effort by any citizen to impose special burdens on, or obtain special benefits from, others as a consequence of the initial decision to distribute manna in a collectivist, rather than individualistic, form.

41. FREE SPEECH, FREE COMPETITION, FREE LOVE

The Assembly was driven to the Master Designer by a very particular conversational embarrassment. Since *any* particular system of property holding—individualist or collectivist—was of questionable legitimacy, the way out of the dilemma was to engineer a transactional framework that gave each citizen the power to repackage his initial property rights in the way he thought best—given an equal power by every other citizen to do likewise. The transmitter-shield is but a specification of this aspiration.

Yet while I have generated the transmitter-shield in response to dialogic necessity, my thought-experiment casts light beyond the confines of my particular theory. Historically, the area we are investigating constitutes the core of the liberal tradition. While many liberals can comfortably ignore the entire problem of genetic or educational or material disadvantage, the idea of free exchange is nothing less than a preoccupation. There are countless efforts to draw a conceptual line around a protected sphere of individual freedom, countless ideals that mark the liberal heartland: free expression, free competition, free love. What is needed is a sense of the way these particular ideals are related to one another. The idea of transactional flexibility provides, I think, just this kind of organizing framework.

Consider, first, the clear and precise meaning that can be given to a prohibition of censorship in our ideal world. Quite simply, the principle translates into a flat ban against jamming another's transmitter so as to disable it from either sending or receiving information about any *R* whatever. The ban is both universal and absolute. *Nobody* can tamper with the transmitters; *no* message may be blocked, regardless of its content. If anybody tries to impose special restrictions on my transmitter, I can insist on knowing why he thinks he is entitled to greater transactional freedom than I myself possess. And unless he can come up with a Neutral answer, a liberal Commander must block his effort at self-aggrandizement.

This freedom from censorship is but an aspect of an even broader right to free competition. Not only may I *learn* of competing offers but I may *accept* one of them without your imposing some special sanction upon me. While you have the right to refuse to deal with me, you may not go beyond this and take affirmative action to block my favored relationship. Thanks to our wonderful shields, moreover, the line between refusal to deal and the imposition of special injury may be drawn with preternatural clarity. Quite simply, you are guilty of the charge of monopolization if you make *any* effort to sabotage my shield so that you can impose a special sanction on me for dealing with one of your competitors.

This clean definition of monopolization, finally, permits us to fulfil Mill's promise by locating an important category of self-regarding actions that are, in principle, immune from state suppression. The traditional solution has been cast in terms of an action's harmfulness: if it causes harm to others, then the government may properly control it; if not, not. Unfortunately, this test threatens Mill's principle with trivality: it is hardly possible that the government will regulate conduct unless *somebody* complains about it; and people will never complain unless they conceive themselves harmed in one way or another. Consequently, a great deal of energy has been devoted to defining the sorts of harms that fail to qualify as really harmful. The favorite effort has been to deny that "merely" psychological harms are harmful. Yet this venture generates familiar difficulties. Not only is it hard to distinguish the "merely" harmful from the "really" harmful, but one wants to know why psychological affront is necessarily less serious than other kinds of hurt. The answer is generally nothing better than an impassioned plea about the need to draw a clear line "somewhere" if individual liberty is to be assured.

While the liberal Commander can sympathize with the passion, she tries to mark its meaning by a different compass. It is, of course, only natural for Mill and other utilitarians to define self-regarding action by refining the idea of harmfulness. Indeed, there is nothing a utilitarian *can* do but to draw lines after balancing "harm" against "benefit." In contrast, the ideal liberal polity refuses to pass judgment on the net benefits generated by its citizens' actions; instead of evaluating outcomes, it holds *any* outcome legitimate so long as it has been generated through a legitimate transactional *process*. Hence, the character of self-regarding actions is not to be judged by asking whether they cause "harm," but whether they have been accomplished without anyone's committing an offense against the ideal transactional process. In short, the category of privileged self-regarding conduct includes *all* actions that do not require censorship or monopolization before they can be effected.

To apply the definition, imagine that Manic and Depressive want to engage in a sexual rite that Noble considers offensive. Given our ideal technology, Manic and Depressive have the right to communicate the fact of their mutual inclination in any way they choose; moreover, they have an equal right to shield their talk and actions from the rest of the world. If, however, they choose to make a "gift" of their R to others by allowing it to pass through their shields, Noble need only preprogram[3] his shield so as to block R from his perceptual field. In short, our ideal technology is equal to the task of protecting *both* the rights of Manic and Depressive to engage in their favored form of association *and* the right of Noble to be free of special sanctions imposed by others.

This is not to say, however, that the outcome generated by our transactional network will satisfy the demands of a clear-thinking utilitarian. Even though Manic and Depressive are out of sight, they need not be out of Noble's mind. Noble may be outraged at the thought that somebody somewhere is doing something of which he disapproves. Indeed, his distress may outweigh the joy of sex felt by Manic and Depressive. Moreover, I do not assert that Noble's harm is not really a harm or that it has not been caused by Manic and Depres-

---

3. Noble's shield must be designed in such a way as to permit him to exclude offensive R's from his perceptual field without experiencing each one. That's what it means to have a *shield*.

sive's conduct. Instead, I shall grant all this and still deny that Noble has reason to expect a liberal state to recognize his grievances as stating a legitimate complaint.

The argument should be familar. Noble clearly cannot say that Manic and Depressive are doing something the state may label bad in the face of the couple's contrary judgment. Nor can he say that he has the special right to censor their transmitters or tamper with their shields. What then *can* he say? If Noble cannot translate his distress into a liberal conversation, Manic and Depressive have an absolute right to engage in their favorite rites regardless of Noble's condemnation. Noble's difficulty, in short, is not psychological but cultural—his incapacity to make his claim intelligible within the bounds of liberal argument.

A dialogic reformulation of Mill's principle,[4] however, does more than restore its analytic power in areas, like sexual freedom and privacy, where its use is familiar. Liberalism's protection of such rights does not spring from some special solicitude for bizarre forms of sex play; instead, it is grounded in each citizen's ideal right to use his transactional power as he sees fit so long as he does not engage in any act of censorship or monopolization. The argument for sexual freedom is but a special case of the argument for freedom. Every person has a dialogic right to use his transmitter-shield in the way he thinks best. So long as you have equal transactional rights, you have no right to restrict my power simply because you think I am using it to join with others in a form of life you think despicable.

42. A GENERAL THEORY OF INITIAL ENTITLEMENTS

We can now redeem an early promise by describing a power structure that would permit our explorers to live together in a way that could be perfectly legitimated through Neutral dialogue. So long as our spaceship is inhabited by liberally educated citizens, none of whom genetically dominates another, the polity may achieve a perfectly legitimate initial distribution of new world resources by providing each citizen with a transactional mechanism that permits him to shield

4. My thinking about this problem was clarified by Thomas Scanlon's essay on "A Theory of Freedom of Expression," *Philosophy and Public Affairs* 1 (1972): 204. While Scanlon's arguments are different from mine, they helped me greatly in suggesting the plausibility of a non-utilitarian interpretation of Mill's principle.

an equal share of manna if he fails to find more advantageous relationships on his ideal transmitter.

Depending on his conception of the good, each citizen will use this transactional freedom in the way that seems best to him. Some may club together and establish one or another kind of tightly knit community. Others may choose to define *all* their relationships through an ongoing process of arms-length bargaining. And many may design more complicated arrangements—retaining some rights for themselves while ceding others to different groups governed by different decision-making principles.

On another level, different people will reach different agreements about their use of the transmitter-shield itself. Some people will agree with their like-minded friends to switch off their transmitters forever and settle down to the task of making their particular communal arrangements work. Others will insist upon their right to use their transmitter-shields in the future to form and reform relations over time in the light of their evolving experience, opportunities, and values. Within the common framework established by liberal conversation, people will be free to establish a communal life as complex and diverse as their search for meaning requires—all based upon principles of free exchange and mutual advantage.

This said, I do not wish to make any predictions as to the way our explorers will make use of their freedom as they begin life on their new world.[5] Even if all citizens lived identical lives, the resulting pattern of association would be entitled to as much respect as a pattern

---

5. There are many relationships between my ideal transactional structure and general equilibrium models familiar in contemporary microeconomic theory. While an extended technical discussion does not belong in this essay, perhaps a few orienting remarks will be useful.

Most important is the way that the liberal's *normative* analysis dovetails with the neoclassicist's *positive* analysis of the conditions under which a system of free exchange generates a Pareto–efficient set of economic outcomes. As is well known, unfettered free exchange will only lead to Pareto efficiency under very special conditions. For an accessible statement, see Francis M. Bator, "The Simple Analytics of Welfare Maximization," *American Economic Review* 47 (1957): 22. Nonetheless, the transactional system required by liberal ideals would vindicate several of the key assumptions neoclassical theorists require before they can make a link between free exchange and Pareto efficiency. Thus, the perfect shield permits each citizen to exclude any other person from any of the goods under his control—thereby making the neoclassicist's assumption of *universal markets* into an empirically accurate description of an ideally liberal world. Similarly, the neoclassicist's assumption of *costless negotiation* is vindicated by the design of the ideal transmitter. Finally, given the spaceship-computer's capacity to generate perfectly accurate empirical predictions, the citizenry should not have much difficulty arranging a set of efficient futures markets.

When the neoclassicist turns from the transactional technology to the demand functions prevailing in my ideal world, he will experience greater difficulties. Most importantly, liberal

that reflected the overwhelming diversity of human aspiration. No citizen's freedom of association depends on some political elite's approving the use he has made of his freedom. Indeed, the entire point of our earlier liberal conversations was to set the stage for a world in which everybody could use his *legitimate* initial endowments in the way he thinks best. So long as initial endowments have been distributed on a dialogically Neutral basis, each citizen can justify his choices by saying to every other: "While you may think I should spend my life in the pursuit of some other good, I'm afraid I must disagree. Moreover, I deny that you have the right to say that I'm mistaken. For my judgment in these matters is at least as good as yours is."

This is the closing line of an ideally liberal political conversation. The promise of ideal theory is a world in which all may speak in the accents of individual freedom. Yet while liberal dialogue permits each of us to gain public recognition as an autonomous person responsible for his own conception of the good, it cannot promise more than this. In particular, it cannot guarantee an end to the human suffering that comes with the exercise of moral freedom. Consider, for example, the fate of Michelangelo Crusoe, whose liberal education has convinced him of the importance of a single-minded commitment to a life of artistic creation. As he searches the associational options open to him, he finds that none of his fellow citizens thinks his art worth a damn. Not that Crusoe is a victim of genetic domination; he can function quite nicely in at least some forms of life that some of his fellow

---

ideals permit citizens to select any utility function they think best; hence interdependent utility functions cannot be excluded by assumption. Nor is there any reason to expect the over-all demand for particular commodities will exhibit the conditions of "gross substitution" that makes the general equilibrium theorist's life a happy one. See Kenneth Arrow and F. H. Hahn, *General Competitive Analysis* (San Francisco: Holden-Day, 1971), pp. 221–33. Hence the neoclassical theorist *cannot* guarantee the liberal Assembly that its ideal process of exchange will converge upon a *unique* equilibrium that satisfies Paretian conditions. While this *may* well happen if utility functions take particular shapes, there can be no guarantee that it *will* happen.

This means that the theory of exchange presented here is, in principle, incomplete. To finish the story, I would have to consider two final problems. First: if, as a result of demand conditions, multiple equilibria are possible, is there any liberal way of picking the particular equilibrium point toward which exchange ought to converge? While perhaps a fair lottery may serve as an adequate answer here, cf. § 61.6, a second problem is much more difficult. Demand conditions may sometimes make it impossible for *any* stable equilibrium to exist. If this is true, the liberal Assembly is faced with the task of designing constraints on the process of free exchange sufficient to assure stability. I suspect that modern game theory might be used to clarify greatly the issues at stake in the case of unstable equilibria. I am, however, hardly confident that the issues, once clarified, will admit of easy conversational solution.

citizens consider good; and the nature of these options is suitably displayed on Crusoe's transmitter-shield. The only trouble is that Crusoe considers the Rs open to him entirely worthless. Despite the judgment of his fellows, Crusoe thinks it better to devote himself entirely to his art in utter solitude. Looking forward to starvation and early death, Crusoe turns from his transmitter in protest:

CRUSOE: I have been abused by the powers that be!

COMMANDER: Well, I agree that you are terribly unhappy. But you must tell me why your unhappiness should be attributed to an unjust power structure. After all, everyone can't be happy in a world with finite resources. What then is your complaint? You have received an equal share of manna, like the rest of your fellow citizens.

CRUSOE: But what is manna without the capacity to use it in a meaningful form of life?

COMMANDER: I quite agree, and that is why you have been provided with this wonderful transmitter-shield.

CRUSOE: What's so great about it? No matter how loud I shout into the machine, nobody ever seems to say Yes.

COMMANDER: But you must admit that the transmitter *has* gotten your message to those most likely to think it worthwhile.

CRUSOE: Yes.

COMMANDER: And you have not had trouble using the transmitter to express the sort of relationship you have in mind.

CRUSOE: No trouble at all.

COMMANDER: And nobody else has been given a special right to punish your audience if it accepts your offers.

CRUSOE: Right.

COMMANDER: And nobody is taking advantage of your art without your consent!

CRUSOE: My shield is good for that at least.

COMMANDER: Then what are you complaining about?

CRUSOE: Very simple, dimwit. Nobody has recognized me for the great artist that I am.

COMMANDER: Surely it is not up to me to say they are wrong about that.

CRUSOE: But I am going to die if you don't do something!

COMMANDER: Everyone must die; there is nothing I can do about that.

CRUSOE: But I'm going to die *soon*.

COMMANDER: You could live longer if you accepted some of the offers that are coming in on the transmitter.

CRUSOE: Absolutely not; life on those terms is not worth living.

COMMANDER: You said it. I didn't.

CRUSOE: How can you be so heartless and unfeeling? I am in pain. Why won't you help me?

COMMANDER: Because helping you requires hurting somebody else. And you have yet to explain to me why you think this step is justified. Do you, for example, think you are entitled to more manna than the next fellow or that your offers of association are entitled to a privileged position in the transactional network?

CRUSOE: Enough of this quibbling. Isn't there *anybody* out there who will help me?

Now this last cry of help *need* not go unanswered in a liberal state. Nothing stops private citizens from responding to Crusoe's call.[6] They are free to give voluntarily what the Commander cannot force them to give through the exercise of illegitimate power. Nonetheless, Crusoe may fairly symbolize the tragic aspect of the liberal vision. People suffer not because they vainly imagine themselves to equal the gods in their wisdom but because the Commander refuses to engage in such godlike posturings and cannot bring herself to judge the intrinsic merit of Michelangelo's vision compared to those pursued by others. Yet, while its form is different, the root of the liberal tragedy remains the same as the Greek: a recognition of the limits imposed by a kind of ignorance that no human order should seek to surmount.

It would be a great mistake, then, to view the Commander's treatment of Crusoe as grounded in some naïve belief in the survival of the fittest. Instead of denying the tragic element of human life, liberal theory makes it central to an interpretation of social justice. So long as relative scarcity remains a feature of social existence, there can be no hope of a political solution that will end frustration and disappointment. While voluntary acts of benevolence and solidarity may ease one or another pain, they cannot end our common predicament until *all* of us are *absolutely* satisfied with what we are and have. While the liberal can understand, affirm, and participate in efforts to reach out

6. Except if Crusoe decides to commit suicide by shielding his pain from all people who might respond.

and ease the pain all of us feel, he builds a theory of justice on different ground: the right of each individual to interpret his own predicament in his own way without others presuming to judge the ultimate merit of his particular interpretation.

It is this right that links Crusoe's tragedy to a more common melodrama. Consider, for example, a variation on a script offered by Robert Nozick.[7] During the time our spaceship careens toward its destination, Wilt Chamberlain has been perfecting his hookshot with the aid of a perfect liberal education. When we arrive, Chamberlain's transmitter reveals that his talents are in very great demand. How is he to deal with the messages flooding his transmitter?

Like any other citizen, Chamberlain has the absolute right to use his transmitter to locate the offers that best fulfill his conception of the good. It is up to Chamberlain to decide whether to play basketball at all, whether to charge for every performance, whether he will play on the team with Noble or Depressive—making these decisions in the light of all the offers that his transmitter suggests are open to him. Nobody has the right to distort Chamberlain's decision by tampering with his transmitter so that he is kept in ignorance of some of the opportunities that are in fact open to him. Nor does anyone have the right to tamper with Chamberlain's shield so that he may be subjected to special sanctions if he has the temerity to reject a particularly noble offer. It is up to Chamberlain, and nobody else, to say how he will use his freedom; however trivial, however profound, at least the decision will be *Chamberlain's*.

Needless to say, these rights can only be taken as absolute in an ideal world that perfectly fulfills the other requirements of a liberal power structure. Thus, Chamberlain's messages cannot be given a privileged place in the transactional network; nor can his athletic abilities give him genetic dominance over any of his fellow citizens; nor may the educational system enshrine basketball in the holy of holies of public value; nor may Chamberlain begin adult life with more material assets than the next person. If all these conditions are fulfilled, however, then we have shown that *regardless of the use he makes of his freedom*, Chamberlain can justify his power position in a thoroughgoing Neutral dialogue.

From the vantage of liberal theory, then, Nozick's spirited defense

7. *Anarchy, State, and Utopia* (New York: Basic Books, 1974), pp. 161–63.

of Wilt Chamberlain's absolute right to make use of his talents is less wrong than it is myopic. For Nozick, of course, does not want to defend Chamberlain's rights in some ideal world but in the real world in which we live today. To put the point into our terms, Nozick's views would require us to adopt a striking position on the proper way of doing second-best theory. His unconditional defense of Chamberlain's freedom would make liberal sense *only* if it were sensible to address real-world problems *as if* we were *already* inhabiting the ideal utopia we are presently constructing in the mind's eye. This is, of course, an extreme position on the proper relationship between political ideals and social reality. Indeed, it will be the task of the theory of exploitation, developed in chapter 8, to demonstrate that Nozick's position is dialogically indefensible in a world deeply scarred by illegitimate domination. Our political problem is far more difficult than Nozick imagines; rather than a single-minded defense of absolute transactional freedom, the task is to defend the principle of free exchange while taking effective steps to remedy injustice in genetic, educational, and material endowments that have been unearthed by liberal dialogue.

43. THE LIBERAL CRITIQUE OF INDIVIDUALIST PROPERTY

For the moment, however, I shall put to one side all questions of the relationship between transactional freedom and the underlying injustice in the distribution of wealth, education, and ability. Even so, a critical issue remains: when we focus single-mindedly upon the existing transactional network, it plainly falls short of perfect flexibility. This means that, even when we heroically assume away the existence of injustice in initial endowments, Nozick's paean to the free market is unacceptable. Second-best limits on voluntary exchange can be defined only after liberal statesmen confront the serious inadequacies of a private-property regime in a world that remains chock-full of transactional rigidities.

43.1. *Negotiation Costs*
While we remain distant from the perfect transmitter, recent advances have permitted a quantum leap in our power to realize liberal transactional ideals. Such humble things as cheap mail and telephone

service have vastly increased each person's power to engage in a far-ranging search for relational possibilities; a cheap transportation system permits people to follow up initial probes with more intensive face-to-face communication. While liberals greet this new flexibility as an unambiguous advance, elitists use the new technology to tighten their repressive control: the mails are censored; conversations are bugged; transportation is controlled by restrictive "internal passport" systems. All this is intolerable in a liberal state.[8] While so much is clear, there are any number of perplexities. The most obvious involve technologies of mass communication: print, radio, movies, television. Given the high costs of entry, ordinary people must convince one of the established gatekeepers that their message is worth carrying. A critical question, then, is the criteria gatekeepers use to screen transmissions. Do they deny access to all messages except those that favor one or another dominant conception of the good? Or are gatekeepers under continuous pressure to accept any message that any considerable group may want to hear?

The liberal's fear of monopoly provides a starting point for analysis. If there are lots of competitive gatekeepers, each knows that some competing gatekeeper may accept any transmission he turns down. This may give each gatekeeper an incentive to maximize the audience tuning into his channels, even though the gatekeeper personally considers the message of no intrinsic value. It should be emphasized, however, that even a relatively diffuse system will be far from ideal. However diligent gatekeepers are in searching for new audiences, economies of scale will often make it far cheaper to serve large groups than small ones. To the extent that gatekeepers are liberated from market incentives, however, there is the ever present danger of a cartel decision to exclude opinions that the gatekeeping elite finds offensive. The problem of design cannot, then, be resolved by any simplistic formula. While monopoly in *any* form, governmental or private, is an unambiguous evil, liberal designers will often disagree on the way of diffusing gatekeeping authority to best fulfill liberal ideals—depending on their reading of technological possibilities, organizational realities, and cultural traditions. The object throughout must be to provide dissident citizens with networks that give them—no less than their more conventional fellows—the power to locate

---

8. Subject to national security and other third-best restriction. See §§ 53.1 and 63.5.

like-minded associates for common enterprises that seem mutually beneficial.

But there is another side to the question of access: the right of each citizen to choose which communications he wants to hear. In ideal theory, each receiver is equipped with a screening device that permits each citizen to block out all messages that he thinks are a waste of time. Once again, however, our present design capacities fall far short of this ideal. On the one hand, an unregulated "free market" in information suffers from any number of well-known defects: most obviously,[9] an ignorant person may, precisely *because* he is ignorant, pass up the chance to buy a bit of information that would redound greatly to his advantage. This means that laissez faire will systematically give some people special transactional advantages to exploit ignorance in ways they could hardly justify in a Neutral conversation. On the other hand, governmental efforts to protect the ignorant suffer from very different vices and virtues. While a person may be very grateful for receiving information he would never have purchased on his own, he may also be obliged to listen to a lot of stuff he would rather not waste his time on. The dilemma is familiar to all students of consumer protection, as is the variety of solutions whose plausibility depends on innumerable contextual elements.

However these problems are resolved in detail, only one thing is clear: negotiation costs will predictably remain substantial for many citizens. This means that an individualistic property solution cannot entirely escape dialogic critique. Groups of like-minded people who *could* have located each other with perfect transmitters will fail to find one another in the real world. To the extent that government regulation of individualistic property rights permits the reduction of negotiation costs, these measures can be readily justified in dialogic terms.

43.2. *Externalities*

As we go about our life in the real world, we do not make claims on a single manna-like good but on a multiplicity of things which are, at

9. Less obvious, but no less important, is the fact that people have incentives to over-invest in activities that others will use for the purpose of solving their problem in information-processing. See, e.g., A. Michael Spence, *Market Signalling* (Cambridge: Harvard University Press, 1973). Market signalling raises particularly acute normative problems when some citizens are prevented from making market-signalling investments—e.g. when employers use the race or sex of applicants as a proxy for information about candidate abilities that would otherwise be too costly to acquire. See Barbara Underwood, "Law and the Crystal Ball: Predicting Behavior with Statistical Inference and Individualized Judgment," *Yale Law Journal* 88(1979): 1408.

best, imperfect substitutes for one another: bauxite and limestone, oil and wood, land and air. This simple fact further compromises the dialogic legitimacy of laissez faire.

Not that the mere multiplicity of resources leads to serious perplexity. If that were the only problem, my story would simply end with each citizen holding a bundle containing equal amounts of many raw materials rather than a single all-purpose good. While this complexity would place added strain on the transactional system—as I seek to trade my share of limestone for a quantity of bauxite I value more highly—there is nothing analytically new here.

Serious problems arise only when it is recognized that some things can be shielded far more cheaply than others. If I want to build a car, I can cheaply exclude people who don't cooperate with me in its production. If I want to breathe clean air, I cannot cheaply exclude people who want to take a free ride on my efforts to preserve the environment. Given differential shielding, it is, ceteris paribus, harder for me to induce others to join in a mutual effort to clean the air than to build a car. This, of course, compounds the dialogic difficulties of a spokesman for a laissez faire specification of initial property rights. Not only does the classic form of private property impose transaction costs upon the like-minded; imperfect shielding encourages certain forms of association at the expense of others. None of this would be legitimate in an ideal framework, where no one has a special power to sanction anyone that is not possessed by everyone.

44. THE LIBERAL CRITIQUE OF COLLECTIVISM

It is not enough, then, for the second-best statesman to remain content with the pattern of search and shielding costs that evolve "naturally" from a political commitment to the classic system of unregulated "free" markets. Before such a system can be dialogically legitimated, the polity must correct the systematic biases costly negotiation and imperfect shielding impose upon the citizenry. The goal is clear enough in principle: those citizens unfairly disadvantaged by an individualistic property system may demand that government intervene to help them approximate the outcomes they would have reached under an ideal transactional network.

Implementing this goal, however, will predictably generate new second-best difficulties.[10] Just as the like-minded may protest against the systemic costs generated by an individualist regime, so too the deviant may protest against high exit costs imposed by a collectivist starting point. Imagine, for example, that many people are dissatisfied with prevailing levels of air quality and would be willing to sacrifice a good deal to improve their collective situation. If they begin transacting from an individualistic starting point, however, they will find it difficult or impossible to solve the negotiation and free-ride problems generated by an individualistic property structure. In contrast, if the air shed is treated as a collective asset, the polity will confront the problem of deviants who *truthfully* assert that they would be unwilling to pay for cleaner air *even in a world where they could not free ride on others' clean-up efforts*. So far as ideal theory is concerned, these people—no less than Wilt Chamberlain—have a perfect right to refuse to contribute to an activity if they think they have better ways of spending their time and manna. Unfortunately, however, recognizing this right under second-best conditions may open the door to the free-riding difficulty that made collectivism so attractive in the first place. Unlike the situation in ideal theory, here deviants cannot be readily deprived of cleaner air upon their refusal to pay a share of the costs. Thus, a person will have a strategic incentive to obtain a free ride merely by announcing that he is a deviant when in fact he would be willing to sacrifice a good deal for clean air under ideal conditions. The liberal state is, then, driven to a standard second-best perplexity: *both* the like-minded *and* the deviant may link their demands for collectivism and exit respectively to the liberal ideal of transactional flexibility. How, then, to respond?

45. LIBERAL SOLUTIONS

45.1. *Federalism*
The thing to avoid is a solution suggesting that only one side has a good argument. Even where air is concerned, there is no physical necessity that all of us breathe air of precisely the same quality. Instead, the world may be divided up into federal regions with *different*

---

10. I will focus exclusively on normative difficulties that will predictably attend collectivist interventions. Quite apart from these, there are serious practical difficulties in implementing collectivist solutions—which, in every case, must be soberly considered in shaping second-best policy. See § 63.

tax–air-quality combinations. Citizens who prefer dirty air and lower taxes may be expected to avoid the cleaner regions, and vice versa. Of course, such limited freedom of choice is a long way from the perfect shielding postulated by ideal theory. The world is not big enough to permit every conceivable air-tax combination to find a place in the sun. Even if a citizen disagrees with his region's air-tax trade-off, he may find the costs of moving to a more congenial region prohibitive. Despite these serious imperfections, however, a federal regime is far better than some all-or-nothing solution that would force *all* deviants to pay for a collectively specified level of good air or force *all* environmentalists to suffer with bad air merely because they cannot transcend the organizational hurdles imposed upon them by an individualistic property-holding system.

45.2. *Lindahl Solutions*

A bias toward federal solutions, however, is only one part of the liberal effort to design mechanisms that recognize that *both* the like-minded and the deviant have legitimate transactional interests. Thus, within each region, an effort should be made to link decisions about collective goods to the hypothetical responses of people equipped with an ideal transactional technology. Imagine, for example, that we were able to determine how much each inhabitant of our region would be willing to sacrifice for air quality before he would prefer to spend his material resources on other goods. For simplicity, assume that: clean air is more important to me than it is to you; you and I are the only inhabitants of our region; and only three levels of air quality (A, B, C) are feasible. The costs of each, as well as our willingness to bear them, are displayed in the following table:

Air Quality	Total Cost	*My* Willingness To Pay	*Your* Willingness To Pay
A	400	200	150
B	300	175	125
C	200	100	75

In a world with perfect shielding, you and I would not agree on A-quality air. While I am willing to sacrifice 200 manna units, I cannot force you to place the same high value on environmental purity. When confronted with the fact that you are willing to spend only 150 units on A-quality air, I have no right to declare you deviant and force you to hand over the extra 50 units you would rather spend on something else. It follows that the best second-best form of property ownership would *also* deny me the right to impose a 200 unit tax on you in the name of clean air. Cleanliness has precisely the same status as godliness in the liberal state—neither can be given a transcendent place in public values. If, however, we are too solicitous of the rights of the deviant, it may be easy to generate a transactional structure that will give us both so many free-ride incentives that we will end up with C-quality air, *worse* than the level we would have found mutually beneficial in an ideal system. The aim is to design a system that will generate a solution like B, where each of us is making a tax payment equal to the marginal benefit we are receiving from the collective good. This is the solution that would have been reached under ideal transactional conditions.

It is at this point that liberal theory makes contact with an important branch of economic theory. Students of public finance will recognize that the characteristics of the B solution are those specified by Lindahl in his classic analysis of the problem of public goods.[11] This means that the liberal statesman can take advantage of a rich body of theoretical and applied work in determining the decision-making structure that best approximates the Lindahl norm. Not that this literature suggests that the task of institutional construction is an easy one.[12] To the contrary, even in the best of all possible second-best worlds, some people will bear costs, and others will gain free rides, that would not have been acceptable in a world with an ideal transactional structure. Despite these inevitable imperfections, it *is* possible to move beyond heavy-handed collectivism and naïve laissez faire and design a set of institutions that respond to the problems posed by free riding while preserving exit rights for genuine dissidents. Armed with the principles of federalism and public finance, it is not too much to hope that

11. Erik Lindahl, "Just Taxation: A Postive Solution" in Richard A. Musgrave and Alan T. Peacock, eds., *Classics in the Theory of Public Finance* (London, New York: Macmillan, 1958) p. 168; see generally, Richard A. Musgrave and Peggy B. Musgrave, *Public Finance in Theory and Practice* (New York: McGraw-Hill, 1973), chap. 3.

12. Despite some clever new institutional schemes that aim to eliminate strategic incentives for dishonest free riding, e.g., Nicholas Tideman and Gordon Tulloch, "A New and Superior Process for Making Choices," *Journal of Political Economy* 84(1976): 1145, it is predictable that a host of imperfect devices will, depending on particular institutional contexts, be relied upon in an effort to approximate Lindahl solutions—ranging from the imposition of duties of fair play, A. John Simmons, "The Principle of Fair Play," *Philosophy and Public Affairs* 8 (1979): 307; through complex legal rules of civil liability, Guido Calabresi and A. Douglas Melamed, "Property Rules,

we may generate increasingly sophisticated structures for accommodating the interests of people who, for all their common citizenship, wish to impress radically different meanings upon their joint and several existences.

45.3. Privacy

There are issues—clean air is one—in which even the best available liberal solutions will fall far short of the liberal ideal. It may be possible to give people a choice between a few different levels of regional quality; it may be possible to link air quality to the willingness of each region's inhabitants to sacrifice other good things of life on its behalf; it may even be possible to distribute the costs of clean air in a way that tends toward a Lindahl equilibrium. Nonetheless, physical constraints will place definite limits upon the liberality of the decision-making structure: the earth is not big enough to permit each group of like-minded persons to select the precise level of clean air for which they are willing to pay.

In other cases, however, there *are* things a liberal statesman can do to ameliorate further the second-best tension between collectivist property and exit rights. Recall, for example, Noble's rage at the thought that Manic and Depressive were engaging in some despicable form of sexual activity behind their transmitter-shields. While we saw that Noble's rage could not be translated into a Neutral complaint, the problem increases in complexity under second-best conditions. People in the real world must confront the fact that it is very costly to insist on a perfect shield. While it may be possible for Proust to survive with his shield (virtually) intact, most of us find it advantageous to pursue a more public form of existence. Thus, when Noble, Manic, and Depressive leave their bedrooms without their shields, they must establish terms upon which their interactions will take place. Suppose that Manic and Depressive would prefer to conduct their public, as well as their private, dealings in the nude, while Noble is of the clothed persuasion. How, then, to manage the conflict that ensues when, thanks to imperfect shielding, both find themselves riding the same bus to work?

Liability Rules and Inalienability: One View of the Cathedral," *Harvard Law Review* 85 (1972): 1089; through sophisticated tax and subsidy schemes, William J. Baumol and Wallace E. Oates, *The Theory of Environmental Policy* (Englewood Cliffs, N.J.: Prentice-Hall, 1975), Bruce Ackerman, *Private Property and the Constitution* (New Haven: Yale University Press, 1977).

Once again, a federalist solution must be taken seriously. Noble has no right to complain if a group of nudists are allowed to establish regions in which it is they, and not he, whose preferences establish the background terms for interaction on collectivist property. In contrast to the air-pollution case, however, far more can be done to protect the exit rights of citizens who find that their values are inconsistent with those that rule the region. Deviants must have the right to use the entitlements they hold in the individualistic form to pursue their ideals. Thus, a group of nudists in a clothed region may nonetheless establish nudist beaches, parks, and business establishments by notifying their fellow citizens to keep out unless they are prepared to accept the deviant ground rules, and vice versa in nudist regions. The mere fact that such "unnatural" activities upset the region's nobles never suffices to justify special restrictions upon transactional freedom.

Such ambitious deviant projects, however, presuppose the existence of a significant minority group willing to pool their individualistic bits of property together to form the basis of a substantial communal life. A deviant's dialogic rights, however, are not dependent upon the number of people who agree with his conception of the good. Suppose, for example, that Nudist takes advantage of a second-best negotiation system to find that there are only a handful of citizens in his region who share his beliefs—too few to establish a rich collective life with one another. Moreover, while more substantial populations may exist in other regions, Nudist finds that other benefits of living in his region outweigh the benefits of a move to more natural environments. Making the best of his situation, then, he invites his fellow nudists to his home, where they may live out a shadow of their mutual ideals. Here the right to privacy plays a strategic role in the liberal ideal of transactional flexibility. *Not*, mind you, because liberals have a special fondness for nudity or other forms of personal intimacy. If it were physically possible to permit each person to determine his own air quality, each citizen would have an equally fundamental right to exit from his region's collective determinations. Only it happens that the structure of the air-pollution problem makes this exit right infeasible, while the structure of the nudity problem makes it entirely possible to permit many forms of exit from the collectively established interactional norms. While it may be very costly to shield Nobles when they confront Nudist on the bus, no similar defense can be seriously entertained when it comes to the bedroom. Rather than representing a good-faith effort to manage conflicts between Nudists and Nobles in a world of imperfect shielding, bedroom regulation only makes sense as an effort to suppress deviant forms of life. Respect for the right of privacy serves as a litmus test for a collective commitment to the liberal ideal of transactional flexibility.

46. CONSENT AND UTILITY IN TRANSACTIONAL THEORY

Having glimpsed once more the perplexities of second best, step back to consider the overall shape of the transactional theory we have constructed. To begin, notice the way the theory challenges a convenient dichotomy that has gained currency in recent political philosophy. It has become popular to divide the question of legitimacy into two, almost watertight, compartments—in one box are "micro-questions" addressed to the fairness of individual transactions between particular people; in another, are "macro-questions" implicating basic social institutions. Thus, Nozick tries to specify principles of fraud and duress as if this effort had nothing to do with the principles regulating other dimensions of the power struggle; Rawls returns the compliment by restricting his principles of justice to something called the "basic structure," specifically exempting all issues involving the fairness of particular transactions.[13] In contrast, the dialogic principles regulating free exchange are an inextricable part of a larger liberal theory of social justice. Without transactional flexibility, a liberal state cannot defend the property system—be it individualist or collectivist—under which initial claims to material wealth are distributed. If a citizen has obtained a transactional advantage over his fellows, he must respond to the same question of legitimacy that confronts the holders of genetic, educational, or material advantage. Rather than drawing an arbitrary limitation on the scope of its principles of legitimacy, liberal dialogue governs *all* dimensions of the power struggle—whether they concern micro-interactions between two individuals or macro-dealings between generations.

The pursuit of liberal dialogue, however, does more than reveal a

13. Compare Robert Nozick, *Anarchy, State and Utopia*, chap. seven and especially pp. 204–12, with John Rawls, *A Theory of Justice*, pp. 7–11, and especially, "The Basic Structure as Subject" in A. Goldman and J. Kim, eds., *Values and Morals* (Dordrecht: D. Reidel, 1978), pp. 41–71.

self-imposed limitation of recent work. It provides a framework within which the concerns of traditional liberal theories may both be refined and reformulated.

46.1. *Contract*

In protecting *any* relationship that is the product of a free exchange between consenting adults, ideal liberal theory attempts a rapprochement with voluntarist ideas central to the contractarian tradition. Nonetheless, differences remain. Most important, my theory does not deal in the *imagined* consent accorded by primitives emerging from a prepolitical state of nature hypothesized by classic writers. Nor do I join Rawls in appealing to a *hypothetical* consent said to be forthcoming from citizens who have stripped themselves of self-identity and all understanding of their particular social situation. Rather than making a metaphor of consent, ideal theory focuses upon the *explicit* agreements made by flesh and blood people on the basis of their particular insights into the concrete opportunities that social life affords them. Rather than imagining that all citizens assent to a *uniform* social compact, ideal theory permits adults to enter *diverse* forms of consensual community that best express their particular ideals. Yet, for all this, liberal theory retains an affinity with contractualist concerns—at least if the core of this tradition is an insistence that the forms of social life be rooted in the self-conscious value affirmations of autonomous individuals.

Even at the moment of its greatest triumph, however, this voluntarist impulse is anchored in a larger dialogic theory of legitimacy. Citizens have a perfect right to demand that all special forms of association be based on consent only in a world endowed with a perfectly just power structure—in which the transactional framework, educational system, and distribution of material wealth and genetic endowment can all be justified in perfectly Neutral dialogue. Mutual dialogue, not individual will, is the center of the system. Freedom of exchange emerges as one—but only one—of the conclusions of a political discourse that denies one citizen the right to assert his moral superiority over another.

Even this, however, suggests too unequivocal an endorsement of contract. In the end, ideal theory provides a platform from which one may question the contractarian's deepest intuitive certainties. To see the problem, imagine a citizen—I shall call him Shifty—contemplating his future under an ideal technology of justice. As he emerges from the spaceship at the age of twenty, Shifty is committed to a rigorously ascetic form of communal life; unhappily, the ship's computers also predict that there will come a time (say, age forty) when he will desert his sackcloth and enter upon a libertine phase. Assume further that after canvassing his relational options, Shifty has selected subcommunity X as the one best suited to his present (ascetic) purposes, and that the other members of the subcommunity much prefer a subcommunal compact that demands lifelong commitment from all its members. When faced with this demand, Shifty has three options. First, he may try to obtain a special contractual exit right by undertaking specially onerous obligations during the twenty-year period of his membership. Second, he may choose to live in some other subcommunity, Y, which is otherwise less satisfactory but whose compact allows exit at the age of forty.

Finally, and most interestingly, the twenty-year-old Shifty may condemn the predicted views of the forty-year-old Shifty and seek to make it as difficult as possible for his future self to pursue its libertine ways. On this scenario, Shifty gladly affirms a contractual term authorizing the Xers to take all the necessary steps to curb his future effort to depart from the commune. If the young Shifty follows this course, the liberal polity will confront a peculiar problem when the older Shifty tries to escape from the ascetic commune and his fellow Xers seek to bar his way. Shifty has set himself against himself, and the Commander will then be obliged to determine which of the mutually inconsistent conceptions of self is to be given respect. Is it to be the views of the twenty-year-old Shifty inscribed on the subcommunal compact or the views of the flesh-and-blood forty-year-old who stands before her?

Perhaps there is an answer to this question somewhere in the metaphysics of time and self. At present, however, I am unwilling to assert that a convincing case can be made on behalf of any single view; perhaps the best that can be done is to restrict the field to a number of plausible theories.[14] For purposes of the present essay, I shall interpret the Neutrality principle to permit the Commander to adopt *either* view of the Shifty case. If she holds Shifty to his contract, she may

14. For a selection, see the views collected by John Perry, ed., *Personal Identity* (Berkleley: University of California Press, 1975) and Amelie Rorty, ed., *The Identities of Persons* (Berkeley: University of California Press, 1976).

legitimately say: "Twenty years ago, you said that this contract was the best way of fulfilling your conception of the good. And I will not listen now when you wish to put this assertion into question." If, however, she permits Shifty to escape his contractual obligation, I shall permit her to say: "I'm not interested in what Shifty said at some half-forgotten time. It is the talk of the flesh-and-blood speaker before me that is of overriding concern. And once this is conceded, I must protect his right as a citizen to exit from associations imposed upon him by the system of property holdings in which he finds himself."

In raising the problematic aspect of contract, however, I mean to do more than confess myself unequal to its satisfactory theoretical resolution.[15] For the ambiguities beclouding the liberal position compare favorably, I think, to the simplistic certainty with which a contract theorist would analyze Shifty's problem. However different contractarians are from one another, all agree that the paradigmatic case in which a person is *justly* bound by the principles of a social compact is one where he has actually given his free and knowing consent to its provisions at a previous point in time. If people are not fairly bound by contracts to which they have given their *actual* consent, why should they be bound to a social contract to which they have only given their *hypothetical* consent?

To free Shifty from his *express* agreement, then, threatens to shake the very foundations of the contractarian's effort to found society on a *hypothetical* contract. In contrast, dialogic theory permits us to question the basic premise upon which the contractualist endeavor proceeds. As the Shifty case demonstrates, it is *not* clear that citizens who give their knowing and explicit consent to a contract should always be held to its terms. There may be a place for the law of bankruptcy, as well as the law of contract, in the ideal liberal state.

A final assessment of contractualist themes in transactional theory demands, then, a complex accounting. On the one hand, dialogic theory, like its contractarian counterpart, is committed to each individual's right to determine his own ends in life. On the other hand, it is dialogue, not contract, which serves as the central bond between citi-

15. The practical implications of this theroretical indeterminacy are not so serious as they may first appear. Even if the Commander were to take the extreme (and surely untenable) view that the elder Shifty should *always* be legally free to dishonor the younger's promises, citizens will still be able to engage in a wide range of associational activities. Non-enforcement would simply increase the risks involved in these activities (and hence their cost), thereby inducing citizens marginally to prefer (at any particular timeslice) patterns of life which entail less long-term risk.

zens. This means that liberalism permits itself a more questioning attitude towards contractual behavior than can its competitor. On the level of policy, this attitude will be reflected in a continuing insistence that the claims of free contract be appraised against the background of power relationships established by the transactional framework and the distribution of wealth, education, and ability. On the philosophical level, the liberal can have the courage to question the doubtful notion that a promise, once fairly made, must *always* be kept. Freed from the emphatic certainties about the self and time implicit in the contractarian's position, he can permit himself to wonder about these mysteries without discrediting the master concept organizing liberal thought.

46.2. *Utility*

Despite its affinities with contractarian thought, there is much in the dialogic analysis that will find favor in utilitarian circles. Like the utilitarian, the liberal does not make a fetish out of free contract; both theories try to locate the value of exchange within a larger noncontractarian framework of analysis. Moreover, both scrutinize this larger transactional setting with similar questions in mind. First, like the liberal, the utilitarian will scrutinize the facilities for negotiation provided by the transactional system; so long as one assumes that each adult is in the best position to know what will make him happy, low negotiation costs increase the chances that the contracting parties have located the exchanges that will make them as happy as scarce resources will allow. Second, the utilitarian will agree that externalities represent a serious problem. As soon as the contractors can impose disutilities on others without first obtaining their agreement, it is no longer clear that overall utility will rise as a result of a free exchange. As a consequence, collective ownership of an asset may—depending on the costs of government intervention—be a happier solution. Third, when collective ownership is justified, the utilitarian will agree that the best use of the asset should not be determined by the fiat of some political elite but by a calculus that measures the costs and benefits imposed on all concerned citizens.

But important differences remain. From the liberal point of view, the utilitarian trivializes the issues of principle raised by transactional structure. A cheap negotiation system is not merely one among countless ways of increasing felicity; it is critical to the dialogic legitimation of the individualistic elements of the prevailing property system. Similarly, the protection of privacy and other exit rights is a critical element in the dialogic legitimation of the collectivist elements of the system. It follows that a citizen cannot be denied such rights simply by showing that this will make other people happy. Instead, an effort must be made to convince him that the transactional system, taken as a whole, represents a fair approximation of the liberal ideal of perfect flexibility. Doubtless there will be room for good-faith disagreement on this issue. Nonetheless, I hope to show, in chapter 8, that there *are* serious limits on the extent to which statesman can compromise liberal ideals without depriving the polity of its dialogic legitimacy.[16]

Despite these differences, however, it is hardly surprising that dialogic theory can find the greatest common ground with its competitors in precisely the area where the liberal tradition is richest: in the affirmation of the right of every citizen to exchange goods, services, and meanings with his fellows on terms that do not require him to concede that his search for the good is any less important than his fellows' pursuit of happiness.

16. On a more technical, but hardly trivial, level, liberals and utilitarians will disagree on the standards for managing collective resources. For the liberal, the aim is to reach an outcome that would have been achieved under ideally flexible conditions. In defining this goal, the liberal statesman wants to know how much of his material assets each citizen would be willing to sacrifice for a given level of collective output. In contrast, the utilitarian will not define his objective in terms of the citizenry's willingness to sacrifice *material* assets but in terms of the citizenry's *subjective* satisfaction. For the liberal, this effort to move beyond revealed preferences represents an illegitimate effort to measure disparate ideals by a common yardstick. See § 13.1. This reluctance to move beyond revealed preferences is one of the many features that liberal theory shares with contemporary welfare economics.

7

TRUSTEESHIP

47. THE QUESTION OF INHERITANCE

Imagine that the founders of our new world have achieved a success beyond their dreams. Each and every power structure—genetic, educational, material, transactional—has been arranged in a way that supports a perfectly Neutral dialogue of justification. Within this legitimating framework, the first generation lives out its life, each citizen using his rightful powers to impose (or discover) a meaning that may (or may not) be shared with others in one or another of the communities that abound in our liberal world.

Then there is death. Foreseeing the inevitable, the first generation attempts to set the terms on which the second will continue after their parents are gone. How does liberal dialogue constrain the use of this final power?

Consider the likely position of the parental generation when it lets go. While in the beginning a material equality prevailed among an undominated citizenry, in the end there will be a great disparity in personal histories. Some will have used the transactional system to gain enormous wealth; others will die with nothing but their name. Some with few material possessions will exercise great moral leadership in one or another community; others will amass material fortunes to find themselves the objects of widespread contempt. Still others are solitary and poor—some brutish, some wise. As this multitude nears death, most will wish to influence the future in a way each thinks good. If each is allowed to use his power as he sees fit, the second generation will begin with a power structure very different from the one with which the first began. Instead of undominated equality,[1] some children will obtain enormous wealth, while the dispossessed will begin with nothing but their labor.

---

1. "Undominated equality" is being used as a shorthand for all the conditions enumerated in the preceding chapters.

And what is wrong with that? As we have seen, Michelangelo Crusoe, Wilt Chamberlain, and the rest *generally* have a right to use their time and manna in the way they think best. Why, then, can they not decide to give a head start to their children—or anybody else they think deserving? What, if anything, marks "intergenerational" preferences off from other, entirely legitimate, preferences?

As Robert Nozick's recent book makes plain,[2] this question can be answered in a way that calls into question the importance of all our work up to this point. According to Nozick, so long as the first generation began from a just starting point at Time One, individual seniors may pick out particular juniors for special favor—by gift, inheritance, or otherwise. The fact that a rich junior can trace his title through a series of voluntary actions to an initially just Time One discharges him—so far as Nozick is concerned—from any claim of injustice made by his second-generation contemporaries. In principle, all eternity could be barred from all claims of injustice so long as a single generation had attained a just starting point for a single moment.

This extraordinary conclusion, I shall argue, is entirely inconsistent with the principles generated through liberal dialogue. Even if I were wrong, however, this would be of very little practical importance to our present social predicament. For it should be fairly obvious by now that the human race has *never* in its long history approached a single moment at which a single generation's starting point was arranged in a way that approximated the liberal ideal of undominated equality. We are, in short, at generation zero. It will suffice for us to build the foundations for generation one; we may, as a practical matter, safely leave the status of generation two to our children. Practicalities aside, the problem of inheritance is of such great theoretical importance that we must confront it head-on if we hope to grasp the shape of liberal ideals.

48. TRUSTEESHIP: A SIMPLE MODEL

Begin with a simple model. Assume that Manic and Depressive are the only members of the first generation and that they have two children, neither of whom genetically dominates the other. Both Manic Junior and Depressive Junior are in the final stages of a perfect liberal education. As they approach full citizenship, their parents approach death.

2. *Anarchy, State and Utopia*, pp. 149–82.

The model's critical assumption is that the two generations share only a single moment during which both coexist as full citizens, each charged with the full burden of dialogue. During this moment, the first generation asserts its right to determine each child's initial wealth.

48.1. *Minimal Trusteeship*

To simplify further, assume that Manic and Depressive have, mirabili dictu, ended where they began—each with a single grain of manna under his control. On their deathbeds, each announces his intention to pass on half a grain to his namesake; the two seniors, however, propose to spend the other half on a giant fireworks display commemorating their achievements. Upon hearing this announcement, the two juniors rise in protest. The death scene, then, is dialogue:

SENIORS: Let there be light!

JUNIORS: Not if we have anything to say about it.

SENIORS: Why are you being so selfish? Isn't half a grain enough?

JUNIORS: This is a question of justice, not selfishness. After all, when you started out in life, each of you received a whole grain as your initial endowment.

SENIORS: True.

JUNIORS: And why should we start off with less?

SENIORS: Well, you weren't there when we began.

JUNIORS: Why should that matter? Do you think that citizens who are born early are intrinsically superior to those who are born late?

SENIORS: We can't say that. It would violate Neutrality.

JUNIORS: Well, then, how *can* you justify the fact that your starting point was better than ours promises to be?

SENIORS: (*Silence.*)

JUNIORS: While you are searching for a Neutral reason, let us give you one to support our claim. We think that all citizens are at least as good as one another regardless of their date of birth. If we're as least as good as you are, we should start out in life with at least as much manna as you did.

So far as ideal theory is concerned, the bad trustee stands no better than any other kind of thief.[3] To see this, recall the grounds upon which the Commander legitimates her effort to deter thievery of the

3. See also the dialogue rehearsed at § 25.

garden-variety kind.[4] When a thief is stopped from stealing his victim's manna, the Commander does not deny that the thief may suffer a very real disappointment; nor does she even say that the utility loss sufferred by the thief is outweighed by the utility gains obtained by the victim (as well as the rest of society). Instead, the reason why the thief is *rightly* deterred is that he is attempting a power play that he cannot justify without asserting his moral superiority over his fellow citizens.

And the same holds true for a breach of trusteeship, for what is the difference between taking your neighbor's initial endowment and taking the endowment of a citizen who you know will be your neighbor? While it is true that the aggrieved victim will not challenge the action immediately, we have stipulated, in this model, that there *will* come a time when Senior will be called to account for his conduct by Junior. And at that time, Senior will find nothing Neutral to say in defense of depriving Junior of his right to an equal starting place. In short, unless Senior has fulfilled his trusteeship obligation, the Commander knows that an illiberal power relationship will come into existence. And if she hopes to maintain a perfect liberal order, she must intervene here no less than in the case of simple theft.

48.2. *Trusteeship and Equality*

Assume now that both seniors have fulfilled their minimal trusteeship obligation by engaging in a "minimal investment strategy," which assures that each junior will have at least one grain of manna with which to begin his adult life. Manic Senior, however, is not content with this minimal commitment. Instead, he has worked his grain of manna long and hard so that he might pass on five grains to his only child; Depressive, in contrast, contents himself with passing only a single grain to his counterpart. Can Depressive Junior maintain a legitimate complaint in a deathbed dialogue with Manic Senior?

DEPRESSIVE JUNIOR: I want some of the extra gains of manna you've produced.
MANIC SENIOR: You can't have any.
DEPRESSIVE JUNIOR: Why not? I'm at least as good as you are.
MANIC SENIOR: And you're starting out in life with one grain of manna just like I did. If you want to accumulate five grains, you can

4. §§ 19.3 and 19.4.

try to achieve this ambition within a perfectly legitimate interactional structure—just as I did. So what are you complaining about?

DEPRESSIVE JUNIOR: I don't object to *your* holding the five grains. I simply deny that you can give them to Manic Junior.

MANIC SENIOR: Why can't I use this manna in the way that seems best to me? Surely you couldn't complain if I used my four grains of "supertrusteeship" manna in a gigantic fireworks display. Why, then, can you complain if I give it to Manic Junior instead?

DEPRESSIVE JUNIOR: When you began with one grain, everybody else did too. Now you're trying to deny me the good of initial equality. Why should I be worse off simply because I'm a member of generation two rather than generation one?

MANIC SENIOR: You mean to say that you feel bad simply because others start out richer than you?

DEPRESSIVE JUNIOR: That's right.

MANIC SENIOR: That's what I call envy, pure and simple.

DEPRESSIVE JUNIOR: Call it what you like—envy or a proper sense of my moral dignity. The point is that you had this good of initial equality and I do not. Why, then, should I not start out on the same terms you did?

MANIC SENIOR: (*Silence.*)

DEPRESSIVE JUNIOR: Well, until you come up with a Neutral answer, you have no right to use your power to my disadvantage.

This is not to say that Manic Senior is entirely barred from giving a gift to his posterity. So long as he divides his gift among the *entire* second generation, his act of benevolence does not infringe the rights of any of the younger Manic's peers. Each will begin adult life under conditions of initial equality that mirror the first generation's, and none will complain about their extra stock of manna.[5]

48.3. *Waiver*

But isn't there still a way in which Manic Senior may legitimately provide a special advantage for a favored youth? The key here is that

5. A second generation Ascetic may, however, respond by refusing to make use of the gift. See § 15.1. It should also be plain that Senior's age-mates in generation one have no right to protest his gift to generation two. So far as they are concerned, Senior's gift to his successors is no different from any other use that he might make of his transactional freedom. See the dialogue of Michelangelo Crusoe, § 42.

Manic Senior is under no *obligation* to hand over *any* of his "super-trusteeship" assets to the second generation. So long as each junior receives a single grain, neither can complain that he is the victim of discrimination on the basis of his date of birth. Thus, imagine that Manic Senior responds to the last conversation by announcing a plan to spend his four extra grains of manna on a fireworks display:

MANIC SENIOR: Well, if you say I must give out the manna equally, I'm going to make sure that my surplus is all spent before I go. Start off with a grain apiece, and I'll go out with a bang while you whimper. . . .

MANIC JUNIOR: But, Dad!

MANIC SENIOR: Sorry, but you'll have to talk to that little snit Depressive Junior, not me. If he wants justice, justice is what you'll get.

DEPRESSIVE JUNIOR: But you haven't been listening to me carefully enough. While I have a right to insist on an equal division, I didn't say that initial equality was a pearl beyond price. In fact, I'm willing to put a very particular price on it.

MANIC SENIOR: What do you mean?

DEPRESSIVE JUNIOR: If you give me one of your extra grains, I won't object if your little Manic takes the other three.

MANIC SENIOR: I don't get it. Do you or do you not have a fundamental right to initial equality?

DEPRESSIVE JUNIOR: I have the right to insist on a bundle of rights no worse than yours. And, as far as I'm concerned, this would be true if I traded my right to initial equality for the right to an extra gain of manna.

MANIC SENIOR: Well, then, where do I stand?

DEPRESSIVE JUNIOR: That's for you to say. It all depends on whether you value your big bang more than an outcome that gives your boy four grains of manna while I get two.

Any realistic application of the waiver dialogue will, of course, confront serious second-best complexities. Most obviously, it will be necessary for generation one to determine its trusteeship investment policy at a time when generation two is still in toddling clothes. Since the younger generation can't explicitly tell its elders the extent to which it is willing to waive its birthrights, the proper application of the waiver rationale will inevitably be controversial. Given the importance of this issue I shall return to it in Part Three after developing a more general framework for second-best decision making.[6] I raise the problem now only to caution the partisans of unequal bequest that the concept of waiver is hardly a royal highway beyond the liberal commitment to undominated equality.

49. COMPLEXITIES: THE PROBLEM OF CONTINUITY

Our simple model generates a stark contrast in the legitimate ways a citizen may deal with people in different generations. On the one hand, seniors may not deprive their juniors of their prima facie[7] right to a starting point of undominated equality; on the other hand, the Crusoe dialogue of the last chapter[8] establishes that citizens of the same generation may ignore the pleas of a contemporary for special assistance. Intragenerational freedom is married with intergenerational trusteeship.

Having established this basic pattern, we must apply it in a more realistic world. Thus far we have pictured the intergenerational transfer of power as if it were an abrupt shift from one age cohort to another. But, in fact, the transfer is continuous in at least two senses. First, people of different ages do not confront one another for a single moment of time; instead, they coexist as full citizens for long periods. Second, generations are not neatly divided into groups born N years after one another; instead, citizens enter and leave the social world continuously over time. How do these facts change the substance of our conclusions?

From one perspective, very little. Even within a continuous model, the fact remains that every individual does have a moment of entry into, and departure from, the adult world. And at these moments, the dialogues of the simple model remain relevant. Thus, at the moment of his induction into full citizenship, we may imagine a junior making a dialogic demand upon those seniors who are about to die—demanding, as before, a Neutral explanation if any of them wishes to use his powers of bequest to violate the entering citizen's right to a starting point of undominated equality. The fiscal system that emerges from this dialogue is one that is constantly transferring wealth from

6. See §§ 57 and 62.
7. Prima facie because of the conceptual possibility of a waiver argument.
8. See § 42.

those who are leaving the system to those who are entering it. At one end, there is a taxing system that, at the very least, discharges the dying citizenry's minimal trusteeship obligation; at the other end, each entering citizen receives a share of material wealth that is *equal* to that of others who are roughly contemporary and *no less* than that received by his predecessors. Inequalities of material endowment are authorized only to the extent that it is reasonable to anticipate a unanimous waiver by entering juniors.

A new issue arises, however, when a junior turns from the departing seniors to those elders with whom he will share the new world for much of his life. Elders are *both* predecessors and contemporaries. Yet under the first characterization, they are bound by strict trusteeship; under the second, they are granted the most perfect freedom. What is needed is a set of characterization rules indicating the occasions when elder-junior relations are analyzable under one rubric rather than the other.

49.1. *The Domain of Intergenerational Freedom*

Begin with an easy case. Here, while the parties to the relationship are of different ages, they have never encountered each other before the younger participant reached the age of full citizenship. I shall argue that in all such cases, the elder-junior relation should be regulated by the Crusoe dialogue. To fix ideas, imagine that Noble Junior has, after a liberal education, chosen architecture as his career. As soon as he qualifies for full citizenship at Time Two, Noble Junior transmits his plans for a dream house into the communications network. His designs meet with a positive response. In particular, Manic Elder, aged forty, wants to pay Noble Junior to build the house for him. Just as the deal is to be sealed, Depressive Junior intervenes:

DEPRESSIVE JUNIOR: You are getting an unfair advantage over me!

NOBLE JUNIOR: How? Do I dominate you genetically? Am I starting out with more manna than you are?

DEPRESSIVE JUNIOR: No, but you have this nice offer appearing on your transmitter-shield, while I don't.

NOBLE JUNIOR: I've heard this before. It's Crusoe's complaint. But I thought we agreed that Crusoe's complaint was no good. How is yours any different?

DEPRESSIVE JUNIOR: Manic is not one of our age-mates.

NOBLE JUNIOR: So what? How has he used the power his age gives him to your disadvantage? Did *he* start out with more than you do? Does *he* genetically dominate you?

DEPRESSIVE JUNIOR: No, but he has destroyed my right to start off equally with you.

NOBLE JUNIOR: I don't understand. You *have* started off equally with me. But it's no longer Time Two. It's Two + N. And both of us have a right to select the associational options that seem best to us. Manic just happens to be in my set of possible options.

DEPRESSIVE JUNIOR: But he isn't in mine. And that's unfair!

NOBLE JUNIOR: But did you have a fair chance to convince him of the merit of your project as compared to mine?

DEPRESSIVE JUNIOR: Yes, both of us sent our messages through the transmitter system. Only yours got a positive reply and mine didn't.

NOBLE JUNIOR: This *is* precisely Crusoe's complaint!

DEPRESSIVE JUNIOR: Not quite. Manic, you see, was a full citizen before we were.

NOBLE JUNIOR: So what? Are you saying that simply because Manic is older than we are, he is obligated to accept your offer rather than mine?

DEPRESSIVE JUNIOR: That would never pass the Neutrality constraint.

NOBLE JUNIOR: So, then, what are you saying?

DEPRESSIVE JUNIOR: (*Silence.*)

NOBLE JUNIOR: Well, until you find something to distinguish the case, I claim that the Crusoe dialogue applies to our present power struggle.

So long as Manic Elder did not know Noble Junior before Time Two, Noble Junior cannot be said to have gained a special transactional advantage from Elder's superior age. Yet if this is true, then the Crusoe dialogue establishes that Depressive cannot justly complain simply because Manic has selected a competitor's offer over his own.

49.2. *The Domain of Intergenerational Trusteeship*

To construct the "easy" case on the other side of the conversational line, imagine that Manic Elder has been intimately involved in Noble Junior's upbringing—as natural parent, primary educator, and principal guardian. Assume, however, that when Time Two tolls, Manic Elder finds Noble Junior an altogether despicable person with whom, ordinarily, he would have nothing to do. Nonetheless, Manic Elder has a strong view of the obligations of paternity. Despite his distaste for his child, he sits through the induction ceremony at Time Two, and then, at Two + N, approaches him with a gift. Depressive Junior once again intervenes:

DEPRESSIVE JUNIOR: What's going on here! I thought Noble and I were supposed to start off equally.

NOBLE JUNIOR: Well, we have. At Time Two, both of us received a grain of manna, no more, no less.

DEPRESSIVE JUNIOR: And now you're getting lots more!

NOBLE JUNIOR: Haven't we just gone through this? Tell me, you wouldn't have an objection to this gift if I had received it from an elder whom I never met before Time Two.

DEPRESSIVE JUNIOR: But this is no ordinary elder. This is your parent.

NOBLE JUNIOR: So what?

DEPRESSIVE JUNIOR: I didn't have a fair chance to persuade him to favor me rather than you during all that time before Two.

NOBLE JUNIOR: That couldn't be helped. Both of us had to receive a liberal education, and the only way this could be done was to distribute particular children to particular grown-ups.

DEPRESSIVE JUNIOR: Yes, but we're talking about a power not entailed by this initial educational decision. Just because Manic was your principal educator up to Time Two doesn't mean you should also have the special power to call on your past relationship once you are an adult. What right do you have to exploit this power over Manic when I am denied an equivalent power? Do you think you are intrinsically better than I am?

NOBLE JUNIOR: But how can you be so sure that I've received this gift as a result of the special access I've had to Manic?

MANIC ELDER: Well, I'm afraid Depressive's right on that one. If you weren't my child, I would have never singled you out.

DEPRESSIVE JUNIOR: I told you so!

MANIC ELDER: Not so fast. The fact remains that I *have* singled Noble out. And I fail to see why my preference should not be honored. After all, it's my manna, isn't it?

DEPRESSIVE JUNIOR: But as our earlier dialogues demonstrated, the grain of manna you took at Time One was impressed with a trusteeship. You can't use your temporal priority over me to deny me my initial rights to undominated equality.

49.3. *Conflict between the Principles*

And now for the harder cases. Here Manic has learned to love his child over their long time together. Thus, when Manic offers Noble Junior a gift at Time Two + N, he no longer need make the damaging concession that provided the key to the previous dialogue:

MANIC ELDER: I'd prefer Noble Junior to Depressive Junior even if Noble weren't my child.

DEPRESSIVE JUNIOR: Why?

MANIC ELDER: I find Noble more lovable.

DEPRESSIVE ELDER: That's because you got to know him better before he and I were full citizens. Yet his preferential access to you cannot serve as a reason for depriving me of my initial rights to undominated equality.

MANIC ELDER: Why are you so sure that my present affections are entirely the product of my past associations? Surely a liberal polity cannot say it's a bad thing for a parent to become a friend. And remember that you would have no objection if I fell in love with some complete stranger and lavished gifts upon him!

DEPRESSIVE JUNIOR: You have a point. I've already conceded as much.

MANIC ELDER: And I tell you that I would befriend Noble even if he had been a stranger.

DEPRESSIVE JUNIOR: You tell me so, but how can you be so certain?

MANIC ELDER: Well, I can hardly be entirely certain about hypothetical speculation on such personal matters. But, by the same token, you can't be so sure I'm wrong.

DEPRESSIVE JUNIOR: Where does this uncertainty lead us?

MANIC ELDER: To the recognition that ours is a hard case. If I would have chosen Noble anyway, then my right to give the gift is justified; if not, not.

DEPRESSIVE JUNIOR: But as a practical matter, we can't know which side of the line you fall on. What, then, are we going to do?

MANIC ELDER: Given our uncertainty, I guess the sensible thing is to recognize the relevance of both the principle of intergenerational trusteeship and the principle of intragenerational freedom.
COMMANDER: Well, then, how are we to accommodate these conflicting norms?
DEPRESSIVE JUNIOR: How about this? Generally speaking, the trusteeship norm should be emphasized when parents give large material gifts. It is here where the child gains a general transactional advantage over his age-mates. In contrast, the norm of free exchange should apply to more intimate forms of association. Here it is difficult for the law to intrude without threatening each citizen's right to pursue the good.

While this dialogue begins with ideal theory, it ends with second best: Depressive's proposal depends upon a host of institutional judgments that require contextual development. It is enough here to state the main point: Whenever a group of citizens established a privileged acquaintance before Time Two, their efforts to create special adult relationships after Time Two will create theoretical tensions that can only be sensitively accommodated, rather than definitely resolved.

50. COMPLEXITIES: "IRREPLACEABLE" RESOURCES

Up to now, I have measured compliance with trusteeship in terms of my favorite unit: manna. This simplification is not as unrealistic as may first appear. While it is often costly to shift specialized land and capital from one use to another in the short run, many resources are much more fungible in the longer run. And presumably, it is the longish run that is relevant to a practical assessment of trusteeship compliance. Hence, over a large area of the economy, it will make sense to ask whether the senior generation has, through capital formation and technical innovation, passed on a stock of manna-like resources that permits their juniors to begin in a material position made no worse by the passage of time.

Nonetheless, some objects are entirely irreplaceable and many more cannot be replaced except at enormous cost. Imagine, for example, that our new world contains two kinds of good. On the one hand, there is the Grand Canyon, which can be used in only one of two ways, as a source for uranium or as an object of natural majesty. On the other hand, there is a slightly modified form of manna that is capable of producing anything except natural majesty upon the command of its rightful owner. Assume, finally, that there is no way of mining the Canyon's uranium lode without destroying its natural aspect—mining and majesty don't mix. Given this two-good world, the ideal Commander now gives out initial material endowments in two forms. In addition to an equal share of manna, each citizen also receives an equal share in Canyon Corporation, an entity charged with controlling the use of this special resource.

50.1. *Energy and Majesty*

It is now Time One + N. The corporation devotes its first meeting to a market study of consumer demand for energy and majesty respectively. After a brief interval, the ideal transmitter system displays a compelling picture. Apparently the citizens of generation one are willing to pay an astonishingly high price for the Canyon's energy resources, a price so high that all the corporation's conservationist shareholders are willing to sell their stock to energy users. Despite the corporation's unanimous vote, should the government intervene to prevent Canyon development?

If this were the ordinary case, the answer would be a straightforward No. A liberal government cannot declare that the activities made possible by an enhanced energy supply are intrinsically inferior to those made possible by the use of the canyon as a sanctuary. Nor can it say that nature lovers are intrinsically better than energy users. Since, by hypothesis, the distribution of initial endowments is just and the transactional system perfectly flexible, it follows from the Crusoe dialogue that the rightful owners of the Canyon can use it in the way they think best.

Yet before we permit the miners in, consider whether the trusteeship rationale may be deployed with special effect. Trusteeship requires one generation to arrange its affairs so as to refrain from making members of the next worse off than the present occupants of our planet. And in our two-good world, this obligation cannot be satisfied merely by passing on a *manna* stock sufficient to give each junior at least as much as each senior received: before the next generation's condition is equivalent to the present, their use of the Grand Canyon must also be protected. Is mining the Canyon consistent with this obligation?

Begin with an easy case, one in which trusteeship does *not* prevent the corporation from acting on its mining decision. To make the analysis straightforward, indulge some technological pyrotechnics: imagine that at Time One + N, the liberal Commander can command the services of a Master Estimator, who perfectly predicts the values that will be adopted by each member of the second generation after he completes a liberal education. The Master reports that the second generation, like the first, will place a higher value on energy than it will on majesty. Note that the Estimator need *not* assert that nature lovers will be entirely absent from generation two. Instead, he merely must say that like their fellows in generation one, the conservationist shareholders of the corporation will find their share of the profits from energy use too good to refuse. Given this finding, trusteeship does not prevent generation one from mining the lode—for the simple reason that the first generation's temporal priority has not in fact caused the nature lovers of the second generation any harm they would not have otherwise sustained. At best, the nature lovers have an argument against their age mates; but the Crusoe dialogue is sufficient to take care of such a complaint.

This is not to say that the corporation is free of all significant trusteeship obligations when mining the lode—only that trusteeship should be measured in terms of energy, not majesty. Thus, if the first generation removes X megawatts of energy from the Canyon, trusteeship requires it to make up this deficit by an investment in research and development. This compensating investment, however, need not occur in the vicinity of the Canyon. So long as generation two receives the same per capita energy resources as generation one, trusteeship is content.

So much for the easy case.[9] Difficulties begin when the two generations differ as to the best use of the Canyon. Assume the Master Estimator reports that the second generation will place such a high value on the Canyon's majesty that nature lovers will willingly compensate energy users to forego Canyon development. Given this finding, a new dimension of intergenerational conflict is revealed. While generation one would prefer to fulfill its trusteeship obligation by making up the megawatts it has consumed, the second generation

---

9. There remains, of course, the preservationist argument, developed at pp. 102–03, which permits the protection of the Canyon as a symbol of liberal agnosticism. This rationale becomes increasingly attractive as the cases get harder.

wants trusteeship defined in terms of the Canyon's majesty. When different generations disagree about the best use of a nonfungible good, which generation's characterization should dominate the interpretation of trusteeship?

When put in this way, the basic liberal answer is clear enough:[10] *Neither* generation has the right *always* to determine the metric by which trusteeship should be measured. The first generation cannot say its firstness entitles it to measure its Canyon trusteeship *exclusively* in megawatts; nor can the second say its secondness permits it to measure the Canyon solely in terms of majesty. Yet in one way or another, a functioning liberal state must fasten upon a particular interpretation of trusteeship, and given the mutual incompatibility of the two generations' dominant characterizations, how is this to be done?

With difficulty. Yet some hard cases will be easier than others. Imagine, for example, that the Canyon's uranium lode amounted to a small fraction of the total energy supply when the possibility of using manna as energy is taken into account. Assume, moreover, that the Estimator reports the Canyon will be centrally important in the life definition of the conservationist members of the second generation; so important, in fact, that they would not trade their interest in the Canyon for any other good. In contrast, assume that the energy users of the first generation concede that they could adapt, with only a modest inconvenience, even if the Canyon were withdrawn from exploitation. In such a case, second-best principles would point toward protection of the Canyon's majesty. If the government is unwilling to impose even modest inconveniences upon the energy users, it could only be because this interest group is deemed intrinsically superior to its competitors. And it is this claim of moral superiority which is inconsistent with the legitimating dialogue of a liberal state.

Unfortunately, however, it is easy to build harder cases. Assume that the Canyon is the source of *all* the world's energy as well as *all* its majesty. In managing the trusteeship conflict here, liberal government will be reduced to desperate expedients. Each side, after all, credibly explains how its conception of the good is threatened if the

10. Indeed, the paragraphs that follow are nothing more than an application of the same principles developed in § 45 to manage conflicts over indivisible resources like clean air. The task here, however, is more difficult. Instead of managing the conflict by permitting different regions to pursue different policies in different *spatial* areas on the planet, we are faced with the job of permitting different generations to use the same resource differently during different *time slices.*

other wins, and the liberal statesman can hardly say that the grievous injury to one good is better than a similar injury to the other. At this point, the Solomonic instinct runs strong: Is it *really* impossible to permit *some* Canyon mining without retaining *some* of the place's majesty?

50.2. *Crystal Ball Gazing*

Thus far, I have simplified the problem by conjuring up a Master Estimator capable of reporting with perfect accuracy whether future citizens would agree or disagree with the present generation's preferred characterization of its trusteeship obligation. As soon as we dispense with this device, however, a new problem emerges. Some mechanism must be designed to discriminate between hard and easy cases, for without such a mechanism, powerful elites will transform trusteeship into a rhetorical cover for their personal aggrandizement. Reconsider, for example, the case of Michelangelo Crusoe. While all of his contemporaries consider his art to be junk, can he not argue that someone sometime in the future will consider it more precious than the Grand Canyon? How, then, can the liberal state justify preserving the Grand Canyon while permitting, on Crusoe's death, the artist's canvases to be recycled for the energy value?

The general form of the answer is clear enough. Before Crusoe's canvases present an easy case for burning, a liberal government must find that future generations will prefer to define trusteeship in terms of energy rather than Michelangelos; if the Canyon is a hard case, it is because the future prefers to measure the Canyon in terms of majesty rather than energy. But if we lack a powerful empirical theory for predicting the evolution of future values, how are we to make the required discriminations?[11]

A short answer: The interpretation of trusteeship represents a supreme test for liberal education. Each citizen must try to sort out his own preferences from those that, on the basis of his liberal education, he recognizes as within the probable range of moral evolution. While

11. It is easy to lose sight of the force of this question by forgetting that, under the terms of the hypothetical problem, the present generation wants to use *both* the Canyon and the Crusoe canvases for their energy value. After all, if (as is true right now) the present generation places a higher market value on the Canyon's majesty, it will preserve the Canyon regardless of the preferences of succeeding generations. It is only when the present generation wants to use the Canyon for energy that the preservation of its majesty will depend upon an interpretation of trusteeship obligations.

much must be left to individual insight, there are several guidelines that may be deployed to inform, if not control, good-faith judgment. One is history: the dominance of a value structure in the past suggests that, ceteris paribus, its reemergence is a serious possibility. A single generation of atheists should not be permitted to transform all Christian shrines into parking lots. A second factor involves the overall pattern of objects protected under trusteeship: Does it reflect a sense of the rich variety of possibility that the future may have in store? Or does it, under the guise of a spurious certainty as to the inevitable path of historical development, only protect objects that rank high in the value scheme of those groups that happen to be powerful at the moment? Third, there is the simple passage of time: If a thousand years were to pass without a single generation placing a higher value on the Canyon's majesty than its energy, the possibility that even this irreplaceable object represents an "easy" case for energy development must be seriously confronted.

51. POPULATION CONTROL

51.1. *Principles of Harmonious Policy*

We can now complete the generational cycle by viewing the concept of trusteeship against the discussion of birthrights with which the present part began. In chapter 4, I argued that the Commander had no right to impose a population floor on the size of the next generation: if each and every member of generation one decided that he had better ways of spending his time and manna, the first generation could become last. If, however, members of the first generation *do* choose to have children, the dialogues of the present chapter establish that each child is entitled to an endowment that is no worse than:

1. that provided to any of his agemates.
2. that obtained by any older citizen with whom the younger citizen can converse.

In bringing these ideal principles down to earth, a second-best state must recognize that:

1. The content and distribution of ideals held by future generations may well be different from the present, and take steps to protect particular objects if this seems a fair way of mediating the intergenerational conflict.

2. Unequal inheritance may spur economic productivity to such an extent that even those relatively disadvantaged by initial material inequality may waive their prima facie rights upon learning of the benefits that they will in fact gain from the increased growth.

Good-faith differences in implementing these second-best principles are to be expected. It will be the task of the next part to consider the way they may be legitimately resolved in a functioning liberal state. For now, though, it is enough to say that if the dialogues in chapter 4[12] are read together with those we have just rehearsed, the result is a liberal commitment to a "harmonious" population policy— one that allows *no more children into the world than can be provided for under the trusteeship principles we have just summarized.*

Note that "harmony" does not require any particular quantitative limit on the size of the next generation. If, for example, there are a million people on our spaceship and a million grains of manna in our new world, we may, if we think it good, have *two* million children so long as we embark upon an investment strategy that will yield at least two million grains of manna for distribution at the time when our children come of age. Harmony is not the same thing as zero population growth.

Yet this difference may itself be the subject of dialogic challenge. Imagine, for example, that generation one does decide to double the population from one to two million, embarking upon the harmonious investment policy this decision requires. At the moment of dialogic truth, can't some junior challenge the legitimacy of this decision to double the number of his agemates?

JUNIOR: You have unfairly exploited the fact that you came first!
SENIOR: How so?
JUNIOR: You have created a situation in which there are more citizens associating with me than there were with you.
SENIOR: But you have received as much manna as I have. How then have you been disadvantaged by the simple fact that there are a larger number of citizens?
JUNIOR: I just don't like so many people swarming around!
SENIOR: But you can use your transmitter-shield to exclude anybody you don't want to deal with.

12. § 25.

JUNIOR: Even so, I dislike the idea of people swarming around out of sight. It gives me the creeps.

SENIOR: I'm afraid you'll have to do better than that if you hope to make a convincing trusteeship argument.

JUNIOR: Why so?

SENIOR: Trusteeship requires me to assure you only those rights that I myself possess, no less but no more.

JUNIOR: That's right.

SENIOR: But you are now claiming a right I myself don't possess. While I can shield out an offensive object, I cannot go further and suppress it. Your argument is no different from the prude who is upset by the thought that someone somewhere is engaging in offensive forms of sexuality.

Ideal theory, then, sets no absolute quantitative limit on the size of the legitimate population. So long as the seniors come up with harmonizing investments, juniors cannot articulate a Neutral reason for preferring a policy of zero population growth.

Predictably, the clarity of this conclusion does not survive the shadows of second best. Here the critical issue is the interpretation of the idea of a "harmonizing investment." In a world without perfect shielding, for example, it will not be enough for seniors to give each junior a quantity of manna equal to that with which each senior began. Instead, seniors must also compensate those juniors who like their solitude for the extra[13] shielding costs they will experience as a result of the doubling population. The fair estimate of such costs and the design of an appropriate administrative mechanism for the transfers will be a complicated question, open to an enormous range of contestable judgments. As always, ideal theory can only set the master question for practical policy without pointing to a unique solution to the difficult issues that will arise in implementation.

51.2. *Allocating Birthrights*

Imagine, next, that a second-best liberal government concludes that the foreseeable rate of resource growth is harmonious with a population growth rate of no more than X percent. Unfortunately, if every-

---

13. The only shielding costs relevant here are those *marginal* costs generated as a result of the move from one to two million people. While there will, of course, *also* be shielding costs imposed in a million-person second-best world, this is a problem dealt with by the liberal theory regulating *intra*generational externalities developed in chapter 6, § 45, not the theory of *inter*generational trusteeship.

body who wants a child is allowed to have one, population will increase at a rate of $2X$ percent. How, then, can a liberal polity allocate scarce birth rights among the contending citizenry?

An excursion into ideal theory will clarify the issue. Here the Commander may resolve the issue quite simply and decisively: Anyone can have as many children as he likes so long as he promises to invest his initial grain of manna in a way that will permit him to provide "his" children with a grain of manna apiece upon maturity. Thus, if you (together with the other members of your "family") are willing to invest in a way that will yield three grains of manna for distribution to the next generation, you can have three children; if, however, you want a child without paying the trusteeship price, then your exercise of power is illegitimate:

> CHILD-LOVER: But I *want* a kid!
> COMMANDER: A liberal state cannot guarantee a citizen everything he wants. I say that your use of power to bring a child into the world is illegitimate.
> CHILD-LOVER: Why?
> COMMANDER: Because if your power play is permitted today, an illiberal conversation will foreseeably result a generation hence when the juniors come to claim their manna.
> CHILD-LOVER: But having a child is *terribly* important to me.
> COMMANDER: If it's so important, why don't you invest part of your manna so that it will yield a whole grain a generation hence?
> CHILD-LOVER: But such an investment will deprive me of the wherewithal to pursue other valuable activities.
> COMMANDER: True, but none of us can hope to escape the dilemmas of resource scarcity. Which, then, do you think is more valuable—having a child or using your manna in some other way?
> CHILD-LOVER: However much I love children, I think the goods I shall lose are even more precious.
> COMMANDER: You said it; I didn't.

Such a short and simple dialogue, however, will only suffice in an ideal world where undominated equality has been achieved in genes, education, material assets, and transactional advantage. In more familiar power structures, there are serious problems in an allocation scheme that requires everybody to buy an insurance policy that guarantees a "trusteeship" payment to each child when he reaches maturity. Most obviously, it will be difficult for young adults to *prepay* an insurance policy that *guarantees* that the child will receive his trusteeship assets on maturity. Yet if a liberal government contents itself with a *promise* to pay premiums over time, what to do when defaults arise? And then there is the hard fact (developed at greater length in the next chapter) that the present distribution of initial endowments is unjust. Given pervasive injustice, an allocation of birthrights on the basis of willingness to pay would only serve to exacerbate the existing conditions of illegitimate exploitation. While there is no easy solution to third-best problems of this kind, it would be very wrong to ignore their existence. Perhaps an appropriate response would be an allocation mechanism that distributes birthrights on an egalitarian basis. Here, the government allocates an equal number of birthrights to each citizen, regardless of his conception of the good. It is then up to each citizen to decide whether he will exercise his birthrights or sell them to others who think childrearing relatively more important. While there are difficulties with the scheme, at least it will not force people who already are unjustly impoverished to pay for the right to have a child.

52. JUSTICE OVER TIME

Robert Nozick, then, is precisely wrong when he imagines that a first generation starting out under perfectly just conditions would have the perfect right to shape the second's entitlements in any way it wished. To the contrary, if the first generation enjoyed a condition of undominated equality, it is under the plainest dialogic obligation to pass this inheritance on to its children. Nozick thinks otherwise because he fails to confront the fact that temporal priority gives the old a distinctive form of power over the young. Every member of the rising generation will not, however, equal Nozick in his blindness. Many who are disadvantaged by their elders' exercise of power will question its legitimacy. Once the dialogue has begun, those in power have only three options: silence the questioner by the further exercise of power; answer the question by asserting the moral superiority of senior over junior; or respond in a way that recognizes that each citizen's claim to public respect does not depend on his birthday. For the liberal there can be no choice: trusteeship describes the dialogic outcome.

However demanding the obligations of trusteeship, they do not extend without limit. The claims of dialogue cannot exceed the possibility of dialogue itself. Before political dialogue can exist, two bodily creatures must be capable of talking to one another about their mutual predicament in a world of scarce resources. Generations yet unborn cannot participate in the dialogue and, hence, cannot assert their right to come into existence. Their rights must, at best, be conditional: if—but only if—existing citizens think it good to bring more citizens into being, then the elders have an obligation to conduct themselves in a way that will withstand the inevitable questions that the young will raise about their upbringing.

But it is not enough to distinguish dialogic theory from phil-osophies—like Nozick's—that entirely ignore the potential for in-justice arising from the simple fact of temporal succession. Further insight into trusteeship can be gained by a comparison with more traditional methods of liberal political theory.

52.1. *Contract*

Turning to contract theory, we encounter familiar difficulties in using the framework to generate an incisive set of principles to govern trusteeship issues. The best way of locating the methodological prob-lem is by a study of the most ambitious contractarian treatment of intergenerational justice, the one developed by John Rawls.

Consider first his treatment of population growth.[14] As always, Rawls sets up the problem as it might appear behind the veil of igno-rance. Ignorant of how they will fare in society, the contractors con-sider the consequences of a policy that allows population to grow without limit. At some point, growth will hurt, rather than help, the representative member of the worse-off class. Since Rawls thinks that the welfare of the worst-off is a decisive factor in everyone's calculus behind the veil, his contractors unanimously vote to restrain the popu-lation growth below this hurtful rate. On the surface, then, Rawls seems immune from my complaint about the vagueness of contracta-rian treatments of trusteeship questions. But appearances are deceiv-ing, for Rawls has generated a pointed response only by manipulating the veil of ignorance in a way that he does not even attempt to justify. To see the problem, think your way into the original position. How would you respond to a term in the social contract permitting a limita-tion on population growth?

Well, if I were self-interested (as Rawls assumes), I would want to

14. *A Theory of Justice*, pp. 161–64.

know whether or not I would be one of the people who would remain unborn as a result of the population restraint. If I knew I would still be alive, I would cast my vote for Rawls's proposal so long as I was exclusively concerned (as Rawls assumes) with my worst possible outcome. *But if I thought I might be deprived of existence by the birth limit, I would have a very different attitude.* I would now be exclusively concerned with the prospect of being deprived of life itself and vote against all growth restraints. Rawls's conclusion follows, then, only if the veil of ignorance is rigged to transmit a vital bit of information about each contractor's personal fate in the real world—namely, that the population limit carries no threat to his personal existence. Yet as soon as this is seen, Rawls's conclusion seems more to beg the question than answer it: Why is it fair to design the original position so that contractors are *certain* of winning from birth control?[15]

In the absence of a convincing answer to this question, it is perfectly proper for opponents of birth control to redesign the veil to suit their tastes. As soon as they stipulate that contractors *cannot* be certain that they will survive a societal commitment to birth control, a very different answer emerges from the Rawlsian machine. Given his contractors' notorious skittishness about downside risks, they may well assert a principled opposition to birth control in all its forms. Rather than leading to an incisive answer, Rawls's approach leads to as many answers as there are different designs for the veil of ignorance.

But population size represents only one aspect of Rawls's theory of intergenerational justice. Once an upper bound on population growth is set, Rawls considers—as if it were a separate question—the quantity of material resources each generation may rightfully expect from its predecessors.[16] Once again, his surface position seems clear enough. According to Rawls, it is not enough if the per capita wealth of the second generation is *equal* to that of the first, as it would be under the liberal theory of trusteeship. Instead, he insists that the first generation must embark on a "just saving" program under which the second's worst-off class (WOC) is made *better* off than its predecessor. The image is one of steady progress, in which the position of the worst-off is continually ameliorated over time.[17]

15. This point, along with many other incisive ones, is raised by R. M. Hare in his "Rawls' Theory of Justice," *Philosophical Quarterly* 23 (1973): 144, 241.

16. *A Theory of Justice*, pp. 284–98.

17. Rawls adds the proviso: "Justice does not require that early generations save so that later ones are simply more wealthy. Saving is demanded as a condition for bringing about the full

   This clear and incisive picture dissolves, however, as we explore its relation to the larger contractarian whole. To see the problem, return to the original position and compare "just savings" with the principle of liberal trusteeship that I have developed. Under trusteeship, the first generation contents itself with assuring that future WOCs are not worse off than its own. Thus, if the representative member of the first-generation WOC receives, say, three units of welfare, then every subsequent WOC is assured of three units, but no more.[18] In contrast, the "just savings" program will do better for you if you are lucky enough to be born into a late generation, which reaps the bounties of compound interest. Unfortunately, you will almost certainly obtain *less* than three units of welfare if it turns out that you're born early. After all, "just savings" requires the first generation to deprive itself of some extra consumption to help out future WOCs; and it is unlikely that this extra saving will only come out of the hide of the first generation's upper classes without touching the worst-off group. Which program, then, would you choose from the original position—where you are stripped of knowledge of your particular position in the generational sequence?

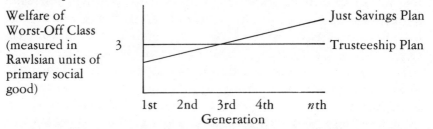

Welfare of
Worst-Off Class
(measured in   3
Rawlsian units of
primary social
good)

                                                                    Just Savings Plan

                                                                    Trusteeship Plan

         1st   2nd   3rd   4th   *n*th
                      Generation

   Whatever your answer, one would expect to have little trouble in guessing Rawls's. If *anything* is fundamental to *A Theory of Justice*, it is the claim that rational contractors will, when making their fundamen-

realization of just institutions and the fair value of liberty. . . . In fact, beyond some point, it [great wealth] is more likely to be a positive hindrance, a meaningless distraction at best if not a temptation to indulgence and emptiness" (*A Theory of Justice*, p. 290). The greater the weight given this passage, the less important will seem the following paragraphs, which detail the differences between "just savings" and "liberal trusteeship." There is a danger, however, in giving this passage too great an importance. Rawls's talk about "indulgence and emptiness"— however much it may appeal on the level of personal morality—provides an unlikely foundation for a *liberal* theory of intergenerational justice which tries to eschew such contestable value judgments about the amount of wealth necessary for the pursuit of a truly satisfying life. Contrast my discussions at §§ 15.1 and 50.
   18. Intergenerational gifts are, of course, possible, but they cannot be demanded as of right. See § 48.2.

tal choices, focus exclusively upon their worst-possible outcomes. In the present case, this means the contractors will be unimpressed by the fact that "just savings" generates higher welfare to people lucky enough to land in the later generations. Instead, they will concentrate upon the sacrifices "just savings" imposes on those who come earlier. Following maximin, one would expect Rawls to predict that the *liberal principle of trusteeship* would be the unanimous choice of his original contractors, for they end up worse off under "just savings" if they find themselves in the first generation after leaving the original position.

The only trouble is that Rawls says just the opposite.[19] He tells us that the contractors must conceive of themselves as family heads who are concerned with the welfare of their entire bloodline; why a person can't be a bachelor (or at least know of the possibility) is left entirely obscure. Yet even this first manipulation will not suffice. After all, *why* must a responsible family head want more for his children than he gets for himself? Why is it not enough to bring the child to a level of welfare equal to that the parent himself enjoys? It is always possible to short-circuit these questions simply by stipulating that *all* contractors have the psychology of the quintessential Jewish mother, but this stipulation will hardly convince parents of other temperaments. Moreover, the altruistic psychology attributed to contractors considering *inter*generational questions starkly contrasts with the self-interested psychology of contractors confronting *intra*generational conflicts. This is a contractarianism at its worst, where hard questions are dismissed by painting the "state of nature" to suit one's pre-philosophical fancies.

52.2. *Utility*
The same cannot be said of the utilitarian's approach to trusteeship: the measure of intergenerational justice no longer depends on one or another question-begging manipulation of the original position; instead, it rests on a calculation that is clear in principle if fuzzy in practice. The only trouble is that the utilitarian's answers are clearly illiberal.

Begin with the question of whether we have an obligation to bring our successors into existence. Liberal trusteeship makes no such demand—its obligations are purely conditional: *if* you have a child,

19. *A Theory of Justice* pp. 288–92.

then you must be prepared to answer his predictable questions of legitimacy. In contrast,[20] a utilitarian may well applaud a decision to *force* people to have children. Not that the utilitarian is oblivious to the pains of the reluctant parent; but he must balance this off against the joys of the potential child. Moreover, extra children may increase the pleasure of other citizens. It follows that a utilitarian Commander will sometimes think it justified to induce adults to have children when they would prefer to use their time and manna in other ways.[20]

Of course, a point will come when the utilitarian will call a halt. On the one hand, as the population target increases, ever more reluctant parents must be recruited into the child-rearing effort. On the other hand, crowding and the aggregate pressure on resources will diminish the marginal benefits gained overall by an additional child. To maximize utility over time, a utilitarian will want to arrange the world so that no less than X children enter the world—and will fail to understand why a liberal Commander will refuse, in principle, to impose this policy on her fellow citizens.

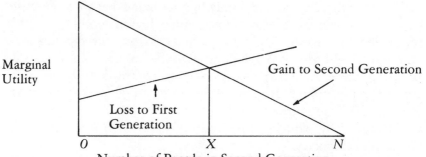

Once the question of population size has been settled, the two theories also differ as to the extent of material provision the young may rightfully demand. Thus, imagine that the second generation will make a great leap forward in happiness if the first denies itself consumption in favor of capital accumulation. Then, so long as the parents' marginal disutility is exceeded by their children's incremental gain, extraordinary levels of parental sacrifice may be demanded. On other occasions, utilitarians may permit parents to consume gobs of available capital, leaving their successors with a vastly depleted stock

20. Subtle forms of inducement will be preferred, for these will be the least costly. Financial inducements (family allowances and so forth) provide happier forms of incentive than jail terms.

of natural wealth. It all depends on whether parents or children get the greater happiness from the resources in question. In contrast, ideal liberal theory imposes a trusteeship that does not depend on the shifting patterns of sentiment over the generations.[21] So long as each generation does not deplete the per capita share of capital available to the next, further accumulation may not be demanded in the name of trusteeship; nor can less be justified by an appeal to the general good.

The difference between liberal and utilitarian, then, shows itself on every basic issue of intergenerational justice. This sustained substantive dispute is simply a symptom of a basic difference in method. For the utilitarian, the liberal makes much too much of the fact that unborn generations cannot ask and answer the question of legitimacy. Despite their absence from the public dialogue, no fair mind can doubt that future citizens—like all other sentient beings—will be capable of happiness. It is this fact that serves as the guiding principle in the utilitarian's search for intergenerational justice.

In contrast, the liberal rejects the idea that a political community may legitimately further a collective good and call it happiness. For him, the overriding fact is that he finds himself among a large number of individuals, each one of whom affirms his own good—which may or may not include the reproduction of the species. If one of his fellow citizens refuses to have a child, it is not for him to say that this decision is mistaken. Instead of pretending to the moral certainties of a god, it is enough to insist that each parent be in a position to answer each child's questions of legitimacy in a way that respects the child's claim of common citizenship. This is the essence of the liberal solution to the problem of justice over time.

21. Except for second-best problems generated by irreplaceable resources, see § 50.

PART THREE: FROM IDEAL TO REALITY

8

EXPLOITATION

53. STATESMANSHIP

53.1. *Ideal to Reality*

So it *is* possible to conceive a world that fully lives up to liberal ideals, where each citizen both enjoys a right to undominated equality and preserves it for his posterity. This act of political imagination is enough to establish the conceptual coherence of liberalism, to reveal the liberal method of dialogue as one that can, in principle, generate a harmonious vision of social order. The harmony is of a distinctive kind. It does not promise an end to ambiguity, disagreement, disappointment; it does not promise an idyllic social union where all mankind loses itself in lyric praise of cosmic order. Instead of the standard utopian reverie, it offers each citizen the chance to achieve self-understanding without subordinating himself to the meanings imposed by others; it bids us glimpse a deeper harmony in the dialogue that provides the social foundation for all subsequent disagreement.

Yet there is a darker, and equally valid, way of looking at the achievement of ideal theory. Even conceding (no small thing) that an ideal power structure is *conceivable,* have we not also shown that its attainment is *impossible* in the world as we know it? Time and again, I have been obliged to invent a "technology" of justice as a necessary condition for specifying an ideal set of power relationships. But it is plain that this technology does not exist. What is the use, then, of all this ideal talk? Does it have any practical value in the world in which we are fated to live?

The problem—relating ideal to reality—serves as a critical test for any political philosophy. On the one hand, a theory that cannot serve as a practical guide is merely utopian fantasy, an inferior form of fiction. On the other hand, a book that offers a detailed action program is merely a symbol of the theorist's power lust, an inferior form of autobiography. It is not, however, enough to say something without saying everything. If one is to avoid the fate of Polonius, the sayings cannot be empty maxims whose content is left entirely to the states-man's discretion. The task is to show how theory permits *both* an affirmation of the autonomy of liberal statesmanship *and* the imposi-tion of principled constraints upon the exercise of practical judgment, to demonstrate that theory establishes its own self-denying ordinances without denying itself entirely.

Begin, then, by reexamining the fundamentals of ideal theory to see what remains of lasting value in the world as we know it. Looking back, there are three things that make ideal theory ideal. First, there is a perfect technology of justice, a sure and costless way of rectifying injustices revealed by dialogue. Second, there is the unswerving commitment by the Commander to the process of Neutral dialogue it-self, the determination to use the technology in only those ways that can be legitimated consistently with the three principles. Third, there is the neat way that technology and dialogue interact to generate determinate substantive results. That is, we can show that a power system that respected each citizen's right to undominated equality passes the test of liberal dialogue, while a great many other power structures do not.

These three elements survive the journey to realer worlds in dif-ferent ways and degrees. While condition one—a perfect tech-nology—is far beyond us, condition two—a commitment to dialogic process—need not be. Indeed, I shall define second-best theory as nothing other than a description of the way a citizenry committed to condition two will deal with the problem of technological im-perfection. Putting a new condition one together with the old con-dition two leads, unsurprisingly, to a new condition three. When we inspect the stream of second-best discourse, we will find that an all-embracing commitment to perfectly undominated equality does not survive the test of this more complicated dialogue. The range of sub-stantive disagreement prevailing under second-best conditions is far wider than that tolerated by ideal theory. Nonetheless, I hope to convince you that our new condition three is not infinitely elastic. Instead, I mean to generate convincing second-best arguments that establish the illegitimacy of many proposed or existing power struc-tures.

While second-best theory, as defined here, will be our primary focus, my definitions allow for yet a third body of theory—which, tediously, I shall call "third-best." Here the statesman must reckon with the fact that every existing society is scarred by entrenched patterns of domination which resist change, not because of some technological constraint, but because those favored by the *status quo* will fight for their advantages. Indeed, it is a fair question whether Neutral dialogue can have an important, let alone supervening, influence in the world of power. People love power and will fight to keep it; the more powerful the group, the more tenacious the grip; the more powerful the group, the greater the temptation to suppress, rather than answer, the questions of legitimacy advanced by the oppressed. Power corrupts.

There can be no underestimating the challenges of liberal statesmanship: to confront the power lust within oneself and channel it to legitimate ends; to confront the power struggle in the world and chart a realistic strategy that exploits the liberal possibilities of the ongoing conflict. Indeed, there are social conditions that will defeat the most inspired political action; societies whose history reveals a ceaseless change from one form of tyranny to another with no gain in liberal values. Nonetheless, this book does not pretend to be a practical manual for statesmen. I do not aim to isolate the necessary or sufficient empirical conditions for one or another liberal advance. It will be hard enough to discharge the task of second best and describe the way a polity committed to Neutral discourse will confront the task of doing justice in a world whose technology was not designed by a benign liberal Maker. I will leave the agony of third best to other times and places.

53.2 *Second-Best Argument*
I shall portray second-best argument as involving nothing more than a single conversational gambit—albeit one of enormous power and complexity. To see this, imagine a liberal community talking about rights in two stages. In the first phase, the citizenry talk as if there were no costs involved in the institutional effort to identify and remedy injustices identified through dialogue. This, of course, is precisely the stance adopted by ideal theory. After developing the conversation sketched in the preceding chapters, each citizen finds that he may defend his right to undominated equality in a legitimate way. This conclusion inaugurates the second conversational phase, as some citizen argues that the present power structure makes him a victim of injustice:

CITIZEN: But my fellow citizens have denied my right to undominated equality. If this is a liberal state, as you claim, this condition cannot be permitted to continue.

STATESMAN: We need not right this wrong.

CITIZEN: Why not? Do you deny that I would be entitled to undominated equality under a perfect technology of justice?

STATESMAN: Not at all.

CITIZEN: Then why not here?

STATESMAN: Our technology of justice is radically imperfect. It is simply impossible for us to achieve a world where undominated equality reigns supreme in all power relationships.

CITIZEN: But surely you will try to right some wrongs. Not every use of power is legitimate.

STATESMAN: Yes, I must agree to that. Otherwise I would violate the first principle of Rationality.[1]

CITIZEN: Why, then, don't you use your admittedly imperfect technology to right the wrongs committed against me rather than those perpetrated against others? Are they any better than I am? Why should they obtain public protection while I am left to fend for myself?

All of second-best theory can be understood as an effort to frame answers to this last question, answers that pass the test of Neutrality. A liberal statesman cannot support a challenged power structure unless he can give such an answer—subject, of course, to further third-best argument. Second-best theory does not displace ideal theory; rather, it continues the *same* conversation, correcting earlier conclusions only when this can be justified by Neutral argument.

53.3. *Tyranny and Statesmanship*

How, then, can the existence of an imperfect technology of justice justify the denial of *prima facie* rights?

In at least two, quite different, ways. Most obvious is the problem caused by human ignorance. Unlike the ideal Commander, the liberal statesman cannot call upon a master geneticist or educator or designer to devise a costless way of implementing the demands of liberal dialogue. Our technological mastery is fragmentary, our practical wisdom full of errors. Even when we attain a modest level of instrumental

---

1. See the conceivability test imposed under Rationality, § 11.2.

rationality, the pursuit of liberal justice will be very costly. All earthly resources would not be enough to purchase a perfect transmitter-shield system or universal liberal education—let alone the entire bundle of rights encompassed by the ideal of undominated equality. It follows that, unlike the ideal liberal Commander, the statesman cannot aim for the ideal liberal power structure. Instead, he must prepare a "structural budget" indicating the resource costs the polity should accept in the effort to ameliorate genetic domination, enrich education, guarantee the initial equality of wealth, provide transactional flexibility, and assure a just trusteeship for future generations.

This demanding exercise is made doubly difficult by a second basic failure in the technology of justice. Even if we could tap the skills of the Master Geneticist and his friends, we surely cannot count on government by an ideal Commander who single-mindedly devotes herself to the realization of dialogic legitimacy in a disorderly world. To the contrary, there is the constant danger that government officials will transform themselves into imperious overlords, whose actions mock the liberal rhetoric that legitimated their acquisition of power in the first place. This means that, in devising his response to denials of prima facie rights, the liberal statesman must take into account the dangers of authoritarian tyranny that arise from a hyperactive and overly concentrated government bureaucracy. To make judgment more complex, the rich and powerful who are endangered by governmental initiatives will predictably exaggerate the risk of tyranny—protraying the smallest governmental steps toward undominated equality as giant strides down the road to serfdom. Yet this fog of overexcited rhetoric should never obscure the point that power *does* corrupt. The ongoing liberal dialogue is endangered *whenever* a small group—be they "public" bureaucrats or "private" plutocrats—have enough power to suppress questions of legitimacy they find threatening.

It is only in the next chapter, however, that I will give the problem of tyranny the importance it deserves in an overall account. To make matters analytically tractable, I propose to introduce the basic problems confronting liberal statecraft one at a time. Assume, then, that you are a liberal statesman operating within the framework of a liberal constitution that has succeeded in reducing the risk of tyranny to tolerable limits. This permits you to concentrate single-mindedly on the problem posed by human ignorance. All around you are costly and imperfect programs for securing one or another dimension of the liberal ideal. How are you to choose among them?

53.4. *The Shape of the Structural Budget*

In the end, the answers you give to this question will find their way into a massive document detailing the costs of assuring each right and explaining why the programs selected achieve their objects more cheaply than do plausible competitors. But implicit in all this important detail will be an answer to two questions that will give the entire document its characteristic structure. The first problem is raised by the fact that, beyond a certain point, further increases in the structural budget demand a cut in the resources allocated to each adult citizen for the purpose of fulfilling his ends in life. To adopt a shorthand, the structural budget, B, competes with self-regarding expenditure, S. This means that the statesman must assess the gains in liberal value achieved by marginal increases in B and compare them with the losses in liberal value suffered as a result of the decrease in S. One principal task of second-best theory is to guide this trade-off, which I will call the problem of *overall budget size*.

Assume now that this problem has been resolved, at least in a provisional way. Given a decision to reserve an S of a particular size, the maximum structural budget, B, may be obtained by subtracting S from the total resource base, T. A second question then comes into view. Since $T - S$ will be exhausted long before all prima facie rights can be secured, the statesman must confront the problem of *budgetary distribution:* which prima facie rights should be protected and which should be sacrificed?

These two questions, dealing with the distribution and size of the structural budget, will be our central concern here. While I develop the argument through a series of examples, these discussions are not intended to be exhaustive. My main aim is to clarify the distinctive relationship between principle and decision characteristic of liberal statesmanship. On the one hand, I hope to show that second-best theory imposes powerful constraints on the kind of structural budget a liberal statesman may legitimately support. On the other hand, these constraints hardly bind judgment so tightly as to reduce the statesman to a preprogrammed automaton. A wide range of issues remain that not only demand difficult assessments of fact but contestable judgments of value. Moreover, I hope to show that this pattern of constraint and discretion is not the product of an ad hoc accommodation between theory and practice. A systematic pursuit of theory itself leads to a picture of a statesman that is of human scale, neither heroically free of all principle nor entirely bound by an iron lattice of rules.

This conclusion leads naturally to a central concern of the next chapter. If certain second-best decisions are plainly forbidden, while others are essentially contestable, this black-and-gray pattern has strong implications for proper governmental design. On the one hand, the second-best constitution must specify the way a government can come to a definite policy on those numerous occasions when liberal statesmen can be expected to disagree. On the other hand, the constitution must specify a procedure for preventing those outcomes plainly forbidden to liberal statesmen. In the face of this dichotomy, I shall argue that Neutrality permits questions of the first kind to be resolved by majority rule, while decisions of the second kind demand a different kind of dialogic process, one associated, in the United States at least, with judicial review by the Supreme Court. In short, by the end of this third part, we shall have rebuilt, from the ground up, the skeletal structure of the liberal-democratic state. But I have gotten ahead of myself; now that I have motivated the distinction between black and gray, it remains only to make it.

54. EQUAL SACRIFICE

Begin with the negative dimension of the inquiry—defining the acts of statesmanship that, prima facie, fail to qualify as legitimate in a liberal state. Once we paint in the black, it will be easier to distinguish the shades of gray. To do this, I shall first concentrate on the question of budgetary distribution. Provisionally assume that the statesman has reserved S for self-interested expenditure and is now trying to define the best structural budget costing no more than $T - S$. Since $T - S$ is too small to right all wrongs, the statesman must choose among claims that are all prima facie valid. Is it possible to write a dialogue that constrains this power of choice?

Imagine that Disadvantaged is denied one of the prima facie rights that make up his claim to undominated equality—say, his right to an initial equality in material endowments. He encounters one of his fellow citizens who is relatively advantaged in this regard and engages him in dialogue before a statesman charged with the task of resolving the dispute.

DISADVANTAGED: By what right do you start off life with more than I do?

ADVANTAGED: Because you're black and I'm not.

DISADVANTAGED: But I thought this was a liberal state.

ADVANTAGED: It is. You would have gotten an equal share under a perfect technology, but the pursuit of justice has heavy costs in our imperfect world. And we have to cut costs somewhere, you know!

DISADVANTAGED: But why not cut costs somewhere else? Say, where your rights are cut back and mine are not?

ADVANTAGED: I would oppose that. I think that since someone has to bear imperfection costs, it should be the morally inferior party.

DISADVANTAGED: And who might that be?

ADVANTAGED: You, of course.

DISADVANTAGED: Well, if we're reduced to this level, I say that whites are inferior to blacks!

STATESMAN: Enough of this name-calling. All of it violates the Neutrality principle. Moreover, it strikes me as quite unnecessary.

ADVANTAGED AND DISADVANTAGED: How so?

STATESMAN: Well, constrained by Neutrality as I am, it seems plain that I must say that each of you is at least as good as the other.

ADVANTAGED AND DISADVANTAGED: Yes, that was the conclusion of an earlier dialogue.

STATESMAN: And, if that's true, it follows that neither of you can justly call on the other to bear the entire burden of imperfection.

ADVANTAGED AND DISADVANTAGED: But what should we do?

STATESMAN: Accommodate imperfection in a way that requires *each* of you to make an equal sacrifice of your ideal rights.

ADVANTAGED: But what if I could show you that my larger wealth *is* consistent with the principle of equal sacrifice.

DISADVANTAGED: How are you going to do that?

ADVANTAGED: While I have more wealth than you, you have better genes or education than I do. Given your advantage in these other power domains, we can achieve overall equality only if I start off with more material wealth.

STATESMAN: A pretty complicated argument, but it's conceivable that you can make it work within the constraints of Neutral power talk.

DISADVANTAGED: But if he fails, does that mean I get the money?

ADVANTAGED: Not necessarily. I have other arguments. Perhaps it's in your advantage to concede me an initial wealth advantage.

DISADVANTAGED: How so?

ADVANTAGED: The chance of giving me a special bequest gave my parents special production incentives—which, in turn, permitted the state to increase its tax revenues, which, in turn, meant that you received a better liberal education and more flexible transactional capacities than you would have otherwise.

DISADVANTAGED: Talk about complicated arguments!

STATESMAN: Well, I see we're in for another long talk. But before we get too deeply immersed in it all, can we at least agree on one thing?

ADVANTAGED AND DISADVANTAGED: And what might that be?

STATESMAN: That unless I hear some convincing Neutral reason for doing otherwise, we should not require only one of you to bear the brunt of imperfection costs while the other's ideal rights are fully secured. Instead, each of you should make an equal sacrifice of his prima facie rights.

ADVANTAGED AND DISADVANTAGED: I guess so. Whatever our private pretentions to moral superiority, we can't really hope to gain a power advantage on the basis of them while remaining in a liberal state.

Simply because a statesman must deny protection to *some* ideal rights, it hardly follows that he may single out a few of his fellow citizens and make them bear the brunt of the burden of imperfection. Instead, a statesman must begin second-best analysis by asserting that each citizen should bear an equal share of these costs. Once again, the principle of equal sacrifice merely establishes a prima facie case. The advantaged remain free to defend their privileges on grounds that do not offend the Neutrality principle. Before considering such second-stage defenses of advantage, however, carefully examine the notion of equal sacrifice to which dialogue has already led us.

55. EXPLOITATION AND AFFIRMATIVE ACTION

I introduced the notion of equal sacrifice in a relatively unproblematic context. If, ceteris paribus, two people begin adult life with assets whose market value is unequal in money terms, the poorer citizen has been called upon to make a greater sacrifice than the richer. Equal sacrifice means identical sacrifice, measured in terms of a common metric—though even here there are some problems.[2] Similarly, there are nonmonetary cases where the interpretation of equal sacrifice does not seem difficult. If one citizen cannot be imprisoned for a crime unless he is proved guilty beyond a reasonable doubt, equal sacrifice is violated if another citizen is convicted on a lesser showing of probability. Nonetheless, there are many cases where the measurement of equivalence will not be so simple.

55.1. *Problems of Particular Comparison*

Begin with cases where the principle of equal sacrifice is plainly consistent with very great differences in the treatment of particular people. Education provides obvious examples. Even if an ideal liberal education were possible, different children would be treated in vastly different ways depending upon their primary socialization and genetic makeup.[3] And there is no reason to imagine that second-best educational programs will be any less diverse.

Even here, however, more may be involved. Imagine, for example, that when a spokesman for educational program A is asked to justify his system of pedagogy, he candidly avows its exclusively authoritarian purposes. Rather than developing the child's capacity for critical reflection upon, and choice among, a range of life plans, the system emphatically suppresses each student's effort to question his preordained mission in life. In contrast, program B actually succeeds in developing among many of its students a capacity for critical self-reflection, as well as the basic skills needed to explore the diverse life experiments characteristic of a liberal society. On these facts, there can be no doubt that we are in the presence of an easy case, where it is *plain* that the children victimized by program A are making a far

2. Most important will be the problem generated by the second-best decision (§§ 43–45) to collectivize ownership over certain forms of material wealth. If both of us get the same amount of money but you breathe better air than I do, you have gained an initial material advantage over me that is of questionable legitimacy.

3. See chapter 5, especially §§ 35–36.

greater sacrifice of their prima facie rights to a liberal education. Nor would this judgment change if the per pupil dollar cost in the A schools were far higher than those in B schools. This would merely show that it is more expensive to run a glorified prison than a liberal school.

But this is the easiest possible case. That there *are* easy cases is one of my main points; nonetheless, it is also right to ask about the boundary separating the *plain* violations from the cases of *contestable* equivalence. Imagine, for example, that neither A nor B is pursuing explicitly authoritarian goals; nonetheless, can it ever be *plain* that A imposes a greater sacrifice than B?

There is at least the conceptual possibility of an affirmative answer. Suppose, as the dialogue between A and B proceeds, it is possible to show that B accomplishes all of A's liberal ends, and achieves others as well. To trivialize, imagine that A prepares its children for life options [A . . . M], while B prepares for [A . . . N]. It would follow that B was plainly more liberal than A, and that those subjected to A were making the greater sacrifice of their prima facie rights. But, of course, this notational example begs any number of questions involving the skills and traits of character necessary for one or another range of life patterns, as well as the pedagogic methods that will best elicit them. Only in extreme cases could one side demonstrate through dialogue that its system dominated the rival in the decisive way we have denoted.

More common will be the intermediate case of *contestable* equivalence. Here the dialogue between A and B reveals that B equips the child for an insightful encounter with ranges of experience far more "diverse" than that provided by A. Yet A does prepare better for some ranges of experience. The hard question, of course, is whether B's greater breadth should count as a reason for calling it a more liberal eduation than A. Here there may be room for good-faith disagreement, depending on a number of contextual variables. Speaking generally, however, there will be great reluctance in declaring that B's advantages of breadth and flexibility justified the sacrifice of A's peculiar depth. The case for tolerating A is made stronger by the general danger to liberal values threatened whenever a small central group of "educational leaders" attempts a close curricular scrutiny.

So much for education. The need for discriminating judgment will be no less great in the evaluation of other power domains. Nonetheless, it will serve no good purpose to proliferate illustrations, which would inevitably be too brief to be decisive. For the present, simply imagine that after countless dialogues a particular statesman has identified those citizens who would be called upon to accept (either plainly or contestably) an unequal sacrifice if one or another proposal regarding genetic, educational, material, or transactional advantage were adopted. Even so, a final exercise remains before the principle of equal sacrifice may be intelligently applied.

55.2. *Exploitation and the Aggregation Problem*

Call it the aggregation problem. Before a statesman can say whether citizen A is sacrificing more rights than B, it will not be enough to see how these competing citizens fare in any single power domain. Even if A is plainly disadvantaged in education, he may possess an equally plain advantage over B in some other domain—say, material wealth. And when this is true, the statesman will predictably encounter an aggregation problem as he attempts to determine whether, overall, the imperfect technology has exacted an equivalent sacrifice from A and B. For he will be obliged to determine whether B's educational advantage outweighs, or merely equilibrates, A's wealth advantage. Yet how is the liberal statesman to make such trade-offs between such dissimilar goods?

I do not mean to minimize the seriousness of this difficulty. Nonetheless, aggregation is most emphatically *not* a problem in every important case. For example, imagine a society, X, where power is packaged in only two sizes. Assume that one group, the blacks, not only receive a smaller share of material resources but are shunted into an authoritarian educational system that prepares them to accept a limited number of subordinate roles, later to confront a transactional network that drastically limits a black's access to the means of communication and transaction. The whites get just the reverse: more wealth, privileged access, and an educational system that makes at least a half-hearted effort to awaken them to their moral freedom. On these facts, it is as easy as pie to add up each particular disadvantage into one outrageous violation of the principle of equivalent sacrifice. I shall call such conditions—where the move from particular disadvantages to overall judgment is *entirely* unproblematic—ones that involve the *exploitation* of one group by another.

Before exploitation exists, it is not necessary for one group to have an advantage over the other in each and every power domain. Assume, for example, that genetic domination is altogether absent from society, with each citizen, regardless of race, enjoying a perfectly legitimate relationship in that power dimension. Such a condition of perfectly equal (in this case, zero) sacrifice in one power domain cannot compensate for the systematic disadvantages encountered in other domains. To put the point arithmetically: equals added to unequals maintains the initial inequality. This means that X would not cease being an exploitative society simply by moving to end disadvantage in one or another particular power domain. However important such triumphs may be, exploitation continues so long as all the remaining disadvantages favor the whites.

Having grasped the conceptual features of exploitation, it remains to deploy the idea under more complex social conditions. For starters, complicate the black-and-white model by stipulating that severe genetic disabilities are distributed throughout the population on principles that do not respect the color line. Hence, the prevailing power structure now defines four different groups: handicapped/black (h/b); "normal"/black (n/b); handicapped/white (h/w); and normal/white (n/w). Assume, finally, the handicapped are given no special assistance to compensate them for their plain genetic disadvantage.[4] In such a case, the pattern of exploitation is no less clear: citizens who fall within the n/w class exploit *all* the others, while those in n/b exploit those in h/b. The hard case arises only when comparing the sacrifice demanded of h/w with that of n/b. Here the concept of exploitation does not apply; since the patterns of disadvantage do not move in only one direction, the problem of aggregation arises with full force. Nonetheless, this difficulty does not at all undercut the fact that *both* the blacks and the handicapped are, on the facts hypothesized, *plainly* exploited by the "normal" whites. While the power relationships between certain groups may be hard to evaluate, the exploitative character of other relations can be entirely uncontroversial.

And, of course, it is possible to get as complicated as necessary to describe all the important power relations obtaining in a particular society. Thus, I myself live in a world where, in addition to obvious victims of racism and genetic handicap, many citizens are disadvantaged by being: (*a*) born into families whose parents are not capitalists

4. For the second-best complexities involved in the definition of genetic domination, see § 29.2.

or communist party members, as the case may be; or (*b*) born female and subjected to a more authoritarian education than their male counterparts. In such a world, only normal white capitalist males (n/w/c/m) unequivocally exploit *everyone* else, while everyone except handicapped black female proletarians would have a more complicated relationship to exploitation. Consider, for example, the tripartite analysis required to understand the position of the normal white proletarian males (n/w/p/m): While they are exploited by (n/w/c/m), they exploit (n/b/p/m), (n/b/p/f), (h/w/p/m), (h/w/p/f), (h/b/p/m), and (h/b/p/f); finally, they stand in a more ambiguous position with regard to (n/w/c/f), (n/b/c/m), (n/b/c/f), (h/w/c/m), and (h/w/c/f). In such a society, identifying a person as a proletarian hardly means that he is invariably the victim of exploitation in all his relationships; while he is exploited in some roles, he is the exploiter in others.

Exploitation, in short, can be a complex business. Since this very complexity may prove an initial stumbling block, let me indulge a preliminary defense before doubt solidifies into prejudice. Consider, then, that the theory I am advancing flies in the face of two simpler opinions. First, there is the conventional liberal approach, which views all talk of exploitation with suspicion.[5] Then there are the more radical folks who, though they greet exploitation talk with great enthusiasm, typically speak as if exploited and exploiter can be neatly sorted into two grand classes containing all humanity. Hence both camps can be expected to join forces against a view that not only says that exploitation talk makes sense but that it makes a *complicated* kind of sense. So far as liberals are concerned, the proof of this claim is the entire dialogic framework presented here. It is my disagreement with the conventional radical notion, deriving from Marx, that can be clarified usefully here. Most important, I do *not* deny that the notion of exploitation *can* have very straightforward applications; indeed, I began analysis with a black-and-white model in which exploiting and exploited classes could be distinguished neatly enough. My claim is that this simple view makes sense only in a world where *all* the people in one class, call them now capitalists, get *each* and *every* advantage, while *all* the people in another class, call them proletarians, receive *each* and *every* disadvantage generated by the power structure. Put differently, if

---

5. I shall discuss liberal attitudes toward exploitation more thoroughly at § 59. The liberal suspicion of such talk ripens, of course, into affirmative disgust in conservative circles.

the real world corresponded to the (vulgar) Marxist picture of it, then I would agree that all proletarians are unambiguous victims of capitalist exploitation.[6] The problem is *not* that my abstract conception of exploitation is terribly complex; the problem is that *the world is complex.* If the social system distributes different kinds of power advantage in different ways, then a theory of exploitation should not be faulted for taking this into account.

Moreover, the complexity we have described does not disturb the clarity of some central second-best judgments. Even in the more realistic situation we are now modeling, there are millions upon millions of people who occupy an unambiguously exploitative position over all the rest, while millions more exploit countless others. All of this involves a breach of each citizen's prima facie right to demand that others, no less than himself, be called upon to sacrifice their ideal rights before the altar of second-best necessity.

55.3. *The Core of the Aggregation Problem*

Nonetheless, there *are* harder cases. Consider, for example, the comparison between the (h/w/c/f) and the (n/b/p/m) in the society we have hypothesized. How is the statesman to decide whether the special sacrifices imposed on a citizen's power by virtue of sex and physical handicap are greater than the sacrifices imposed on another by color and wealth?

Such questions admit of only despairing conclusions, despair no less epistemological than moral. The distinction between *ordinal* and *cardinal* judgments, borrowed from welfare economics, can usefully clarify the point. When making an *ordinal* judgment, the statesman contents himself with saying that A has more of some quantity than B; in contrast, a *cardinal* judgment requires him to specify *how much* more of the quantity A has. Thus, when working with the concept of exploitation in the last section, all we required was an *ordinal* judgment in each of the particular power domains that defined the overall relationship between A and B. So long as A had, in some domains, a plain advantage over B, while B had no advantages over A, then the statesman could confidently assert the existence of exploitation on

6. It should be emphasized that my notion of undominated equality is different from the Marxist one of "surplus value." Nonetheless, *if* the world actually conformed perfectly Marx's model, I would agree that the (white, normal, male) capitalists were plainly exploiting the proletarians.

the basis of ordinal rankings only. In the present comparison, however, the statesman must make cardinal judgments, comparing the value of the powers sacrificed by wealthy, but handicapped, white females to the powers lost by normal, . . . but impoverished, black males. Only two things are clear: first, however a particular statesman may resolve such dilemmas, he will be quick to concede that another may reasonably resolve it differently; second, such judgments of comparative degradation will fuel the statesman's demand for an ongoing reform of the power structures that make them necessary. Simply put: In a world where racism, sexism, and the like did not afflict the basic power structure, there would no longer be any point in considering the particular examples we have been offering. Rather than playing one group of oppressed citizens off against the others, liberal government must aggressively question the need for exploitation in all its forms.

55.4. *Compensation*

Yet an all-out attack on all root causes is beyond our present powers. In saying this, I do not mean to point to the obvious power of illiberal forces who struggle to retain their exploitative advantages; that would be to invoke third-best factors prematurely. Even if we restrict ourselves to the terms of second-best argument, it is simply beyond our present technological capacity to remedy unequal sacrifice in some power domains. Genetic disadvantage provides straightforward examples. A child is born blind; assume[7] that this defect qualifies him as a victim of genetic domination, and that the blindness is incurable under present medical technology. This means that the statesman cannot hope to root out genetic domination at its source. To fulfill the requirement of equivalent sacrifice, he will be obliged to compensate the blind citizen by giving him advantages in other power domains. Yet this makes a confrontation with the aggregation problem inevitable: how many educational, material, transactional advantages must the blind child receive before he is compensated for his initial disadvantage?

The unavoidable difficulties can at least be clarified if the compensation effort is divided into two analytic phases. The first is marked by a concern with "negative" compensation. The object here is to assure

7. For the problematics of second-best classification, see § 29.2.

the victims of blindness that their initial disadvantage will not be exacerbated further by their treatment in other power domains. Thus, negative compensation requires that the blind child be provided an education *no less liberal* than that provided others. He can no more be deprived of the tools necessary for an understanding of his life options than can any other child. The fact that the blind suffer one injustice does not warrant their suffering another. Nor can the demand for "negative" compensation be satisfied by a showing that per pupil expenditure upon blind children is equal to that invested in more gifted citizens. The liberality of an education is not to be measured by money spent but by insight gained, by the success with which children attain an actual sense of the domain of their moral freedom. Nonetheless, a point must come where the statesman must draw the line on further negative compensation and say that the (enormous) imperfections that remain in the blind child's education are no greater than those that afflict other children. The precise location of this line will, quite obviously, be a matter upon which different statesman may appropriately disagree with one another in good faith. Nonetheless, while statesman will differ on the line-drawing question, none will deny the blind child's prima facie right to an education equivalent in liberality to that received by his contemporaries.

I have labored this simple point because it prepares the way for another that will be greeted with greater resistance. I aim to prove that a liberal statesman cannot settle for a negative compensation policy. He must move beyond and act affirmatively on behalf of those, like the handicapped, who suffer from irremediable domination. Like its negative counterpart, moreover, affirmative action will engender a ceaseless good-faith debate when it comes to the question of implementation. The existence of this ongoing debate, however, should no more discredit affirmative action than does the identical pattern of clarity and controversy discredit negative compensation.

So much for the conclusions. The first step in the affirmative argument is to prove that liberal statesmen must *necessarily* conclude that negative compensation is *plainly* insufficient to satisfy the principle of equivalent sacrifice. To do this, assume that a compensation program, N, exists that is universally agreed to satisfy the negative principle. Thus, N assures the blind citizen that in each and every power domain—other than genetic—he is asked to make a sacrifice of his ideal rights that is no greater than that required of his fellows. To prove that N is nonetheless unacceptable, simply display the salient features in a table where = stands for the condition of equivalent sacrifice, while − or + stands for deviation from this standard.

Power Relations After Negative Compensation

Citizenship Rights	Blind	Sighted
Genetic Abilities	−	+
Liberal Education	=	=
Material Wealth	=	=
Transactional Flexibility	=	=
Trusteeship Rights	=	=
Overall Evaluation	−	+

Given this display, the proof of N's illegitimacy is obtained by simple addition. To end exploitation, it is not enough to eliminate one or another form of illegitimate dominion. *Exploitation continues so long as the remaining patterns of advantage favor the same group.* Moreover, N's exploitative character may be ascertained by engaging in an uncontroversial act of *ordinal* judgment, without the need to ask *how much* worse off a blind person is than a sighted one. It follows that a statesman who wants to conform to the prima facie principle of equivalent sacrifice must move beyond negative compensation. A blind citizen has a right to insist that others make a *greater* sacrifice of their rights in nongenetic domains if overall equivalence is to be achieved. In terms of the chart, it is only by placing a compensatory + in at least one of Blind's remaining rows, with a corresponding − in Sighted's row, that a compensation program can escape the charge that it is *plainly* incapable of ending exploitation.

But while the principle of affirmative action may be generated from second-best theory by anybody who understands the difference between a + and a −, the proper implementation of this obligation is a very different matter. The precise identity of the power domain(s) in which victims of irremediable disadvantage are best compensated depends heavily on particular contexts and contestable judgments concerning the ways in which the blind's claim to equal respect can best be supported in the overall public dialogue. Despite the contestability of any particular program, however, the statesman cannot flinch from the need for decision. While working in a dim half-light may be unpleasant, one thing remains worse: accepting a policy of negative compensation that is *demonstrably* inadequate to the task of ending exploitation.

So much for blindness. I have chosen the example of genetic domination to emphasize that the case for compensation—affirmative as
well as negative—does not require proof that a group has been shame-
lessly exploited in the past by oppressors who proudly justified their
action by explicitly authoritarian pronunciamentos. Instead, we have
been dealing here in second-best, not third-best, terms: Even a polity
that had *throughout* its history been devoted to liberal principles
would have to confront the need for some forms of affirmative action
if it hoped to redeem its dialogic commitments in a world without the
Master Geneticist. The conclusion that emerges is that the principle of
affirmative action can be rooted far more deeply in liberal theory than
is conventionally believed.

55.5. *Statesmanship: A Partial Synthesis*

We may summarize our story in terms of a three-phase process of
deliberation. When asked to prepare a budget with an overall size of
B_i the statesman's first concern is with the problem of exploitation.
The existence of an overall budget constraint does not justify a decision to lavish protection on some people while others are denied equal
rights as a "cost-saving" measure. Since everybody is at least as good as
everybody else, each must make an equal sacrifice of his rights unless
he can justify his advantage in a way consistent with Neutrality. While
there are many occasions for disputable judgment in applying this
standard, the half-light of contestable equivalence cannot obscure the
existence of power structures that blatantly exact unequal sacrifice.
The statesman's first prima facie obligation is to free the polity of such
exploitative structures.

Even after all exploitative budgets have been eliminated, however,
many budgetary options will still seem plausible. This means that the
statesman must carry on the process of elimination to a second stage.
Here he must make the cardinal judgments necessary to judge the
seriousness of different violations of equal sacrifice. After making
these judgments, he must eliminate all B_i-sized budgets that fail to
yield a system of rights that satisfies his contestable understanding of
the concept of equal sacrifice.

And even when the winnowing process has reached this point,
there is no assurance that only one budget will remain standing. At
this stage, all of the admissible budgets distribute structural resources
in ways that satisfy the statesman's notion of equal sacrifice; nonetheless, one budget might contain large expenditures for liberal educa-

tion and small ones for transactional flexibility; another may reverse these priorities; and so forth. It follows that a second round of contestable judgments is required where the statesman must trade off the value of additional investments in education against competing investments in transactional flexibility and other areas of structural concern.

Now, as I warned earlier, I shall be saying very little about these "particular" trade-offs between different forms of liberal investment—not because these decisions are unimportant, but because so much depends on context. Thus, a small increase in investment may sometimes yield great returns in liberal education, while enormous expenditures will be worse than useless on other occasions.

The picture of statesmanship that emerges from this initial survey, then, has precisely the black and gray quality promised at the outset. Given a B_i-sized bundle of structural resources, it is relatively easy for the statesman to identify a subset of exploitative budgets that are prima facie unacceptable; harder to select from the remainder the subset that satisfies his affirmative understanding of equal sacrifice; harder still to select the particular budget that, within the preceding constraints, promises the most adequate realization of liberal values. This tripartite structure of statesmanly judgment, moreover, can be expected to control the texture of political discourse in a liberal state. Thus, we may glimpse a political dialogue that permits its participants to distinguish the fundamental from the problematic, that enables liberal statesmen to affirm their common opposition to exploitation while differing as to the shape of power that best captures the liberal ideal in a given time and place.

56. EXPLOITATION AND OVERALL BUDGET SIZE

We can now lift the analytic blinkers that have previously encumbered our statesman. Rather than stipulating a structural budget of a given overall size, he is now given the power to choose any B_i that he thinks best. How, if at all, does second-best theory constrain this choice?

56.1. *Intrinsically Exploitative Budget Sizes*
Once again, the concept of exploitation plays a fundamental role. To see how, we must build upon the preceding theory of budgetary choice under a fixed B_i. We saw there that the statesman's first task

was to eliminate all particular budgets (b_i's) that enforced an exploitative regime. After this clearing operation took place, he could then consider the happier—if conceptually more problematic—task of choosing amongst the nonexploitative budgets that remain live options. Now that B_i is permitted to assume any size, however, a darker prospect comes into view. What if the statesman chooses an overall budget size *so* small that it is simply impossible to remedy all the clear cases of exploitation generated by the prevailing social structure? Recall, for example, our model exploitative society—scarred by racism, sexism, genetic handicap, and initial inequality of wealth. Unless the budget is of a certain overall size, B_{min}, there will be no way of transforming all these forms of exploitation into *any* structure of even contestable equivalence. All "subminimal" budget sizes, B_s, are *intrinsically* exploitative. Thus, the question is whether the theory of exploitation can be extended to condemn an entire budget size, B_s, as prima facie illegitimate.

I shall need one empirical assumption before answering this question in the affirmative. And that concerns the size of the minimal budget. For if B_{min} is so large that it exhausts all available resources, then *all* feasible Bs are intrinsically exploitative, and the only relevant question would be the form of exploitation that was least intolerable. If, however, there is at least one B_{min} that will not exhaust all resources, the following dialogue is applicable:

BLACK: I am exploited. If this is a liberal state, I'm entitled to more power.

STATESMAN: Sorry, I can't do anything about it.

BLACK: Why not?

STATESMAN: Well, if you must know, the government has just gone bankrupt. There's nothing left in the till to fight injustice.

BLACK: That's no reason at all.

STATESMAN: Why not?

BLACK: It was within your power to propose a minimal but nonexploitative budget rather than this outrageously small one.

STATESMAN: Yes, that's true.

BLACK: So why have you used your power over the budget in one way rather than the other?

STATESMAN: Do I have to answer that?

BLACK: You do if you want to qualify as a liberal statesman. The Rationality principle gives you no choice.

STATESMAN: Well, then, look at the problem I'd be creating for myself if I used my power the way you suggest. I'd have to raise taxes to increase the budget.

BLACK: But why is that a problem?

STATESMAN: Because of the people whose taxes would be increased: I'd have to tax the powerful.

BLACK: Right again. You can't end exploitation by imposing all the extra taxes on me. But I still don't see why this makes for a problem.

STATESMAN: Isn't it obvious? I don't want to annoy powerful people.

BLACK: *Of course* my exploiters will be annoyed if you take their power away from them; similarly, I'll be annoyed if you don't respond affirmatively to my demands. But the truth is that none of us can rightfully expect to gain anything through a show of pique. In a liberal state, the only way to gain power is through dialogue.

A critical dialogue, I think. Moreover, in an effort to make Black's conversational victory straightforward, the script failed to probe an important weakness in the statesman's already inadequate defense. When, near the outset, the statesman announced, "There was nothing left in the till to fight injustice," he must have been exaggerating. If there were *absolutely* nothing left, the government could no longer resolve *any* disputes. And in that case, it would no longer qualify as a government at all—for I take it to be definitional that a government must undertake to settle at least *some* conflicts.[8]

It follows that *at the very moment the bankruptcy dialogue is taking place,* the government is in fact resolving *some* disputes between people struggling over scarce resources. Indeed, it is very likely that some of the disputes involve blacks charged with "theft" of one kind or another. Thus, we can imagine a black trying to conduct the bankruptcy dialogue at his criminal trial. More generally, the dialogue of bankruptcy threatens the statesman's legitimacy not only when he enforces the laws of property, but when he seeks to compel obedience to any other aspect of the power structure.

8. This is not to say that a place without a government is inconceivable. It would simply be a world where everybody is free to grab anything he can without ever being obliged to justify his conduct before any institution charged with settling disputes. Might would make right, and the powerful could cut off the question of legitimacy whenever it got uncomfortable. It is enough, for now, to say that this condition of anarchy is inconsistent with the first principle— Rationality—of liberal theory. See § 11.2.

A grim prospect. Yet it casts a shadow upon a power structure that has long preoccupied partisans of the liberal tradition. The statesman who is most likely to choose an intrinsically exploitative budget is precisely the advocate of laissez faire. While proposals for "minimal" government differ in detail, I take their essence to be a refusal to permit the state to question the overall distribution of power in society. The distribution of private property is, of course, the traditional center of concern, but laissez faire also extends to the distribution of genetic, educational, and transactional opportunities.[9] After insulating all these issues from governmental "interference," the partisan of laissez faire characteristically turns activist—and urges his watchman state to punish anybody disturbing the sanctity of those personal and property rights whose legitimacy he has not been permitted to question. Billions for police, but not a penny for dialogue.

So long as exploitation scars the power structure, the bankruptcy dialogue haunts the watchman state. Not that it inevitably serves as the last word on laissez faire. As we shall see,[10] a regime of unequal sacrifice may sometimes be justified at a subsequent stage in the political conversation. Nonetheless, the dialogue does suggest the harm done by those who work to confuse the spirit of liberalism with the outworn husk of laissez faire ideology.

56.2. *Beyond the Minimal Budget*

As always, exploitation only excludes options; it does not provide the statesman with a unique solution to his choice problem. After all subminimal budgets are put to one side as prima facie inadmissible, a large range of budget sizes may well remain open, and the selection of a particular size will require a final trade-off.

One side of the equation is obvious enough. As the budget increases, the statesman will find room for intrinsically worthy projects that the costs of an imperfect technology excluded previously: an enriched education, greater transactional flexibility, more certain protection for property rights in material wealth. On the other hand, a point will come where further increases in the structural budget will reduce the material wealth distributed to each adult for the purpose of fulfilling his ends in life. In shorthand: an increase in B_i competes with resources available for self-regarding expenditure, S_i. Thus, the

9. The trusteeship question is barely glimpsed.
10. See the appeal to general advantage, § 54, and the problem of tyranny, § 63. The standing of laissez faire is discussed further in §§ 58–59.

statesman must somehow assess the gains in liberal value achieved by marginal increases in B_i and compare them with the losses in liberal value suffered as a result of decreases in S_i. Now, I want to say that liberals can, in good faith, adopt a very wide range of answers to this question. But I should like to reach this conclusion by first isolating a single response that, I think, is incontestably inappropriate.

Imagine, then, that a statesman takes a "purist" position on the trade-off between B_i and S_i. So far as he is concerned, it is *always* worthwhile to invest in increases in the liberality of structure, whatever the cost in self-regarding expenditure. Given our grossly imperfect technology, this purist commitment can have only one result. Save for the minimal amount necessary to keep the citizenry alive and talking for the next period, everything will be spent on structure—and even that will prove inadequate to obtain the ideal of perfectly undominated equality. A bizarre prospect: billions of citizens, condemned to bread and water, spending all their time building, say, a "better" transmitter-shield system!

Rather than challenging the premises of liberal theory, however, such daunting images suggest that the purist has mistaken a part of the liberal ideal for the whole. The ideal liberal state is not a place where a citizen's only consolation is the tedious repetition of the mantra "Because I'm at least as good as you are." To the contrary, given a costless technology of justice, all that is required of any citizen is that he enter the dialogue once to claim his rights. Then, if other things interest him more, he may simply instruct his transmitter-shield to provide a recorded announcement to answer others if they wish to challenge the legitimacy of his rightful exercise of power. Neutral dialogue is only a *necessary condition* for legitimating each citizen's desire to use his power in pursuit of the life he thinks worth living. To force all citizens to exhaust their lives in the service of dialogue is to render it pointless; it is to enslave all to the very ideal that would make them free.

The ideal Commander cannot, of course, make this mistake. By definition, she has a costless technology of justice at her disposal; hence, the pursuit of legitimacy does not entail any sacrifice in self-regarding investment. But to avoid the mistake under second-best conditions, the statesman must recognize that the quest for the best feasible structure, regardless of cost, is self-defeating in terms of the liberal ideal itself. While this much must be recognized, we will soon predictably find ourselves in the gray area of fair dispute. Granted that *some* substantial sum must be allocated to adults to spend as they like, how much is enough to escape the charge of misguided purism?

The question is made more difficult when the relationship of structural investment to the exercise of adult freedoms is kept clearly in view. When the polity provides a handicapped child with special care, when it assures all of us a good liberal education and flexible means of transaction, these steps not only respond to each citizen's demand for equal respect; they also provide each citizen with tools for self-realization that are no less essential than the receipt of some material assets upon maturity. Since investments in *both S* and *B* are critical for self-realization, the best way of trading off increments will be a deeply contestable matter. Since there will be no prospect of a single "right" answer emerging, day-to-day governance will largely consist in a discussion of particular proposals. Thus, a modest investment that some statesman believes will vastly increase the flexibility of transaction will seem to others nothing better than an expensive toy doomed to failure. And so forth.

While active participation in this debate will have its peculiar rewards, many will find the detailed trade-off talk boring and spend most of their time on other pursuits they find more rewarding. Nor can they be denied this right. Engaged liberal statesmanship, after all, is only *one* of the good lives made possible by a liberal state; citizens have the right to ignore the daily trade-offs of liberal politics and yet have their views treated with respect when they turn, from time to time, to governance. Indeed, the proper relationship between full-time politicians and the relatively apolitical mass of the citizenry is an abiding concern of liberal constitutional theory.[11] I shall merely remark here, however, upon a single principle governing the ongoing process of accountability between professional politicians and the mass of the citizenry: the concept of exploitation. However contestable and complex day-to-day governance, it will be easy to pierce the fog if the resulting budget turns out to support an exploitative power structure. Plain breaches of the requirement of equal sacrifice can never be treated as part of the humdrum affairs of state. They are prima facie illegitimate, and before they can be tolerated, the victims are entitled to a clear explanation of why special privilege is consistent with their fundamental standing as free citizens of a liberal state.

11. And one that will bulk much larger in my next book than it does in this one.

56.3. *The Worst of All Possible Liberal Worlds*

We shall shortly turn to consider this second round of second-best discourse, where citizens try to defend deviations from equal sacrifice in ways consistent with Neutrality. Before doing so, however, I must remark upon a grim prospect raised by the first stage of the analysis. Thus far, we have been talking as if it were always possible to divide the range of statesmanly choice into three distinct regions: those budgets that are intrinsically exploitative; those that are indefensibly purist; and the middle range over which liberal statesmen may legitimately differ. It is possible, however, for the two extremes to crowd out the middle. Here the *only* nonexploitative budgets available exhaust so large a proportion of total resources that nothing substantial is left over for purposes of self-regarding expenditure. The image is not of a citizenry on a starvation budget for the sake of perfect transmitter-shields, but one where starvation follows from the *equal* distribution of even a minimal set of liberal rights. If, then, the *only* choice is between purism and exploitation, in which direction should it be made?

To put the dilemma in practical terms, suppose powerful political movements in both China and India prepared realistic programs that promised the ultimate construction of a liberal power structure. While most of the work was to be done at home, the plan would demand from richer nations assistance valued at hundreds of *billions* a year for a generation. I say demand, not request: If the people of China and India proposed to build their own domestic relations on liberal principles, would they not have an equal right to regulate their relations with others on the same basis? Are they not as good as anybody else is?

To refuse such a demand, the rich people of the world would be obliged to respond in a plainly exploitative fashion. They would be forced to say that they were entitled to more simply because they were born on one side of an arbitrary geographic boundary rather than another, that Americans were intrinsically superior to Indians, Japanese to Chinese. We have, of course, heard all this before. Worse yet, there is a recurring need to paper greed over with a complex vocabulary—sometimes nationalist, sometimes racist, often both, but always hostile to liberal principle. When this husk is stripped away, however, the kernel of dilemma remains. The fact is that accepting the Asian demand could well engender the purist nightmare—with *all* starving in the name of legitimate freedom. Which, then, do you choose—starvation or exploitation?

This much, I take it, is clear enough: the people living on the rich side of the line would be obliged to make serious sacrifices in self-regarding investment if they hoped to show their liberalism to be more than gross pretense. Beyond that, though, there can only be two terrible answers: freedom without legitimacy or legitimacy without freedom. This is the final dilemma of a liberal world where population growth has outstripped resource development.

There can be no easy way to manage this tension. While there are, I am sure, more and less illiberal ways of managing the intractable dilemmas of foreign policy, I cannot say anything particularly useful about them. Beyond the necessity of a *substantial* aid program to undeveloped countries of a liberal tendency, I can manage only one other principle of statecraft. And that is to take vigorous steps to assure that the intractable difficulties of international relations should not infect the integrity of liberal politics on the national level. When we successfully struggle against domestic forms of exploitation, we not only build our own society on firmer foundations, but give an example to others of the liberal meaning of freedom—an example that they, in turn, will find useful in interpreting their own experience. By deepening the foundations of liberal dialogue at home, we can only increase its power abroad.

57. THE APPEAL TO GENERAL ADVANTAGE

Let us return, then, to the domestic dialogue of the richer half of the world, which does not confront the stark choice between purism and exploitation in domestic political life.[12] Here we may imagine each liberal statesman selecting an overall budget size, B_i, in the "intermediate" zone where B_i is neither so small that it is intrinsically exploitative nor so large that it is impossible for each adult to engage in substantial self-regarding investment.

Given B_i, the statesman will select a particular budget, b_i, which he thinks best approximates liberal ideals within the constraint of equal sacrifice. It is at this point that each statesman reaches the final stage of second-best argument. Up to now, the statesmanly decision was sharply constrained by the concept of exploitation. At every critical stage,

12. Am I overly optimistic? Must even America recognize that some citizens—say, the desperately handicapped—may properly be sacrificed to avoid the dilemmas of purism?

I have not made the empirical study needed to answer this question soberly. My aim here is to show the grievous dialogic breach implied by an affirmative reply, cf. §§ 29, 56, and 59.2, as a caution to those for whom talk of triage comes cheap.

exploitative solutions were excluded as prima facie inadmissible. It now remains to ask whether this prima facie constraint can ever be removed, whether the statesman can *ever* justify lifting the constraint of equal sacrifice, and thereby reject b_i in favor of some other budget, b_s,[13] which gives some citizens special rights that others do not possess. As always, the bar against exploitation can never be breached unless the statesman can justify special advantage in a way consistent with Neutrality. He cannot say that the advantaged are especially superior people or that their goals in life warrant special public approbation. But if these moves are closed, what remains open?

The basic response is clear enough. Call it the appeal to general advantage. Rather than proclaiming the moral superiority of the advantaged class, the statesman makes an instrumental case for special privilege. Even though b_i stands as the best budget given equal sacrifice, it hardly follows that the citizenry will live in the best of all possible worlds. Scarce resources and an imperfect technology will require the statesman to deny a multitude of legitimate "structural" claims—for fuller genetic compensation, deeper liberal education, greater transactional flexibility, and a more ample vindication of trusteeship. Similarly, b_i will provide each adult citizen with an equal, but very finite, share of material resources with which to pursue his aims in life. Thus, it is at least possible for the rights of all to be enriched by giving special advantages to a few. To make this conceptual possibility into a concrete reality, however, will require an argument that indulges a complicated set of empirical—hence contestable—premises.

Call it the incentive-tax argument. To make it work, the statesman must assert, first, that the prospect of one or another special advantage will serve as an incentive for the increased production of some scarce resource that would not have been supplied under the regime of strictly equal sacrifice; second, that he can design a tax scheme that will deprive the advantaged of some of the extra resources they produce, without leaving them fewer rights than they would have possessed under the equal-sacrifice regime, b_i; and third, that the extra taxes will be spent in a way that gives the disadvantaged a richer set of liberal entitlements than they would have had under b_i. If all three of these

13. As defined, b_s, is an exploitative budget equal in overall size, B_i, to the preferred nonexploitative budget, b_i. I do not see any special difficulty, however, in generalizing the paragraphs that follow to govern choice between b_i and exploitative budgets of overall sizes that are different from B_i.

conditions apply, the empirical groundwork has been laid for a successful claim of general advantage.

This is, of course, a very abstract way of putting the argument. Nonetheless, I can confidently leave its concrete elaboration to the elites of any society who are forced to face the challenge of liberal dialogue. Elites are notoriously quick to imagine that their special advantages redound to the benefit of all. When given the chance, they will press this conversational opening with all the energy and ingenuity they can muster, seeing a counterproductive loss of incentives in every move that threatens their meanest privilege. Moreover, they may be relied upon to dress their fears up in the most impressive empirical forms, defending their advantage with reams of computer printout if this will make their case seem more credible.

All such "demonstrations" will serve as acid tests for liberal statesmanship. First, elaborate care must be taken to assure that the "demonstration" is not merely the result of superior access to technocratic tools. Special arrangements must assure that the empirical case for equal sacrifice is argued with the same energy and technical sophistication as the one mounted on behalf of special privilege. And even if this requirement is satisfied, the fact remains that the merits of particular tax-incentive arguments will inevitably remain within the competence of a small number of specialists. While there is a difference between facts and values, a policy that gives too great a weight to technocratic argument runs the risk that technocrats, to advance their own moral pretentions, will abuse their claims to factual accuracy.

After all is said and done, however, it remains possible that the rich and powerful may sometimes be right on the facts. And if the empirical showing is sufficiently persuasive to overcome the suspicion of self-interested propaganda, the statesman is justified in giving attention to the claim of general advantage. At this point, however, a second difficulty must be confronted—one involving values, not facts.

The problem may best be explored through an illustrative case. Imagine that the statesman is considering an inheritance law that violates trusteeship by permitting rich parents to give their children twice as much money as their poorer generation-mates. Suppose, further, that if parents are given this incentive, they will engage in activities that permit an increase in tax revenues which, in turn, will be invested in an education for all children which is judged more liberal than the one provided by a regime committed to egalitarian inheritance. To beg a critical question for a moment, denote this added increment in liberal education by the index number e, while the liberality of the inferior education is indexed at i. Thus, if the statesman *rejects* the unequal inheritance proposal, the next generation will look like this:

	"Rich" Children	"Poor" Children
Education	i	i
Material Assets	=	=

While if he accepts it:

	"Rich" Children	"Poor" Children
Education	$i + e$	$i + e$
Material Assets	+	−

On these facts, the liberal statesman cannot justify the appeal to general advantage by means of a straightforward ordinal judgment. Instead, the question necessarily requires a cardinal comparison of an essentially contestable kind.[14] The prospect is for unending debate. Sometimes the weight of statesmanly opinion will place a relatively small value on the principle of initial equality of wealth—what will seem of prime importance is the depth of the poor child's liberal education, the flexibility of his transactional system, the quantity of his self-regarding expenditure. Here the tax-incentive argument may have a wide range of application. At other times and places, most statesmen will consider initial material equality a vital social prop for the equal respect that is proudly proclaimed in public dialogue. Here the tax-incentive argument will operate as a narrow exception, justified only when the benefits to the disadvantaged group are plainly enormous. Given the fundamental character of this dispute, it is easy to predict that the appeal to general advantage will often generate angry disagreement. Yet however bitter any particular battle on special privilege, the hard fact is that the outcome will always be essentially contestable; the collective judgment is always subject to reconsideration—if not tomorrow, then by a new generation confronting fresh facts and a new sense of the possibilities for the realistic development of the liberal ideal of undominated equality.

Indeed, it is only this collective sense of the *contestability* of special advantage which stands as a permanent value that must be preserved at all cost. Elites would vastly prefer a political discourse that did not require them to justify their privileges on the instrumental—hence,

14. § 55.3.

problematic—ground of general advantage. Instead, they would gladly convince themselves and others that their special advantages are tokens of their intrinsic superiority over the mass, that any challenge to their privileges shakes the order of the moral universe. This sense of irritation with Neutral dialogue only increases with the size of the special privileges an elite has obtained. Power corrupts; when further special privileges put the future vitality of liberal dialogue at serious risk, the time has come to draw the line.

58. CAPITALISM, SOCIALISM, LIBERALISM

How, then, does the liberal statesman propose to bridge the gap between ideal and reality?

Through conversation—by offering up a concrete program that can be defended as the most appropriate means to the end of Neutral dialogue. What I have done here is not to be confused with this creative act of statesmanship. Instead, I have provided an abstract account of the process of dialogic justification. Not that a statesman can afford the time necessary for the exhausting process I have outlined. Instead of beginning, as I have done, with a universe consisting of all possible budgets of all possible budget sizes, the statesman will inevitably take a far less comprehensive view. Time pressures will narrow serious discussion to a relatively small set of policy options. Nonetheless, if he hopes for a liberal legitimacy, the statesman must accept my dialogic outline as the one that should, in principle, govern his inevitably more partial efforts at justification. On this understanding, it will be useful to attempt a final summary.

The first stage involves the selection of a budget that prima facie serves as the best approximation of liberal ideals. The process may be analogized to a mathematical problem in constrained maximization. The constraint is the idea of equal sacrifice: since everyone is at least as good as everyone else, no one can be called upon to sacrifice more of his ideal rights than anyone else. Within this constraint, the statesman's task is to choose the budget that best fulfills the liberal ideal of undominated equality.

Neither aspect of this exercise in constrained maximization is selfdefining. So far as the constraint is concerned, the concept of exploitation only serves to mark out a core of clear cases; the statesman must confront a wide range of contestable cardinal judgments before he can articulate a well-specified conception of the nature of equal sacrifice. Similarly, the effort to maximize liberal ideals will raise a host of contestable questions involved in the evaluation of inevitably imperfect systems for compensating genetic disadvantage, assuring liberal education, and guaranteeing transactional flexibility.

A different pattern emerges at the second stage of decision, where the statesman considers whether it is in the general advantage to relax the collective commitment to the principle of equal sacrifice. Here the watchword must be caution. The temptations for elite abuse are overwhelming: moreover, the facts necessary for the incentive-tax argument will change over time. Solid empirical foundations may disappear; other claims, previously unrealistic, may take on greater weight. It is only when the empirical evidence is compelling, and the general advantage is substantial, that the incentive-tax argument may be taken seriously in political decision.

All in all, a project that will exhaust a Hercules of dialogue. Rather than expecting any single statesman to explore the entire universe of argument, each must be alive to the possibility that others may have glimpsed something valuable in the vast universe of possibility. It is possible, then, for the whole of the political dialogue to be greater than the sum of its parts, with statesmen actually convincing one another to change their minds in ways each previously thought unimaginable. The theory I have presented can be no more than a skeleton—which only a collective commitment to statesmanship can transform into a form of life.

Nonetheless, I hope I have said enough to permit a contrast with more familiar notions of statecraft inherited from the century long debate between laissez faire capitalism and Marxism-Leninism. Consider, first, the night-watchman figure familiar in laissez faire theory. As we have seen, the liberal statesman cannot accept the notion that his job is limited to propping up the power structures generated by the owners of private property. Before these power wielders can call upon government assistance, they must legitimate their power through dialogue. And when the only thing they can say offends Neutrality, the exploitative character of their domination must be unmasked. Not that private property owners must *inevitably* find themselves embarrassed in a dialogic test. It *is* possible, I suppose, to imagine an invisible hand arranging history so that members of a particular generation find that they have gotten exactly what they are entitled to under the principles of equal sacrifice—each obtaining genetic, educational, material, and transactional opportunities of arguable equivalence. If such a happenstance occurred, there would be no need for liberal government to concern itself with exploitation. Moreover, as chapter 6 established, the liberal state *is* deeply committed to the ideal of free exchange—*provided* that mutually beneficial trade occurs within a power structure legitimated by liberal dialogue. Thus, if a liberal deity made life easy for us and arranged history so that a just structure evolved without conscious direction, it would be possible to defend a laissez faire position.[15] But there is no reason to think the invisible hand will ever lead us to the promised land without any assistance on our part. The end of exploitation will come only through self-conscious political action—as citizens seek to shape an intractable reality so that it may conform, however crudely, to the requirements of liberal dialogue.

In distancing himself from the invisible hand, the liberal statesman resembles the leader of a Marxist party, who is similarly unimpressed by the claims of private property to "natural" right. Nonetheless, the liberal's questioning of the existing power structure does not lead to the familiar posturings of the Leninist dictator. Rather than ramming his views down another's throat in the name of "democratic centralism," the statesman can never imagine that his particular version of second-best policy is the only acceptable approximation of liberal ideals. If he ever finds himself the only one talking, he knows he has failed in his great ambition. It is dialogue, not monologue, that provides the only legitimate way to establish a just society.

The liberal statesman, in short, offers a qualitatively different form of leadership than that promised by familiar extremists of the right and the left. From the liberal point of view, the best form of socioeconomic organization is the one in which the pretentions to eternal truth inevitably advanced by the powerful are kept most firmly in check; where emerging structures of exploitation are destroyed before they take root; where free people affirm their own visions of the good after considering the virtues of alternative experiments in

---

15. Though, even here, the argument is not open and shut. There will, generally, be *many* power structures that pass the test of equal sacrifice, and the invisible hand may have chosen one that fails to gain the support of a majority of liberal statesmen. If such be the case, the next chapter will argue that a liberal polity should choose the solution preferred by the majority over the one thrown up by the invisible hand. See § 62.

living. From this vantage point, a centralized socialist economy makes it all too easy for a small elite utterly to destroy all dissident groups, while simple laissez faire makes it impossible to remedy the wide range of illegitimate domination tolerated—indeed generated—by the invisible hand. Instead of glorifying either state bureaucracy or private market, the task is to use each structure to check the illiberal forms of domination encouraged by the other. It is this goal which unites those in the West committed to the mixed economy and those in the East committed to market socialism. While both Eastern and Western approaches have many imperfections, both provide a basis for liberal advance within the particular historical context of each nation and region. Indeed, it is one of the important tasks of second-best theory to make the common aspirations of Eastern and Western liberalism clearer. Only in this way will we discard the ideologies of the past century and see that the ultimate question is not capitalism against socialism, but liberalism against elitism.

59. PHILOSOPHICAL FOUNDATIONS FOR LIBERAL ACTIVISM

But I am hardly the first to try to free liberalism from its bondage to laissez faire. The history of the past century is littered with such efforts, and it will clarify my proposed solution if it is viewed against the background of earlier liberal attempts. Once again, I shall restrict myself to a stylized treatment of utilitarian and contractarian themes.

59.1. *Utility*
Consider two familiar ideas by which modern utilitarians hope to move beyond laissez faire to an active, yet principled, conception of governmental regulation. The first argument revolves around the notion that marginal utility declines with increasing income. Granted this premise, the utilitarian can devise a rationale for redistribution: since the rich lose less utility than the poor gain, there may be room for a well-designed program of redistribution that maximizes utility. When contrasted with the liberal notion of exploitation, however, the argument from declining marginal utility is narrower, softer, and weaker than its liberal counterpart. Narrower, because it is limited to the distribution of wealth; indeed, as our prior comparative surveys revealed,[16] utilitarianism may well legitimate exploitation in the fields

16. §§ 30.1 and 37.2.

of education and genetic manipulation. Softer, because it depends on notoriously slippery exercises in interpersonal comparisons of utility. While the liberal notion of equal sacrifice is also contestable, the narrower concept of exploitation singles out certain power structures that *plainly* fall within the class of prima facie illegitimacy. There is no escape from the compelling claim made by a group of poor ghetto blacks who have been processed by an illiberal educational system and who confront a transactional system where whites use race as a proxy for individualized data on personal abilities. Whatever the difficulties of interpersonal comparisons of utility, the liberal is perfectly clear that these blacks are the victims of exploitation.

Finally, the utilitarian argument provides a weaker foundation for an assault on exploitation. Imagine, for example, that a group of exploited blacks could be cheaply taught to be happy with their lot. On this finding of fact, the utilitarian statesman might be tempted to sponsor a "reeducation" program rather than engage in a painful project of social reform. So long as it is cheaper to change psychology than alter social structures, the utilitarian statesman will lead us to 1984— not precisely a liberal utopia. Declining marginal utility fails to draw a sharp line between liberal statecraft and elitist tyranny.

A similar problem afflicts a second basic utilitarian route to the activist state. This is the notion of market failure. Modern economics has described countless ways in which a laissez faire regime fails to allocate resources efficiently. To recite only part of the litany: the theories of monopoly, public goods, externalities, information imperfection, all suggest important ways in which government may improve upon the efficiency of the invisible hand. A broad path is thereby opened for discriminating state intervention to correct market failures. This, by itself, is no bad thing; indeed, the liberal statesman will make heavy use of microeconomic theory as he strives to achieve a realistic version of transactional flexibility.[17] My problem is with the illiberal uses that a utilitarian may make of the market-failure rationale. For example, it is quite easy to show that the market in ideas is subject to a variety of market failures that guarantee the inefficient production and dissemination of information.[18] Thus, a clear-thinking utilitarian might conclude that government regulation of speech would sometimes maximize the production of happiness-inducing

17. §§ 43–45.
18. See, e.g., Ronald Coase, "The Market for Goods and the Market for Ideas," *American Economic Review* 64 (1974): 384.

ideas. In contrast, the liberal theory of transactional flexibility is not
grounded on some asserted link between communication and overall
happiness; instead, government attention is narrowly focused on an
effort to design a transactional structure that will facilitate each person's equal right to communicate with those who want to listen to him.

In drawing these contrasts with utilitarianism, however, I do not
want to exaggerate. My point is not that utilitarianism *must* lead to
tyranny, only that it *may* do so—depending on the statesman's view of
the facts. Indeed, the risk of tyranny might be further reduced by the
familiar trick of "rule utilitarianism." Here, the statesman is forbidden
to apply his master principle on a case-by-case basis. Instead, a set of
rules is advanced that will—when applied systematically to the run of
cases—maximize utility in the long run. And it may well be that the
best rule-utilitarian approach will turn out to be far more liberal than
my horror stories imply. Indeed, rule utilitarianism may even serve as
a useful stepping stone to liberalism: If the utilitarian is to guide his
concrete actions by "intermediate" rules, I am happy to propose the
three principles as candidates. If we are to pursue utility indirectly,
why not restrict official actions to those rules that can be justified
through Neutral dialogue?

I shall present more fundamental arguments for liberalism later on;
but if the rule utilitarian finds my three principles useful, he is welcome to them.

59.2. *Contract*
While utility is a weak constraint on activist statesmanship, contract
is no constraint at all. As Hobbes showed, so long as the theorist is
willing to paint the "state of nature" in dark enough tones, it is easy to
prove that tyranny is a good bargain. If the idea of contract is to
discipline activism, all will depend upon a cogent description of the
original position from which the terms of the compact are derived. It is
here where John Rawls is important. Almost two centuries have
passed since anybody has made a comparable effort to provide the
vague contractarian idea with a systematic structure. How, then, does
Rawls's conception of statecraft compare with the one advanced here?

A similarity in aspiration is evident: Rawls also tries to liberate
liberalism from laissez faire without lapsing into tyranny. The way the
Rawlsian statesman seeks to achieve a discriminating activism is, however, quite different. Rather than seeking to justify decisions through

Neutral dialogue, the Rawlsian focuses his attention upon a hypothetical choice situation in which contractors are deprived of all knowledge of their actual social position. Once placed behind a veil of ignorance, Rawls believes people will find that laissez faire imposes intolerable risks for their well-being if they should end up propertyless. Indeed, they will settle for nothing less than the maximin principle of justice—which requires statesmen to improve the position of the worst-off class without regard to the interests of the more fortunate.

While countless commentators have criticized Rawls's claims for maximin, I shall not rehash this familiar controversy. Instead, I want to extend the Rawlsian framework by asking how his ignorant contractors might respond to the liberal statesman's approach to the problem of exploitation.

With some surprise, I must conclude that Rawlsian contractors will, if given the chance, desert maximin and choose liberalism as the better bargain in their dim world. At first, this claim may seem silly. What could conceivably provide a more complete assurance against downside risk than maximin? Yet, on a more careful inspection, the Rawlsian contract contains fine print that undercuts the contractors' confidence in its promises.

To see the problem, consider the position of a contractor, X, who finds, upon lifting the veil of ignorance, that he is a victim of a crippling set of genetic disadvantages that greatly restrict his freedom of action. As we have seen,[19] X will have no difficulty establishing himself as a victim of exploitation of a kind that, prima facie, requires special assistance in a liberal state. In contrast, Rawls is quite explicit in *denying* that X may invoke maximin directly on his own behalf. Instead, it turns out that he—and his kind—are only a submerged fragment of the "worst-off class" as Rawls understands it. Rawls's discussion is brief but clear.[20] It consists of little more than two alternative rules for class definition, together with an assertion: "I suppose that either of these definitions, or some combination of them, will serve well enough." Rawls's first approach to class is truer to the concept's Marxist roots. Here, the worst-off group is defined by focusing upon "a particular social position, say that of the unskilled worker" and grouping all those no better off into a single R class. Rawls's second proposal

19. §§ 29 and 55.
20. *A Theory of Justice*, pp. 97–100.

has a more contemporary technocratic tone to it. Here, the worst-off R class contains "all persons with less than half of the median income and wealth." While the difference between these two standards is substantial, they both imply that people afflicted with severe genetic disabilities fall into the same class as healthy proletarians.

The implications of this are, quite simply, enormous. After all, there are many *more* healthy proletarians than people with crippling birth defects, and if the interests of a small minority gets in the way of the welfare of the larger group, the minority's claims must be sacrificed to maximize the position of the class as a whole.[21] In contrast, the liberal theory of exploitation takes the chance of being X seriously. From the liberal statesman's view, it is simply grotesque to respond to X's plight by telling him all the good things that have been done for healthy white male proletarians. As a citizen of the liberal state, X's status *cannot* be subordinated to the goal of maximizing another's interests, whatever his particular attributes. Such a conversational move attacks Neutrality at its very core. Worse yet, Rawls's broad definition of class does not merely subordinate X's rights to a group that stands at the

---

21. This is *not* an idle pipe dream. The issue is raised very explicitly in contemporary discussions of welfare reform. Traditional relief programs try to draw a bright line between "needy" people who are entitled to full relief payments and the rest of the citizenry who must work for a living. Reformers criticize such exercises in "categorical" line drawing on the ground that it imposes an enormous penalty on anybody who wants to leave the relief rolls for a (low-paying) work opportunity. Rather than depriving the marginal worker of his entire relief check, the reformers propose a "negative income tax" that removes public assistance at a rate keyed to income. Thus, a person would no longer be forced to choose between a $4,000 relief check or a $6,000 job; instead, even if he took the job, he would still receive a payment, say $1,500, as "negative income tax."

However advantageous this reform may be to healthy proletarians, it has a more sinister aspect for the severely handicapped. Negative income tax programs inevitably contemplate substantial payments to people (like the $6,000 wage earner in the preceding paragraph) who would get nothing under traditional categorical programs. This means that if they are to contain the overall welfare budget within manageable bounds, the reformers have only one option. They can pay the marginal worker something only at the cost of paying the unemployed "needy" person *less* than he would receive under a categorical program. See Christopher Green, *Negative Taxes and the Poverty Problem* (Washington, D.C.: Brookings Institution, 1967), chapters 5 and 6. In short, the interests of the healthy proletarians are at odds with people whose handicaps make them (relatively) unemployable. Who is to be preferred? While Rawls's broad R-class gives comfort to the negative income tax proponent, the utilitarian may well come out on behalf of the handicapped—on the ground that the *rich* feel sympathy toward them and hence will be utility gainers from the categorical proposal. Cf. Harold M. Hochman and James D. Rodgers "Pareto Optimal Redistribution," *American Economic Review* 59 (1969): 542. In contrast to both, the liberal theorist can explain why such trade-offs between the interests of exploited groups are especially difficult, § 56.3, and why it would be best to design a more complex strategy that, despite heavy administrative cost, tries to identify *severely* handicapped citizens entitled to aid levels that are far more generous than those prevailing under the typical negative income tax proposal.

same level of power disadvantage as he does. Instead, many of X's classmates—notably healthy white workers—stand in an unambiguously exploitative power relationship over him.[22] Thus, Rawls's approach to class permits the statesman to justify X's continued degradation by heaping benefits on a subset of his exploiters.

These facts discredit maximin as it competes with liberalism behind the veil of ignorance. Maximin requires each contractor to gamble that he will be a healthy proletarian rather than somebody as powerless as X. And it is precisely this kind of gamble with degradation that Rawls considers irrational. In contrast, liberalism assures the contractors that however powerless they may be, their demands for justice will never go unheard. We come, then, to the promised paradox: If Rawls's version of social contract is taken seriously, it is liberalism, not maximin, that emerges from the original position.

But let us probe this paradox further in search of its ultimate cause: *Why* has Rawls explicitly chosen to exclude the most powerless among us from the concerns of the activist state. Surely the answer cannot be found in meanness of spirit; a deep sympathy with the victim of misfortune is one of the most striking features of both the man and his work. Instead, my hypothesis is that Rawls's broad conception of class is forced upon him by his own principle of justice. To see why, consider the consequences of saying that X—and *only* people like X—are members of the worst-off class. Then, given the "maximizing" character of maximin, it would seem to follow that *the entire social universe* should be organized for the convenience of a small number of the world's worst basket cases. After all, even after the rest of us have done *everything* possible for these powerless people, can we *ever* say *with confidence* that they are at least as well off as we are? The fact is that *we* can walk and see and move on our own, and they cannot. Yet, despite the force of this point, Rawls cannot bring himself to say that justice requires society to transform itself into an enormous hospital ward. To escape this embarrassment, he suppresses the question by opting for a conception of class that sacrifices the most powerless people to the interests of those somewhat higher up in the power structure.

If this diagnosis is correct, Rawls's broad conception of class is only a symptom of a deeper problem—the fact that maximin insists on

22. See § 56.2.

maximizing the power of the worst-off class. Yet it is precisely this preoccupation with maximization which is lacking in liberal theory. Instead, the statesman's first goal is to end clean-cut cases of exploitation. So far as the victims of genetic disability are concerned, we have shown that this goal itself breaks down into two phases. The principle of negative compensation requires X to receive an education and transactional system that permit him to explore those (perhaps very limited) options that his genetic equipment leaves open for him. These compensatory systems, moreover, need *not* be perfect, for the resources provided even "normal" children hardly provide *them* with an ideally liberal education or perfectly flexible system of transactions. Instead, negative compensation insists that X be provided with a chance of realizing his genetic possibilities that is *no less imperfect* than that provided others.

Now I do not deny that even this standard is terribly difficult to apply in the terrible cases we are now considering.[23] It is one thing to describe a compensatory educational effort that would provide ghetto blacks with an education no less liberal than that imperfect variety provided suburban whites, quite another to decide whether a "comparable" education for X requires the investment of enormous sums in an effort to teach him to control his own wheelchair. Indeed, any philosophy in which the assessment of X's claims is positively *easy* condemns itself to superficiality. Nonetheless, whatever the strain placed on statesmanly judgment, the standard of negative compensation does *not* impose the insatiable demand implied by a maximizing principle.

Nor is the liberal duty of affirmative action equivalent to the Rawlsian insistence on maximization. Without belittling X's deprivation, liberal statesmen can never say *for certain* how much crippled limbs are "worth." Given this epistemic limitation, statesmen cannot accept the naïve idea that X may insist that his power be "maximized" until a point is reached where it is comparable to that enjoyed by a healthy proletarian. Once outright exploitation is eliminated, X must accept the epistemically problematic character of all efforts at affirmative action. There can be no hope of compensating him so that he is *clearly* as well off as his healthier contemporaries.[24]

23. Cf. note 12, p. 257, *supra*.
24. To accomodate this kind of objection, Rawls proposes the construction of an index of "primary social goods" which tries to indicate each group's prospects in terms of several different

To sum up, political discourse in a liberal state is both more narrowly focused and more complex than in its Rawlsian counterpart. And once we have come this far, it is possible to grasp a third distinctive feature of the liberal conception of activist discourse: its breadth. Paradoxically, breadth is achieved in part through the very act of "narrowing" Rawls's broad conception of class to liberal proportions. However valid X's claims against his fellow citizens, it hardly follows that his treatment can serve as the exclusive touchstone of economic and social policy in a just society. There are millions of other people who are victimized by exploitation even though they do not qualify as "worst-off." Middle-class blacks and women *also* have legitimate grievances about the way they are subordinated by the power structure; and so, of course, do all people born to poverty. While it is true that these grievances are not so profound as those suffered by people marked out by poverty *and* by race *and* by sex, they are deep grievances and cannot be tolerated in a world dominated by liberal statesmanship.

To this the Rawlsian may respond that he is not so narrow as I imagine him. Once the position of the worst-off is maximized, he is perfectly willing to agree that the position of the "next-worst" class should then be improved, and so forth. Yet this alternative formulation is defective for at least two reasons. First, in liberal theory, there is no reason to think that only one group can lay claim to the next-worst position. Instead, different groups defined in different ways will have equally plausible claims to being nth worst. Who is worse off: middle-class black males or poor white females? Since these groups have very different interests, maximin will once again lead to very different social policies, depending on the answer. In contrast, the liberal statesman does not imagine that there is *any* easy answer to conflicts between exploited groups. Rather than seeking to rank their status in a precise hierarchy of degradation, he will instead seek solutions that recognize that *both* have valid claims for special assistance.

---

kinds of variables: rights and liberties; opportunities and powers; income and wealth; and, perhaps most important of all, self-respect. To construct a satisfactory welfare index, however, one must explain how a single index of overall welfare is to be constructed from the many different goods Rawls enumerates. Yet Rawls does not seriously attempt such a formidable enterprise: "We admittedly rely upon our intuitive capacities in compiling the index" (*A Theory of Justice*, p. 94, discussed further in my § 32.2). Rather than this desperate effort to "solve" the indexing problem, the better part of wisdom is to separate the clear cases of exploitation from the large number of contestable judgments involved in affirmative action. See § 55.

This leads to a second difference between the liberal and Rawlsian conceptions of breadth. For the liberal, there is no need to belittle the grievances of people quite high in the overall power structure who find that their claims to liberal education and flexible transaction have been denied because of their race, sex, or unpopular conception of the good. Rather than engaging in the simple kind of class struggle suggested by Rawlsian theory, the liberal statesman tries to induce *all* exploited groups to recognize that their particular struggles are linked together through a common form of dialogue. In this way, it is possible to hope that an assault on exploitation will not generate class war and its familiar risks of tyranny but a deeper recognition—by both oppressed and oppressor—of the value of the dialogue that defines their common predicament.

9

LIBERAL DEMOCRACY

60. DISAGREEMENT AND TYRANNY

Imagine a Hercules of liberal statecraft. For him, the demanding process of judgment we have just described is not a lofty ideal but a living reality. Hercules actually does canvass all his budgetary options and puts to one side the many exploitative budgets that are prima facie illegitimate; out of those remaining, he selects the one he thinks gives each citizen an equal right to the best system of genetic, educational, and transactional possibilities that his optimal structural budget will allow.[1] Finally, he cautiously considers whether the equal sacrifice constraint should be lifted and a better budget proposed that serves the advantage of all citizens. After doing all this with sobering care and conscientiousness, Hercules comes before the rest of us to announce his judgment: Program A seems the best second-best path to social justice in a state that falls far short of ideal conditions.

Even so, the rest of us can reject A. Although Hercules has executed the decision procedure perfectly, this does not mean that his conclusion is uncontroversial. To the contrary, only the first part of his exercise can claim this precious merit. Exploitation, after all, simply requires the use of ordinal judgments—identifying power structures that unambiguously disadvantage a group in one power domain without giving them compensating advantages in any other.[2] And if Hercules *is* Hercules, his effort to cleanse politics of all exploitative proposals should save us needless labor. As far as the second and third stages go, however, Hercules' judgments remain controversial. Suppose I think that Hercules is silly in spending so much on liberal education and so little on transactional flexibility. I do not have to canvass all the options before pointing to one that I think represents a better compromise of competing liberal ideals. And so we come to a

---

1. Nor will he forget the obligations of trusteeship.
2. The distinction between ordinal and cardinal judgments was introduced in § 55.3.

first difficulty of second-best government: What decision rule should be used when liberal statesmen disagree about the best way to compromise the liberal ideal of undominated equality? Call this the problem of good-faith disagreement.

A second problem follows from the fact that all of us don't even try to emulate Hercules. For many, the task of government is not to approximate liberal ideals but to shape social reality around a particular conception of the good—which they are only too happy to provide. The danger, then, is plain enough: would-be tyrants will try to break the collective commitment to liberal dialogue by tempting their followers with the joys that come from brutally exploiting an underclass. The task is to design a constitution that can withstand the predictable pressures. Call this the problem of tyranny.

Conceptually speaking, disagreement and tyranny are distinct from one another. Even in a world miraculously free of all risks of tyranny, there would still be disagreement among liberal statesmen about the best second-best way of approximating liberal ideals. In more realistic settings, the risk of tyranny complicates the problem of disagreement. Surely the embryonic dictator will, when it serves his purposes, disguise his designs beneath a cloak of liberal rhetoric; surely the noblest Hercules will be reluctant to trumpet his liberal virtues too loudly— only a charlatan or a fool can be confident of absolute immunity from the authoritarian temptations of governmental power. While a complete constitutional theory must confront these strategic complexities, we will make the most headway by taking up the problem of tyranny after we have dealt with the "pure" problem of good-faith disagreement.

61. THE "PURE" PROBLEM OF GOOD-FAITH DISAGREEMENT

61.1. *The "Easy" Case for Majority Rule*

Begin, then, with a world that is free of would-be tyrants. Not, mind you, that any of our citizens are Hercules; they do not attempt the impossible task of canvassing *all* possible structural budgets in their search for the best second-best governmental program. Instead, each makes do with a fragmentary understanding of the shape of political possibility. When asked his opinions on second-best policy, however, no citizen is a slave of his own self-interest. Nobody is willing to support an exploitative program simply because it will lead to personal profit; aping Hercules, each frames a proposal that he thinks best supports a liberal conversation under the second-best conditions the polity confronts. To make things simpler still, assume that our citizen-statesmen have no trouble with the first labor of Hercules. They too can sort out and uncontroversially put to one side all exploitative budgetary proposals. Thus, it is only at the second stage of decision, where an effort is made to identify the budget that maximizes liberal ideals subject to the constraint of equal sacrifice, that the reality of disagreement emerges. Moreover, it should be clear by now that the chorus of dispute will range over a broad scale of key issues. Yet, ultimately, these dissonant voices must be resolved into a single, if tentative, harmony. Of all the plausible second-best compromises, only one can emerge as the binding law of the liberal state. How, then, is this act of resolution to be accomplished?

Never underestimate dialogue. Since nobody remotely achieves a Herculean perspective, each citizen-statesman may learn a good deal from the others. If the hermit and the opera star try to listen to one another, they may both gain a deeper understanding of the place of transactional flexibility in the larger scheme of liberal value. Yet, while dialogue may transform each *individual's* opinion, it does nothing to assure *collective* consensus. Indeed, it is quite possible that political opinion will be more fractionated after the debate than it was before.

Yet there remains one final move before we need despair of a dialogic solution to the problem of disagreement. Granted our citizens are fated to disagree about the *substance* of second-best compromise. It does not follow that they are fated to reach a conversational impasse when the question arises as to the *procedure* that offers the best way of resolving their substantive disagreements.

The only way to find out is to think through the conversation in the usual manner. Imagine, then, that two citizens, Democrat and Elitist, find they disagree as to the most statesmanlike solution to a second-best problem. Democrat argues that despite their disagreement, the polity should enact his favorite solution, B, into law and reject Elitist's, solution, A.[3]

3. For the present, I shall assume that the policy set includes *only* A and B, deferring to § 61.7 the problems that will arise when three or more options are within the policy set. Social-choice buffs will note that this simplification also permits me to avoid an analysis of requirements, like the Independence of Irrelevant Alternatives, that apply only to social choices among three or more policy options.

DEMOCRAT: Well, we've talked ourselves out on A and B. It's time to decide, and I think we should choose B.

ELITIST: But I think A is better. What gives you the right to jam B down my throat?

DEMOCRAT: A good point. Rather than putting my word against yours, let's count hands and see which program commends itself to more of our fellow-citizens. [*Does so.*] Look: the B's have it, fifty to forty-nine.

ELITIST: Yes, they do. But I fail to see why that should be decisive.

DEMOCRAT: Isn't it obvious?

ELITIST: Not at all. There are plenty of other decision rules that can resolve our dispute. Why is majority rule better than the others?

DEMOCRAT: Do I have to answer that?

ELITIST: Rationality requires it.

DEMOCRAT: O.K. Let me try.

ELITIST: And please, no noise about how you folks in the majority are intrinsically superior to us in the minority! What I want is a Neutral reason.

DEMOCRAT: Well, that will require some more thought.

ELITIST: Take your time. Only don't impose majority rule on me until you've come up with an answer.

Up to this point, the conversation is quite unremarkable. All that Elitist has done is apply the general requirements for Rational and Neutral discourse developed in chapter 2[4] to the particular power struggle that is now at center stage. What *is* remarkable, however, is the sequel. I shall show that after giving the matter some thought, Democrat *can* successfully defend majority rule through a process of Neutral dialogue. Hence, the "easy" case for majority rule promised in the subtitle.

Even at its easiest, however, the argument for majority rule is not free of difficulty. First, I want to show that it is only our assumption of a "tyranny-free" world that permits Manic to defend simple majoritarianism in a Neutral way. As soon as the problem of tyranny enters the conversation, all liberal statesmen must respond to the danger that a majority may use its power to deprive minorities of the rights they may justly claim through Neutral dialogue. Second, even within

4. §§ 11 and 12.

the limits of our tyranny-free world, majority rule emerges as one—
but only one—of a larger set of legitimate solutions to the problem
of disagreement.

61.2. *The Relevance of Social-Choice Theory*

A familiar scene in the liberal Assembly: Hundreds of citizen-
statesmen advance, each with his favorite solution to the problem of
good-faith disagreement. The proliferation of decision rules raises an
initial problem of its own. The Assembly requires an economical way
of organizing the political conversation lest it consume several
lifetimes while Democrat tries to defend majority rule against each
and every counterproposal invented by an ingenious citizenry.

It is here where the conversational enterprise is greatly assisted by
some recent analytic breakthroughs in the theory of social choice.
Over the past thirty years, a group of political economists have devoted themselves, with unprecedented success, to the rigorous analysis of conceptual solutions to the problem of disagreement. Unhappily, this literature has not had its full impact upon the broader current
of political speculation, in part because social-choice theorists have
adopted the language of symbolic logic to prove their points. A bit
of translation from formal logic into the vernacular, however, will
provide a conversational path that can be traveled by all who would
reconcile majoritarianism with the principles of liberal dialogue.

A theorem proved by K. O. May provides the basic framework.[5] To
state the conclusion first, May shows that majority rule is the *only*
decision procedure that satisfies four simple conditions that we will
call *universal domain* (U), *anonymity* (A), *outcome indifference* (O), and
positive responsiveness (P). A good technocrat, May himself does not
consider whether U, A, O, and P are normatively desirable properties
of a decision procedure. He contents himself with the conditional
conclusion that *if* you approve of U, A, O, and P, *then* you are logically
committed to majority rule. For us, however, the interest of May's
theorem is not its technical virtuosity. Since the formal proof is available in any good book on social-choice theory,[6] I will leave the techni-

5. "A Set of Independent, Necessary and Sufficient Conditions for Simple Majority Decision," *Econometrica* 20 (1952): 680.
6. See, e.g., Amartya Sen, *Collective Choice and Social Welfare*, (San Francisco: Halden-day,
1970) pp. 71–73, whose proof I find easier to follow than May's original. In labeling the
conditions, I have departed from the standard terminology in one particular. May calls my
condition O the Neutrality Condition. My adopting this term, however, would cause unnecessary confusion.

cal argument on the intuitive level. Instead, I shall concentrate upon the *dialogic* use that Democrat might make of May's logical conclusions in his confrontation with Elitist. I shall show that Democrat can defend each of May's conditions as normatively desirable with arguments that remain within the constraints of Neutral conversation. But if this is so, it follows from May's theorem that Democrat can successfully defend majority rule as a legitimate way of resolving his dispute with Elitist. For May's theorem teaches that *only* majority rule is consistent with U, A, O, and P. Hence, to defend the legitimacy of U, A, O, and P *is* to defend majority rule.

61.3. *U, A, and O*

Begin, then, with the least problematic of May's conditions: universal domain. By setting down this requirement, Democrat wants to bar silly rules of the following kind: "All votes that indicate a preference for B over A will be counted; we refuse to say, however, how a preference for A over B will be counted." More abstractly, condition U requires all acceptable decision rules to specify *some* social outcome[7] under all conceivable concatenations of individual preference orderings. We do not need, I think, to spend much time on this requirement. It is implied by the demand, discussed much earlier,[8] that all distribution rules be *complete* if they hope to satisfy Rationality. Just as a citizen has a right to learn how much manna he will receive on leaving the spaceship, he also may insist on knowing how much political power he will have if, as a statesman, he casts his vote for A rather than B.

The second of May's conditions is only slightly more demanding. Here Democrat wants to bar rules of the following form: "Program A requires a two-thirds vote for passage if Elitist is opposed to it; but if Elitist favors the program, 60 percent will suffice." Instead, any legitimate aggregation rule must be *anonymous:* if it requires X percent support to assure enactment, it must keep X constant regardless of the particular citizen-statesmen who constitute the decisive coalition.

7. A rule does not violate U if it specifies conditions under which the liberal polity is *indifferent* as to whether A or B is the preferred social outcome.
8. § 11.1.

ELITIST: And what's so great about anonymity?

DEMOCRAT: Well, isn't each of us trying to ape Hercules in an effort to select the best second-best program?

ELITIST: Why are you so sure of that?

DEMOCRAT: Are you saying that any of us are would-be tyrants?

ELITIST: I guess our present conversational ground rules forbid this charge.

DEMOCRAT: Then I say that each liberal statesman's opinion is at least as good as any others. None can demand greater political power on the basis of some feature—like his name—that he possesses independently of his conception of the good.

ELITIST: Haven't I heard this before?

DEMOCRAT: Indeed. To deny what I am saying would require you to offend the bar against unconditional claims of superiority imposed by the Neutrality constraint.

Yet anonymity is not enough to make out the "easy" case for majority rule—as is suggested by a glance at the following proposal: "Unless two-thirds of the statesmen prefer program B, program A will be enacted into law." Now this proposal satisfies both U and A. However, it violates the third of May's tests for an acceptable aggregation rule, the one I shall call *outcome indifference.* Condition O states that it should be *equally* difficult for competing programs to gain public enactment into law:

ELITIST: And why, Democrat, do you think outcome indifference is such a good thing? Why *not* permit A to pass on a showing of one-third approval but insist that B gain two-thirds of the vote?

DEMOCRAT: Because B is no less a legitimate solution than A.

ELITIST: Why do you think so? After all, *I* think that A is the better second-best compromise.

DEMOCRAT: And I respect your right to have an opinion different from mine. Only you yourself must recognize that your own judgment is fairly contestable.

ELITIST: Why? I don't think *all* my judgments are fairly contestable. For example, if B were an exploitative proposal that forced some group of citizens to bear an unequal share of the burden of imperfection, then I'd have no trouble saying that *all* liberal statesmen *must* recognize B's prima facie illegitimacy.

DEMOCRAT: Yes, but that's just the kind of choice we don't confront.

ELITIST: How can you be so sure that an exploitative proposal hasn't been forced onto the agenda?

DEMOCRAT: Don't you remember that this is the second stage of our decision procedure? During the first stage, we eliminated all exploitative proposals from our agenda so as to concentrate on presumptively legitimate solutions like A and B. Moreover, our present ground rules require us to assume that we have executed this first labor of Hercules to perfection.

ELITIST: O.K. I'll accept the stipulation—but only for the purpose of this conversation. What follows?

DEMOCRAT: Since neither A nor B is uncontroversially the inferior liberal compromise, a rational decision procedure should not make either one easier to enact than the other.

Notice, once again, how sensitive the conversation is to the assumption of a tyranny-free world. Just as the "easy" argument for anonymity required Manic to assume that the polity was composed entirely of liberal statesmen, so too the "easy" argument for outcome indifference requires an agenda that has been purged of all exploitative proposals at an earlier stage of the decision-making procedure. Condition O is unproblematic only as a solution to the "pure" problem of good faith disagreement; a liberal citizenry can never be indifferent to the prospect of tyranny.

61.4. *Minimal Decisiveness*

The dialogic defense of U, A, and O serves to eliminate a vast number of elitist decision rules from the Assembly's agenda. Nonetheless, these three conditions will not suffice to exclude all competitors to majority rule. Consider, for example, citizen Diviner's proposal: according to him, God has provided a solution to our disagreement if we would but consult Him. The particular details of the divination procedure are of little interest; it may be as simple as flipping a coin or as complex as reading entrails. Similarly, I shall permit Diviner to justify his decision rule by appeal to any transcendent principle whatever; he can justify a random coin flip by glorifying the role of fortune in human affairs or come up with a complex theology in defense of entrail reading. The critical point is that the outcome generated by the divination procedure be *completely* independent of the

considered judgments on A and B rendered by particular members of
the liberal community. So long as this is true, it will be easy to design a
divination procedure that satisfies the first three May conditions. Divination can satisfy U as long as it tells us how to resolve all conceivable patterns of citizen disagreement; it will satisfy A since the outcome
is (by definition) insensitive to the preferences of particular citizens,
and it will satisfy O since the fate of the competing proposals depend
upon the same decisional factor: God's favor. Nonetheless, there is a
compelling dialogic objection to this effort to short-circuit the problem of good-faith disagreement.

DEMOCRAT: There seems to be a disagreement. How should we
resolve it?
DIVINER: I say that we should leave the decision in the hands of
this black box that God has been so kind as to provide.
DEMOCRAT: If that's all you can say, I insist that you take *my* word
for it and declare that B is the law of the liberal state.
DIVINER: Why is your word any better than God's?
DEMOCRAT: I don't say it is. I only assert that your way of divining
God's will is entirely misconceived.
DIVINER: You're wrong about that!
DEMOCRAT: Perhaps, but your say-so is insufficient to dispose of
my objection in a liberal state. The Neutrality principle forbids the
claim that you have privileged access to the meaning of the universe.
DIVINER: A good point. But can't I turn it around with equal
force? After all, *you* don't have the right to insist on B simply
because *you* think it's best!
DEMOCRAT: True, but I am not trying to be a dictator. While I am
happy to concede that my opinion may be outweighed by the contrary opinions of my *fellow citizens,* I am unwilling to have my views
ignored merely because you believe that your *divination procedure*
provides a better way of resolving our policy problem than my
considered judgments on the liberal merits.

The script does not imply that a citizen should always get his way.[9]
Instead it simply assures each citizen that his views are *taken seriously*
in a minimal, but fundamental, sense. A polity that ignores a citizen in
favor of Diviner's unresponsive black box is telling the citizen that his

9. Such a claim would be excluded by the dialogue reported at § 15.2.

views have *no* political standing *whatsoever*. More formally, each citizen has a right to a *minimal degree of decisiveness* (condition M): the polity cannot appeal to some completely unresponsive procedure when it remains possible to resolve a political disagreement by consulting the opinion of a liberal statesman whose judgment has not yet been solicited on the matter. While M is a limited right, it does have a broader scope than may be imagined. Suppose, for example, that Diviner does not appeal to his favorite black box upon the first hint of citizen disagreement, but makes a more modest proposal: while he is willing to enact one or another program so long as it obtains two-thirds of the vote, he wants to use his black box to determine all "close" questions—where more than one-third of the vote is cast on both sides. To set the stage, assume that there are 99 statesmen in the Assembly, and that after 66 votes are tallied, the count is 33–33:

> DIVINER: Well, this seems a close question. Rather than proceed with the balloting, I say we should consult my black box!
> UNCOUNTED: What do you mean? I haven't yet spoken on this matter!
> DIVINER: So what? I say that my black box is a better way of deciding this result.
> UNCOUNTED: I protest. I say that the outcome should depend on *my* considered judgment rather than your divination procedure! You have no right to overrule my opinion simply on the basis of some black box that suits your fancy![10]

In short, minimal decisiveness gives *each* of us the right to have our *particular* opinion constitute the favored means of breaking all tied votes that arise in a liberal decision procedure.

61.5. *The "Easy" Argument Completed*

It is, I think, easy to see the sense in which majority rule satisfies minimal deciveness. If, say, there are 99 people in the Assembly, then

10. We have encountered this conversational move before at another critical, if substantively distant, point in the argument. Recall the argument in support of every citizen's right to refuse to have children, § 24. In discussing this key issue of population policy, the Assembly was obliged to confront a citizen whose claim was very much like Diviner's. This citizen claimed the right to speak on behalf of generations yet unborn; according to him, these disembodied spirits wanted bodies, and the Assembly would do wrong in denying this request from the spirit world. Before affirming the right of the existing generation to reject procreation, the Assembly was obliged to reject the claim that any of its members was the authoritative spokesman for the spirit world. In short, the liberal arguments for *both* democracy *and* abortion ultimately turn on the very same conversational move.

majority rule gives me a decisive voice when the rest of you are split 49–49; and the same is true of your decision as well. When confronted with the prospect of a tied vote, the majoritarian does not appeal to some unresponsive decision procedure, but instead recognizes each citizen's right to have his considered judgment determine the social outcome. Using the technical language of social choice, I will say that majority rule satisfies condition M by *positively responding* to the considered judgments of any citizen when this will serve to break a tie.

Yet this simple observation will not suffice to make out the "easy" argument for majority rule, for any number of other voting rules *also* exhibit positive responsiveness (or condition P). Consider the standard "two-thirds" rule as an example—say, a procedure that declared A the winner unless two-thirds of the citizens voted for B. While this rule differs from simple majoritarianism, its difference does not reside in condition P. *Both* decision procedures specify a particular distribution of citizen preferences under which you or I could play a decisive role in the social decision. The only difference is that under one rule the social decision positively responds to my vote when everybody else is divided 49–49, while the other rule makes the outcome positively respond to my vote when everybody else is split 33-68.

This is not to say, of course, that there is nothing wrong with a two-thirds voting rule when analyzed from a liberal point of view. To the contrary, I have already written a script[11] showing that it offends the principle of outcome indifference and hence is an inadmissible solution to the problem of good-faith disagreement. It would be tedious, however, to deal in a similar fashion with every other positively responsive rule, showing the respect, if any, in which each competitor to majority rule violates A, O, or U. And it is here where the immense analytic convenience of May's contribution can be appreciated. For May's concern is precisely with the large class of decision rules that give each of us the power to play tie-breaker: the class of *positively responsive* rules. Having defined the class in a way that meshes remarkably with our argument, May proves that majority rule is the *only* procedure that *simultaneously* satisfies positive responsiveness, *as well as* outcome indifference, anonymity, and universal domain.

It follows, then, that the easy case for majority rule may be concluded:

11. See § 61.3.

DEMOCRAT: So you see, Elitist, when B beats A by a vote of fifty' to forty-nine, I do not have to say that program B is *indisputably* the best second-best approximation of liberal ideals. Nor do I have to say that I am a better liberal statesman than you are. Instead, I can say that majority rule—under tyranny-free conditions—provides a way of resolving our good-faith dispute that is consistent with the idea that you're at least as good a liberal statesman as I am.

ELITIST: How so?

DEMOCRAT: Well, you don't deny that a good decision rule must have a universal domain?

ELITIST: To do so would be ir-Rational.

DEMOCRAT: And I haven't heard you deny that a good decision rule ought to satisfy the requirements of anonymity and outcome indifference.

ELITIST: So long as you don't let the risk of tyranny enter the conversation, I can't see how I can talk my way out of these requirements.

DEMOCRAT: So that leaves the question of minimal decisiveness. Surely you don't think that somebody should appoint himself God's prophet and impose his favorite black box upon the rest of us.

ELITIST: Not unless that somebody is me. Since I have no hope of forcing you to accept my claim to prophetic status, I concede that we cannot completely ignore your opinion and have our decision turn on some completely unresponsive decision-making procedure.

ELITIST: And how does majority rule fare under the test of minimal decisiveness?

*DEMOCRAT: It passes. We have not ignored your opinion in favor of some unresponsive black box. Indeed, if there had been a tied vote, your opinion would have determined the outcome.

ELITIST: But surely there are other nonmajoritarian decision rules that give me this tie-breaking power.

DEMOCRAT: Yes, but May has shown that all other positively responsive decision rules violate one of the other requirements—A, O, or U—whose legitimacy you have recognized earlier in this conversation.

ELITIST: You mean that unless I can verbalize a complaint about one of the moves revealed in this conversation, I'm stuck with majority rule?

DEMOCRAT: You said it.

ELITIST: But I still think that A is a better solution then B! If I'm crossed in this, I'll be awfully unhappy!
DEMOCRAT: Citizens can't always get everything they want. All they can rightly demand is a share of power that can be justified through Neutral conversation. And the decision-making power granted to you by majority rule passes this test.

While this conversational victory is important to me, I do not wish to overstate its significance. The script shows that majority rule *can* be vindicated within the framework of a dialogic theory of legitimacy; it does *not* show that it is the *only* rule that can be conversationally justified under liberal ground rules. In this, of course, the last dialogue is no different from the many others we have rehearsed. As I emphasized earlier,[12] I have no proof of the conversational uniqueness of *any* of my results. In this case, however, I have more to offer than the hope that you will try to write scripts that generate radically different conclusions while remaining within the bounds of liberal discourse. Instead, I can provide a particular example of a script that does in fact generate a legitimate competitor to majority rule.

61.6 *The Responsive Lottery*

Of the four conditions specified by May, the first three seem beyond dialogic challenge. To deny U is to violate Rationality; to reject anonymity or outcome indifference will transparently require un-Neutral noises—so long as our model remains tyrant-free. If there is a dialogic competitor to majority rule, then, the verbal challenge must be directed at P.

To detect the weak link, reflect on the point at which my dialogic argument joined May's conceptual analysis. While May begins analysis by restricting his concern to the class of *positively responsive* rules, condition P does not have an equally fundamental place in the conversations I have written. Democrat does *not* sing praises to P as a good in its own right. Instead, the center of democratic concern is a more abstract principle: *minimal decisiveness.* While Democrat does not insist that his views must always govern, he does protest if the polity ignores his views and appeals to some black box to solve its good faith disagreement. It is only this dialogic insistence on condition M that gives a liberal point to May's P. P is valuable precisely because it

12. See § 16.

defines a class of decision procedures that are certain to satisfy M. Since all *positively responsive* rules give each of us the power to break all tied votes, they guarantee each citizen that his considered judgment will never be ignored on behalf of someone's transcendent appeal to an unresponsive black box. In short, May's theorem is of conversational interest because P is a sufficient condition for a decision rule satisfying M.

Yet, if this is so, then we must beware the logical difference between necessary and sufficient conditions. While *all* P rules satisfy condition M, it does *not* follow that *only* P rules satisfy M. If, then, we can identify a rule that violates P but satisfies M, we are on to a democratic alternative to majority rule that may be justified on liberal principles—while May has proved that majority rule is the only procedure that satisfies U, A, O, and *P,* he has not proved that it is the only procedure that satisfies U, A, O, and *M.*

It is this path of reflection that leads me to focus upon the following procedure as a liberal-democratic alternative to majority rule: As before, each of us is asked to indicate whether A or B constitutes the best second-best liberal program. This time, however, there is no effort to count up our votes to determine the majority winner. Instead, each writes down his preference on a slip of paper, which is then placed in a large black box. After all of us have dropped our ballots into the box, a single paper is selected at random. If it happens to announce a preference for A, A is enacted; if B, B. I shall call this procedure a "responsive" lottery. Is its use consistent with democratic theory?

Different people, I have found, have different intuitions on this subject. Moreover, they can buttress their intuitions by appealing to different historical precedents. Those sympathetic to the responsive lottery can invoke the ancient practices of Athenian democracy, where most representative positions were filled by lot.[13] Those devoted to strict majoritarianism appeal to modern democratic practice, which consigns the lottery to the periphery of social choice.[14] The task, however, is to move beyond private intuition and selective history by a dialogic method that, in principle, is accessible to all citizens. I shall show that the responsive lottery does indeed have a foundation

13. See A. H. J. Greenidge, *A Handbook of Greek Constitutional History* (London: Macmillan & Co. Ltd., 1896), pp. 138–39.

14. Though even today the lottery is sometimes relied on to resolve particularly intractable issues. See Guido Calabresi and Philip Bobbitt, *Tragic Choices,* pp. 41–44 (New York: W. W. Norton, 1978).

in liberal discourse. More particularly, I want to locate the precise point at which the conversational defense of the lottery diverges from the majoritarian dialogue we have just rehearsed.

To state my conclusion first, the point of conversational divergence is marked by the asterisk you must have noticed when reading the last dialogue. To see why the two conversations run parallel to the final dialogic turn, consider the way in which the responsive lottery satisfies each of the criteria defended by Democrat. Taking them up in the order discussed in the majoritarian script, there is no problem with U, for the lottery generates a social decision for every conceivable concatenation of individual preferences; nor is there a problem under A, for the outcome does not give any advantage to the opinions held by particular statesmen; nor is O troublesome, for it is no more difficult for program A to gain political victory than program B.

Complexity arises only when we reach minimal decisiveness. Like majority rule, the responsive lottery does not permit my considered judgment to be overruled by a political outcome generated by a completely *un*responsive procedure. Instead, if my opinion is overruled, it is because some other *citizen* has conscientiously concluded that a different program constitutes a more liberal choice. Unlike majority rule, however, the lottery does not satisfy minimal decisiveness by giving each of us the right to break tied votes. Instead of satisfying positive responsiveness, the lottery provides an anonymous and outcome-indifferent procedure for picking out *one* statesman's judgment to trump the views of all the others. Despite its failure to satisfy P, however, the proponent of a responsive lottery can justify his procedure under condition M:

ELITIST: And how does the responsive lottery fare under the test of minimal decisiveness?
*DEMOCRAT: It passes easily. Either your slip will be drawn from the black box, in which case you *will* be decisive; or some other citizen's slip will be drawn, in which case you will be overruled by the contrary judgment of some other citizen. In no case will you be overruled by a procedure that is completely unresponsive to the considered judgment of any citizen.
ELITIST: O.K. Let's draw a slip out of the box and see what happens. (*Does so.*)
DEMOCRAT: The slip says B.

ELITIST: But I still think that A is the more liberal program!

DEMOCRAT: Citizens can't expect to get everything they want. All they can rightly demand is a share of power that can be justified through Neutral conversation. And the decision-making power granted to you by the responsive lottery passes this test.

But *why* is it possible to write two different dialogues that pass through the conversational filter established by Neutrality? Why are there two distinct, but dialogically defensible, ways of understanding the idea of minimal decisiveness?

Because there are at least two different ways of understanding an even more fundamental idea: call it political responsiveness. The more familiar way of making a political outcome responsive to a constituency is to *add up*[15] the judgments of individual citizens to form an overall total representing the view of society. Once this "cumulating" view of responsiveness is accepted, it would seem there is only one way of satisfying each citizen's demand for minimal decisiveness, and that is to give him the right to break tied votes appearing on the cumulative scoreboard.

As the responsive lottery establishes, however, there is a second way of relating citizen views to political outcomes. Under this "probabilistic" approach, every citizen is given a finite chance of deciding the political outcome. So long as nobody is allowed to stuff the black box with slips signed "God," this procedure will satisfy the requirement of minimal decisiveness. Yet it no longer makes any sense to speak of people having the right to break "ties"; as votes are no longer added up, there *can be no ties*. As a consequence, the responsive lottery escapes May's proof, which concerned itself exclusively with the class of *positively responsive* decision rules.

It follows, then, that there can be no hope of discriminating between rule by majority and rule by responsive lottery on the basis of any of the criteria that have emerged thus far in the conversation. While it is easy for a liberal to insist that a rational[16] decision procedure be anonymous, outcome indifferent, and minimally decisive, this

---

15. I do not mean to suggest, however, that the only way of "adding up" individual judgments into a societal total is by arithmetic. A decision rule may cumulate individual judgments into an overall total through some more complex mathematical procedure. Hence the "cumulating" conception of responsiveness, rather than the "additive" conception.

16. As noted (§ 61.3) the requirement of universal domain is rooted in the Rationality, not Neutrality, principle.

only serves to eliminate elitism and divination from the field of admissible argument; the dialogue does not permit a liberal community to reason its way to a judgment between two competing forms of democratic procedure. To discriminate further, it will be necessary to write a liberal script that will justify a choice between the cumulating and probabilistic conceptions of political responsiveness. Can such a dialogue be written?

I will leave this question hanging in the air for now. My effort to find a satisfying answer has made only one thing clear to me—that there exists an unresolved tension between the theory and the practice of contemporary liberal democracy. On the level of theory, thinkers faced with the problem of pure procedural justice have often looked to the lottery as a mechanism that might fairly resolve some kinds of dispute.[17] On the level of political practice, however, we have tended to resolve good-faith disagreements by an appeal to majority rule. Rather than ignore this tension, we must make it the subject of self-conscious reflection. Aided by the dialogic method, it is possible to see that responsive lotteries and majorities have more in common than superficial appearances suggest. Perhaps future dialogues will establish the undisputed primacy of one procedure over another. But, at present, the important discovery is that *both* methods commend themselves to liberals for precisely the same reason: their promise of a solution that recognizes each citizen's standing as a statesman whose political judgments are entitled to equal respect.

61.7. *Condorcet Paradoxes*

Assume that after canvassing the relevant arguments, the liberal Assembly adopts majority rule, rather than the responsive lottery, as its primary technique for the resolution of good-faith disputes.[18] Even after this threshold is crossed, a final obstacle must be confronted before a liberal polity may fully rationalize its majoritarian commitments. To focus on the difficulty, simply suppose that our Assembly is composed of 100 statesmen, rather than 99, and the vote splits 50–50 on the merits of A and B. Here an appeal to majority rule will not suffice to resolve the Assembly's problem. Moreover, the principle of Rationality requires power holders to justify themselves in *every* case.

17. See, e.g., Rawls, *A Theory of Justice* (1971), p. 86.
18. And if citizens disagree, how is this disagreement to be resolved—by majority rule or responsive lottery?

Since simple majority rule cannot conceivably provide us with the legitimation required by our first principle, it requires conceptual supplementation before it can pretend to serve as a complete[19] solution to the problem of disagreement.

If the 50-50 case were the only case of incompleteness, we might learn to live with this regrettable hole in the majoritarian's armor. Unfortunately, the problem takes a more threatening turn as soon as I add a single complexity to my initial statement of the problem. Up to now, I have posited the simplest possible case of good-faith disagreement, where opinion is divided between two—and *only* two—second-best programs. Yet it will be common for liberal opinion to be divided among a larger number of contenders. Imagine, for example, that a liberal policy discussion fastens political attention upon three mutually inconsistent programs: A, B, and C. After talking themselves to exhaustion, liberal statesman find themselves divided into three groups of equal size, whose policy preferences are displayed in the following chart:

		Voting Blocs		
		1	2	3
Order	First Choice	A	B	C
of	Second Choice	B	C	A
Preference	Third Choice	C	A	B

An inspection of the matrix indicates that two groups of statesmen (1 and 3) will vote for A in preference to B; that two (1 and 2) will prefer B to C; *and* that two (2 and 3) prefer C to A. In this situation, the winning program will be determined by the group in charge of parliamentary procedure. If the citizenry is first required to choose between B and C, B will emerge victorious, with groups 1 and 2 voting against 3. If B is *then* paired against A, A will be victorious, with groups 1 and 3 voting against 2. In contrast, if A and C are first put up to the voters, A will be defeated on the initial vote; C emerges victorious from the first round of balloting only to be defeated by B on the second round, with 1 and 2 voting against 3! And it is easy to specify yet another order of balloting where C emerges as "the" majority winner.

Call this the problem of agenda manipulation. Not that the problem—first articulated by Condorcet—inevitably afflicts majority

19. For the relationship between completeness and Rationality, see § 11.1.

rule when the agenda contains more than two options. Instead, it occurs only in situations of the kind portrayed in the chart—where no program is the clear favorite of 51 percent of the voters and minority factions so disagree as to the relative standing of A, B, and C that each program gets one first-place vote, one second-place vote, and one third-place vote. Nonetheless, even when cut down to size, Condorcet's paradox does mean that the "easy" argument we have developed for majority rule is seriously incomplete. When Condorcet's conditions obtain, they open up a new dialogic path that requires exploration. To see why, simply continue the dialogic defense of majority rule where it broke off, this time stipulating that there are three programs—A, B, and C—that generate a Condorcet split in the opinion of liberal statesmen:

DEMOCRAT: The B's have it—this time by an overwhelming majority.

ELITIST: I protest! I still think that A is the better program.

DEMOCRAT: This is getting boring. Haven't we talked this through before?

ELITIST: Yes, and I'm prepared to concede your general argument on behalf of majority rule.

DEMOCRAT: So where's the problem? B has just emerged victorious out of a majoritarian political process.

ELITIST: Yes, but the victory was merely an artifact of the order of balloting. If the voting agenda had been manipulated in a different way, A would not have been defeated by C on the first round of balloting, and so would have emerged victorious in the end.

DEMOCRAT: So what? I won, didn't I?

ELITIST: Yes, but your victory is not attributable to the features of the decision-making process—U, A, O, P—which you have so cogently defended. Instead, your victory over me is entirely owing to the decision of the agenda manipulator to choose one order of voting over another. And how can the use of *this* power to favor you over me be defended?

Now there *is* at least one decision procedure that may be developed in response to Elitist's new challenge. Quite simply, Democrat may propose a mechanism for establishing ballot order whose only merit is that it *cannot* be consciously manipulated by a particular person or group. Here, after a series of straw votes reveals the existence of a

Condorcet paradox, the polity makes use of a random-number machine to announce the order in which A, B, and C will be paired against each other:

> ELITIST: What's so great about a random-number machine anyway?
>
> DEMOCRAT: Consider the alternative. Surely none of us can claim the exclusive right to manipulate the agenda in a way that will systematically favor his particular program.
>
> ELITIST: I guess you're right about that. After all, the agenda manipulator can't say he's a better liberal statesman than the rest of us.
>
> DEMOCRAT: You're learning fast, my good Elitist. And at least the random-number machine permits us to proceed without requiring any of us to violate the conversational ground rules.
>
> ELITIST: That isn't much of a recommendation, if you ask me.
>
> DEMOCRAT: But it *is* something. And given our commitment to Rationality, something beats nothing every time.

Once again, the lottery appears at a critical stage in the liberal argument for majority rule, but this should not blind us to the very different conversational role the lottery plays in its second performance. Earlier, the responsive lottery appeared as a democratic *competitor* to majority rule; now the *un*responsive lottery is being used to *complete* the dialogic defense of majoritarianism in situations where—thanks to the Condorcet paradox—its implications would otherwise be indeterminate.[20] As a consequence, the particular design of the appropriate lottery differs greatly in its two appearances. The first time, each statesman placed his *substantive opinion* in the hopper and the lottery gave each *statesman* an equal chance to determine the result; this time, each possible *ballot order* is placed in the hopper and the lottery gives each possible *agenda* an equal chance of realization. Similarly, the dialogic standing of the two lotteries is altogether different. The first lottery might, in principle, displace majority rule if a decisive dialogue could be written rejecting the cumulating view of political responsiveness in favor of the probabilistic view. The second lottery has a

---

20. But doesn't the use of the unresponsive lottery in this context violate condition M? No. Minimal decisiveness only gives me the right to protest if the polity ignores my view *entirely* in favor of some unresponsive procedure (§ 61.4). In the present case, however, my view has *not* been ignored; indeed, if it had been, the vote would not have added up to 50–50! Rather than *violating* condition M, the unresponsive lottery appears as an answer to the following question: How should a dispute be resolved when the solution remains indeterminate after each citizen's right to minimal decisiveness has been recognized?

much weaker foundation—based as it is on the claim that *all* other solutions to the problem of agenda manipulation will require the agenda manipulator to assert his unconditional superiority in violation of Neutrality. Indeed, far from threatening the foundations of majority rule, it is not even clear that Democrat is correct in making the sweeping assertion advanced in the preceding dialogue. Perhaps there *is* a way of resolving Condorcet paradoxes that avoids a lottery and yet can be justified within the constraints of liberal discourse. If such a procedure could be proposed, the liberal-democratic argument for an agenda randomizer would be shown to rest on a false premise. Instead of committing the agenda to a random-number machine, we might discover that the alternative procedure—call it Q—has dialogically satisfying properties.

It is not clear, however, that Q *does* exist. Recent developments in social-choice theory do not give great cause for hope. Indeed, the classic work of Kenneth Arrow[21] can be seen as generalizing themes articulated by Condorcet. Arrow shows that Condorcet-like paradoxes are not a peculiar property of majority rule; instead, they afflict a very broad class of initially attractive decision procedures. Yet, while any serious work must contend with Arrow's conclusions, it is not clear that they condemn all efforts to narrow (or entirely eliminate) the range of Condorcet indeterminacy tolerated by majority rule. Since my dialogic framework has not guided the research agenda of social-choice theory, it is possible that solution simply awaits the creative worker who takes time enough to do justice to the problem.[22] It was only in the 1950s that May came upon a formulation that could provide the framework for the dialogic defense of majority rule; it is far too soon to think that the last word has been spoken on the incompleteness problem that remains for satisfying conversational resolution.

62. CIVIL DISOBEDIENCE AND THE LIMITS OF MAJORITY RULE

Imagine, now, that program B has emerged from the basically majoritarian regime we have described—assisted, when necessary, by

21. *Social Choice and Individual Values* (New Haven: Yale University Press, 2d ed., 1970).
22. Indeed, my friend Gerald Kramer may already have hit upon on a solution that will prove defensible through liberal dialogue. I shall defer an analysis of his proposal, however, until he publishes it.

a randomized agenda setter or some other device yet to be discovered by a future Condorcet. Even so, B does not necessarily represent the best of second-best responses to the imperfections of our technology of justice. Recall Hercules: It was not enough for him to select a program that maximized liberal ideals subject to an equal-sacrifice constraint. After this demanding task had been accomplished, it remained to consider whether it was not best for all concerned to lift the equal-sacrifice constraint and propose a budget that *did* impose admittedly unequal sacrifices on different citizens of the liberal community.

The key here is the tax-incentive argument developed in the last chapter.[23] To put the point in process terms, imagine that after the citizenry adopts program B as the best equal-sacrifice solution, Democrat proposes an amendment.

> DEMOCRAT: I say that we should allow unequal inheritance of material assets, permitting the children of rich parents an initial material endowment twice the size given to citizens who happen to have poor parents. Let's call this amendment X.
>
> EGALITARIAN: But your amendment requires a substantial revision of program B, which presently assures each young adult an equal right to initial material possessions, regardless of his parentage.
>
> DEMOCRAT: Nonetheless, it seems to me that amendment X will serve the general advantage. Unequal inheritance will give many people a powerful incentive to work harder and produce more. This, in turn, will permit us to increase the overall size of the structural budget from B to B + Y; and this in turn will permit us to increase the liberality of the education we give each child. While some citizens will start off poorer, they will be compensated by a deeper insight into the range of their moral opportunities. Even if I take the view of a poor kid of the next generation, this seems to me a liberal trade-off well worth making.
>
> EGALITARIAN: That's quite a complicated argument you've got there.
>
> DEMOCRAT: Complicated or not, I haven't said anything un-Neutral, have I?
>
> EGALITARIAN: I guess not. Still, I'm not convinced.
>
> DEMOCRAT: What's troubling you?

23. See § 57.

EGALITARIAN: First, as an empirical matter, I'm far from certain that your optimistic budgetary predictions will come off. Moreover, as a normative matter, I have even more doubts.

DEMOCRAT: How so?

EGALITARIAN: Well, I don't think that your enriched liberal education is all that fantastic. Money isn't everything, you know; and I worry about how a poor child will interpret the news that his classmate will be getting twice the bundle he will receive on stepping out into the adult world.

DEMOCRAT: But that's not *so* important—compared to all the liberalizing things we've placed in the kid's environment! (*Enumerates them.*)

EGALITARIAN: Once again, there's something to what you say. But the educational case would have to be far more compelling before I'd let it offset the prima facie injustice of initial inequality.

DEMOCRAT: Well, then, we disagree. I can't say I'm surprised. After all, this is an essentially contestable matter, involving cardinal, not ordinal, value judgments.

EGALITARIAN: How, then, are we to resolve our disagreement?

DEMOCRAT: By majority rule, of course. If that was the right procedure for selecting program B, isn't it also the right way to deal with amendments?

Democrat's majoritarian proposal seems a natural one. Nonetheless, his parting shot should not be treated as a rhetorical question with an obvious answer. Our "easy" argument for majority rule did not vindicate the principle as appropriate for the resolution of *all* disputes. Rather than an unquestionable assumption, majority rule dropped out as a conclusion of a Neutral argument about the requirements a liberal community might rightly impose upon a legitimate decision-making procedure. Before extending majority rule to a new class of disputes, we must ask each time whether the conditions that made our dialogic argument "easy" still apply with the same force.

62.1. *The Limits of the Easy Argument*

The importance of caution is underscored by this first, seemingly natural, extension of the majoritarian principle to the "third" and final round of our idealized decision-making procedure. Even here, where so little has changed from the previous situation, the "easy" argument fails to go through:

296   FROM IDEAL TO REALITY

EGALITARIAN: I deny that the arguments you have made for majority rule cover the instant case.

DEMOCRAT: What's giving you the problem?

EGALITARIAN: The requirement you called outcome indifference.

DEMOCRAT: You mean my claim that a good decision procedure should not make it any harder to enact program A into law than it does for program B.

EGALITARIAN: Yes, that's the one. It is, I take it, an essential part of your "easy" argument?

DEMOCRAT: Right. If you deny O, then majority rule is no longer uniquely identified by the rest of May's conditions.

EGALITARIAN: And denying O is precisely what I want to do.

DEMOCRAT: But why? How is this dispute over B and X different from the "easy" case presented by a disagreement over B and A?

EGALITARIAN: Recall your previous argument on behalf of outcome indifference. In response to an earlier question, you made much of the fact that neither A nor B was plainly a better liberal solution than the other.

DEMOCRAT: So I did. It was precisely because A and B were both presumptively legitimate solutions that oucome indifference made so much sense. After all, if there is no reason to think B is a plainly better liberal solution than A, why should it be any easier to enact B into law than its competitor?

EGALITARIAN: And why were you so certain that A and B were both plausible candidates for adoption by a liberal state?

DEMOCRAT: Because all the presumptively illegitimate options had been excluded from the agenda during the first uncontroversial stage of our decision procedure.

EGALITARIAN: But it is *precisely* this that *cannot* be said of X in this final stage of our decision procedure. X plainly contemplates unequal sacrifice—indeed it was one of the proposals that we placed to one side during the first stage of our procedure!

DEMOCRAT: I guess so. After all, nobody denies that X requires one group of citizens to sacrifice more of their ideal rights than it requires of another group. And that's the definition of exploitation.

EGALITARIAN: So, unlike the choice between two presumptively legitimate options like A and B, we are presently faced with a choice

between a presumptively legitimate option like B and an X that is
prima facie illegitimate.

DEMOCRAT: And what follows?

EGALITARIAN: That the "easy" argument for outcome indifference, hence majority rule, no longer applies. Rather than being
indifferent to the choice between B and X, a liberal polity should
make it much harder to enact an option that is prima facie illegitimate.

Egalitarian's point can be dramatized by means of a cartoon case.
Suppose that among the amendments waiting on the agenda was one
N that proposed the wholesale replacement of program B by the
official platform of the Nazi party. Suppose, further, that when N's
turn came, nobody even tried to justify it by making the complicated
appeal to general advantage which Democrat has just attempted. On
this scenario, surely no liberal statesman could say that a legitimate
voting procedure should be indifferent between outcome B and outcome N. It is not the act of voting but the act of dialogue that legitimates the use of power in a liberal state. When an outcome is not
justified through Neutral dialogue, a liberal voting procedure *cannot*
remain indifferent about its adoption. Even if an overwhelming majority is shouting its support for the extermination of the Jews, this din
does nothing to legitimate the outcome. Of course, liberal principles
may not suffice to save some exploited group; the forces of oppression
may simply sweep away all the restraints of Neutral dialogue. But we
are presently discussing the status of majority rule within the framework of liberal theory, not the power of the majority to destroy a
liberal state. And within this framework, outcome indifference—
hence, majority rule—is only appropriate for collective choices between options of *equivalent* liberal legitimacy.

Of course, from Democrat's point of view, this analogy to Nazism is
a symptom of poor judgment bordering on silliness. So far as Democrat is concerned, there *are* convincing Neutral arguments for making
the value trade-off that X entails. Unlike the Nazi, he aims to enrich,
not to destroy, the liberal state. Yet despite these considered and
conscientious judgments, Democrat *cannot* say that Egalitarian is
plainly wrong in saying that X is just another exploitative effort to
oppress the poor. For a comparison between B and X requires each

statesman to make the kind of cardinal judgments that are essentially contestable in a liberal state. However reluctantly, Democrat must concede that Egalitarian is *within his conversational rights in denouncing X as an expression of authoritarian domination rather than an act of liberal statesmanship.*

Such a dialogic concession undermines the liberal polity at its very foundation—which is nothing other than the effort by *all* citizens to ground their power relations upon a political culture that *all* may recognize as falling within the conversational limits defined by Neutrality. Once the Democrat concedes the legitimacy of the dissenter's characterization, he must himself admit that a liberal decision procedure cannot be indifferent between X and B. If B is enacted, *nobody* can plausibly deny its liberal legitimacy; if X, *some* people can and will deny it in ways that the others cannot hope to refute decisively. This is itself a serious political cost that must be considered in *every* effort to override a substantial charge of exploitation by an appeal to the general advantage. A legitimate decision rule must reflect this fact by making it easier to enact a presumptively legitimate program (like B) than one that plainly imposes unequal sacrifices upon different groups in the community (like X).

62.2. *Beyond Majority Rule*

But *how* much harder should it be to enact legislation in the teeth of a credible charge of exploitation?

There is, I think, no easy answer to this question. Indeed, it is not even apparent that all appeals to the general advantage must be forced to transcend the *same* special procedural obstacles. While some Xs might be rejected unless they meet with two-thirds approval, others will so deeply alienate minorities from liberal discourse that even a broader consensus must be demanded before the polity will recognize that the asserted benefits of X outweigh its dialogic costs. Or perhaps we should move beyond simple majoritarianism by invoking a second procedure that has no less claim to liberal legitimacy: the responsive lottery. The advantage of the lottery, of course, is that it gives the egalitarian minority at least *some* chance of determining the political outcome in a way consistent with its conscientious beliefs; this fact emphasizes the polity's recognition of the essentially contestable standing of *any* appeal to general advantage.

62.3. *Civil Disobedience*

Suppose, then, that Democrat submits his amendment under a special rule requiring approval by a supermajority, a responsive lottery, or some system that he conscientiously believes does justice to the dialogic stakes involved in overruling a charge of exploitation. After another round of sustained substantive debate, the matter is put to decision, and X emerges triumphant over all obstacles. What next?

EGALITARIAN: But you will stigmatize these poor kids!

DEMOCRAT: The harsh fact is that we do not live in an ideal world, and we say that they're better off well educated.

EGALITARIAN: You're wrong. You're exploiting them on behalf of the rich. This is tyranny!

DEMOCRAT: We do not wish to belittle your complaint. But, after all, you must recognize that you're not the only statesman in this commonwealth! And if we let you veto our decision, this will, we think, impoverish our common pursuit of the liberal ideal.

EGALITARIAN: So what are you going to do?

DEMOCRAT: We hereby declare X to be the law of this liberal polity.

EGALITARIAN: And what is this law to me?

DEMOCRAT: Isn't it time for you to recognize that we, no less than you, are in good faith in this matter? We are not tyrants, my friend, but fellow citizens trying to make the best of an imperfect world. Surely you will not sever the bonds of citizenship that we have so painfully built through our common dialogue? Surely you will not disobey the law?

Hear the sound of liberal conversation at the breaking point. The dominant group urgently invites the dissenters to reaffirm a common commitment to mastering the world of power by the force of dialogue. Yet they cannot, by definition, say that the dissenters are unreasonable in asserting the exploitative character of the dominant arrangements. Thus, liberal theory requires democrats, no less than dissenters, to recognize that the political conversation has not yet reached an end. While the dissenters may respond affirmatively to the last dialogue, they may also reject Democrat's invitation and pursue the political conversation in a new form—by undertaking acts of civil disobedience. Here a citizen refuses to obey a law his fellows have imposed upon him on the ground that it requires him to give his support to intolerably exploitative conditions. At the same time, he also refuses to abandon his dialogic ties with his fellows. Hence, after violating the law, he submits to the punishment the law establishes—making his own body, as it were, a counter in the continuing dialogue that binds all citizens together despite their profoundest disagreements.

> EGALITARIAN: I do not deny our mutual commitment to the dialogic mastery of the world, but I cannot explain this law to myself in terms that pass the test of Neutrality.
> DEMOCRAT: But we cannot go on talking forever. We must resolve this dispute, at least for a time, so that we may turn to the main business of life: the pursuit of the good in all its diverse forms.
> EGALITARIAN: Easy for you to say. As for me, I am entirely unwilling to turn to the pursuit of *my* good so long as the power structure is premised on illegitimate exploitation.
> DEMOCRAT: We too detest illegitimacy. Only we believe that our decision will enrich the liberal rights of all citizens.
> EGALITARIAN: But I cannot accept your characterization.
> DEMOCRAT: So what should be done with you?
> EGALITARIAN: That's for you to say. The only thing clear to me is that your laws are intolerably exploitative.

But why shouldn't the dissenter go yet further? Why can't he simply declare his fellows to be tyrants and deny the legitimacy of *any* punishment for his acts of disobedience?

I do not wish to deny the legitimacy of liberal revolution. To the contrary, the limited liberal achievements of the present day would have been impossible without the blood of our predecessors. Nonetheless, I *do* wish to deny the legitimacy of revolt under the special conditions of our present problem. Recall, for the last time, that we are dealing with an idealized world where each citizen resembles Hercules in his effort to approximate liberal justice; where the liberal political community has given a serious indication, by its adoption of supermajoritarian decisional procedures, that it takes the question of exploitation seriously. Under these conditions, a committed liberal—no matter how seriously he contests the terms of the trade-off between exploitation and general advantage—cannot forget that the matter requires cardinal judgments of a kind upon which good-faith disagreement is inevitable. To use such an essentially contestable issue as a justification for rebellion is simply juvenile. Even if Egalitarian's revolution succeeded, he could not reasonably hope to establish a political order in which alienated liberal minorities did not find themselves in the same position he currently occupies. Better, then, to force the majority to an even deeper reconsideration through civil disobedience than use so contestable a cause for severing the dialogic bond and unleashing forces that may readily destroy all hope of reestablishing civil dialogue.

63. TYRANNY

63.1. *Toward Realism*
The easy case for majority rule is not so simple after all. Maximum clarity is achieved only at the core of liberal politics, where a single presumptively legitimate program gains clear majority support against all of its competitors. Here the majoritarian will have no difficulty defending his principle against countless elitist solutions to the problem of good-faith disagreement. Conversational difficulty arises only in a confrontation with fellow democrats who argue that the responsive lottery, rather than majority rule, better expresses each statesman's claim to equal respect in collective decision making. The easy argument is complexified further by Condorcet's paradox, which teaches that the majority principle will not always identify a single policy as preferable to all the rest. While, as we have seen, this conceptual problem may sometimes force the polity to randomize its agenda-setting procedures, this complexity should not obscure the dialogic affirmation that *is* possible when a single policy does indeed command the unambiguous support of a majority.

More fundamental limitations on majority rule enter only when the problem of exploitation comes into view. Each citizen has a prima facie right to the undominated equality vouchsafed by ideal theory. While the hard facts of second-best require a compromise of liberal ideals, a legitimate decision procedure cannot be indifferent between a presumptively legitimate outcome and one that requires some citizens to make great sacrifices of their ideal rights while others are permitted to enjoy their freedoms undisturbed. A legitimate decision procedure must instead recognize the contestable character of all appeals to general advantage and take steps to assure the minority that its claims of exploitation are treated with the seriousness they require.

Even supermajoritarian procedures, however, cannot be expected to forestall all principled challenges to liberal authority. The most we can demand is that alienated minorities express their opposition through civil disobedience rather than outright rebellion.

Even at its simplest, then, the vision of liberal democracy that emerges can hardly be reduced to a single image of the populace heading to the polls on election day. While voting is a necessary condition, it is hardly sufficient for a government to claim liberal legitimacy. Instead, the way statesmen manipulate the political agenda and the way they talk about the issues they define are no less important in the theory of liberal democracy. And if this is so in the "easy" case, it is even truer in more realistic models of liberal politics.

The realist begins with an irrefutable fact: No liberal government can expect all its citizens to behave like liberal statesmen all of the time. Not that all acts of statesmanship require the labor of Hercules, nor even the subtlety of Metternich. What is needed, above all else, is the spirit of toleration—while each of us commits himself deeply to a particular vision of the good, we can never lose sight of the countless moral possibilities that any particular life must leave unrealized. The critical skill is to use liberal dialogue as a means for reinforcing this fragile awareness of unrealized possibility that all of us can sometimes glimpse—so that government does not become an arena where each person tries to suppress all that is foreign to him but a place to reaffirm our separate identities as free and autonomous persons.

All this is easy to say and hard to achieve. Each statesman must recognize that neither he nor anybody else is immune from the corruptions of power. Yet this perception is only the beginning, not the end, of realistic liberal statesmanship. Once the temptations of tyranny are recognized as the ultimate threat to liberal government, they can be made the subject of Neutral conversation. Can we design mechanisms that will contain, if not cure, the authoritarian instincts with which all of us must deal?

63.2. Three Strategies

There are, I take it, three strategies we may pursue to reduce the risk of tyranny. The first tries to control the inputs into the political process. Perhaps the crudest form is to bar some citizens from governmental office on the ground that they aim to overthrow the liberal state. But there are other, more indirect forms of input control: manipulating the educational system to assure a steady flow of citizens of statesmanly virtue, combating undue concentrations of economic power, and so forth.

The second strategy structures governmental processes in ways that make it costly for statesmen to indulge authoritarian pretensions. The key to most process strategies is the artful division of power to give officeholders personal incentives for checking and balancing one another when they try to act out their authoritarian ambitions. The American Constitution is, perhaps, the most familiar example of this device.

And finally there are the strategies that try to impose direct controls over governmental output. This is the tactic taken by the draftsmen of bills of right, when they try to specify, in legally binding form, particular outcomes that shall forever be beyond the power of government to achieve.

Now it is hardly my purpose to provide a blueprint for would-be statesmen who lack the wit to combine these strategies in ways that make sense of their own historical situation. To the contrary, the point of the following survey is that *all* these strategies have weaknesses as well as strengths, and that statesmen who make a fetish of some particular strategic formula risk failure at the times of greatest crisis. Rather than mistaking a particular strategy for a final solution to the problem of tyranny, we must keep our eyes on the ultimate objective, which is to take those concrete steps that will deepen the institutional foundations of the ongoing dialogue that constitutes the liberal state.

63.3. *Input Controls*

Of the three strategies, input controls have the most obvious dangers. When I exclude you from positions of government, there are always two possible interpretations. On the one hand, I may have concluded—with the reluctance of Hercules—that this step is necessary to save the state from a totalitarian coup d'etat. On the other hand, it may be I, and not you, who pose the more serious threat to the integrity of dialogue. All this liberal talk of mine may simply be a pose, a public-relations gimmick disguising my own lust for unquestioned despotism.

Surely this second danger is real enough to preclude crude exclusions from political power except under the most extraordinary conditions. Yet, even here, the principle of universal political participation cannot be made into an absolute rule. Imagine a totalitarian clique taking advantage of an economic crisis to exploit popular discontent. The propaganda machine spreads the word: If only Adolf or Benito or Vladimir were in command, they would have the wisdom to make the sun rise once more in the heavens. This messianic message gains a powerful political following, both on the streets and in the ballot box. What then?

Depending on a host of particular factors, it may not be a mistake to ban the authoritarians from the governmental positions to which they would otherwise be entitled by their electoral victories. This may, after all, be the best way to weather a temporary storm without doing grievous damage to the rights of millions of citizens. Nonetheless, even a temporary exclusion cannot help but damage liberal dialogue. Once left alone upon the commanding heights, the so-called liberals may come to resemble the totalitarians below with appalling speed.

A similar complexity arises when governing roles are reversed and it is the liberals who are leading the revolution against established authority. Here, too, the liberal revolutionary must fight a war on two fronts. As a *liberal,* each statesman is committed to the central importance of dialogue in a legitimate state; yet as a *revolutionary,* he is equally committed to the fact that talk is presently fruitless and that violent upheaval is a necessary preliminary for legitimacy. There is, of course, nothing logically inconsistent with this stance: the world is full of states in which power elites refuse to permit their claims to be tested by dialogue, where the question of legitimacy is simply answered by repressive force. It may well be foolish to expect much from talk under such circumstances.

Nonetheless, liberal revolution requires a special complexity in statecraft. On the one hand, central control is required both to smash the old regime and to prevent others from fashioning a new tyranny to replace the old one. On the other hand, the statesman must try to make the liberal principle of dialogue a living political reality as soon as possible. It follows that there are two ways a liberal revolution may fail. Either liberal forces spend so much time talking that they are overwhelmed by hostile military power, or the revolutionary leadership becomes so transfixed by hostile threats they create a police state that mocks the very ideals that inspired the revolution in its early stages.

Even when we put moments of revolutionary crisis to one side, the case for input controls cannot be lightly brushed aside. Of course, crudities like barring totalitarian groups from parliament must be recognized as the acts of desperation they are. However, it is possible to imagine structural measures that will affect the long-term liberality of the social forces that push their way into the governmental arena. The question here is political education in its broadest sense. Preaching the spirit of tolerance is no good unless people sometimes see a practical value in allowing others to go their own way. At the very minimum, there must be competition among different elites, with at least a few gaining a mass following. It is only then that both elites and mass may come to see the need for toleration to achieve a stable form of community life. And it is this basic lesson in toleration which liberal politics seeks both to refine and to deepen.

63.4. *Process Controls*

There are social conditions that will defeat the most inspired acts of liberal statesmanship. The liberal's ceaseless questioning of legitimacy is never exactly popular, and, as we have just seen, liberalism cannot readily be imposed by a small elite on a hostile mass. Nonetheless, liberals are not fated to remain forever on the sidelines, philosophizing on their own powerlessness. History reveals that the liberal spirit has sometimes become a powerful social reality. Assume, then, that we inhabit one of these more hopeful times and places, where a liberal government can confidently open its doors to all adult citizens who wish to engage in political life. Even so, liberal statesmen can hardly be indifferent to the way formal institutions structure participation in the power of command. A mistake in institutional design can needlessly damage—even utterly destroy—a promising liberal politics. Moreover, no single blueprint can be expected to function in all social settings; worse yet, we do not have powerful theories that explain why some institutional frameworks work tolerably well in one social setting and fail so abysmally in others.

One thing is clear: the inadequacy of the model that served as the backdrop for the constitutional conversations sketched in the first half of this chapter. Democrat and Elitist spoke to one another as if they lived in a world where the entire body of citizen-statesmen could get together from time to time to manage affairs of state, with full-time civil servants, if they existed at all, safely under control. Yet the age of the polis is long passed; moreover, a liberal statesman will not mourn its passing. Only an extensive republic will embrace the diverse population required to provide the social foundations for a liberal politics. This means that the best we can hope for is a representative democracy, in which the dialogues between Egalitarian and Democrat are refracted by the problematics of representation.

The problem is simple enough: representatives, once selected, have the chance to abuse their office for personal advantage. Rather than serving as a focus of the larger liberal conversation within their constituencies, they will use their authority to immunize their power from further challenge. Power corrupts.

It is here that the idea of process controls becomes a central liberal preoccupation. The goal is to remove law-making authority from the hands of a single statesman or easily organized clique. No official's word becomes law when it is spoken; each power holder is constitutionally obliged to persuade others whose tenure does not depend on their passive acquiescence. This idea is taken to its extreme in the American system, where President, Supreme Court, and the two Houses of Congress are deprived of the power of unilateral command in the hope of forcing each to engage the others in a convincing effort at conversation. And when the talk reaches an impasse on official levels, the competing sides have an incentive to focus attention on their disagreement at the next general election. Thus, the aim of the separation of powers is to channel the politician's tendencies toward self-aggrandizement into the service of a broader liberal dialogue.

A similar instinct is apparent in a second classic mode of process control. The aim of this federalist strategy is to decentralize political decisions geographically, creating local polities with sufficient legal power and independence to check authoritarian impulses emanating from the center, and *vice versa*. Federalist structures also permit the polity to make creative use of the fact that many second-best problems admit of a wide variety of legitimate solutions. Since there is often no need to impose the same solution throughout an extensive republic, many critical issues may be left to the decision of different local majorities.

Yet, in the end, process strategies run up against very serious limitations. While they may well reduce the risk of governmental tyranny, they often increase the risk of private exploitation. A government can be checked and balanced into immobility. It may become impossible to change the status quo unless an overwhelming majority favors the change. This may be tolerable so long as the status quo can be reasonably understood as one of the presumptively legitimate outcomes that could emerge from a sober second-best dialogue. Yet there is little reason to expect the status quo to pass this minimal test. As we have seen, the liberal question of legitimacy is no respecter of the "natural" rights that the powerful invariably claim to justify their control over property, their dominion over dependent spouses and children, their enjoyment of genetic advantage. While it is possible to imagine a benign deity distributing these endowments to each generation in a liberal way, there is no reason whatever to believe that God, in his inscrutable wisdom, has created a liberal version of the garden of Eden, where legitimacy can be achieved without effort. Instead, a ceaseless struggle is required if the conditions for liberal dialogue are to be remotely approximated. If we hope to make liberalism a living reality, the government must intervene on an ongoing basis: to aid the handicapped, educate the young, equalize material wealth, increase the flexibility of transaction, and protect the interests of future generations. Under real-world conditions, a government immobilized by checks and balances loses its legitimacy if it simply uses its coercive force on behalf of the status quo without seriously dealing with the claims of exploitation raised all around it.

The second–best government is *not* the one that governs least. Checks and balances are not valued for their own sake but rather as tools to force government officials to talk to the rest of us as moral equals rather than dominating overlords. Yet this goal is only part of the larger liberal project. We do not merely aim for a world where government officials are stripped of their pretentions to moral superiority; we aim for a structure in which *all* power held by *all* people is justified through a dialogue worthy of free and rational beings. The statesman can never mistake a part for the whole without impoverishing the liberal vision.

63.5. *Output Controls*

Isn't there an easy way to guard against the weaknesses of a process strategy? Why not promulgate a bill of rights defining intolerable conditions of exploitation and legally require the government to fulfill the bill?

But output control has its own problems. Most obviously, the strategy requires Herculean effort by those who take it upon themselves to impose a bill of rights on future processes. For this power, like any other, can be used tyrannically. It is as easy to write a bill of rights that enshrines slavery as it is to proclaim a commitment to undominated equality. And if a bill of rights is abused in this way, the political conversation of a liberal state will be off to a very bad start indeed.

Yet even if a particular generation finds that the time is ripe for a liberal bill of rights, it must confront a second perplexity of a more conceptual kind. For a liberal statesman, the most basic right of any citizen is the right *to have his question of legitimacy answered in a liberal conversation.* Yet this right to a dialogic *process* cannot be unproblematically reduced to any particular set of *outcomes* under second-best conditions. At best, a statesman can describe an exploitative power structure, X, that gives rise to prima facie illegitimacy. Yet it is always possible that a particular X can be justified as legitimate, under particular social conditions, by an appeal to the general advantage.

This means that the liberal statesman immediately encounters a dilemma as he begins writing his bill of rights. On the one hand, the whole point of his exercise is to specify some outcome, X, which should not be tolerated in his particular second-best polity. On the other hand, if he tries to forbid X in clear and unambiguous terms, a time may come when future generations will rightly regret the earlier decision to write an "absolute" prohibition into the bill of rights. Even if X is plainly illegitimate at the time of the original bill, historical conditions may evolve in a way that makes X dialogically justifiable.

This tension between precision and overbreadth does not, of course, demonstrate the impropriety of clear and absolute language in a bill of rights. It merely suggests that such a strategy is no more a panacea than the others we have canvassed. Nonetheless, a few well-specified output controls may sometimes play an important role within the overall constitutional structure.

Take free speech for example. As a citizen of a liberal state, I have an ideal right to use the communications network to transmit any message I think worthwhile. While this ideal of transactional flexibility will not completely survive second-best cost considerations, I may still rightfully protest against exploitation if I am asked to sacrifice my speech rights when an equivalent restriction is not imposed on you. Imagine, for example, that I want to use the telephone to transmit message X while you want to use the phone to transmit Y. The gov-

ernment is doing something presumptively illegitimate if it denies me
the right to transmit X and lets you say Y whenever you like. Yet,
despite this conclusion, it is possible to imagine cases where a governmental restriction on my rights may be justified by a conversational
appeal to the general advantage. Suppose, for example, that X is a
secret war plan whose general publication will predictably lead to the
destruction of the liberal state. Surely it would be appropriate for a
democratic government to find that restricting my rights to transmit X
enriches the bundle of liberal rights held by *all* citizens in the not-so-
long run. Yet an "absolute" bar on governmental efforts to impose
content restrictions on communicative utterance would make this restriction unconstitutional.

Even so, it may be sensible for a second-best statesman to frame his
prohibition on content control in absolute terms. Not, mind you, that
he will take such a step with a light heart; indeed, he may secretly hope
that if the fate of liberal dialogue *did* hinge on the publication of a war
plan, his successors would have the good sense to ignore the "absolute" language of his bill of rights. Yet, a liberal statesman might
rightly fear that a constitutional provision giving officials *some* power
to censor *some* substantive talk *some* of the time would be used as an
excuse for a more sweeping official censorship over the substance of
communication. Once officials are conceded the right to turn off the
flow of critical talk whenever they like, the days of liberalism are
numbered. If the mode of "absolute" prohibition appreciably reduces
this risk, it may be worth the gamble.

Government officials, however, are hardly the only threat to liberal
values in a second-best state; a bill of rights may also be a useful tool in
forbidding state support for "private" efforts to exploit the powerless.
The primitive case is the institution of chattel slavery. Here the law
recognizes only the master as a legal person and treats the slave as if he
were just another piece of manna whose fate was the master's private
affair. Surely the fact that the master can be described as a "private-
property owner" rather than a "public official" should not preclude
the absolute prohibition of slavery in the bill of rights. Instead, each
person may be guaranteed an absolute right to challenge the legitimacy of *any* power play that adversely affects his interests. Any effort
by the government to lock the courthouse door may be placed on the
list of forbidden outcomes.

But citizens of a liberal state have more than the right to complain in court when others frustrate their desires. They have a right to relief when their fellows prove incapable of justifying their power through Neutral dialogue. Thus, a bill of rights may go well beyond a minimal guarantee of legal personality—the right to sue and be sued—and give a richer substance to the absolute rights of citizenship. In some or all the areas of basic concern—genetic handicap, liberal education, material wealth, transactional flexibility—a bill of rights may try to specify minimum output levels that must be received by every citizen on pain of a finding of unconstitutionality. The definition of these minima will, of course, be a subject of reasonable disagreement *but no more than any other provision of the bill of rights*. As we have seen, *every* exercise in output control necessarily runs up against the problem of overbreadth. In each case, the statesman must frame his guarantee after recognizing that the outcomes he prohibits may, under certain empirical conditions, prove justifiable. The decision to add a right to the bill can occur only after the statesman judges that the risks of overbreadth are offset by the risks that an uncontrolled process will systematically deprive citizens of their fundamental rights.

63.6. *Judicial Review*

But perhaps the difficulties of output control are only of our own creation. Up to the present point, I have treated the output strategy within the constraints imposed by the most familiar myths that surround the promulgation of a bill of rights, a story in which a group of master statesmen have somehow obtained the power to hand down a few clear "Thou shalt nots" to guide a grateful populace determined to protect its rights against authoritarian threat.

Now, if such a thing came to pass, I would be among the first to applaud the miracle. Building a liberal state is hard enough under the best of circumstances; the task of the statesman is to make the best dialogic use of the materials given to him by history; if history contains some splendid utterances by liberal founders, so much the better for us all. Yet, a few dead heroes are neither necessary nor sufficient for the creation of a sound liberal state. Even at its best, the promulgation of a bill of rights is hardly the ideal conceptual vehicle for the protection of fundamental rights. A list of prohibited outcomes cannot by its very nature protect the most fundamental right of citizenship—the right to stand steadfast before my fellows and refuse to give ground until they explain Neutrally why they, not I, may exercise the power we both seek. The question arises, then, whether we cannot design a mode of output control that does not so heavily rely on a momentary spasm of heroic statesmanship to curb the constant temptation toward authoritarian self-aggrandizement.

Imagine, for example, a special body of dialogic policemen established by the polity to serve as a supreme court. The task of the court is *not* to second-guess the second-best trade-offs inevitable in any realistic version of liberal politics. These are left to the democratic processes that seem most likely to generate a steady pattern of liberalish outcomes given the particular historical situation. The task of the supreme court, instead, is to assure the liberal quality of each outcome, X, by exposing it to a final test of legitimacy. This test is not conceived, however, as one of determining whether X falls within the forbidden class of outcomes specified by the master statesmen of long ago. Nor does the court try to imagine what the master statesmen would have thought if they knew the facts now available for all to see. Instead of an act of inspired guesswork, the court proceeds to the dialogic heart of the matter. X's legitimacy, after all, is ultimately a question of what its *present* proponents can say on its behalf; and what better way to find out than to require its proponents *to answer the question of legitimacy* before the court itself?

Thus, when some citizen disadvantaged by X comes before the court, X's beneficiaries are not permitted to greet the question of legitimacy with a resolute silence. For if a citizen's question gets no answer, the court is empowered to declare X unconstitutional. The mere grant of such a judicial power is an act of high symbolic import. It not only vindicates the challenger's standing as a citizen of a liberal state, whose questions must be taken seriously; it also expresses his fundamental right to a liberal answer, by promising the nullification of all power that cannot be mediated by liberal conversation.

Of course, if this threat of nullification is institutionally credible, the supreme court will typically find X's proponents in a talkative mood. Indeed, their imaginations will know no bounds as they try to legitimate X within the constraints imposed by liberal conversation. Two gambits will be especially favored. First, since it is always possible to dream up a second-best world, Z, where X is a dialogically plausible policy, Xers will try to convince the court that the world outside the courtroom in fact resembles Z in all relevant respects. Needless to say, the questioners will bend every effort to paint the facts with different hues, making Z an entirely implausible portrait. Second, the Xers will be tempted to develop dialogic rationales that were never seriously considered by the democratic institutions that enacted X in the first place. Thus, laws that would never have gained a majority's support without demagogic appeals to the basest authoritarian impulses will be dressed up in a most remarkable manner within the four walls of a courtroom. The complainants may play the same game if this suits their private interest—trying to persuade the court that the most Herculean acts of statesmanship are in fact the product of the basest power lusts.

And so we come to the ultimate weakness, as well as the strength, of this final constitutional safeguard against tyranny. Even at its best, policing the dialogue will make Herculean demands on the statesmen called to the supreme court. Moreover, the judges can no more pretend to Herculean virtue than the rest of us. They too will succumb to the temptations of tyranny and exploit the haze of rhetoric to impose judgments that go beyond their special role as output controllers.

Yet, a liberal constitution is not defenceless against such possibilities. Just as the output strategy can be used to control the deficiencies of input and process approaches, so too these other strategies may be deployed to ameliorate the abuse of output control. Thus, the supreme court may itself be checked and balanced in numerous ways to constrain its authoritarian pretensions. Similarly, an input strategist might dream of providing the bench and bar with a proper sense of their calling in a liberal state, one that emphasizes the special mission of the supreme court without making it a cause for yet another elitist celebration.

63.7. A Realistic Conclusion

It bears repeating that no particular strategy is worthy of uncritical support at all times and all places. Doubtless if we were lucky enough to live in a place where a particular institutional matrix sustains liberalish talk and action, it would be silly to destroy a tolerable framework to achieve some speculative liberal advantage. Nonetheless, even a viable structure will rapidly decay if its inhabitants forget the basic aspirations of liberal government.

Liberal government, in the end, is an expression of hope—that citizens, by reasoning together, can domesticate the power struggle that is an unavoidable part of their social situation. This aspiration is constantly at war with another reality— that government is itself a central focus of the power struggle, permitting exploiters to cement their power over their fellow citizens. There can be no hope for a "final" institutional solution to this tension between aspiration and reality. Yet, without the constant effort to repair and construct liberal institutions of government, the aspiration will come to seem a childish dream. With liberal institutions in decay, it is only a matter of time before one or another zealot will sieze the chance to impose his private nightmare on the rest of us.

64. ALTERNATIVE FOUNDATIONS FOR LIBERAL DEMOCRACY

My essay began bravely in search of a new world of liberal ideals; I have been scrambling back to earth ever since. Not that we have reached the end of the journey. The matter of third-best compromise remains before us. There is no reason to think that vested interests will meekly retire before the triumphant voices of liberal dialogue. Success, instead, may involve playing one set of exploiters against another to achieve a perceptible liberal advance. But I, at least, can offer no advice on this matter that is worth your time. I have no "science" of historical development which can save the statesman the hard work of studying the dynamics of the particular society in which he lives.

I must leave you, then, at the second-best turning of the road, the point at which the ideal polity of undominated equality has been transformed into more familiar political images: men and women arguing things out under ground rules that deny their pretensions to innate superiority; political decisions made by democratic means, but only after the prevailing statesmen make a conscientious effort to hear what the others are saying. Even the majority, however, cannot maximize its own convenience by exploiting their fellow citizens. Inequality of right can only be justified when it furthers the dialogic rights of *all* citizens. Otherwise, legalized exploitation is itself an assault on the very dialogue that legitimates majority rule in the first place. Liberal dialogue is not only the lifeblood of public life; it serves to mark the limits of majority rule itself. Second-best government, in short, turns out to be nothing other than old-fashioned liberal democracy.

It is a hard thing to rediscover the familiar. What was the good of all this spaceship talk if it simply returns us in the end to the place where we began? All it does is suggest that our liberal parents were not always the fools they sometimes seemed, that their failures are our failures, and that we have yet to achieve our own successes.

Yet it is this awkward recognition that eludes us when we use the metaphors of contract and utility to illuminate our commitment to liberal democracy. Rather than providing an incisive account of the dilemmas of democratic politics, these familiar philosophies only succeed in obscuring the distinctive attractions of liberal-democratic ideals.

64.1. *Utilitarianism*

Liberal democracy: the very terms seem to jumble two incompatible ideals to form a pleasing, but unsatisfying, political confection. Isn't a *democrat* someone who thinks that the people should rule? Isn't a *liberal* someone who thinks that certain individual rights are so fundamental that they can never be violated by any collective body? What, then, does a "liberal-democrat" say when the people deprive individuals of their fundamental rights? If he protests, isn't our hybrid just a liberal in disguise? If he goes along, isn't he a democrat without the need of a hyphen?

Obvious questions. And no theory of liberal democracy is any good if it fails to answer them. Before liberal democracy can be anything more than confectioner's sugar, a philosophical act of reconciliation is required. Democratic rule must be justified by principles that delimit its application to a subset of all possible issues. Individual rights must be generated in a way that leaves some room for democratic rule. To make the juggling act more difficult, only one ball can be in the air at any moment; in principle, issues should be classifiable *either* as appropriate for democratic rule *or* as appropriate for the vindication of a fundamental right, but not as both.

As always, utilitarianism is equal to this formidable challenge. Yet it succeeds only at the cost of trivializing the ideals that the liberal-democrat seeks to reconcile. The basic strategy is familiar. Utility is the sun around which all lesser political ideas revolve. When words like "majority rule" and "individual rights" look as if they are about to collide, this is only a sign of the speaker's disordered mind. If he only would take proper account of the sun, the orbits of the planets can be calculated by an elegant bit of triangulation.

Begin by placing majority rule into perspective. A useful idea, this, so long as it is not made into a fetish. Consider, for example, a simple case: three people, A, B, C, voting on two options, X and not-X. If X is enacted, A and B each gains ten utiles of happiness; if not-X, C gains ten utiles. Recognizing these facts, A and B form a majority on behalf of X, while C votes not-X. Simple arithmetic indicates that utility requires that the majority should rule: twenty is bigger than ten, isn't it? More generally, majority rule maximizes utility if three conditions are fulfilled: (1) each affected individual has the same utility stake in the issue up for decision; (2) every interested person goes to the polls; and (3) each votes his self-interest.

Sophistication is required, however, whenever these simple conditions do not obtain. Imagine, for example, that the suffrage were extended to its furthest plausible limits, embracing everybody over sixteen. Imagine further that all three assumptions were perfectly fulfilled for this entire constituency. Nevertheless, a clear-thinking utilitarian will remain dissatisfied whenever a law affects the interests of children or other sentient creatures who cannot protect themselves through the ballot box. The happiness of all such creatures has a standing equal to that of voters in the utilitarian scheme.[24] Yet there is no good reason to think that these nonvoters will receive their felicific due within the simple model of self-interested majority voting I have advanced. How, then, are we to protect these individuals?

It is here where the notion of "fundamental rights" makes a useful appearance in constitutional argument. Since children and animals cannot protect themselves at the ballot box, it may well make sense to entrench their interests in a bill of rights and empower a supreme court to review legislation to make sure that the disenfranchised are given their proper weight in the overall accounting.

So much for the fashionable canard that utilitarians fail to take rights "seriously." To the contrary, a bill of rights seems affirmatively desirable *even when majority rule is operating at maximum efficiency*. Of course, a utilitarian's bill of rights will look quite different from one drafted by a liberal statesman. For example, the rights of animals would occupy a prominent position that would be absurd in a liberal bill.[25] Yet this simply suggests that the utilitarian's understanding of majority rule leads him to take *different* rights seriously. Moreover, with a bit of pushing and shoving, it may not be too hard for a utilita-

24. See §§ 22.2 and 37.2.
25. § 22.2.

rian to include many familiar items on his list. Consider, for example, the model's third assumption, that each affected individual votes his self-interest. This requirement for utility maximization can be used as the ground for a constitutional right of free speech. For how are individuals to learn their self-interest without ongoing and robust political debate? Thus, the utilitarian's bill of rights may well contain strong guarantees for free speech and free press. Similarly, the model's second requirement—that all affected individuals vote—can permit an even more straightforward argument for a constitutional prohibition on all efforts to bar racial or other groups from the polls.

Arguments based on violations of the first assumption—that the political decision has an equal impact on all voters—are more complex but no less important. To return to our simple three-person world, assume now that A and B will gain ten utiles by voting for X, while C loses one thousand utiles; here majority rule produces an unhappy result. Thus, utilitarians may view a bill of rights as a useful instrument for the protection of "passionate" minorities against the tyranny of "apathetic" majorities.[26]

And so forth. It is hardly my intention to build the utilitarian's castle for him. It is enough to suggest that a recognizable building of the liberal-democratic type[27] *may* reward the utilitarian's labors. Of course, the structure will differ in many ways from the pattern built up by a liberal state. At every important stage of life, from birth through education to maturity to death, the citizen of a utilitarian polity will find his right to undominated equality compromised in the name of greater happiness. Since I have already indicated the grounds of these substantive disagreements in earlier chapters, there is no point repeating them here.

I wish instead to emphasize the shallow foundations upon which the utilitarian builds his intricate and imposing structure. A thought experiment will permit us to get to the root difficulty. Imagine that our liberal-democrat gets the special chance to submit his master plan to Jeremy Bentham himself for final approval. Arriving at the place of final judgment, our designer learns that he is not the only statesman to

26. See, e.g., Robert Dahl, *A Preface to Democratic Theory*, (Chicago: University of Chicago Press, 1956), chap. 4.

27. The utilitarian structure will, almost certainly, rely upon majoritarian processes and ignore all appeal to "responsive lotteries" discussed in § 61.6. Given the utilitarian's strong commitment to a "cumulating" view of social welfare, I am quite confident that he would reject the "probabilistic" conception of political responsiveness upon which the lottery is based.

receive the call. Before him stands a rival draftsman whose technical skill is no less formidable than his own. His rival, however, does not depend upon the self-interest of voters to generate a utilitarian solution; instead, his constitution calls upon an elite—call it the Party—to lead the nation to its greatest happiness. The elitist constitution contains elaborate provisions for selecting and educating the best and the brightest for positions of leadership. All children will be called for preliminary political education, but few will be chosen. The chosen few, however, will be deeply impressed with the responsibilities implied by their selection. They are not to use the power of government to stuff their bellies and line their pockets. Instead, they must learn to define their self-interest in terms of the common good. Their indoctrination program will call upon them to sacrifice themselves for the public good in ever more demanding ways; recruits who fail these tests of benevolence will be remorselessly purged from the elite's ranks. Only the best of the best will be permitted to advance and advance— and lead the nation to ever greater happiness for all.

Now, of course, our elitist draftsman will recognize the risks entailed by his design. And, no less than the democrat, he will have taken steps to reduce unnecessary pain. Just as the democratic design entrenches "individual rights" to guarantee against majoritarian failure, the competing constitution will contain ingenious efforts to reinvigorate the elite's dedication to the greatest happiness for the greatest number.

The issue, then, is clearly drawn. Which constitution will gain the approval of the Master Builder himself?

BENTHAM: I smell some unhappiness about. Perhaps my judgment will be useful to you?

ELITIST AND DEMOCRAT TOGETHER: Just the thing we need! This squabble is wasting time we could be spending on more useful collaborations. We'd love it if you helped us out.

BENTHAM: Well, then, I've inspected your documents. Brilliant contrivances, both. Each is designed with a deep understanding of the people for whom the constitution is intended; neither is taken in by all the claptrap about Democracy or the Party. Such principles have value only when they work for the public happiness.

DEMOCRAT: Right you are. And that is why I've taken every sensible step to control the unhappy features of majority rule.

ELITIST: And I too have been alive to the misery elites may cause. Hence, the squabble. Which of us has done the better job?

BENTHAM: Well, let's begin by facing facts. Nobody is perfect. Despite your clever contrivances, both constitutions will sometimes generate unhappiness.

ELITIST: True. Mine will fail if, despite my best efforts, the elite will act selfishly to maximize its advantage, forgetting about the larger public.

DEMOCRAT: And mine will fail if, despite my bill of rights, the majority will find many opportunities to maximize its advantage and selfishly impose great unhappiness on the minority.

BENTHAM: Given these humbling facts, I can see only one way to resolve this dispute. Each of you must look into the future and try to guess the likelihood and seriousness of your relative failures. The constitutional regime that has the least unhappy consequences is the one to choose.

ELITIST: And when I look into my crystal ball, I see my elitist system working well under conditions in which liberal democracy would permit majorities to oppress passionate minorities in a scandalous way.

DEMOCRAT: But I too can foresee futures where a liberal democracy functions tolerably well under conditions your elite would exploit in harsh and selfish ways.

BENTHAM: But which constitutional failure is the more likely?

DEMOCRAT AND ELITIST: The one generated by my competitor's design!

BENTHAM: You really must both refine your predictions!

DEMOCRAT AND ELITIST: Isn't there anything more useful you can say to us?

BENTHAM: I'd love to help you out. But there is no sense being dogmatic when the future is uncertain.

ELITIST: Well, given our uncertainties, it may be best to hedge our bets. Perhaps the Party should rule some of the time, the majority should rule some of the time, and individual rights should govern on other occasions!

DEMOCRAT: Too clever by a third. I still think liberal democracy is the best bet.

BENTHAM: Well, perhaps you are right. We really must talk again a couple of centuries from now and see how things turn out.

The liberal-democrat's conversational problem can be located without undue difficulty. As a utilitarian, he is obliged to look upon liberal democracy as a machine for cranking out happy results. Since it is easy to show that this machine operates unreliably under some conditions, it is always possible that a well-designed elitist machine will crank out happier results. Until this possibility has been refuted, the foundations of liberal democracy remain insecure. Yet, if this is so, the foundations can *never* be fully secure. While I sincerely hope that liberal democracy may add up to something the collective calls happiness, only a fool can be sure about this gamble.

No such doubts erode the democracy built up by liberal dialogue. At no point is liberal democracy conceived as if it were some potentially defective happiness machine. Instead, it emerges as a means by which citizen-statesmen can resolve good-faith disagreement without claiming the right to impose their idea of happiness upon their fellows. By respecting the principle of anonymity, the majoritarian asserts that no citizen is intrinsically a better statesman than any other; by respecting the principle of minimal decisiveness, the majoritarian asserts that each citizen's judgment is worthy of greater respect than the view imputed to some transcendent being; by respecting the principle of outcome indifference, the majoritarian recognizes that there are many plausible ways of approximating the liberal ideal of undominated equality. It is these more fundamental principles that make majority rule an acceptable means for resolving good-faith disagreement. The fact that some citizens predict that the majority's solution will have "unhappy" results is beside the point. So long as the rule can be justified through Neutral conversation, its legitimacy has been established within a dialogic theory of legitimacy.

Given this understanding of majority rule, the liberal statesman will also have a very different understanding of institutions designed to protect individual rights. The point of a bill of rights or a supreme court is not to secure lodes of utility that would otherwise be ignored in majoritarian politics. Instead, such guarantees aim to assure the integrity of the ongoing liberal conversation—especially each citizen's right to protect himself against exploitation in the name of the greater happiness. Yet it is just this right that eludes the Benthamite. Rather than denying the elite's right to impose their idea of happiness on everybody, the utilitarian is reduced to clever arguments about the comparative design of happiness machines. But liberal democracy is trivialized when conceived as an exercise in social engineering; it is instead an expression of the power of men and women to shape their world by reasoning together in a manner consistent with their standing as free and rational persons.

64.2. *Contract*

At least contract theory does not trivialize government by reducing it to a machine for cranking out public happiness. Instead, government is the creation of independent individuals who use it as a tool for furthering their fundamental interests. Since each contractor is out for himself, he will be unimpressed by the most advanced utilitarian course in social engineering—even if the instructor conclusively demonstrates that liberal democracy does the greatest good for the greatest number. Since each contractor is looking out for Number One, he will only sign on the dotted line if liberal democracy is shown to be in *his* best interest.

This formulation shakes the utilitarian theory of liberal democracy to its very foundations. Unfortunately, it does not do equal service when the time comes to rebuild liberal democracy on firmer ground. Recall the formal puzzle that every blueprint must solve: every liberal democrat must explain why his commitment to democracy does not preclude the protection of individual rights, and *vice versa.*

Whatever the superficiality of utilitarianism, at least it had the merit of providing a plausible-looking solution to this basic problem in political architecture: *both* majority rule *and* individual rights may be justified by a third principle: utility maximization. Whatever the depth of his critique, the contractarian has trouble keeping the roof from caving in: while social-contract theorists can justify either individual rights *or* majority rule, they find it difficult to justify them both at the same time.

The first part of the job is almost too easy. While different contractarians generate different "rights" from their constructions, they usually have no difficulty finding some that are so fundamental that they must be respected by a legitimate state. After all, the whole point of the social contract is to permit Number One to do better than he was doing in the state of nature. If government makes a person worse off than this, it has failed to deliver on its side of the bargain. Even Hobbes thought each individual had a natural right to disobey the sovereign when confronted by imminent death. And theorists, like Locke or

Rawls, who take a more benign view of the negotiating situation will naturally take a more generous view of a person's fundamental rights.

But a liberal democracy cannot be built with rights alone. Room must also be made for the principle of popular rule, and it is here where contractarians tend to crumple. Not that they deny the importance of government in remedying the inconveniences of the state of nature. What they find difficult to explain is why *majoritarian* government is preferable to less democratic varieties.[28]

Imagine yourself in the state of nature. If things are as bad as Hobbes describes them, you'll sign on with the nearest potentate before sunset brings more terrifying dangers. If things are better, you'll naturally try to strike a harder bargain. Imagine that you're already capable of launching a pretty effective defense of your person and the bit of acreage you call home. Well, then, you won't want to give carte blanche to the first potentate who comes along. Indeed, you might be tempted to insist on your right to veto any governmental initiative that threatens your preexisting advantages. Of course, if you insist on a veto, others will as well—leading to the rule of unanimity, nor majority, as the natural beginning point for the bargaining that yields the social contract.

But the rule of unanimity only serves as a starting point in each contractor's calculus of consent. A unanimity requirement will generate enormous bargaining costs, as each voter tries to use his personal veto to appropriate the entire gain from governmental action. Less than unanimity may reduce these costs, but only at the cost of increasing the danger that governmental power will be used to make Number One worse off than he would have been in the state of nature. Hence, the task will be to select the decision rule that minimizes the sum of bargaining and victimization costs. As Buchanan and Tullock show, it would be quite remarkable if all contractors agreed that majority rule fulfilled this requirement.[29]

Writers like Buchanan and Tullock treat the state of nature in a

---

28. I have argued (61.6) that rule by responsive lottery must be taken as a serious liberal-democratic competitor to the more familiar majoritarian principle. Moreover, I can imagine that some contractarians might be attracted to the "probabilistic" conception of political responsiveness upon which the responsive lottery is based. At present, though, I am not aware of any contractarian treatment of the responsive lottery, and so will ignore this democratic option in the discussion that follows.

29. See their *Calculus of Consent*, (Ann Arbor: University of Michigan Press, 1962), part 2. Indeed, there is no reason to think that *all* contractors would converge on the *same* solution.

neoclassical way, as a pseudohistorical event in which flesh-and-blood people coolly calculate their self-advantage. Taking the Rawlsian turn places majority rule in a different, but not more manageable, light. Rawls himself does not explicitly consider the way his hypothetical contractors would think about majority rule, yet it is easy to see that they would be scared silly by the prospect. Once the veil is lifted, I might find myself enslaved by majority vote; this is a risk that Rawlsian contractors could not readily accept. It is no surprise, then, that when Rawls discusses majority rule at a later stage in his argument, it is viewed as a practical expedient without deep roots in the theory of justice.[30]

A more sympathetic view can be gained, however, by a modest redesign of the original position. As is well known, Rawls forbids his contractors to have *any* knowledge about their personal abilities, values, or chances of gaining any particular social outcome; moreover, he limits their empirical knowledge only to the most general and least controversial facts about society. Majoritarianism becomes attractive if we permit two thin rays of light to pass through this thick veil of ignorance. First, instead of keeping the contractors completely in the dark about outcomes, tell them they have an *equal* chance of ending up with any outcome generated by the political process. Second, fill in the empirical picture a bit by telling them that voters can be expected to cast their ballots to fulfill their self-interest. On these assumptions, the contractors will unanimously prefer majority rule over any other voting rule. Since they have an equal chance to be any voter, they might as well select a rule that puts them on the winning side as often as possible. And, as Douglas Rae has shown,[31] it is precisely majority rule that will give them this assurance.

While this is an important result, too much should not be made of it by those who wish to rebuild liberal democracy on contractarian foundations. Rae's construction builds up majoritarianism only by permitting the principle of individual rights to collapse. Since majority rule now seems the best way to protect their self-interest, veiled contractors will reject any effort to restrict the range of its application by

30. See *A Theory of Justice* (1971), § 54.
31. See his "Decision Rules and Individual Values in Constitutional Choice," *American Political Science Review* 63 (1969): 40. It should be noted that Rae's argument does not depend on a narrow, materialistic conception of self-interest; even altruistic voters will want their particular notions of altruism to be reflected in political outcomes rather than the competing altruistic ideas advanced by others. Cf. § 15.1.

insulating (what must seem to them) arbitrarily selected "rights" from the political process. Rae's original position generates an argument for simple majoritarianism, not liberal democracy. Moreover, Rae's results, no less than Rawls's, are vulnerable to the slightest modification of his favored version of the original position. Thus, suppose Rae's second ray of light is extinguished: the contractors are no longer told that people beyond the veil vote their self-interest. Indeed, they are told nothing special about politics at all, but are asked to ponder the fact that they have an equal chance of receiving any social outcome. Then, Harsanyi has shown that the parties will reject both Rae's majority rule and Rawls's maximin on behalf of a very utilitarian objective. Since they know they have an equal chance of being anyone, everyone will want to maximize the average utility obtained by the people living beyond the veil.[32] Yet, as we have seen, an objective of this kind will support liberal democracy only if one is persuaded that a benevolent despotism will not do greater good for greater numbers.

So far as I can tell, then, no modern contractarian has succeeded in vindicating majority rule without, at the same time, undermining the foundation of individual rights.[33] Even if some future contractarian solved the formal puzzle, however, I would remain dissatisfied—for the contract myth obscures the very essence of the liberal experiment in self-rule. Liberal democracy cannot thrive if the present generation thinks it is enough to live up to a social contract written down at some hazy point in the distant past. However great the liberal achievements of the past, they cannot do our own work for us. Nor can the spirit of liberal democracy be captured by a retreat behind a veil of ignorance. Rather than attempting a privatistic act of self-forgetfulness, we must quit the solitary darkness and encounter one another in a public forum if we hope to build a liberal state. It is only there that you and I can put each other to the test; it is only there that we can ask and answer the questions of legitimacy that the struggle for power forces upon us.

32. See his "Can the Maximin Principle Serve as a Basis for Morality? A Critique of John Rawls' Theory," *American Political Science Review* 69 (1975): 594; and Cardinal Welfare, Individualistic Ethics and Interpersonal Comparisons of Utility," *Journal of Political Economy* 63 (1955): 309.

33. This conclusion forces us back to the classic treatment most sympathetic to the democratic principle—Rousseau's *Social Contract*. I cannot devote the space required for a study of this profound document in the context of Rousseau's other writings. Yet surely a superficial reading of Rousseau only confirms the contractarian's difficulty in building a harmonious theory reconciling democratic rule with the protection of individual rights.

Liberal democracy can readily survive the death of social contract. What it cannot survive is a social condition under which the masses render an unquestioning obedience to the authority of one or another elite. So long as people continue to question the legitimacy of their subordination, elites will have little choice but to respond with a mixture of force and moral pretention that will never seem very convincing to the oppressed. It is only when people forget the meaning of the question of legitimacy that the liberal spirit will have been dealt a mortal blow.

But questioning is not enough. The reality of a liberal constitution is measured by the extent to which questions get answered and answers bring relief from wrongful exploitation. There can be no hope that this constitutional project will ever be complete.

PART FOUR: FIRST PRINCIPLES

10

CONTRACT, UTILITY, NEUTRALITY

65. HIGHER JUDGES AND THE LIBERAL TRADITION

Begin again from the beginning. The first page presented the basic elements of my problem: on the one hand, a plurality of individuals, each seeking to fulfill his ends in life; on the other hand, a set of scarce resources permitting some, but not all, of these ends to be fulfilled. Given these conditions, conflict is inevitable; you and I confront one another, and each demands to know why the other is entitled to frustrate his purposes. The fundamental problem for liberal political theory is to determine what you could possibly say that might convince me of the legitimacy of your claim to power.

If so much is conceded, then I wish to remark upon the peculiarly indirect way both standing liberal traditions try to answer the central question of legitimacy. Rather than engaging the parties in a dialogue in which they themselves participate in formulating an answer to their own question, the traditional strategy has been to appeal to the judgment of some *hypothetical third party* whose opinion is said to determine the just resolution of the flesh-and-blood contest for power. It is true, of course, that the two standing liberal traditions differ in the way they go about constructing the hypothetical person who will be given the status of final judge. From the vantage point of contract theory, the final judge is somebody who has the choice of entering society or remaining indefinitely in some prepolitical state. In contrast to this notion of a potential entrant, utilitarianism proffers the ideal observer, whose situation seems even further removed from the human predicament. While we wish to fulfill our own particular projects in the world, the observer is content simply to consider society from afar; while *we* want more scarce resources, *he* wants nothing for himself; while *we* wish to maximize our particular conception of the good, *he* is concerned only with the collective welfare of the sentient creation that struggles on below him.[1] While the differences between the potential entrant and the ideal observer are important, it is even more important to recognize their common deficiencies.

Perhaps the best way to do this is by inviting you to put this book down and actually try to put yourself in a frame of mind that approximates your understanding of an ideal observer or a potential entrant. We can then compare notes about what we find. Speaking for myself, I must confess that I cannot reach the platforms from which these transcendent beings view the world. Moreover, in both cases the reasons for my failure are quite similar. Turning first to the ideal observer, the first stage of the ascent seems to me quite easy. That is, I am not so caught up in my own ideas and projects that I cannot distance myself from them, recognizing my conception of the good as but one of the countless ways in which a sentient being can define his happiness. The trouble comes at the second stage: after distancing myself from my own happiness, I must then define the way in which the ideal observer will understand the nature of happiness and maximize its sum.

Consider, for example, the problem raised by a slave society in which half the inhabitants are in bondage to the other half; the masters live the way great nobles should, while the slaves are miserable. Imagine, further, that if slavery is abolished, the society will transform itself into a second-best liberal state in which the general population will share in different triumphs, different miseries. After embroidering the story to suit your taste, you are called upon to judge each society from the vantage point of the ideal observer. Which form of organization increases overall utility?

On first thought, the answer seems easy. I feel very certain that the ideal observer would find the liberal state happier than the slave society, even after full allowance is made for the peculiar miseries suffered by some in the liberal condition. Yet, as soon as I make this judgment, doubts begin to form: the convergence between my own personal views and those of the ideal observer strikes me as downright suspicious. While I have in fact made a conscientious effort to distance

1. While the utilitarian imagines a supremely *benevolent* ideal observer, it is quite possible to imagine ideal observer theories that impute different motivations to this mythic being. See Roderick Firth's essay "Ethical Absolutism and the Ideal Observer," *Philosophy and Phenomenological Research* 12 (1952):317, which states some formal requirements an argument must satisfy before it may plausibly qualify as an ideal observer theory. My criticisms of the utilitarian's use of this mythic device carry over, I think, to less purely benevolent conceptions of the ideal observer.

myself from my own principles, and preferences, and prejudices, have I only succeeded in unconsciously projecting my deeper beliefs onto the ideal observer?

With these doubts rising to the surface, I return to my two imaginary worlds with renewed concern. Perhaps, after all, I have been unduly unsympathetic with the great delights of lordship; perhaps I have overestimated the secret agonies of servility. Similarly, given my particular place in American society, it is only natural for me to overstate the joys of life in a liberal state. Am I really sure that the ideal observer—aloof and *entirely* removed from my particular aspirations, my particular history—would make a similar appraisal?

At this point I encounter the void. Try as I might, I can discover no criterion for determining whether my original judgment represents the considered opinion of the ideal observer or whether it merely represents a screen upon which I have projected the personal values I initially attempted to suppress. Of course, my predicament would be resolved if the higher judge revealed himself to me in some indisputable way. But in the absence of Revelation, I have little to say to a person whose intuitions concerning the ideal observer's judgment are very different from mine. Thus, at the liberal's moment of truth—when you and I confront one another over scarce goods—I shall have only my contestable intuitions to proffer you if I seek to justify my claim to power by appealing to the ideal observer. And if this is true in an "easy" case involving slavery, the problems of conducting a good-faith dialogue will be quite staggering when we turn to consider even the "easiest" issues that are likely to arise in modern states.

Nor will an appeal to the potential entrant of contractarian theory do me any more good. To see this, however, we must inspect this new persona carefully. While our final predicament will be quite similar, the path of perplexity diverges at important points. Whatever else is true, the potential entrant is not identical to the Enlightment diety who masquerades as the ideal observer. By definition, the entrant is not content to stand aloof from the social struggle, benevolently designing the universe so that it may be the happiest possible place. Instead, he realizes that social arrangements will affect his own ability to achieve his own good, and tries to assure that the social contract protects his basic interests. In all this, of course, the entrant is a more approachable judge than is the observer.

Yet, at the last moment, he eludes me. To grasp his thoughts, I must imagine myself a being who somehow exists apart from the organized society the contract is intended to constrain. Yet this is no simple task, for the fact is that I am not some apolitical being but a resident of an organized society from the moment of my birth. Nor am I merely physically dependent upon others for my continued survival; I am culturally dependent upon them for the very materials I have used in constructing a notion of myself and my ends in life. I simply could never have started my effort at self-definition without an encounter with the models of behavior and the languages made available by my contemporaries and predecessors. This is not to say that there is no sense in thinking of myself as a distinct person with a distinctive personality and objectives; it is rather to say that whatever individuality I possess has not been gained *independently of* society but rather as a result of an *interaction with* society.

Now, if this is so, then the contractarian is really making an extraordinary demand when he asks us to think of ourselves as potential entrants. For this cannot be accomplished by undressing ourselves in the mind's eye and observing what we are wearing underneath. Whatever we find is no less a product of our encounter with organized society than that which we discard. Of course, the suppressed material may be very different from the surface, but I know of no interpretation of its meaning that would entirely ignore its relationship to the social processes through which we define our individuality.

This means that as we search for the potential entrant within us, we shall soon come to a moment of perplexity similar to that which rewarded our attempt to grasp the ideal observer. No matter where we halt in the process of disrobing, the being we observe still bears the marks of our encounter with organized society. Whenever we stop, we shall be obliged to separate the distorted aspects of our social identities from the motives of the entrant within us. Yet, for the life of me, I can discover no criteria for making this fundamental discrimination.[2] Despite my best efforts, I shall be defenseless at the liberal's moment

---

2. In this, as in much else, Rawls represents a logical conclusion of contractarian thought. Taken to its extreme, his theory invites us to strip ourselves of every trace of our own concrete individuality if we are to reach the vantage point of the potential entrant. This would be fine but for the fact that we are then expected to have an opinion on the way such a being would think about social choices. After so completely stripping myself of self-understanding, it is very difficult to guess the way that "I," as a potential entrant, would go about thinking about the question of social justice. Indeed, to the extent that I *do* have guesses, I fear that "I" would "reason" about the choice in ways that I would otherwise consider quite lunatic. See § 66.1.

of truth—the moment I try to make it clear to another person why it is right that I, rather than he, should establish a claim over a disputed thing:

> I: When I look into myself, I am sure that I would have insisted upon this right as a condition for entering into society with you.
> YOU: You haven't the slightest idea of what you would have insisted on in a presocial state. You're simply using the idea of a potential entrant as a screen upon which you can project the deepest desires of your socialized self. But I too have desires; why should mine be sacrificed to yours? And if you insist, it is possible that I too may delve deep into my psyche and find a transcendent grounding for my desires.

It would seem, then, that despite their important differences, both versions of the liberal tradition require very similar movements of the spirit. Both require us to suppress our own identities as social beings—whose identities and objectives are defined through interaction with other concrete individuals—so that we may catch a fleeting glimpse of some transcedent individual who may sit as higher judge of our social conflicts. Yet neither gives us any reason for believing that, even at our most prophetic moments, we shall be able to distinguish the higher judge from our own, imperfectly suppressed, social selves.

Nor is this final failure of nerve accidental. Anyone who wishes to give his personal view of the ideal observer or potential entrant deeper grounding will be required to embrace theological arguments of the very kind that liberalism has historically viewed as its antithesis. To see why, consider your predicament when I explain to you (in perfectly good faith) that I have attempted the spiritual exercises required to commune with the higher judge (as best I understand them) and that my views concerning his will are quite different from yours. It would seem that in order to persuade me to abandon my own views, you have only two moves left. Either you can say that your spiritual exercises are better than mine since they more nearly conform to the nature of transcedent reality; *or,* if our exercises seem equivalent, that you have somehow been appointed a superior vehicle for conveying the transcendent will to the rest of mankind.

No wonder, then, that the standing liberal traditions call it quits at this point. While their failure to achieve a principled answer to the question of legitimacy is very serious indeed, it would be even more terrible to abandon liberalism entirely and seek a theocratic solution to our social predicament. This said, I do not wish to understate the significance of the impasse. Here we are, you and I, locked in social confrontation with nothing more to say to each other about our rightful claims over scarce resources. Indeed, we seem worse off than when our conversation began. Before we started talking, there seemed some chance that I might find something to say to you which you might find convincing, and vice versa. Yet now that we have both consulted the higher judge, it turns out that we cannot explain to each other how and why our spiritual exercises reach such different conclusions about justice. We are left to struggle on silently, trusting that our higher judge will not abandon us in the struggle for power that lies ahead.

Now all conversations must end at some point, and wisdom is required to recognize when this moment has come. Nevertheless, it is also possible that the impasse we confront is nothing more than the product of a failure to think clearly about our premises. And there is nothing so pathetic as a person who mistakes the fuddlements of his own mind for the ultimate secrets of the universe.

Yet it is just this charge that I wish to make against the standing liberal traditions. Their inability to answer the question of legitimacy is not a sign of the incoherence of the liberal idea, but a consequence of the tradition's incomplete liberation from the theocratic past. While traditional liberal thought has rejected theology when it comes to a *substantive* answer to the question of legitimacy, it has been strangely uncritical in assuming that the proper *form* of an answer involves an appeal to a hypothetical being who transcends the social situation in fundamental ways. It is this formal characteristic that lies at the root of the traditional dilemma: once it is conceded that the views of a higher judge are relevant, the only way to win an argument is to claim that one's view of the higher judge is somehow better than that of one's antagonist.

And it is here, I think, that my theory makes a real contribution. At no point have I asked my reader to suppress the fact that he is a person with his own goals in life, that he encounters others with competing goals, and that he is in a social situation in which conflicts will be settled in some organized way. It is true, of course, that within these basic constraints, I have indulged any number of "unrealistic" assumptions about the way interactions between individuals could be resolved. But the aim of my "perfect" technology of justice was not to transcend our basic social predicament. To the contrary, it was to insist that in the absence of liberal dialogue, all the technology in the world will never answer the question of legitimacy.

But it is not enough to remark upon the conflict between form and substance that afflicts the standing liberal traditions. Unless this conflict is to bring nothing but despair, what is required is the construction of a new form of liberal discourse in which you and I can talk to one another without hiding behind some third party who neither of us can claim to understand. This, of course, is the promise of neutral dialogue. If I have been successful, I have shown that we *can* talk to one another about power without claiming privileged access to some transcendent judge. Indeed, it is possible to imagine a world in which *every* citizen could justify *every* aspect of his power position in a way that was *perfectly* consistent with the Neutrality principle. Of course, even in this ideal world, many citizens might remain dissatisfied with their meager share of the world's resources. Some people might be so upset with their share of power that they might declare, after sincere private reflection, that their favorite version of the ideal observer or potential entrant would find their present situation intolerable. Even the most passionate protester, however, cannot say that his power position depends on my mysterious effort to commune with the higher judge of my choice. *He cannot say I am unintelligible* when I explain to him, "I should get X because I'm at least as good as you are." To sum up: Neutral dialogue gives us what traditional appeals to a higher judge so conspicuously lack—an *interpersonally intelligible criterion* for judging the legitimacy of a power relationship.

This appeal to the value of interpersonal intelligibility, however, raises at least three good questions of its own. Most obviously, a Nietzschean type can flatly deny that he need be intelligible to the weaklings who surround him; indeed, the demand for interpersonal intelligibility may, so far as he is concerned, be the root of all the degradation he sees before him. Now I shall in time try to deal with such *Ubermenchen* as best I can. Their objection, however, is irrelevant for present purposes. The point of this chapter is to vindicate the superiority of Neutral dialogue over its traditional *liberal* competitors; only in the finale shall I argue for liberalism in its struggle against authoritarianism. Given my present objective, I do not anticipate a serious objection to interpersonal intelligibility as an important value.

At best, the partisan of contract of utility might think that this achievement of Neutral dialogue is outweighed by other merits of their competing theories. But the concept of a publicly accessible standard of right is too entrenched in the liberal tradition to be casually uprooted altogether.

This makes the second question all the more important: Am I right in claiming that Neutral dialogue generates an interpersonally intelligible justification for power? Imagine, for example, this peculiar conversation:

> YOU: Why should you get this scarce resource rather than I?
> I: Because I'm at least as good as you are.
> YOU: Ah, hah! There you go, violating Neutrality again!
> I: How so? Surely I haven't asserted my unconditional superiority; nor have I claimed the right to say that some conceptions of the good are intrinsically superior to others. How, then, have I violated the rules of our conversation?
> YOU: Listen, dunderhead, your violation of Neutrality is just *obvious;* if you don't see that, you don't understand *anything* about English!

We have been in a similar position before.[3] Someone who seems to be speaking English suddenly makes an assertion that is so wild that his linguistic competence is put into question. This conversation, however, represents a polar case: here a person wants to excommunicate me from Englishdom when it is he, not I, who has failed to use the language in a way that intelligibly supports his claim. Rather than it being "obvious" that I have breached Neutrality, it is "obvious" to all English-speakers that I have not.

But I am not happy with this bald appeal to the "obvious." What is needed, instead, is a theoretical account of English grammar which would explain why "you" were speaking nonsense in excommunicating me. Indeed, given the fact that I might be speaking English and "you," Japanese, nothing less than a complete theory of universal syntax, semantics, and pragmatics would serve my purpose. Since I am not equal to this task, I must rest my case with a call upon my reader's intuitions. When you tell me that a private consultation with your favorite higher judge legitimates your claim to X, I am well within my linguistic rights in protesting that I too have tried to consult the same

3. § 18.4.

higher judge and find that he has delivered quite a different message from the one you report; in contrast, if I tell you that I should get X because I'm at least as good as you are, you cannot continue to speak *English* and assert that I have violated the terms of the Neutrality principle.

A third and final question about interpersonal intelligibility raises a very different kind of perplexity. Our last puzzle was conceptually deep but practically trivial: How many "yous" have you met in your life? In contrast, the final problem is conceptually manageable but practically exigent. And that is the communicative difficulties involved in implementing the ideal of undominated equality in a radically imperfect world. While the ideal polity might repose confidence in the Master Geneticist and the rest of his crew, it would be silly for us to take such a benign view of our civil servants. Moreover, decisions made within bureaucratic cubbyholes will sometimes have a greater impact on the power structure than the highly visible debates of parliamentary politics. Yet the bureaucrats will often discuss social problems in a technocratic language that is, practically speaking, unintelligible to the general public.

Given the central place of interpersonal intelligibility in liberal theory, such a fact can only generate intense anxiety. Nonetheless, there can be no hope of forcing all bureaucrats to speak ordinary language all of the time. As we have seen,[4] liberal democracy must undertake ongoing action if it is to escape exploitation in the distribution of genetic, cultural, material, and transactional advantage. Empirical knowledge must play a crucial role in shaping rational means to worthy ends. If mathematical equations and computer models are necessary tools to achieve a sound understanding of empirical reality, we would be foolish to banish their use from our republic. Yet we can never let the languages of instrumental rationality become our masters. Technocratic mumbo jumbo is not an end in itself: when liberated from Neutral dialogue, it may merely legitimate a new and awful tyranny that can crush the liberal spirit.

66. BATTLE WEARINESS

A newcomer to a debate enjoys peculiar benefits and burdens. The debaters are poised to exploit the weaknesses revealed by the last turn

4. Chapter 8, especially §§ 58–59.

of the conversation. If they are kind, they will pause to give the new-comer a blow-by-blow description of the most recent goings-on before continuing the debate with one another. Yet, invariably, the late arrival wants more than this. Something about the debate unsettles him; he challenges the old-timers to justify a conversational move that seems second nature to them; then, a moment of silence: everybody fears a lengthy and profitless detour, yet everybody knows that such detours turn out to be worthwhile occasionally. What, then, should we talk about?

This is the position in which we find ourselves. I say that it is a mistake to appeal to a higher judge, but it will take more than my say-so to induce others to stop. To suggest the need for such a drastic step, I shall try to use the ongoing debate between contract and utility to demonstrate its own futility. I mean to show that both sides can mount a powerful offense against the other which each is unable to defend with any great success. Thus, a tiresome cycle is to be antici-pated: a mighty champion launches a powerful attack upon the con-ventional wisdom of the day (be it utilitarian or contractarian), forcing the enemy into a disorganized retreat; after the dust settles, a new received wisdom is established, which may then be routed after a suitable interval by a new champion; and on and on. In philosophy at least, a good offense cannot entirely substitute for a solid defense.

And it is this fact that I hope to exploit in my effort to gain support for Neutral dialogue. By now, each side has been sufficiently bruised by the other that both contractarians and utilitarians are conscious, on some level at least, of their respective points of vulnerability. While these soft spots may not seem sufficient to cause the committed parti-san to switch sides to an enemy whose weaknesses are even more apparent, they may easily provide a sufficient reason to join ranks behind a new theory that promises to resolve a chronic sense of weak-ness. My aim, quite obviously, is to establish Neutral dialogue as the shield that will protect the battle weary from the ravages of endless civil war.

66.1. *The Failings of Contract*

It is a mark of John Rawls's achievement that I must begin with a critique of contractarian theory.[5] A generation ago, it would have

5. This section redeems an early promise (§ 16) of an argument explaining why "The basic framework of the contractarian argument invariably requires its proponents to talk in ways that violate Neutrality" (p. 67).

seemed absurd to take the idea of contract seriously. Yet today it is utilitarian thought which lacks a pre-eminent champion. This is not to say that Rawls has established a new orthodoxy; indeed, it is hard to find a philosopher who is willing to endorse Rawls's particular arguments on behalf of maximin. Nonetheless, the inadequacies of utilitarianism still seem so striking that many are reluctant to ask whether the contractarian idea has even greater flaws. It takes very little imagination, however, to sketch the outlines of a powerful utilitarian attack.

Begin by characterizing the basic structure of the contractarian argument. I take it that, in one way or another, all contractarians want to convince us to approach the problem of justice as if we were (1) some hypothetical person with a particular set of preferences confronting (2) some hypothetical situation that forces us to choose one among a number of options open to us. Once he has decided upon a proper characterization of (1) the ideal chooser and (2) the proper choice set, the contractarian's argument is straightforward: given (1) and (2), he wishes to demonstrate that choosers will reject certain policies within the choice set in favor of other policies open to them. It is these policies that will be inscribed in the social compact that is to structure subsequent social interaction between the parties.

Now, if this characterization of the general argument is accepted, a basic problem seems plain enough. It is just too easy to manipulate the definitions of chooser and choice set to generate any conclusion that suits one's fancy. A trivializing example will dramatize the point. Suppose I wanted to establish that the right to a pound of peanut butter a day is a fundamental part of the social compact. Then, all I need do is stipulate that the hypothetical chooser prefers Skippy to everything else in the world; or that the choice set only permits people to choose between Skippy and Death; or manipulate my characterization of chooser and choice set in any number of subtler ways to the same result. Now, of course, nobody is arguing seriously for Skippy just now, but the ease with which the argument can be made emphasizes the central importance of arriving at a description of chooser and choice set that does not seem ostentatiously question-begging. If people value Skippy above all else, they will choose Skippy if they have a chance; if they fear death, they will insist on protection; if they fear risk, they will opt for maximin. But why impute one characterization rather than another? Call this the characterization problem.

It is here that the utilitarian makes his initial point of critical entry.

According to him, there is no way of characterizing the chooser and choice set that is *not* arbitrary. The entire exercise in characterization is merely a gimmick to obtain privileged status for one's deepest desires in the competition for fulfillment that is an inevitable part of social life. At least the utilitarian does not lower himself to such a shell game; at least his theory proceeds from a straightforward denial that any set of preferences should have a specially privileged position in social assessment. Instead, each person is entitled to have his actual preferences counted in the social calculus without imputing them to some hypothetical contractor. And when preferences conflict, the social solution should depend on an impartial effort to maximize overall satisfaction without giving peanut butter an arbitrary advantage over poetry.

Now it would be nice, to say the least, if the contractarian could come up with a response to this attack. Yet it is precisely my thesis that it is *impossible* to mount a serious defense and stay within the contractarian framework. The one thing a contractarian can't hope to define in a contractarian way is the chooser and choice set that structures the contractarian argument. It is simply futile to say that the answer to the characterization problem should itself be generated by (1) some imaginary chooser selecting among (2) a choice set consisting of alternative characterizations of the choice situation. For this would simply raise the metaquestion of the proper way of specifying the chooser and choice set appropriate for making *this* choice; and so on, in infinite regression. Instead, the contractarian must solve the characterization problem in *non*contractarian terms. Yet to do this is to confess that the idea of contract is but half—and the less important half—of a complete political theory.

To put the same point in a different way, the pseudohistorical character of classic contract philosophy is not an incidental element of the theory which may be extruded without loss. Instead, the pseudohistory performed the central function of providing the theorist with a relatively straightforward solution to the characterization problem. So long as the theorist believed that his description of the state of nature represented a simplified, but essentially factual description of our actual past, then it could seem obvious that the characterization that best conformed to the facts should be preferred to characterizations that were "merely" hypothetical. Once the historical props were removed, however, contractarian theory reached an impasse: entire lifetimes might be devoted to the precontractual "preliminaries" necessary before a satisfactory way of characterizing chooser and choice set could be achieved.

It is from this vantage that Rawls's work takes on real significance. Whatever else may be said, Rawls has hit upon a new way of solving the characterization problem that, taken to its extreme, allows the contract theorist to avoid the charge that he has specified the choice situation in a way calculated to further his own interest (or that of his class). Instead of specifying a particular set of preferences for his contractor, Rawls places his choosers behind a veil of ignorance so thick that none of them knows *anything* about his values or abilities; instead of arbitrarily constricting the choice set so as to make a particular option seem peculiarly desirable, Rawlsian contractors frame a set of principles that are to guide social relations under *all* conceivable social conditions. By setting the choice set at infinity and the chooser at zero, all arbitrariness has been banished from the characterization of the choice situation. At one and the same time, the veil of ignorance evokes the impartiality and universality classically associated with moral judgments. Thus, Rawls's device not only solves a fundamental difficulty in the construction of any contract theory but solves it in a way that endows the initial choice with moral force after we have lifted the veil and returned to our concrete places in social life. Altogether a brilliant idea.

The only trouble is that it can't work. When the Rawlsian Zero confronts the Infinite Choice Set, it is impossible to choose *any* principle of justice until he is endowed by his creator with *some* set of preferences to guide his judgment. Ex nihilo nihil fit. And Rawls recognizes this. Thus, a good deal of *A Theory of Justice* is devoted to explaining just what sorts of information that Rawls will allow to pierce the veil. But as soon as Rawls permits the contractors to know some things and not others, the characterization problem arises with renewed force: What should *we,* the manipulators of the veil, permit the contractors to see? For, of course, their "choices" will be but artifacts of our shadow play. Rawls knows this too, and so spends an enormous amount of energy trying to convince us that his design of the original position is "reasonable." While I shall, in the concluding chapter, attempt a liberal critique of such appeals to intuition, it is enough for now to note that this is just the move that Bentham has taught his followers to savor with delight. For the appeal to intuition makes plain what the utilitarian has long suspected: the contractarian has no reason other than personal preference for designing his choice situation in one way rather than another. And if this is so, is it not fairest to arrange rights so as to maximize everybody's preferences rather than those Rawls is happy with? Yet this is nothing less than the aspiration of utilitarianism.

I hope I have said enough to make the force of the argument apparent. No less important, I want to show that a similar attack will leave liberal state theory unscathed. The contract theorist's characterization problem has its source in his appeal to the view of some higher judge who, unlike us, may continue in his prepolitical state if the contract is not negotiated to his advantage. Once you and I dismiss the appeal to a higher judge, we are no longer interested in characterizing the position of third parties to the debate over power. Hence, we can remain unmoved when the utilitarian unmasks the question-begging character of the search for the potential entrant.

Even more important, we can begin to view the utilitarian's attack, and the contractarian's anguished reply, with a sympathetic understanding unmixed by fear. Like his contractarian comrade, the liberal is also dissatisfied with a utilitarian philosophy that makes an individual's rights depend upon the shifting preferences of his peers. Even if there were only a single person who questioned the legitimacy of his power position; even if the overwhelming majority passionately desired to suppress the questioner; the questioner's right to an answer remains fundamental in liberal theory. To silence this single dissenter would require the dominant coalition to declare that it has the right to treat the dissenter as merely a plaything for their own desires. Such a declaration breaks the dialogic bond that binds all citizens together to form a liberal state.

Yet, like the utilitarian critic, the liberal cannot abide the mythic way in which the contractarian packages his commitment to individual rights. Instead of making yet another heroic effort to grab hold of the potential entrant, the liberal proposes that you and I—in our concrete individuality—answer our own problem by talking to one another in a way that is mindful of our independent identities. By constructing Neutral ground rules, however, we do more than escape the fiats of mythic judges. We also can do our utilitarian critic one better and reveal that he is not so indifferent to peanut butter and poetry as he supposes. For, as we have seen, the utilitarian cannot justify his self-confident hedonism in a conversation conducted under Neutral rules.[6] Not only does the idea of Neutral dialogue serve as a shield for the defender of individual rights, it permits the liberal to turn the utilitarian's favorite weapon—his demand for strict impartiality between different preferences—in an untoward direction.

So much for the characterization problem. While it lies at the core of the utilitarian's critique, it is hardly the only point that causes utilitarians of my acquaintance to doubt their rivals' good faith or mental prowess. I shall limit myself, however, to one other contractarian pattern that conversation convinces me is thought to be of great importance: the distinctively narrow focus of the contractarian's concerns.

Rather than attempting to arrange *all* social institutions in a way that will maximize his preferred set of values, the contract theorist typically concentrates on one or another narrow range of concrete "rights" as if they were the decisive litmus for the legitimacy of the entire power ensemble.[7] Of course, different theorists promote different concrete interests to the rank of fundamental rights. Nonetheless, once they have succeeded in "solving" the characterization problem in one way or another, all contractarians agree that the rights they have generated are of decisive significance. The result, from the utilitarians' perspective, is a peculiar tunnel vision. On the one hand, even a trivial violation of one of the favored rights is cause for furrowed brow and anxious cry; on the other hand, a program involving the welfare of millions will fail to engage the contractarian's attention, let alone concern, so long as it does not trench upon his precious rights. This narrow vision seems to belie the contractarian's proud claim that he aims to vindicate the rights of all mankind; tunnel vision seems more characteristic of the vulgar ideologist intent upon the vindication of his class interest above all else. This is not to say that the utilitarian cannot find a useful place for rights talk; as we have seen,[8] he may well endorse a bill of rights that contains "absolute" protections for inter-

---

6. § 13.1.
7. As has been so often the case, Rousseau's writing stands as a signal exception to the statement made in the text. Rawls's effort to convince us that certain rights are somehow superior to others and should not be traded-off against them is very much in this tradition of contractarian narrowness. See his § 82. For sensitive treatments, see Brian Barry, *The Liberal Theory of Justice* (Oxford: Clarendon Press, 1973), Chap. 7; H. L. A. Hart, "The Priority of Liberty," *University of Chicago Law Review* 40 (1973): 534.
8. § 64.1.

ests that would otherwise be slighted in majoritarian politics. He objects only when rights talk is made an end in itself, unrelated to a more comprehensive method of social analysis.

Once again, I do not wish to quarrel with the real insights of this critique. My aim is to recall the features of liberal state theory which make it immune from similar attack. Very simply, liberal state theory, no less than its utilitarian counterpart, insists upon an exacting scrutiny of *all* social practices that have an impact upon human welfare. Of course, the nature of the test is different under the two approaches: in one it is utility maximization; in the other, Neutral dialogue. But each form of analysis refuses to exempt any social practice from disciplined normative inquiry. Moreover, in assessing the extent to which a functioning society conforms to liberal ideals, the liberal statesman's attitude toward absolute rights will be quite similar to his utilitarian colleague. While "absolute" language in a bill of rights can sometimes serve as a statesmanlike guarantee against the corruptions of majoritarian politics, it should never be made into a fetish that excuses further thought about individual rights.[9] No list of "Thou shalt nots" can ever serve as a definitive statement of our rights in *any* world this side of utopia. The right to a Neutral dialogue can never be captured by a list of substantive outcomes; it can only be assured by an ongoing practice in which you answer my questions of legitimacy and I answer yours. Predictably, the ideal of undominated equality will remain distant; the need for unequal sacrifice must sometimes be grudgingly conceded; but so long as the dialogue continues, the liberal state remains a living reality. It is this dialogue, not any holy right, that serves as the foundation of our life together.

66.2. *The Failures of Utilitarianism*
There is much, then, that is admirable in the utilitarian's critique: his clear-thinking rejection of his rival's question-begging description of a mythical choice situation; his persistent demand for a method that can be deployed in the disciplined analysis of every struggle of social life. Yet there remains one gaping hole in the Benthamite's armor. The principal charge may be stated in a single line: Utilitarianism fails to take individualism seriously enough.[10]

9. § 63.5.
10. Unfortunately, this section was written without the aid of H. L. A. Hart's enlightening essay, "Between Utility and Rights," *Columbia Law Review* 79 (1979): 828.

This failure occurs on at least two levels. First, on the plane of substantive doctrine, utilitarianism conceives each individual as if he were merely an instrument for the greater fulfillment of the idea of happiness that is dominant in the community at a particular time. Thus, if it turns out that the torture of thousands will greatly increase the pleasure of millions of television viewers, the clear-thinking Benthamite may be obliged to master his intuitions and insist that the show must go on. True, the utilitarian may try to ward off this grisly prospect by complicating his doctrine in familiar ways. He may deny that the television audience really gets *so* much pleasure out of torture; or he may emphasize the hidden anxieties of viewers as they wonder when it will be their turn to star in the show; or he may focus upon the institutional difficulty of assuring that torture is kept within felicific limits. While all these arguments may be quite valid in one or another case, they are merely gimmicks when used to avoid the awful truth that there is nothing the utilitarian will not countenance in his single-minded search for the collective happiness. Moreover, it is easy to come up with fairly realistic scenarios in which these gimmicks are quite implausible—where, in fact, the clear-thinking utilitarian must confess that systematic torture and the like may sometimes be an *affirmatively desirable* thing.

It is here that the utilitarian's head seems to have lost touch with elementary decency. Indeed, the elegance and clarity of his analysis only emphasizes the barbarism of his conclusions. *Nobody in his right mind would consent to such degradation.* And it is precisely the point of social-contract theory to put this intuition into disciplined form. Behold: independent contractors pursuing their self-interest in a state of nature; surely each would not sacrifice his self-interest simply to make it easier for others to pursue what–they–are–pleased–to–call–happiness; surely each would refuse to sign the social contract unless it protected his most fundamental interests.

As always, I do not wish to minimize the power of this assault. The single-minded search for happiness *can,* I think, end in systematic brutaility. A clear-thinking utilitarian must live with this fact—just as the contractarian must, in one way or another, muscle his way to a solution of the characterization problem. Indeed, if my only choice were utilitarian ruthlessness or contractarian mindlessness, I would find the utilitarian's brutality the worse evil. Yet the happy fact is that we are not faced with such a desperate choice. Neutral dialogue does provide a medium through which people may reason together without running the risk of barbarism. In the ideal liberal state, there can be no question of reducing some citizens to powerlessness simply because others find this a pleasing prospect.[11] Nor is such a step permitted to liberal statesmen as they grapple with the perplexities of second best. While they will inevitably compromise the ideal of undominated equality, they can never treat a group of citizens as if they were the mere playthings of the dominant class. Unequal sacrifice is legitimate only if it can fairly be said to enrich the rights of *all* citizens. Subordination can never bespeak intrinsic inferiority. Unlike utilitarianism, liberal theory never permits the statesman to lose sight of the individuals whose constant questioning provides the frame of reference for political action. A substantive policy that fails to take this questioning seriously is no solution at all—despite the happiness it brings in its train.

But there is a second, methodological sense in which the utilitarian fails to take individualism seriously. This criticism proceeds from the dizzying quality of the utilitarian's invitation to look at the social world from the perspective of the ideal observer, removed from the slightest tinge of egoism, motivated only by the purely altruistic desire to make this the happiest of all possible worlds. While the contractarian also appeals to a higher judge, at least he does not demand such an extraordinary movement of the spirit. Certainly, one wants to say, such spiritual self-abnegation is worthy of awe, perhaps praise, but to make it the foundation of social justice is quite another thing. This is the stuff that saints are made of, not citizens. Indeed, to *demand* such a spiritual movement deprives it of much of its significance; it is only because individuals have the right to put themselves first that friendship, love, and charity seem such splendid things. In contrast, the contractarian's first principles do not require the citizen to begin his reflections on the state by imagining himself a secularized Saint Francis. The main line of contract theory begins with a state of nature inhabited by self-interested individuals who see the state as a mechanism for furthering their preexisting interests. This way of conceiving the problem does not require a methodological assault upon the legitimacy of self-assertion anything like that presupposed by utilitarians.

11. Though a voluntary association devoted to "torturing" one another would be quite another matter. See chapter 6, especially §§ 41–42.

This is, perhaps, the most fundamental criticism that the contract theorist can hurl at his traditional antagonist. Yet it is easy to see that this weapon falls from his hands when he turns to confront the challenge of liberal dialogue. While it is true that the partisan of contract does not make his higher judge into a *completely* selfless being, he does strip his potential entrant of many of the particular features that mark each person out as a concrete individual. In contrast, the advocate of Neutral dialogue needs no higher judge to free him from the biases of self-interest. Rather than blotting out our particular identities in the hope of communing with the potential entrant, the liberal state permits each of us to talk about the fact that we want different things from life.

67. INDIVIDUAL AND COMMUNITY IN LIBERAL THOUGHT

Try now to view the battlefield without the aid of a higher judge. As the smoke clears, we can begin to see that *both* sides of the traditional struggle have something important to teach us. The contractarian rightly demands that the political community respect the claims of self-interested individuals. The utilitarian rightly insists that no individual promote his self-interest into the public interest without taking others' self-interest into account. The two sides go wrong only when they try to promote their half-truth into the whole truth.

Thus, the partisans of contract carry their commitment to individualism to absurd lengths when they imagine "individuals" treating with one another as if they could survive as independent beings in a prepolitical choice situation. This image requires us to ignore the most fundamental facts about our own individuality. There can be no blinking the fact that the most rugged individualist has not achieved his precious sense of individuality on his own. Instead, his sense of himself as a distinctive person is inexplicable without a reference to the patterns of liberal culture into which he has been socialized. Yet it is just such facts that the contract story asks us to ignore.[12]

Worse yet, this way of setting up the problem permits hostile critics many a cheap victory over liberal thought. Time and again, the isolated

12. True, the most evocative forms of the contract myth try to make themselves credible by introducing socialized elements into their picture of the "original position" in ways I find ad hoc and question-begging. But this is a vast topic in the history of ideas that cannot be treated here.

individuals of social-contract theory are unmasked as pallid reflections of the alienated social conditions of Western life. The contractors' efforts to preserve their asocial selves by a selfish bargain is loudly proclaimed as a token of the impoverishment of the liberal spirit. From this, it is even easier to proclaim a total critique of existing arrangements, signaling the arrival of a new form of social life and consciousness in which alienation will be resolved by a dialectical process whose character cannot, unfortunately, be described at this unhappy hour before dawn. Mythic mistakes multiply; from a single misbegotten seed, whole forests of mystification grow.

They cannot be cleared by the utilitarian's half-truth. Rather than *clarifying* the liberal relationship between individual and community, the utilitarian wishes to clear out all the individualistic underbrush. For him, the great danger is that each individual strives to promote his private happiness into the public good. If this feat is ever successful, all those with different ideas of happiness are transformed into eccentrics, dissidents, outcasts, enemies. To prevent this, the utilitarian must be trained to view himself in an unbiased way—as just another sentient member of the political community. He must not give any extra weight to his preferences when adding up the societal total, for the community's interest *is* nothing more than the sum of individual preferences.

Yet this effort to root out the self-aggrandizement promoted by individualism only serves to promote a false ideal of community. A liberal cannot accept the utilitarian notion that we all must look upon each other as brothers sharing in some mystical communion with the public good. When *I* feel pain, it is *I* who am doing the feeling. I do not necessarily gain consolation from the news that you are feeling ecstacies of delight at the same time. Indeed, I may only become more indignant upon learning that I am considered a plaything for the fulfillment of your desires.

To the contractarian's false individualism the utilitarian responds with a false community. It is our task, however, to seize hold of the half-truths that have led to these distortions and construct a truly liberal relationship between individual and community. We must affirm individualism without denying our dependence on others. While affirming my dependence on others, I must not permit others to subordinate me to achieve their own selfish interests.

This is precisely the promise of Neutral dialogue. Rather than achieving his sense of individuality independently of the political community, each citizen of a liberal state begins his encounter with his fellows with the most naïve kind of self-assertion: "I want it. What gives you the right to deprive me of it?" It is only by trying to talk about this question that you and I gradually gain a sense of the rightful spheres in which each of us may assert our individuality. Moreover, the extent to which *we* succeed in answering this question marks the extent to which *I* have rights against *you* and vice versa. No longer does liberal thought revolve around the dichotomy that opposes individual to community; instead, the substance of individual rights is constructed through a social dialogue; the triumph of individualism, a social triumph.

It is true, of course, that this liberal form of community will strike red-blooded communards as an extraordinarily anemic enterprise. Not only is each citizen of a liberal community free from any obligation to love his neighbor; he is even free to believe that his neighbor is a despicable creature who is wasting his own life and corrupting the lives of those stupid enough to call him friend. While citizens will, of course, have available a rich store of associational networks through which they may achieve their own forms of intimacy and community, the fundamental bond that binds them *all* together is not one of fraternity in any meaningful sense of the word. What is forged instead is a bond that ties citizens together without forcing them to be brothers; liberal conversation provides a communal process that deepens each person's claim to autonomy at the same time that he recognizes others as no less worthy of respect. Liberty, Equality, Individuality are the watchwords of the liberal state.

Given this collective process of self-definition, liberal doctrine is not embarrassed by the fact that each of us is dependent upon our fellows for the very models of behavior through which we define our own individuality. Instead of ignoring our social dependence, liberalism can be understood as making a subtler point about the way this dependence should be structured. In a liberal state, *all other forms of social dependence are subordinated to the dialogic processes of Neutral conversation.* This strict dependence upon liberal conversation, however, does not destroy the variety and vitality of other social processes. By its very nature, liberal dialogue is hardly a jealous mistress. It does not pretend to solve the final mysteries of life; it is forever pointing citizens beyond itself, inviting them to make the sense they can of their place in the universe. Any form of social life that makes sense to any significant group will find a place in the liberal state. It will survive so long as it continues to convince a fragment of the next generation that the ideal it puts forward deserves the respect of a free and autonomous person.

From this perspective, it is possible to see how shallow are the critics of liberalism who look upon it as a peculiarly modern form of consciousness whose beginnings can be traced no further back than Hobbes, Locke, and the Industrial Revolution. However important these modern sources, the liberal impulse runs far deeper in the history of philosophy. As Nietzsche saw, it is none other than Socrates who stands as the emblem upon the liberal standard. This is so not only because his death stands as the paradigmatic political wrong, but because his life stands as the paradigmatic ground of political right—in its insistence that all people submit to questioning about the things they hold dearest; that each of us contemplate the possibility that our moral vision may be distorted; that all of us accept the discipline of dialogue and restrain the temptation to destroy those whom we cannot convince.

11

DIALOGUE

68. BEYOND INTUITIONISM

Suppose I've convinced you that both contract and utility fail to locate the proper place of individual rights in a liberal political community. Nonetheless, it hardly follows that you will join me in building a power structure that we can defend together through Neutral dialogue. In the end, it remains for each of us to decide whether liberalism is worth the struggle: the personal struggle to restrain our own power lust, the collective struggle to advance liberal values in a world of authoritarian pretention. How, then, to judge the ultimate worth of liberalism—or, for that matter, any other political philosophy?

There are two familiar ways of answering such questions. Each, I shall argue, is inadequate for liberal purposes; this critique will, I hope, point to a sounder approach to the validation of the first principles of liberal theory.

I shall call the first method intuitionistic. While I will reject it, I do not deny its initial charm or peculiar depth. To illuminate its familiar virtues, permit me a homely analogy: I shall look on the choice of a political philosophy in the same way I look upon my next venture to the supermarket. I have come—in the normal semireflective way—to hold many judgments about the value of one or another thing that supermarkets have to offer: I like steak, hate soybeans, and so forth. There is, however, a problem in keeping all these concrete judgments in unorganized form. When I go to the supermarket without a shopping list, I am apt to lose perspective and forget some essential item as I wander down the aisles. And so, in the relative isolation of the kitchen, I prepare for my journey by writing up a list. This effort, in turn, provides an occasion for reconsidering my judgments: Is soybean so awful? Do I really want steak this week? How can I get my money's worth? While this weekly reappraisal is not very searching, it does have an impact—especially over time. Though no two consecutive shopping lists are very different, constant reappraisals generate dramatic changes over years or decades.

And the same is true of political judgments. Of course, most people spend more time and energy on their shopping lists than on their political prejudices. Yet, from time to time, the television news or everyday life leads them to reappraise their existing judgments: *Is* abortion so terrible? Do I *really* want this form of equality? What *is* fair anyway?

For the hard-boiled intuitionist, this ongoing activity provides the only valuable foundation for political evaluation. Each person begins life with prejudices passed on by his predecessors; each changes his personal list as he reflects on his particular experiences; slowly, painfully, unconsciously, the temper of an entire nation shifts as individual prejudices are reevaluated. And thus evolves the collective wisdom of a people, compared to which philosophizing is a frivolous nothing.

Since different nations vary wildly in the liberality of their prejudices, great writers of the intuitionist persuasion intuit vastly different things about liberalism. Unsurprisingly, the British are best at taking liberal prejudices for granted; and when treated in the manner of Burke or Oakeshott, these prejudices take on a depth that makes me wish that I too were born on a tight little island where liberalism came as naturally as my taste for steak and potatoes.

Not all intuitionists, however, are quite so hard-boiled as the British. To return to my shopping list, I have often thought it would be worthwhile to spend an hour or two with a nutritionist talking about my weekly problem in a thoughtful way. After all, he has seen hundreds of such lists before and might be able to characterize my own list with an elegance and economy I could never achieve on my own. Once these patterns were unearthed, I might become unhappy with some of my concrete choices. Considered overall, perhaps I eat too much cholesterol; reluctantly I conclude that steak will have to go; I must reconcile myself to the prospect of eating soybean to get my needed protein. Now I have never, in fact, gotten around to seeing a nutritionist. Indeed, I suspect I never will; but if I do, one thing is clear: I would hate to deal with one of those dietitians who take an overly imperialistic view of his mission in life. I would not want my nutritionist to impose his favorite diet upon me; instead, he should begin discussion with *my* shopping list; and if, after our chat, I remain satisfied with my present menu, I would not want the dietitian to think that he has failed. The thoughtful reexamination of my shopping habits is a sufficient justification for the time we have spent together.

And the same is true of the political philosopher. It is my intuitive judgments about equality and abortion, not his philosophical method, that should set the agenda for our talk. Given the time he has spent reflecting on these matters, perhaps he can provide me a framework for organizing my intuitions into an elegant and perspicuous whole. Once these patterns are revealed, perhaps I will not like the overall picture that I see, and so will reluctantly revise my concrete judgments on equality or abortion to achieve a vision that seems to me to make a larger sense. But it is not for the philosopher, any more than the nutritionist, to impose his favorite shopping list upon all comers.

On this approach, the way to begin testing liberal theory is to ask how much liberal doctrine you can swallow without experiencing acute indigestion. Some will find that they have no stomach for any of my conclusions; others, equally rare, that their political prejudices are perfectly rationalized by my prescriptions. More common will be the more discriminating palates, people who find my position on abortion barbarous but love me for my affirmation of affirmative action, or vice versa. Those who find they have liberalish dispositions may also come to see that their particular judgments have a deeper unity than they previously guessed. While, say, they formerly had a few isolated prejudices in favor of liberal education or material equality or aid to the handicapped, they will come to appreciate the way that Neutral dialogue ties them all together in a harmonious whole. Indeed, they may find this demonstration so compelling that they will expose their un-Neutral judgments to a more exacting scrutiny. Do I *really* think that nudism should be flatly prohibited? Do I *really* want to bar all immigrants from my country? Just as I might reluctantly sacrifice steak for soybean, so too you may be persuaded by my dialogues to revise your views on these and other matters. Nonetheless, it is only realistic to expect that you and I will continue to disagree on some things. Yet your decision to stand firm on your intuitions does not in any way suggest that our time together has been wasted. It would not only be unrealistic, but pretentious, of me to blame you for rejecting some items on my favorite shopping list.

From Aristotle to Rawls, this softer form of intuitionism has always had its distinguished partisans. On this view, philosophy's task is to reveal the basic structure of the beliefs you have acquired in everyday life so as to permit their considered reappraisal. By providing an economical and perspicuous account, the philosopher permits you to revise your particular beliefs in the light of a more comprehensive view. If, however, some concrete intuition strikes you as particularly compelling—say, that slavery is natural (Aristotle) or unnatural (Rawls)—you are entitled to hold fast to this intuition and modify the abstract theory until it fits your settled prephilosophical convictions. No philosophical theory can tell you how to achieve your own reflective equilibrium—it is up to you to revise abstract principles in the light of concrete intuitions until you have attained a whole that is worthy of you.

Now it is difficult to resist the image of charming modesty and sensible industry presented by this picture of the philosophical enterprise. Indeed, there is something about the vision that no liberal can ever abandon: its insistence that nobody can ever do another's philosophical work for him, that any philosopher who tells his readers to take something on blind faith knows nothing of the liberal spirit. These important truths, however, should not blind us to the difficulties that the advocates of reflective equilibrium obscure in the background of their pretty picture. Indeed, when this background is inspected with care, it turns out to be nothing other than the foreground displayed with greater pride by more hard-boiled intuitionists. Yet the weaknesses of intuitionism cannot be cured by a more artful rearrangement.

The first, and more obvious, problem is that the intuitionist cannot cope with the charge that his very intuitions have been tainted by unjust social structures. Suppose I have the strongest possible intuition that I am entitled to the wealth and power that I, as the son of John D. Rockefeller or Leonid Brezhnev, have at my command. How am I to respond when my fellows assert that these intimations of self-righteousness are part of the problem rather than the key to its solution?

Once again we glimpse the problem of interpersonal intelligibility that lies at the heart of liberal concerns. How is Leonid Junior to communicate those internal motions of his spirit that convince him that his intuition is not the product of social conditioning but the purified essence of righteousness? As always, Leonid might say that he has consulted with the higher judge of his choice; indeed, he may endow his spiritual communion with a theological significance, claiming that his higher judge is "really" speaking to him in a special language created for the purpose. But such a claim concedes that we remain well within our linguistic rights when we confess our inability to eavesdrop on the divine communication. Moreover, surely Lenoid must himself confess that the provenance of his intuitions are suspicious—that a life spent in his particular environment is precisely the kind that invites the peculiar intuitions he happens to possess.

But let me move closer to home and scrutinize the intuitions of the residents of ivory towers cluttering the Atlantic seacoast during the declining days of the twentieth century. John Rawls quite correctly expects his particular readership to be drawn from that large group of middle-class Americans who would give a great deal for a Harvard College diploma—either for themselves or their posterity. In short, they hate racism; they like free speech, free religion, (and free love?); they are suitably ambivalent about the place of achievement and compassion in social affairs. (They want to go to *Harvard,* after all.) These aspirations, moreover, are transparently the historical product of a given social structure and cultural situation. Nonetheless, Rawls takes these intuitions as *given* in his exercise in reflective equilibrium. How, then, is he to respond to a critic who says that these very intuitions have been tainted by an unjust social structure?

There is only one way we can gain whatever–assurance–we–can–gain on such matters. And that is by exempting *none* of our political prejudices from rational criticism. For a liberal, no exercise in reflective equilibrium can be complete until the legitimacy of *each and every* intuition is vindicated through dialogue. It is precisely the effort to insulate certain subjects from the test of dialogue that engenders the liberal's deepest suspicions. After all, why should one fear the dialogic test, except that one fears to fail it? Moreover, heroic efforts to fence out dialogue seem particularly misplaced when the fact is that our hatred of racism and poverty, our love of freedom and democracy *survive* the test of Neutral justification.

This is not to say that these grand abstractions survive untouched by the process of liberal conversation. To the contrary, these concepts are transformed by the dialogue itself as they are refined and unified into a comprehensive view. If, as a result of this process, the citizen finds that many of his naïve intuitions must be modified, he should greet this fact as the great reward of political philosophy, rather than as an offense to his unexamined sensibilities. It is only by mastering our intuitions through the process of dialogue that we may gain an assurance that our strongest sentiments are not merely the sediment of darker forms of social indoctrination.

Yet the problem of indoctrination—while very real—still does not get to the heart of the liberal's objection to intuitionism. To see why, imagine for a moment that we were the residents of an ideal liberal state with the benefit of perfectly liberal educations. Nonetheless, we would not be entitled to protect any of our political prejudices by blandly proclaiming that they were too "deep" for conversational scrutiny. In saying this, I do not wish to trivialize the sense of "depth" that is at issue. My point, rather, is that intuitions can be deep for two very different reasons. On the one hand, "deep" intuitions may be signaling that my deepest *ideals for personal fulfillment* are being threatened by your demands for power. On the other hand, my intuitions may be signaling that *my rights as a free person* are being endangered by your demands. Yet these two kinds of intuition have different standing in liberal theory. However deep my desire to fulfill my conception of the good, it does not trump your *rights* to a power position befitting a free and rational being. But, alas, my intuitions do not have little return-address stickers attached to them indicating that they have their source in my concern about Rights rather than my ideals of the Good. While they may have a certain depth or intensity, *the only way to find out whether my intuitions signal a violation of my rights is by talking about them.* If I can tell you why my aims in life should be protected against your effort at self-assertion, then my intuitions may signal a breach of my rights; if, however, all I do is pound my breast in silence, there is no reason for you to bow down before me.

At least that is what my brand of liberalism is all about. You can see, then, why I cannot consign liberal philosophy to the role I assign my nutritionist. In the end, it is up to me, in consultation with any higher judge I care to choose, whether I want to have fatty arteries or yummy steak. If, however, you challenge my right to an income sufficient to sustain my meat-eating tastes, it is *not* for me to decide whether I shall answer your question. Nor will it suffice to beat my breast in response. Instead of the depth of my intuitions, only rational dialogue will vindicate my claim to the power I enjoy.

When you ask me, then, why I want Neutral dialogue to regulate our power struggle, I will not respond with a Fourth of July speech on behalf of freedom, equality, planned parenthood, and the other unquestionables of the American way of life. Such aspirations are *legitimated by* Neutral dialogue; they do not serve *to legitimate* these first principles of liberal philosophy. To the contrary, whenever some unquestionable cannot survive the discipline of liberal conversation, it is revealed as a political prejudice that must, in the fullness of time, be discarded. Yet if this is so, how *is* one to validate the first principles of liberal philosophy?

69. BEYOND MONOLOGUE

It is here where a second traditional answer presses upon our attention. Rather than mucking about with particular political prejudices, we are invited to put our power talk within a much more general framework. Consider, then, how dull a world it would be if we spent all of our time talking about the question of legitimacy that is the idée fixe of liberal political philosophy. Rather than our exclusive interest in life, legitimacy talk is but a narrow stream feeding a large sea of talk dealing with a bewildering set of questions of infinite variety: How does a good person live his life? What is happening around me? What can possibly happen in the future? What was the best joke I've ever heard? And so forth.

Moreover, just as we can philosophize about the question of legitimacy, so too we may expose any of these other questions to sustained questioning. Hence, in addition to political philosophy, there are countless other philosophical domains, whose relative importance to one another is itself a controversial matter. Suppose, for example, that you do not begin—as I have done—with the question of legitimacy, but with some other question of greater interest to you— say, the question of truth or beauty or the way a person ought to live his life. Having come to an answer (however tentative) to one or more of these questions, you may find that your answer implies a particular solution to the question of legitimacy. Thus, once Plato answered questions as to the nature of truth, beauty, and the good, the question of legitimacy seemed to him child's play. It could be answered by making a few deductions from the answers he had given to these *other* questions. While many of Plato's great successors disagreed with his substantive answers, they shared his belief that the question of legitimacy depended on the successful solution of some other philosophical puzzlement. Thus, Augustine or Kant thought Plato's answers—

indeed, his basic questions—faulty; nonetheless, once they answered the *right* questions, they thought that the question of legitimacy could be resolved in a relatively straightforward manner. With apologies, I shall call this the *deductionist* approach to the question of legitimacy—denoting the belief that the first principles of political philosophy are really "second" principles that may be *deduced* from the conclusions reached in some other "higher" domain of philosophical discourse.

Now this deductionist strategy surely does avoid the problems of intuitionism. Once the move is taken, it is easy—all too easy—to explain why you should purge yourself of all political prejudices that cannot be defended through a Neutral dialogue:

> YOU: Why should our power struggle be regulated by Neutral dialogue?
>
> I: Here. Read this (*tendering my favorite philosopher*). It contains the truth about humanity's ultimate predicament.
>
> YOU: And why is this truth relevant to my question?
>
> I: Because once you glimpse the truth, it will logically compel you to accept Neutral dialogue.
>
> YOU: But a commitment to Neutral dialogue offends some of my intuitive judgments about politics.
>
> I: Once you have read the truth, you will see it is your job to purify yourself of all inconsistent prejudices. Read then, and the truth will make you free.

This single conversation threatens the thousands of words that have preceded it. After consistently avoiding any claim of privileged access to the ultimate truth, I would have succeeded in grounding my entire structure on the very conversational move I hoped to avoid. If the deductionist strategy is the only alternative, no wonder that liberals tend toward intuitionism, whatever its ultimate weaknesses.

I should emphasize, moreover, that the deductionist strategy is not made any less suspect—only more insidious—if your favorite philosopher happens to be somebody like Kant or Hume rather than Plato or Augustine. Of course, if I were forced down the deductionist path, I would prefer Kant to Plato as I sought to convince you of the metaphysical truth of liberalism. Nonetheless, in making this move, it remains true that I have made liberalism a hostage of a *particular* metaphysical system. Yet it is the essence of liberalism to deny people the right to declare that their particular metaphysic and epistemology contains the truth, the whole truth, and nothing but the truth. If intuitionism is question begging, deductionism begs the peculiar difficulties involved in providing a liberal answer. How, then, to avoid the impasse?

By returning to the last dialogic script and considering whether there are any moves that "I" left unexplored in my previous encounter with You. And when this is done, I think we *can* find a way to talk our way out of the impasse:

> YOU: Why should our power struggle be regulated by Neutral dialogue?
> I: A good question. Would you mind telling me why you find this conversational constraint unduly confining?

At first, bouncing the conversational ball back to you may seem a cheap trick. What is to prevent you from simply refusing the invitation to play the conversational game beyond this point?

While this is indeed the ultimate question, I want to put it in brackets for a time until the more affirmative aspects of this conversational turn appear to view. After all, there is no reason to think that most people will refuse to play the game at this point; moreover, the person I am most interested in, at the moment, is you, the reader of this book. Can *you* put into words the reasons why you find the idea of Neutral conversation troubling?

If you can, then I have something that we can work with in a way that does not offend liberalism's distrust of deductionism. Instead of launching into *my own* monologue on the nature of things, I can respond to *your* efforts to verbalize the particular reasons you chafe under the constraint of Neutrality. Once you verbalize the reasons you are troubled, perhaps I can show you that they are not as persuasive as you might have thought: *that even within your own view of the world,* you should find ultimately unpersuasive the reasons you can give for your initial disquiet. If I am successful in this project, our dialogue will not conclude with my shoving my own words down your throat. Instead, it will end with *you yourself* recognizing that the world, as *you* understand it, makes Neutral dialogue the most sensible way of regulating our power struggle.

70. THE USES OF DIALOGUE

Imagine that there was one, *and only one*, view of the world that made Neutral dialogue seem a sensible way of controlling our power struggle. For concreteness, imagine that this path to liberalism was to be found, as some suppose, amid the baroque embellishment of neo-Kantian philosophy. If this were true, then my effort to sustain a dialogue would be pretty much an empty gesture. Even if you try to verbalize the difficulties you are having with the idea of Neutral dialogue, my own dialectical task would have but two dimensions. On the one hand, your verbalizations might suggest that, like a good bourgeois gentleman, you have already been talking like a neo-Kantian without even knowing it. In this case, my task would simply be one of making you aware of the larger implications of your neo-Kantian commitments—leading you ultimately to the conclusion that they logically require you to adopt Neutrality as the most appropriate way of constraining our political conversation. On the other hand, if your initial response suggested a hostility to a neo-Kantian world view, then I would try to persuade you of the error of your ways and convince you to adopt the requisite neo-Kantian persuasion. In short, my dialogic posture would only be deductionism in disguise—a single-minded effort to induce you to master your political prejudices so that you may more firmly grasp the Kantian truth about the nature of things. Perhaps the dialogic method would be rhetorically effective, inducing some to adopt liberalism who might otherwise have failed to recognize its attraction. But once they had reached the liberal conclusion, they would recognize that the dialogue only had a pedagogic value, that everything important could be said in a monologue that deduces the concept of Neutral dialogue from neo-Kantian first principles.

If, however, there is *more than one path* to liberalism, then the dialogic method takes on an independent significance. Assume, for example, that it is possible for anti-, as well as neo-, Kantians to reason their way to liberal conclusions. Then the dialectical labor on behalf of liberalism is a good deal more complicated. When you tell me what you find troubling about Neutrality, I no longer need to force your words down the preordained path to knowledge. Instead, *I must actually listen to what you are saying* and try to lead you down the paths of argument that *you* will think most persuasive, given the understanding of the world that your initial responses reveal. So long as the path leads *you* to conclude that power should be regulated by liberal principles, my defense of liberalism will have come to a successful conclusion so far as you are concerned. Yet the conversation I have with you can differ radically from the talk I have with somebody else. Predictably, there will be somebody out there who is persuaded by arguments that not only contradict your arguments for liberalism but also strike you as mean, brutish, or perverse. Nonetheless, despite this disagreement, both of you must recognize that you have something in common. *And that is precisely your common ability to find a dialogically satisfying path to the liberal state.*

There is a perfect parallelism, then, between the role of political conversation *within* a liberal state, and the role of philosophical conversation *in defense of* a liberal state. Political talk within a liberal state is a device for organizing people who are otherwise free to follow very different paths to the good. Philosophical conversation in defense of a liberal state is a device for persuading people who are otherwise free to pursue very different paths to understanding. The task of *political* conversation is to make it possible for each citizen to defend his power without declaring himself intrinsically superior to any other citizen. The task of *philosophical* conversation is to make it possible for a person to reason his way to Neutrality without declaring that the path he has chosen is intrinsically better than any other route to liberalism. Rather than using political power to subordinate people to the pursuit of a single common good, rather than using philosophical argument to convert people to a single common understanding, liberal theory invites people to pierce their substantive disagreements and achieve a deeper unity—in the fact that they all are seeking to define themselves through a common process of dialogue.

71. THE RELATIVE AUTONOMY OF LIBERAL THEORY

At this point, medium conflicts with message. Ideally, I must first hear what *you* have to say before continuing the dialogue. Indeed, once I heard your initial objections to Neutrality, I might well decide that I am not the best person to carry on the dialogue in defense of liberalism. Perhaps I lack insight into, or sympathy with, the views you initially express in resisting the Neutrality constraint. Since my role in the dialogue is to help *you* find a path to liberalism, this failure of sympathetic understanding is no trivial matter. If I fail to appreciate your point of view, I will fall too easily into the trap of using dialogue to *convert* you to my point of view rather than to *assist* you in thinking through the implications of your own position. Given the bewildering variety of cultures, values, and temperaments, nobody possesses a sympathetic understanding so universal that he can ask just the right questions that will lead each different person to a reasoned commitment to liberalism. Nobody can pretend to be the perfect liberal Socrates. Yet, despite the very different sympathies and arguments that different dialogues require, all liberal philosophers will be marked with the same Socratic spirit—for they all will use dialogue to lead their partners to see the virtue of professing a certain kind of political ignorance.

The conflict between medium and message signals a deeper tension between audience and performance. This book aims, in principle, to be intelligible to all potential citizens of a liberal state. Given the very different people in this audience, however, any particular argument can be expected to persuade some only at the cost of turning others off. Thus, if I simply tried to tell you why I personally am a committed liberal, this would predictably divert some of you from arguments that you would find more compelling. Given this dilemma, it seems best to dispense with personal declarations of faith so as to better give you a sense of the *different* paths that can lead a thoughtful person to Neutrality. Having gained this sense, you will be the best judge of the books and people who should serve as your next dialogic partners.

In addition to this primary function, a relatively dispassionate survey also reveals the hidden premise of a fashionable authoritarian critique that can both flatter and intimidate by its show of profundity. The kind of critique I have in mind disdains the need to take seriously the surface complexities of liberal doctrine. Indeed, such narrowly focused analyses are said to be positively dangerous forms of "partial criticism." They can seduce the partial critic into an unthinking acceptance of liberal premises that seem—but only seem—far removed from his particular critical enterprise. In striving to free himself from liberal misconceptions, the partial critic merely manages to find new ways of ensnaring himself with liberal preconceptions. The only way out from this impasse is a "total" critique that gets to the root of the problem: liberalism, it appears, is based on one or another metaphysical or epistemological mistake. Once the root error is uncovered, it is possible to see how all the superficial contradictions of liberalism are but symptoms of a deeper metaphysical disease. Rather than liberal reform, nothing short of radical surgery can give relief to those deep spirits who cannot abide the dialectical contradictions of liberal doctrine. The immediate task, then, is to hack at the roots—and any branches that are within reach. This very act of negation is necessary to gain the metaphysical ground we so urgently require to sustain the growth of a new and organic sense of self and community.

Now I hope this parody does more than reveal my distaste with some fashionable rhetoric. I have constructed my cartoon to emphasize the root error of all those who search for liberalism's root error. Quite simply, the entire root-and-branch metaphor is misconcieved. Liberalism does not depend on the truth of any single metaphysical or epistemological system. Instead, liberalism's ultimate justification is to be found in its strategic location in a web of talk that converges upon it from every direction. Each strand is itself sufficient to support a reasoned belief in Neutrality; yet to cut oneself off from a single strand hardly liberates from the web of belief. Instead, you must keep on hacking for a very long time before you can cut your way to freedom. And the freedom you have purchased by your exertion will turn out, perhaps, to be very different from the one you had in mind. Deprived of so many familiar strands that tie us to the world, we shall walk about the planet with a very different step.

Not, mind you, that it is impossible to break free. Human beings have spun the web; human beings can destroy it. And there are would-be heros who have pointed the way by spinning out a radically different pattern of words and actions. I do *not*, in short, claim that you can reason your way to Neutrality *regardless* of the way you understand your place in the world. Instead of proclaiming liberalism's complete independence from other branches of reflective talk, I mean to assert its *relative autonomy*. In order to accept liberalism, you need not take a position upon a host of Big Questions of a highly controversial character. So long as you understand your relation to the world in one of a *number* of familiar—if very different—ways, you will find it sensible to regulate our power struggle by means of Neutral dialogue.

71.1. *The Myth of the Philosopher-King*

To suggest the false depth of the root-and-branch critique, I should like to begin with a few facts of the "superficial" everyday kind. We live in a world where central governments rule vast populations: small states are numbered in the tens, large states in the hundreds, of millions. These central governments rule with the aid of vast bureaucracies; while governmental bureaucracy may be smaller in the "capitalist" world, this shrinkage is accomplished only by tolerating vast "private" bureaucracies authorized to call upon the power of the state whenever authority is challenged. Finally, we are in the midst of a revolution in the technology of coercion and control—the nineteenth century gave us the organized police force; the twentieth century has given us the computer; what power will tomorrow give our bureaucratic overlords?

Short of nuclear holocaust, these basic realities—imperial government, bureaucratic structure, burgeoning technology—are fixtures of our age. Luddite revolts—while predictable—will predictably fail. Rather than fruitless revolt, the task is to master these realities by shaping them into an environment that makes life worth living.

It is not enough, then, simply to muster up the philosophical courage needed to declare, with the appropriate "Eurekas," that you have discovered the good for all humankind. You must also persuade yourself that an imperial, bureaucratic, and technologized government should be given the patent to make use of your discovery in the power plays of everyday life.

Even if you could effortlessly become philosopher-king, granting such a government a patent could well be a hazardous undertaking. After all, the good you have found may not be of the kind that imperial government can impose by bureaucratic decree. Love, friendship, and the like are not readily susceptible of mass production. A vital communal life will not flourish under the watchful gaze of bureaucrats dispatched from the imperial center. Thus, you might well conclude that liberal democracy is the best second-best means you have at your disposal for maximizing the good. For the aim of liberalism is to organize the machinery of government in a way that facilitates informed and flexible exchanges by people who encounter one another under conditions of undominated equality. With no philosopher-king looking over their shoulder, such people may nonetheless find their own way to the very goods you yourself have discovered—after all, you will still be there to guide them. Such continuing acts of rediscovery, moreover, will generate an energy and vitality that bureaucratic centralism can never equal. While liberal democracy may permit some to live bad lives, this same freedom may provide a setting for a renaissance in which the good is realized with incomparable splendor.

Suppose, though, that on considering the matter, you cannot agree. Suppose you have some bright ideas which you are convinced will make people better than they can become on their own. Think twice before you enact them into law. Using power to achieve the good is a tricky business in a country, say, with a quarter of a billion people. Good intentions are not enough; you must be reasonably sure that you have not ignored second-order effects that will sabotage your clever schemes. While you may indeed have a great understanding of the good, there is no guarantee that you have an equal grasp of more humdrum, yet complex, empirical realities. Nor can you place too much faith in your bureaucratic minions to do the job of implementation for you. Time and again, they will find some way of trivializing your good for their self-advantage. Constant vigilance and continuing shake-ups may be your only hope. Yet these moves themselves generate anxiety and timidity that may be bad enough to offset any good you may accomplish.

Nor should your second thoughts merely extend to your capacity to control, let alone inspire, the bureaucratic mass upon whom you will come to depend. You yourself will change once you accept the crown. Will you be the philosopher you once were—when all the world flatters and panders and deceives in the hope of gaining your favor? When all this is soberly considered, how well do you *really* think you'd do as philosopher-king? Why do you think anybody else would do better?

Yet even this is too generous to the would-be authoritarian. There is no reason in the world to think that the fellow who scrambles to the top has ever aspired to be a philosopher-king. Doubtless he will hire some public-relations people to help him with his image, but real virtue is often an obstacle in the struggle for supreme power. A clever opportunist can often overpower a battalion of philosopher-kings—if, as is to be expected, these worthies are constantly struggling to maintain a semblance of virtue in an uncongenial environment. Good government, always precarious, can readily degenerate into an awful parody of itself—with hypocrites using the awesome powers of the bureaucratic state to spy, torture, and kill, merely to aggrandize themselves without any attention to the goods they profess to value. Such hypocrisy is far more corrosive than the failures of a Neutral government. While liberal government *will* undoubtedly be abused from time to time, at least these failures will not be dressed up in the rhetoric of supreme virtue. Indeed, abuses of liberal government will only emphasize the need for people to stand up for their own right to define the good as they see fit. In contrast, a bureaucratic government's hypocritical declarations of virtue can give the good a bad name. So much cheap talk and brazen power may induce widespread despair at the very possibility of living a good life. Given these risks, surely the effort to save souls by governmental decree is a desperate gamble?

These questions have been asked in very different ways, depending on the time and place. They have led deeply religious people time and again to oppose the pretentions of churchmen to secular authority. This religious insistence on a strict separation of church and state need not be motivated by concern for the state's integrity; it is inspired by an effort to preserve the spirit of the church from irremediable corruption. A spiritual community is constantly perplexed by challenges to its authority; in despair, it may well feel itself obliged to excommunicate the intransigent sinner and heretic. Yet, while church members may treat their former brother as if he were a stranger, they cannot go further and destroy his property, his body, or his mind to save his immortal soul. However precious the heretic's soul, such implements of salvation corrupt the visible body of the church in all the ways we have previously described. It is better to recognize the inevitability of sin, and hope for divine salvation, than to play the role of God's avenging angel on earth. It is worse than foolish to try to anticipate the day of final judgment. It is sensible for the religious, no less than the skeptical, to reason their way to an acceptance of Neutrality—for this conversational constraint is merely a device for marking the conceptual boundary on the secular authority of all those who pretend to be God's vice-regent on earth.

None of this, of course, must necessarily convince a true believer—either of the religious or secular variety. On the one hand, he may respond by denying some of the many empirical assumptions I have made in the preceding paragraphs. He may declare the dawning of a new age in which billions of people will live in peace with one another without the need of any centralized bureaucracy; or he may invent a social science so powerful that achieving the good will not be a problem once power is gained; or he may assert that his band of believers is so disciplined they need not fear the corrosive impact of years of petty bureaucratic power. On the other hand, the true believer may artfully define his good so as to accommodate a harsher reality. He may defiantly declare that a moment of collective virtue is worth an eternity of living hell; or he may explain that this life is but a painful preparation for eternal salvation, which can be attained only by abject submission to the secular order established by the lucky few who have learned God's will: or he may proclaim that the dreary bureaucratic reality he has created is really paradise-on-earth and condemn anyone who hopes for more as a right-wing opportunist.

All these things, and more, can be said. But do *you* want to say them?

71.2. *The Good—and How to Know It*

If you do, you will have a lot more to swallow before you can talk your way out of Neutrality. Up to the present point, I have not touched the vital nerve of the philosopher-king myth—that some among us may not only *believe,* but may justly claim to *know,* that they have grasped the *true* good for all humankind. Nor will I do so yet.

Instead, I shall ask some questions about the *methods* a person must follow before he can move from mere belief to true enlightenment. Surely the way I get to know that something is good is different from the way I get to know that locomotives are speedy. While at the end of my quest, the goodness of X may run over me as if it were a locomotive, surely this intuitive certainty comes after a period of doubt? Let us, then, take the view of the doubter and ask how he may deal with his uncertainties in a way that justifies his claim to *know* the good. While coping with doubt is a complicated matter, I think that a crude distinction will go a long way here. On the one hand, a person may *suppress* his doubts, refusing to consider whether they may indeed be justified. On the other hand, a person may *transcend* his doubts: after squarely confronting the possibility that his doubts have merit, the doubter concludes that they are without foundation. Of course, the right way of transcending one's doubts is a matter of some dispute; yet I do not think that many deny that there is *a* difference of *some* kind between their preferred mode of transcendence and brute suppression. And if this is conceded, the next step in the argument is easy enough: surely the only way you can ever come to *know* the good is by transcending, rather than suppressing, your doubts. If you are simply pretending your doubts do not exist, you can never say for sure what you might say if you ever had the courage to confront them head on. Yet if you yourself might well discard your present beliefs, how could you possibly say that you *know* them to be true? At best, you *hope* that X is good.

And this conclusion opens a broad path to Neutrality. Searching for true knowledge, you begin to reflect upon your past experience in an effort to define the future path that will best permit you to transcend your doubts. After some soul searching, you set your interim course in the way that seems to you best. Perhaps you need a period of monastic contemplation; perhaps an immersion in the bustle of life will yield the greatest insight. Yet just as you use your power in the way that seems best to you, you are stopped short by an imperious command. According to this voice, you are to be denied the right to transcend your doubts because the voice *knows* your good better than you do. Cruel paradox: if you are deprived of the means of transcending your doubts, you must needs suppress them and deprive yourself of any knowledge. Now if the voice were God's, perhaps this would be a legitimate command. But surely no mortal being has the right to deny me all hope of obtaining true knowledge of the good! Once again, we begin to glimpse Neutrality at the end of our path.

Only one more step is required. Perhaps you agree that the state should not intervene in the lives of all those who are genuinely struggling to transcend their doubts. But what of the others, the millions who seem untroubled by doubt and are, with manifest self-satisfaction, pursuing affirmatively bad lives?

There are several liberal moves at this point, ranging from the obvious to the profound. To begin with the obvious, how in the world are you going to administer a bureaucratic test that separates the genuine doubters from the contented evildoers? Once word gets around, even the most contented pig will put on the appropriate show of anguish if it is necessary for him to continue undisturbed on the path to damnation. More profoundly, perhaps the moral environment generated in a liberal state is precisely the one that will encourage people to confront their doubts and try to transcend them. Surely my own doubts come to the surface when I consider the fact that others seem to be gaining self-fulfillment from activities I consider meaningless or worse. Deeper still, is it possible for anyone to know whether a period of piggish satisfaction is only a preliminary for the deepest battles with doubt known in the history of the human spirit? Not every person is Saint

Augustine, but there is something of value that any liberal can learn from his *Confessions*.

It is silly, then, to try to distinguish the doubters from more vulgar folk who are simply engaging in an evil activity for the hell of it. We must regulate the use of power by means of a political conversation that does not attempt such refined distinctions.

Yet, once again, my argument is hardly unanswerable. You can dismiss my emphasis on the doubter's point of view as a morbid fixation that distorts my vision. The moral truth exists, like a locomotive, quite independently of whether any particular person takes account of it. Indeed, if I saw you engaged in an orgy of doubt on a railroad track, surely I would be right in pushing you off the track before the locomotive roared by. And the same is true of the good.

But do *you* want to say such things? Have you *so* transcended your doubts that you can look with disdain upon those who are struggling for knowledge of the kind you think you already possess?

71.3. *The Good of Autonomy*

Suppose, though, that you have mastered your doubts—to the point of depriving others of the knowledge that can come only by transcending, rather than suppressing, self-doubt. Even so, you have hardly fought your way free of Neutrality. You may have scaled Mount Olympus only to discover the blazing truth that the good is of a kind that cannot—conceptually cannot—be imposed on another. Take this truth to be self-evident: All people ought to model themselves on Socrates. If this is your view, it would be transparently silly to deprive people of power when all you can say is that you know what's good better than they do—for this way of presenting yourself is the very opposite of Socratic virtue.

So too if Kant turns out to be right: that the only good thing is the capacity to form a rational plan of life. Whenever I offend Neutrality, I offend this good: for, by definition, I must declare that another citizen is to be subordinated to my purposes in the power struggle rather than recognized as a person whose capacity to form a life plan is no less valuable than my own.

In consigning Socrates and Kant to two short paragraphs, I do not mean to demean their achievement. To the contrary, if I know anything about the good, it is that Socrates and Kant are pointing in the right direction. But I will let these great men speak for themselves. For present purposes, the important point is that you don't have to take a strong Kantian or Socratic line on autonomy to reason your way to the liberal state. Perhaps the capacity to develop a rational life plan is not the only good whose existence can be known to us; perhaps there are other things that are valuable in and of themselves. So long as it is morally better to respect my moral autonomy than to force me to achieve one of these *other* goods, the path has been laid for a rational commitment to Neutrality. It is, in short, not necessary for autonomy to be the only good thing; it suffices for it to be the best thing that there is.

And are you prepared to deny this? What could be better for a person than his own development of a plan of life that seems to him good? Of course, if God had set down a contrary law in clear and unambiguous terms, His view would be entitled to respectful attention. But has He done so? How do you know this?

71.4. *Liberal Skepticism*

But can we *know* anything about the good? Sure, all of us have beliefs; but isn't it merely pretentious to proclaim one's *knowledge* on this subject? Worse than pretentious—isn't some loud fool typically the first to impose his self-righteous certainties on others? Rather than welcoming such certainties, they should be taken as a sign that your intellectual arteries are hardening, that you are beginning to mistake your own personal musings for the unheard music of the spheres. The hard truth is this: There is no moral meaning hidden in the bowels of the universe. All there is is you and I struggling in a world that neither we, nor any other thing, created.

Yet there is not need to be overwhelmed by the void. We may create our own meanings, you and I; however transient or superficial, these are the only meanings we will ever know. And the first meaningful reality we must create—one presupposed by all other acts of meaningful communication—is the idea that you and I are persons capable of giving meanings to the world.

Yet this is just the achievement of a Neutral conversation. We begin our struggle in silence, each of us appropriating what we see in front of us; but soon enough we see each other and are faced with the task of giving meaning to our encounter. By speaking to one another in a Neutral way, we both succeed in giving our struggle a meaningful form. No longer is our conflict interpretable only as a blind struggle between two competing forces; instead, we may understand it as an affirmation of our capacities to impress our own meanings on the world. It is only through such an act of mutual reinforcement that we may give a concrete reality to our understanding of ourselves as people capable of living a valuable life in a world without a preordained design.

But, once again, all this can be denied. If there is no master design, the challenge is to transcend all talk of good and evil and master the universe. If God is dead, everything is permitted.

But are you willing to say this? Even if you are, will the charismatic superman fare any better with bureaucratic realities than the philosopher-king?

72. SELF-DEFENSE

These, then, are four of the main highways to the liberal state: realism about the corrosiveness of power; recognition of doubt as a necessary step to moral knowledge; respect for the autonomy of persons; and skepticism concerning the reality of transcendent meaning. Doubtless there are other paths as well. A detailed map, however, would require nothing less than a canvass of all significant cultural traditions from a liberal point of view. Worse yet, such an exhausting labor would, in the end, succeed only in covering over the main point with heaps of erudition. For the end of liberal philosophy is not encyclopedic knowledge; it is to encourage *you* to philosophize on your own, to figure out how you understand your relationship to the world, to decide whether you are willing to cut free of all the strands that unite us in a common recognition of liberal principles; to think for yourself.

Indeed, my principal concern is not with those few extraordinary souls who have broken free of the web that binds the rest of us to liberal conversation; a stable liberal state will find a place for such people to express their ideals—if not in the all-consuming way they propose. My goal, instead, is to confront the more numerous band of speculative diletantes who seek a cheap victory over liberalism without recognizing all that goes with their triumph. So far as the liberal is concerned, the only remedy for such cheap talk is better talk, talk that induces more people to reflect upon the way they understand the world—so that they may build the foundations of liberalism upon an ever deeper foundation of personal understanding of their own place in the universe. No book can pretend to resolve your doubts in an authoritative manner; the value of any book is its capacity to provoke an independent effort at self-definition. The only proper response to liberal political philosophy is more philosophy.

But even as you and I try to achieve self-understanding, we must reckon with the realities of power. So long as you remain in this world, your effort at philosophy may, at any moment, be shattered by a hostile assault. Just as you are making some progress in self-understanding, your attention may be diverted by a rude challenge to the power you possess. Doubtless you would like some more time to reflect before committing yourself to the Neutrality principle. But time has run out. Either you defend your claim to power through Neutral conversation or you respond to the challenge by some other means. How, then, to respond?

Suppose, that, at a moment of worldly challenge, you find that your view of the world—as best you understand it—demands your rational acceptance of liberal principles. If this is your conclusion, then the first line of defense to a hostile attack is clear enough: try to engage the other in Neutral dialogue; and if he questions the ground rules, continue the conversation on a philosophical level in an effort to convince him that he, no less than you, is tied to Neutrality by a web of reasoned belief. Now this conversation can, of course, have untoward consequences for you. It may reveal that your claim to power cannot be justified through a credible form of Neutral conversation. Worse yet, the other may shake your reasoned commitment to Neutral principles, persuading you instead to break through the snares of liberal rationality to grasp a good of extraordinary potency.

Assume, however, that the conversation has no such ending. So far as you're concerned, the dialogue vindicates your claim to power and clarifies your reasoned commitment to liberal ideals. Unfortunately, however, your dialogic partner remains intransigent. So far as he is concerned, the conversation has only made clearer the bankruptcy of liberal ideals. Your talk has merely convinced him that liberalism is but a screen for moral cowards who have become paralyzed by their sickened reason. Resolutely, your antagonist fights off the corrosive doubts inspired by your chatter; he pushes forward to take what is justly his and to make you a vehicle for the greater good. How, then, to respond?

You have only two choices left. Either fight for your rights or hand over the understanding that you have, with some effort, gained for yourself. If you choose to fight, your defense, quite literally, is self-defense—for if you surrender your understanding of yourself to the power of another, what do you have left?

73. IN DEFENSE OF RATIONALITY

But I have done the foes of liberalism too much credit. For every authoritarian who actually thinks his way through to a coherent set of philosophical and empirical premises, there is a multitude who have never given the matter serious attention. Nor are their authoritarian posturings the fruit of a Nietzschean effort to transcend all talk of good and evil. Given the right time and place, most people see the point of Socratic doubt and serious dialogue. And if I am right about the relative autonomy of liberal theory, such conversations will typically permit people to find their own path to a reasoned commitment to the liberal state.

No, the problem is not so much with my inadequate sketch of the web of argument that converges upon Neutrality; it is rather with the role that reflective argument plays in most peoples' lives. Their philosophic moments are so few, so fleeting, that they are soon forgotten amid the constant power struggles that constitute one side of social life. In most concrete confrontations, one side or another will gain in the short run if it refuses to accept the constraints imposed by a Neutral dialogue and takes all it can grab in pursuit of its conception of the good. While each power player may well, in his more thoughtful moments, recognize that this very good does not justify his power position, the ease with which the powerful can live with self-contradiction is passing marvelous to behold. Nor is the powerlessness of philosophy to be attributed solely to the happy marriage of greed and thoughtlessness common among all power elites—though this is no small matter. When a person is callously oppressed for too long, he is not in a talking mood even when the powerful say they are in the mood to listen. So a destabilizing cycle of incivility begins, leading finally to a struggle in which only fools imagine that they can get anywhere by talk. Philosophy is confined to small dark places, far removed from the ebb and flow of social life.

It is this breach between reflective talk and decisive action—theory and practice—which is both a constant threat to, and ultimate enemy of, the liberal spirit. And it is the affirmation of the ideal unity of theory and practice which provides the liberal state with its first principle of Rationality—the insistence that each citizen be prepared to offer a reason in defense of every aspect of his power position when challenged to do so by anyone disadvantaged by his claim of dominion.

Yet, in affirming the overriding need to talk reflectively about power, liberalism does not place Talk in the same privileged position previously inhabited by other gods. Most important, a liberal does not insist that each individual go through some form of talk therapy before he commits himself to a set of personal ideals. For some, such conversations only obscure things that were otherwise clear enough; for others, the rewards of talk are not to be compared with the harvest gained by action; for others, only silence permits insight. All these beliefs are compatible with citizenship in a liberal state. Indeed, it is the very point of Neutrality to permit each citizen to defend his rights *without* requiring him to convince his fellows that his personal good serves the common good. Hence, he can—if he chooses—keep his own definition of the good entirely hidden from some or all of his fellow citizens. So long as he responds, "I should get X because I'm at least as good as you are," the others are not entitled to probe into the innermost recesses of his mind or spirit. This is not to say that, once freed from legal compulsion, the citizenry will fail to talk to one another about the ultimate meaning of life. To the contrary, the diverse forms of modern culture suggest the breadth and vitality of collective discourse possible once it is no longer necessary for the citizen to justify his every form of expression to the bureaucratic guardians of the true, the good, and the beautiful. It is the freedom to explore the depths and define the limits of communication which is itself the fundamental principle of the liberal interpretation of culture.

Nor does liberalism content itself with assuring each individual the right to be incomprehensible to others in vast areas of his private life; it also permits a group of citizens to establish a subcommunity within which even the question of legitimacy is not subject to reasoned discussion but is instead resolved by one or another form of charismatic authority. So long as a citizen voluntarily joins a charismatic commune, the state may not deny him the right to fulfill his good by serving others in silent devotion.[1] Nonetheless, though citizens need

1. See chapter 6 for a more nuanced discussion.

not talk about many things, they *must* respond when somebody challenges the legitimacy of their power position. Even a subcommunity devoted to the silent obedience of its spiritual leader must assign some of its members the task of responding to the question of legitimacy raised by outsiders who reject its leader and seek to appropriate the scarce resources under his control for their own purposes. When faced with such a challenge, an individual *must* talk on pain of losing his membership in the liberal polity. While liberalism affirms man's cultural freedom—his right to spin talk and action into countless meaningful patterns—it does not assert man's complete freedom from culture. To the contrary, it is only the failure to answer the question of legitimacy that conclusively establishes the illegitimacy of an exercise of power.

Yet the very narrowness of the Rationality principle may make its central position seem even more paradoxical. If I can't force you to talk about so many things, what reason can I give for forcing you to engage in a dialogue with me on the question of legitimacy?

Now this question is very different from all the others we have raised in this book. Up to now, I have tried to answer all questions by placing them within the framework of an ongoing dialogue; the task was to convince each participant to talk about his problem under certain conversational ground rules. At this point, however, my basic technique breaks down.

Again and again, I repeat my question: "Why should you, rather than I, exert the power we both desire?" Yet, no matter how loud I shout, I cannot hope to transform a monologue into a dialogue. Perhaps, in response to your silent stare, I begin to present the many reasons that convince me that Rationality is an appropriate principle for regulating our power struggle. Yet, in mounting this harangue in praise of Rationality, I am no longer *reasoning with* you; I am merely *talking at* you. Is my chatter a confirmation of my position in defense of Rationality, or is it an ironic confirmation of your "position," which disdains all talk on this subject?

There is nothing that I can *say* to persuade you to adopt Rationality that is not mocked by your blank stare. Nor can I escape my dilemma by the use of force. Even if I possessed some magic "talk serum" which, when injected into your veins, transformed you into a chatterbox, I would not gain your answer to my question. While the drug would force a voice out of "your" body, this triumph would mock my very enterprise. For the voice I heard would only continue so long as I continued to assert my power over "your" larynx. Rather than establishing a dialogue, I would have developed a new and awful form of ventriloquism in which my own voice was echoed through "your" body.

I can use neither force nor reason to impose dialogue upon you. All I can do is ask my question and await your reply. If you try to stare me down and impose brute force upon me, I will act in self-defense. If, instead, you answer my questions, I will answer yours, and we will see what we will see. The choice is yours.

74. INDIVIDUAL FREEDOM AND SOCIAL OBLIGATION

In reflecting on your choice, recall only this: I do not wish, by some conversational trick, to induce you to grovel before me in the dust. Liberal conversation is not my technique for gaining mastery over you, but a means by which we may both achieve a deeper affirmation of ourselves as individuals entitled to mutual respect.

Think, for a moment, about social life in a well-ordered liberal state. A fellow citizen comes to you and demands to know why he should obey the law when it awards you control over something he prizes. No longer need there be any awkward shuffling of the feet and turning of the head. Instead, you may respond clearly, squarely, and with understanding:

> Yes, I know precisely why you ask this question. You think you and your goals are so important that they simply must be satisfied, and you insist upon the means necessary for their greater fulfillment. But I too am a person with my own ends in life, ends that I think it good to fulfill. So why should you have precedence over me? If you can answer this question, I am only too happy to talk for our mutual enlightenment. But I will not give ground before brute force.
>
> Why, then, do you think that our power relationship should be organized in a way that presupposes your superior moral worth? How can you claim to know that you are better than I am?

Prepared to defend his claim to a limited share of social power, each citizen may turn his attention to the fundamental question that none can evade: the meaning of his own life. And within a power structure based on dialogue, each person may, to the extent he finds it useful, call upon others to engage with him in a common search for meaning.

The overall pattern of culture and life that emerges from this inter-change will constantly change over time, as one generation builds upon, and criticizes, the work of the last. Over time, however, the social life of the liberal state will represent the full range of moral creation that lies within the grasp of citizens who confront one another without pretensions to moral dominion. If I am right, such a power structure would reveal the breadth and depth of human creativity in all its majesty—beyond the capacity of any single individual to survey, let alone evaluate. Yet, even if I were wrong, even if overwhelming num-bers opted for lives that I consider mean and narrow, we should at last learn what human freedom amounts to.

But all this is for another time. We are in fact very far from a well-ordered liberal state in which my share of power can be said to be consistent with your equal right to self-determination. We are born instead into a world where structures of exploitation are entrenched all around us. The diverse means by which the powerful grab hold of their advantages are wondrous to behold: the enterprising Party offi-cial passes his advantages on to his children with no less avidity than does the capitalist entrepreneur. Each nation struggles to exploit all those who are born on the wrong side of the line, as does each race, each class, each caste, and most religions. Each person is told in count-less ways to make the most of the opportunities given him by his genetic abilities and transactional environment—without comparing the opportunities he has received with those obtained by others. All the while, spiritual leaders of all kinds are forever slipping into an elaborate apologia for the status quo—arguing that the existing categories of exploitation represent the highest good for mankind.

When faced with this prospect, the committed liberal must find a new way of expressing Artistotle's great question. He asked whether it is possible for a *good* person to live in a *bad* society. We must ask: Is it possible for a *free* person to live in an *unjust* society? Though the terms are different, the answer remains the same. A free person can-not think himself perfectly free to pursue his good until a similar power has been extended to all in the just society. For it is only under these conditions that a free person may defend the use of his power in a dialogue constrained by the Neutrality principle.

But this is only half the truth. While the committed liberal cannot turn his back on social justice, neither can he resolve the problem of illegitimate domination by insisting that *all* liberals must do *everything* they can to create a more liberal power structure. Given the world around us, such a demand would require all of us to become liberal saints, forcing poets to become plumbers if they thought that this would better serve the cause of social justice (and vice versa). While liberalism needs its saints, it can be damaged by an excess of saintliness. A society composed entirely of liberal fanatics, all eager to sacrifice themselves for the cause of social justice, would soon lose its grip on the ideal that initially motivated its feverish activity. The aim of social justice in a liberal state is not to build yet another community in which all are enslaved in the name of some grand collective ideal. Instead, it is to construct a form of community in which each participant is guaranteed the right to live his own life regardless of what his neighbors may think of him.

In short, the first principle of liberal political practice is to beware the grand simplificateur, the imperious and self-righteous revolutionary as well as the callous and selfish individualist. The liberal ideal is a social order in which *free* people act within a *just* power structure. Neither half of this formula can be forgotten in the ongoing struggle that is liberal politics. Most efforts to advance along one dimension of the liberal ideal will require us to accept something less than we could have achieved if our sights had been set narrowly on some other dimension. While conservative laissez faire or a revolutionary leap forward may, on occasion, represent the least bad liberal strategy, *no* form of practical politics can pretend that it offers the final solution to the liberal tension between individual freedom and social justice. While we can, in the mind's eye, construct a world where this tension *has* been resolved by comprehensive dialogue, this very effort should convince us that the perfect utopia is beyond our present power. Real advances in the real world will come to those who recognize the practical necessity of the tension between elements of the liberal ideal and yet do not lose sight of the whole amid the cry and smoke of battle.

A similar tension afflicts each of us in our personal lives. Privileged people, like myself, must confront the fact that we have no right to use all the power at our command to further our own personal ends in life. Nor can we typically discharge our debt to the exploited classes by one grand gesture. As we have seen, a revolutionary leap forward has its own liberal problematic and can hardly be relied upon to relieve the tensions arising from a self-conscious recognition of personal privilege. Nor can these anxieties be discharged by simply handing over some money to one or another exploited group—proceeding forever more to pursue one's personal goods in a single-minded way. In modern society, membership in the power elite is at least as much a product of an ability to adapt to the values and skills taught by the present educational system—reinforced by the transactional structures prevailing in industrial society—as it is a consequence of superior financial endowments. Instead of seeking some single act of repayment that will magically discharge our debts, many of us cannot escape the fact that we shall exercise power throughout our lives that could not be justified through liberal dialogue.

This means that a privileged person cannot evade an ongoing personal conflict between his pursuit of self-advantage and the demands of social justice. While this conflict may be plainest in such matters as a choice of career, it is not hard to recognize the tension in areas of life more removed from the world of affairs. Of course, some will find managing this conflict easier than others. They may come to believe, for example, that by trying to achieve some personal ideal—whether it be enlightened statesmanship, great poetry, deep philosophy, or simple decency and kindness—they are in fact doing the best they can to achieve a more liberal society. But an overly great insistence on this point belies an underlying anxiety, an anxiety that can never be entirely banished under the present and foreseeable conditions of social life. However I resolve my private conflict between self-fulfillment and social justice, it will remain true that I could have done more to serve social justice; I could have done more to search for self-fulfillment.

Nor is this personal anxiety the exclusive privilege of the privileged classes. There is, I suppose, some solace in knowing that one's present unhappiness is to be attributed in part to social injustice, that if one were only assured of one's rights, one might achieve a degree of fulfillment that has proved elusive. But it is also possible that one's personal failure would have occurred even in a perfectly just world. The liberal state does not abolish scarcity or assure happiness; after establishing his rights through Neutral dialogue, a person may use his power to make a mess of his life, and nobody has the right to stop him from going to hell in his own way. Thus, while the privileged face the task of defining their self in the light of their undischargeable debt to others, the oppressed face the anxiety that follows from the recognition that the job of self-definition and fulfillment would remain even if others could discharge their debts in full.

The basic problem, then, is ultimately the same for all us. None can hope, either in private or public life, to find a final solution to the conflict between self-fulfillment and social justice. The future of liberalism—so far as you and I have anything to do with it—depends upon our ability to confront this unhappy fact. So long as the powerful respond to the tension by trying to suppress the question of legitimacy, so long as the powerless respond by dreaming of the day they will rise to exploit their exploiters, we cannot do justice to the liberal ideal. Instead, our task is to transform our moral dilemma into a source of creativity, to make a life for ourselves which imposes a form on the discordant materials we find at hand, and so, through our personal efforts at imperfect mastery, to provide a clue to the mystery of individual freedom.

INDEX

Abortion, 25, 350, 351; and citizenship, 75; and genetic manipulation, 113, 130; rights to, 127–28; coerced, 130; utilitarian and liberal views compared, 134–35; and child abuse, 145–46; and Rawlsian theory, 223; and majority rule, 282. *See also* Contraception; Procreate, right to; Unborn generations

Adoption: rights of, 125–26; and infanticide, 129; utilitarian and liberal views compared, 134; and primary education, 143

Advantaged: as character in dialogue, 130, 238–39

Adversary presentation of evidence, 153, 259

Aesthetics, 355

Affirmative action: for victims of injustice, 246–49, 264–65, 270, 376–78; and the structural budget, 250–52, and cardinal judgments, 271; and bill of rights, 310. *See also* Exploitation, Racism

Agenda manipulation, 290–93. *See also* Condorcet's paradox

Aggregation problem, 242–49

Aggression: and citizenship, 76, 80–88; and education, 141, 155; and the family, 147–48

Agnosticism: in liberal philosophy of nature, 102, 103; and abortion, 128; and majority rule, 281. *See also* Theology

Alienation, 346–47

Alien beings, 5, 59–60, 108; and citizenship, 72–73, 74, 78, 79

Altruism. *See* Benevolence

America, United States of, 93, 256, 303; and triage, 257; constitution of, 303, 306

Anarchy, 19, 252

Animal rights, 25; in liberal theory, 71–72, 102–03, 315; talking ape, 74; and brain damaged humans, 79–80; in utilitarian theory, 101–03, 315; and abortion, 128. *See also* Nature

Anonymity principle, 288; and majority rule, 277–80, 281, 284, 319; and Neutrality, 285; and responsive lottery, 287

Anthropology, 73

Anxiety, 3–4, 94, 165–67, 377–78

Apes: and citizenship, 74, 80

Apollonian: character in dialogue, 89–92

Aristotle, 352, 375

Arrow, Kenneth, 14, 182, 293

Asceticism, 64, 75; and liberalism, 59–61; and infanticide, 129; and contract law, 196–98; and trusteeship, 205

Association, freedom of, 97–98, 179, 181, 182, 209

Atheism, 217

Athenian democracy, 287

Augustine, Saint, 355, 356, 366–67

Authoritarianism: liberal critique of, 11–12, 14, 16–17, 361–69; critique of liberalism, 12–13, 360–61, 370–71; and inequality, 16–17; between citizens and inanimate objects, 70; and citizenship, 75–78. *See also* Tyranny

Autonomy: as justification for Neutrality, 11, 367–68; and equal wealth, 57–58; and solipsism, 79; and natural rights, 99; and birth control, 111; in liberal theory, 182, 196, 302, 347, 369. *See also* Self-definition

Bankruptcy, law of, 198

Barry, Brian, 341

Basic structure, Rawlsian theory of, 194

Benevolence: in liberal theory, 82, 103, 177, 184, 344; and coercion, 85; in philosophy of nature, 101–03; and primary education, 144; and inheritance, 205; in contract theory, 225, 329–30, 344; and authoritarianism, 317; and majority rule, 322; and utilitarianism, 328, 344–45

Bentham, Jeremy, 45, 46, 100, 101–02, 339; as character in dialogue, 316–18

Bill of rights: in liberal theory, 29, 303, 307–12, 316, 319–20, 342; and citizenship, 71; and utilitarianism, 315–17, 318, 341–42

Biology: and citizenship, 74, 80, 81, 127; and liberal theory, 108

Birth defects. *See* Handicapped persons

Black: as character in dialogue, 251–52; middle class, 271. *See also* Class; Exploitation; Racism